The Life and Times of Lieutenant General Sir Adrian Carton de Wiart

The Life and Times of Lieutenant General Sir Adrian Carton de Wiart

Soldier and Diplomat

Alan Ogden

BLOOMSBURY ACADEMIC
LONDON • NEW YORK • OXFORD • NEW DELHI • SYDNEY

BLOOMSBURY ACADEMIC
Bloomsbury Publishing Plc
50 Bedford Square, London, WC1B 3DP, UK
1385 Broadway, New York, NY 10018, USA
29 Earlsfort Terrace, Dublin 2, Ireland

BLOOMSBURY, BLOOMSBURY ACADEMIC and the Diana logo are trademarks of
Bloomsbury Publishing Plc

First published in Great Britain 2022
This paperback edition published 2023

Cover design: Terry Woodley
Cover image © Portrait of Lt Gen Sir Adrian Carton de Wiart, VC, KBE, CB, CMG, DSO by
Simon Elwes. With kind permission of White's Club.

A catalogue record for this book is available from the British Library.

Library of Congress Cataloging-in-Publication Data
Names: Ogden, Alan, 1948- author.
Title: The life and times of Lieutenant General Sir Adrian Carton de Wiart:
soldier and diplomat / Alan Ogden.
Description: London; New York, NY: Bloomsbury Academic, 2021. |
Includes bibliographical references and index.
Identifiers: LCCN 2021017242 (print) | LCCN 2021017243 (ebook) | ISBN 9781350233126
(hardback) | ISBN 9781350233157 (epub) | ISBN 9781350233140 (ebook)
Subjects: LCSH: Carton de Wiart, Adrian, Sir, 1880-1963. | Generals–Great Britain–
Biography. | Diplomats–Great Britain–Biography. | British–Poland–Biography. | World War,
1914-1918–Campaigns–Western Front. | World War, 1939-1945–Campaigns.
Classification: LCC DA69.3.C3 O33 2021 (print) | LCC DA69.3.C3 (ebook) |
DDC 355.0092 [B]–dc23
LC record available at https://lccn.loc.gov/2021017242
LC ebook record available at https://lccn.loc.gov/2021017243

ISBN: HB: 978-1-3502-3312-6
PB: 978-1-3502-3313-3
ePDF: 978-1-3502-3314-0
eBook: 978-1-3502-3315-7

Typeset by Deanta Global Publishing Services, Chennai, India

To find out more about our authors and books visit www.bloomsbury.com and
sign up for our newsletters.

Contents

Illustrations

Figures

Maps

Acknowledgements

General Sir Adrian Carton de Wiart did not keep a diary nor was he a prolific letter writer. So I am indebted to all those members of the Carton de Wiart family who went to great lengths to help me build this picture of the very private man who lay behind the celebrity image of Britain's best-known soldier. His great-grandchildren: Anthony Loyd, Annabelle Walker, Jane Barkes; his step-grandchildren – Harry and Rosie Sutherland; Jane Sutherland; Deidre Maxwell-Scott; Baron Jean Houtart and his daughter Patricia.

My particular thanks go to Michael Martin and the Trustees of the Gerry Holdsworth Trust who gave me a generous grant towards researching this extraordinary story.

A special thank you to Crispian Cuss, formerly 4/7 Royal Dragoon Guards, for his invaluable advise on matters regimental and to Graeme Green, the Regimental Secretary of 4/7 Dragoon Guards.

My thanks also go to Charles Richards, Robin and Tara Beiber, Kate Fleming, Lieutenant General Sir John Kiszely, Gabriella Bullock, Paddy MacGregor, Moritz Fried, Brigadier Alex Turner, General Sir Mark Carlton-Smith, Brian Beaumont-Nesbitt, Dr Steven Kippax, Dr Roderick Bailey, Sir Anthony Weldon Bt., Fr Nicholas of Our Lady of Lourdes & St Michael Uxbridge, Rachel Rawlings of the Oratory School, Rebecca Maciejewski of the Victoria Cross and George Cross Association; the Fleming family for their kind permission to quote Peter Fleming; and the Chairman of White's Club for his kind permission to use the club's portrait of Lieutenant General Sir Adrian Carton de Wiart VC.

In Germany, my thanks to Hans von Bulow; Margherita Prinzessin zu Hohenlohe-Bartenstein; Graf Markus Fugger von Babenshausen; Stefan Birkle (Fugger-Babenhausen Archives); and Klaus Breyer at Landesarchiv Baden-Württemberg.

In Belarus, many thanks to Katya Makarevich, Dr Ihar Melnikau and Svetlana Verenich for their invaluable help in navigating me through the Pripet marshes and the history of Belarus.

As always, it was a privilege to work with the National Archives; Karen Robson and Mary Cockerill of the Mountbatten Archives (Southampton University); Katrina DeMuro of the Liddle Hart Centre for Military Archives; Antonia Love

of Reading University Library; Andrew Mussell of the Gray's Inn Archive; Fr
Nicholas of the Westminster Cathedral Archive; Jerry Fielder and Julie Grahame
of the Karsh Archives; Anna Stefaniki of the Jozef Piłsudski Institute of Research
London.

The team at Bloomsbury – Emily Drewe and Abigail Lane – has been hugely
supportive throughout and their patience exemplary. Thank you.

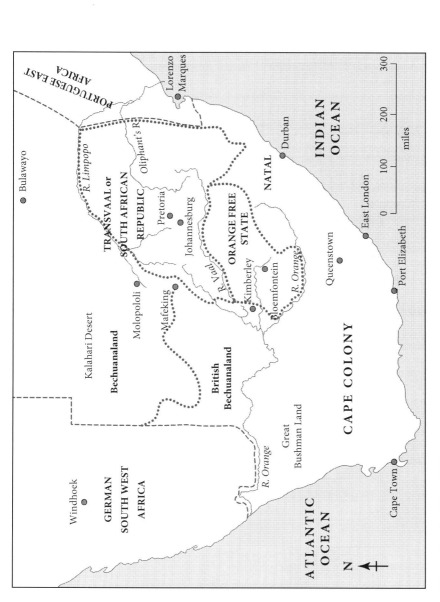

Map 1 South Africa 1899.

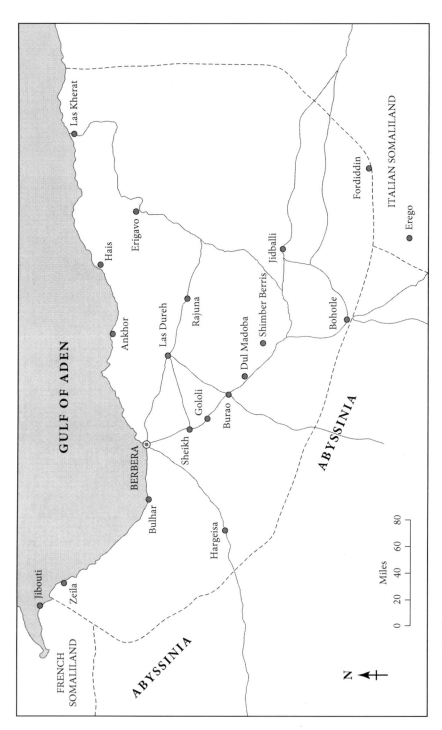

Map 2 Somaliland 1914.

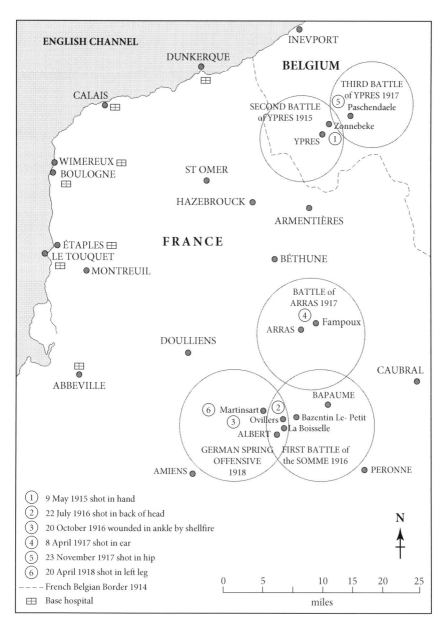

ENGLISH CHANNEL

INEVPORT

BELGIUM

DUNKERQUE

THIRD BATTLE
of YPRES 1917
⑤ Paschendaele

CALAIS

SECOND BATTLE
of YPRES 1915

Zonnebeke

YPRES ①

WIMEREUX
BOULOGNE

ST OMER

HAZEBROUCK

ARMENTIÈRES

ÉTAPLES
LE TOUQUET
MONTREUIL

FRANCE

BÉTHUNE

BATTLE of
ARRAS 1917
④ Fampoux
ARRAS

DOULLIENS

CAUBRAL

ABBEVILLE

BAPAUME

⑥ Martinsart ②
③ Ovillers Bazentin Le- Petit
ALBERT La Boisselle

GERMAN SPRING FIRST BATTLE of
OFFENSIVE the SOMME 1916
1918

AMIENS PERONNE

① 9 May 1915 shot in hand
② 22 July 1916 shot in back of head
③ 20 October 1916 wounded in ankle by shellfire
④ 8 April 1917 shot in ear
⑤ 23 November 1917 shot in hip
⑥ 20 April 1918 shot in left leg
----- French Belgian Border 1914
⊞ Base hospital

N

0   5   10   15   20   25

miles

Map 3 The Western Front 1915–18.

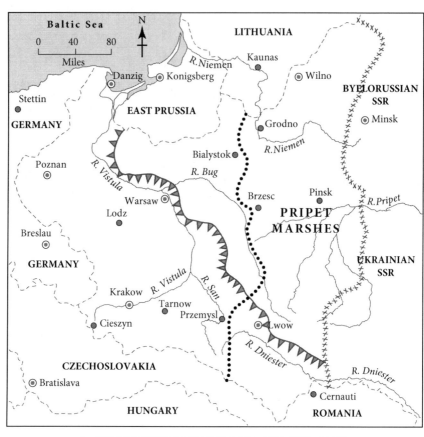

Baltic Sea

0   40   80
Miles

N

Stettin

GERMANY

Danzig   Konigsberg

EAST PRUSSIA

LITHUANIA

Kaunas

R. Niemen

Wilno

BYELORUSSIAN
SSR

Minsk

Poznan

R. Vistula

Grodno

R. Niemen

Bialystok

R. Bug

Warsaw

Lodz

Breslau

GERMANY

Brzesc

Pinsk

R. Pripet

PRIPET
MARSHES

UKRAINIAN
SSR

Krakow

R. Vistula

R. San

Tarnow

Cieszyn

Przemysl

Lwow

CZECHOSLOVAKIA

Bratislava

R. Dniester

R. Dniester

Cernauti

HUNGARY

ROMANIA

●●●●● Provisional Eastern Frontier proposed by Supreme
Allied Council 8 December 1918

▲▲▲▲ Limit of Red Army advance August 1920

✕✕✕✕ Polish - Soviet Frontier Established by Treaty
of Riga, March 1921.

Map 4 Poland 1919–21.

Map 5 Prostyn 1923–9.

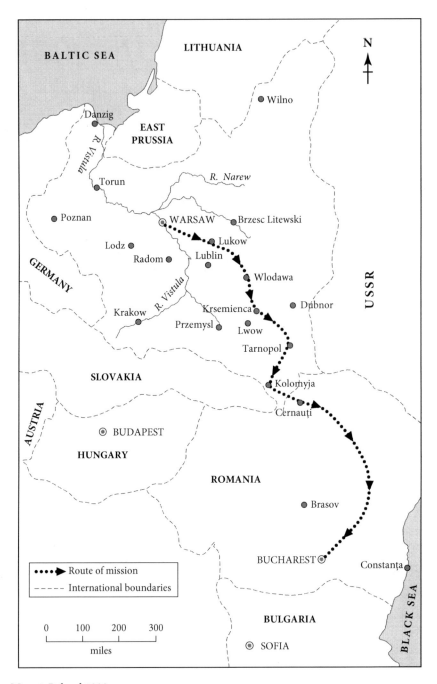

Map 6 Poland 1939.

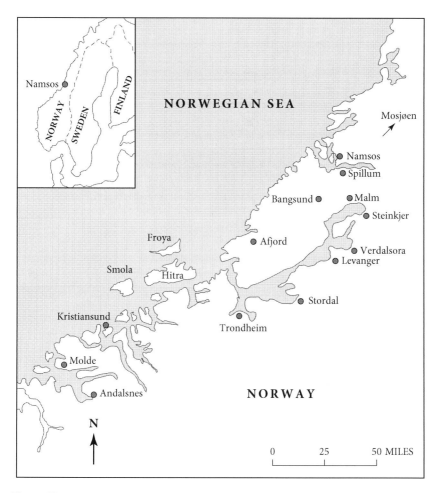

Map 7 Norway 1940.

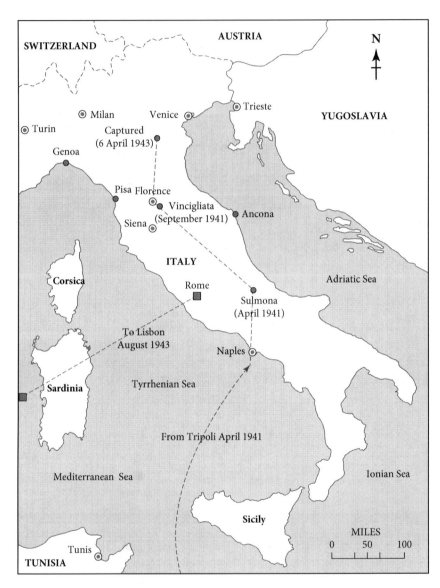

Map 8 Italy 1941–3.

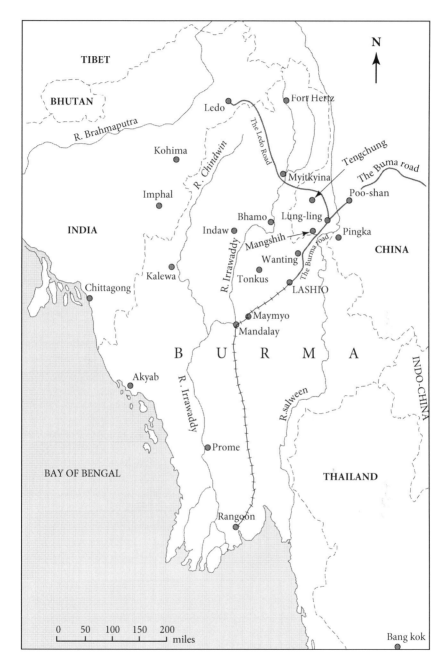

Map 9 Burma 1942–5.

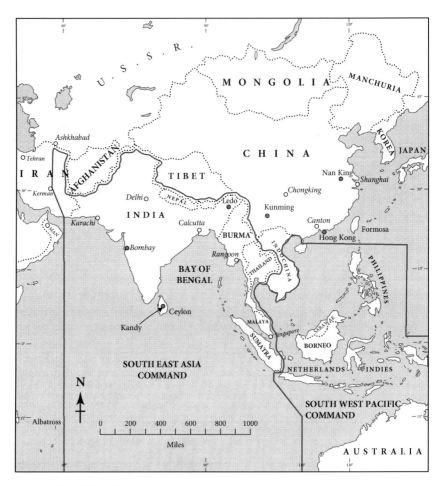

Map 10 SEAC Boundaries 1943–5.

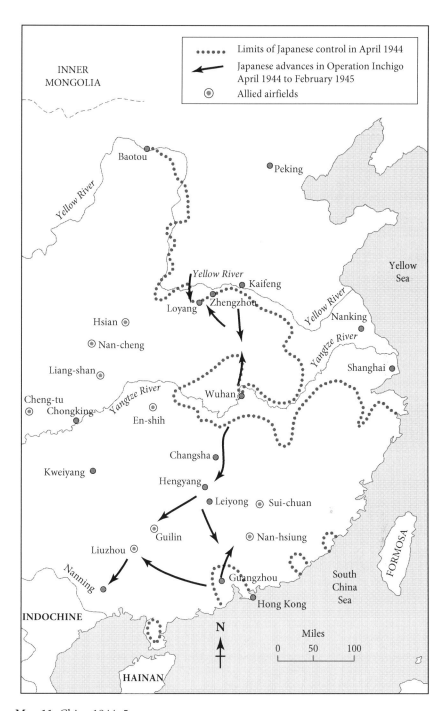

Map 11 China 1944–5.

Introduction

The kind of superficial search that typifies the internet age immediately will reveal General Sir Adrian Carton de Wiart as a most remarkable soldier: his pluck to find the action, the innumerable wounds inflicted when he got there, his luck to survive them and the two highest gallantry awards in the land, to prove it all. In the telling, he almost becomes a figure of fun – as if his catalogue of exploits suffers from an inflationary devaluation. Mostly, it ends there.

More is the pity. Carton de Wiart was far from an adornment; some chivalrous Cavalier from a bygone age who played to the public's imagination of a photo-fit British hero. His life was rich in other, intelligent political accomplishment. It contains the periods of fog and shadow that so often point to a complex soul. He captured the imagination of all he came into contact with: statesmen, diplomats and soldiers. Far from being a red-clawed, unquestioning servant of an empire's martial culture, Carton de Wiart mostly contradicts it.

He was indeed one of Britain's best-known soldiers, with a career spanning the Boer War and both the First and Second World Wars of the twentieth century. Reputedly the most wounded man in the British Army, his aura of indestructibility, accentuated by a Nelsonian eye-patch and empty sleeve, did win him celebrity status. However, that glittering array of nationally recognizable decorations, not least the Victoria Cross, belied the fact that he was not even English. With an Irish grandmother, a Belgian father and in all likelihood a Circassian mother, he could not have been more further from the pedigree of traditional British Army officers. Yet it was in their milieu that he moved with ease and achieved great distinction.

His early record of service in the front line – in South Africa, Somaliland, Picardy and Flanders – is the stuff of legend and deservedly so. At times, his *sang froid* defied belief as he strutted across the battlefields of the Western Front, rocked by artillery and machine-gun fires, encouraging his men with a flourish of his walking stick. Later, as the Head of the British Military Mission to Poland in 1939, he was the first to witness the devastating new military doctrine of blitzkrieg in action. The following year he found himself once more on the receiving end of German airpower, this time in Norway. Yet, far from the one-dimensional heroic soldier he is often portrayed and sometimes parodied as, Carton de Wiart excelled in the nuance of military diplomacy over an extensive period and wide-ranging geography of conflict.

Quintessentially a European by nature (and nurture), French was his first language. He moved effortlessly among multinational circles in Versailles and Poland in the 1920s and later in China in the 1940s. Despite his faintly piratical appearance, there was nothing of the Colonel Blimp about him; more a touch of Thackeray's Chevalier de Balibari. Astute and intelligent, with impeccable manners and an irresistible charm, he found it easy to identify with other cultures and societies, having been spared the upbringing of English imperial superiority. It was this ability to integrate and assimilate that later made him such an effective intermediary with two starkly contrasting leaders – the Polish General Josef Piłsudski and the Chinese Generalissimo Chiang Kai-shek.

His tenure as the British military delegate to the Inter-Allied Commission, and then as Head of the British Military Mission in Poland between 1919 and 1922, covered the dramatic re-emergence of the Polish state post-Versailles. Constrained by a British government policy that eschewed the supply of any meaningful military aid to Piłsudski's government (in stark contrast to France), Carton de Wiart provided a steady flow of military and political intelligence to the Paris Peace Conference and London nonetheless. This included accurate assessments of Denikin's anti-Bolshevik expedition and the defence of Warsaw. His obvious physical courage was matched with a moral determination. Written reports were always to the point, blunt and unadorned. Verbally he never shied from expressing his opinion to Lloyd George, Churchill and their military chiefs. In many instances they disregarded his views, as they did not resonate with government policy. But this never left him deterred from candour.

In the end, the fact that post-Versailles Poland militarily succeeded in prevailing against German revisionism, Ukrainian nationalism and Soviet expansion justified Carton de Wiart's unswerving belief in Piłsudski's leadership. Praise finally followed when the British Ambassador to Poland, William Max-Müller, noted that 'the two foreigners whose advice carried the greatest weight were Sir Horace Rumbold and General Carton de Wiart'. General Sir Richard Haking, Commander of the Allied Contingent in Danzig, had also written to the Chief of the Imperial General Staff (CIGS) that Carton de Wiart 'is the only man [in Warsaw] who Piłsudski really pays attention.'

Aside from sharing a border with Russia, China, his next military-diplomatic posting, had little in common with Carton de Wiart's experiences in Poland.

As the prime minister's personal representative to Chiang Kai-shek, he soon found himself centre stage at the Cairo Conference, where the Americans persuaded their allies to accord China 'Great Power' status. Once in Chongqing, de Wiart quickly established a sound working relationship with both the non-English speaking Generalissimo (mostly through Madame Chiang Kai-shek and her brother T. V. Soong) and with Lord Louis Mountbatten, the youthful British head of the Anglo-American South East Asia Command. Such was the Byzantine nature of the Allied command structure in the China Theatre, before long the antics of US General Stilwell began to impact on Chinese relations with the Allies and cause internal tension within the Anglo-American alliance as well. Grasping the fact that the war against Japan was essentially an American war, Carton de Wiart deftly circumvented the fractious power plays and maintained a position of calm impartiality. At the same time, he never hesitated in advocating for the Chinese point of view, particularly during the Inchigo offensive of 1944, when he temporarily clashed with Mountbatten.

One galling similarity with Poland was the emerging limit of British military and financial influence: Britain had played second fiddle to the French in Warsaw and now found itself in the same position with the Americans in Chongqing. With only a token military force at his disposal, Carton de Wiart had to rely on his personal relations with the Generalissimo's government and senior US commanders to exert any influence. They valued his counsel and insight, which always carried on his civilized, convivial company. It was an arrangement underwritten by mutual trust.

In determining the substantive contribution Carton de Wiart made in his military-diplomatic missions, it is important to note his excellent working relations with British diplomats – Sir Esme Howard and Max-Müller in Poland and Sir Horace Seymour in China. Often there was an underlying conflict of interest between the Foreign Office and the War Office/Admiralty/Air Ministry/Ministry of Economic Warfare (SOE) that required tact and an almost feline sensibility to resolve. These are unusual qualities in a martial figure, which he possessed in abundance. Likewise, while it is a matter of speculation as to whether another British officer could have handled Piłsudski and the Generalissimo with equivalent aplomb, there is consensus among all the major actors – Howard, Max-Müller, Cavan, Ismay, Mountbatten, Churchill, Wedemeyer and many others – that Carton de Wiart pulled it off. Peeling away the layer of *politess* that characterizes official communications (and indeed most of their private correspondence) all were sincere in their accolades. After all, there is always the choice to say nothing.

Behind his exceptional exploits engaged in combat and navigating the labyrinth of political influence, there was a price to pay. Since time immemorial, the peripatetic and uncertain life of a soldier has been at odds with domestic serenity. Circumstances play their part, but often the allures of action beyond the barrack gate encourage people like Carton de Wiart to sally forth in pursuit of their own destiny. He was a curious combination of Achilles, for his prowess in battle, and of Odysseus, for his pragmatism and diplomacy. Either way, he unwittingly cast his wife Princess Rikki Fugger von Babenhausen in the role of Penelope, waiting for her husband to return home from the wars of Troy. After six years of marriage, he journeyed hence and never returned to his wife and two daughters, although they remained in his heart. It was only in his later years, after the death of Rikki, and having hung up his spurs, that he could reconcile himself with the prosaic joys of family life through Joan Sutherland, the last but not the only love of his extraordinary life.

Never a diarist and only a compiler of notes rather than letters, Carton de Wiart left behind only the faintest imprint of his personal life, not even acknowledging the existence of Rikki and their daughters in the pages of his autobiography. The most vexing gap is the sixteen years he spent in the Polesie marshes of Poland between the two world wars. Although it has proved possible to reassemble a skeletal cast of characters, and to revisit the great Radziwiłł sporting estates, the record of his day-to-day existence in these remote European borderlands remains out of reach: no diaries, no game books, no letters and few photographs. This historical void perfectly encapsulates the man and his enduring enigma.

Part I

Early life 1880–1913

1

Who was Adrian Carton de Wiart?

The year 1880 was one of celebrations for the Kingdom of Belgium, beginning with the engagement of fifteen-year-old Princess Stéphanie, the elder daughter of King Leopold II, to Rudolph, Crown Prince of Austria and heir apparent to the Habsburg Empire, and culminating in the spectacular Cinquantenaire exhibition in Brussels which marked the fiftieth anniversary of Belgian independence from the Kingdom of the Netherlands. Neither was a total success. Stéphanie returned home when it was discovered that she had not reached puberty; most of the Triumphal Arch at the Parc de Cinquantenaire ended up hastily constructed out of wood like Potemkin's village.

For Léon Carton de Wiart there was also much to celebrate for his first child Adrian was born on 5 May 1880 in Ixelles. Or was there? For while still suckling Adrian, his twenty-year-old mother Ernestine bolted, and a country girl from Waterloo had to be quickly brought in to continue to feed him.[1] A cloud of scandal enveloped the family.

The Carton de Wiarts originally came from Hennuin which is in today's northern France.[2] In 1719, Gabriel Carton, the officer in charge of the Maquis de Vauban's great fortification at Ath, acquired the lordship of Wiart on the banks of the Dendre. From the mid-eighteenth century onwards, Pierre-Francois-Bonadventura Carton de Wiart and his family settled in Brussels. His son became a lawyer, a profession subsequently embraced by many members of the family including Léon.

Educated at Stonyhurst College in England which had originally been founded in the sixteenth century in St Omer in France to educate English Catholic boys denied a Catholic education in Queen Elizabeth I's reign, Léon read law at Louvain University and then became an *advocat* in Brussels. With the Belle Époque in full swing, business in the capital flourished as Belgium enjoyed the rewards of early industrialization. Fortunes were made in banking and industry as the country became electrified and criss-crossed with railways connecting it to export markets. The jewel in the commercial crown, the Congo Free State, belonged to the king through the Association Internationale pour l'Exploration et la Civilisation de l'Afrique Centrale, an innocuous sounding title that masked a story of atrocities which came to haunt Belgium for the next hundred years.

The circumstances around Léon's marriage to nineteen-year-old Ernestine Wenzig, the daughter of a wealthy German furrier, are somewhat mysterious.[3] Supposedly born in Brussels in 1860, her father Ferdinand Wenzig was married to Pauline Levasseur who came from a distinguished French family which over time had accumulated four maquisards.[4] Some commentators describe Ernestine as Irish but they are confusing her with Léon's mother, Zoé-Marie-Isabelle Ryan, who had been born in Huddersfield in Yorkshire and was indeed of Irish descent.

First, the date of the wedding, 15 October 1879, and then the register of Adrian's birth on 8 May 1890 (three days after the actual event) indicate that he was conceived three months out of wedlock.[5] Secondly, given that her parents lived nearby, why, after deserting her husband and abandoning her baby, did Ernestine completely vanish until surfacing some forty years later when Adrian received a letter from her informing him that she was married with several children and living in Bordeaux? Was this the action of a loving daughter of a respectable family?[6]

Adrian Carton de Wiart later confided that he believed his mother to be a Circassian girl bought by his father in a Turkish slave market 'for at least partly chivalrous purposes'.[7] His cousin Edmond Carton de Wiart told the same story to Adrian's daughter Ria when she was seventeen.[8] The problem with this story is that there is no evidence that Léon as a studious young lawyer would have either been inclined or indeed found the time to embark on a lengthy trip to Turkey or the Levant. However, Ferdinand Wenzig as a furrier would have most probably gone to Istanbul to buy furs for its huge eighteenth-century fur market continued to thrive. Maybe he took pity on a Circassian girl in the Tavukpazari slave market or just acquired her from her parents and unofficially adopted her as his daughter or engaged her as a servant. In these circumstances, the Wenzigs might well have lent their name to her in a hasty wedding.

The notion of a Circassian slave girl at the time is entirely plausible. Ever since the Treaty of Adrianople in 1829 between the Russians and the Ottomans when the latter ceded the Circassian lands to the Tsar, the plight of the Circassians had worsened; and by the early 1860s mass deportations had begun. Some went by land, others by sea from the Black Sea ports; and by the end of the decade more than 400,000 Circassians had been evicted from their homelands and crossed into Turkey. With scant relief available, it was commonplace for refugee families to sell their children in the Ottoman slave markets. Of the families who survived typhus and smallpox in the appalling conditions they endured during their journey, many were settled in Bulgaria,[9] at the time still part of the Ottoman Empire, which could account for a story de Wiart once told Polish Princess Olga Radziwiłł that his mother was a Bulgar.[10] So Ernestine could well have been an orphan adopted by the Wenzigs.

So much for the questions surrounding his mother. What of his father? Would the young Léon with his strict Roman Catholic background and conventional career have risked prenuptial sex with Ernestine? One explanation is that Ernestine had deliberately thrown herself at Léon in the knowledge that under Belgian law she would have the right to sole custody of their child in the event of a separation or annulment and that right could be sold back to the father. Or is there an altogether a different explanation? For many years, it was rumoured that Adrian's real father was Leopold II, King of the Belgians. Leopold's marriage to Princess Marie Henriette of Austria, the granddaughter of the Habsburg Emperor Leopold II, had been in trouble from the beginning – poor Marie had written to her mother, 'I am very unhappy and I pray that I will be dead as soon as possible' – and it was well known that her husband had many affairs[11] and dalliances with courtesans.

Assuming that it was Leopold who was the father, there is a scenario that the Carton de Wiart family may have been approached by courtiers with whom they were friendly to provide a surrogate father for King Leopold's child. The Wenzigs may have been similarly recruited, with money rather than political advancement, to become the parents of Ernestine, who in this scenario was nothing to do with them. The truth will never be known but *Le Roi des Belges et des Belles* never recognized Adrian as his illegitimate son.

Left with a small baby and a wet nurse and doubtless the subject of countless wagging tongues, Léon needed a change of scenery. According to the Register in the Belgian Embassy in Cairo,[12] he is shown as arriving in Cairo on 26 November 1883, his former addresses given as 75 rue de Stassart and 43 rue de Bosquet in Brussels. Little Adrian followed him, arriving on 12 November 1885, and Léon's mother Zoé on 23 February 1887. She returned to La Hulpe in Brabant fourteen months later by which time Léon had remarried.

If this information is correct, it is likely that Léon either left Adrian in the care of his sister Hélène De Ryckman De Betz[13] or his relatively youthful 42-year-old widowed mother until he had established himself in business in Cairo where there was a small coterie of fellow Belgian businessmen, lawyers and entrepreneurs.

There had in fact been another Carton de Wiart in Egypt before him. His first cousin, René (1867–1906) had fought in Egypt when Kitchener was the Sirdar and finished the campaign as a Lieutenant Colonel in the Khedive's army with the honorary title of Bey or Colonel.

This reinforces the idea that Léon was sent by the family to Cairo to set up a legal practice specializing in investment as Egypt was becoming increasingly popular with Belgian investors. Between 1895 and 1912, it is estimated that between 400m and 500m Belgian Francs were invested in forty-four Belgo-Egyptian ventures,[14] mainly real estate, urban transport system like trams and light railways, and electrification. Once the second largest city in the Ottoman Empire after Constantinople, Cairo had resurfaced in the nineteenth century as a vibrant commercial and trading centre when the Suez Canal was opened in 1870. British occupation in 1882 served to accelerate economic growth and in 1883 the Alexandria Stock Exchange was established, followed by the Cairo Stock Exchange in 1903. The number of listed companies in 1907 was 228 with a market capital of about 91 million Egyptian pounds. This was a world where the legal services of Léon were held in high regard[15] and he soon became a director of several companies including the flamboyant Baron Edouard Empain's Cairo Electric Railways & Heliopolis Oases Company in which he personally held 7 per cent of the shares.

Within two years of his divorce from Ernestine coming through, Léon married again, this time to Miss Mary James, a 27-year-old Scots woman whom Adrian describes as formerly a 'companion to a Turkish princess'.[16] Little is known about her except that her family came from Cardiff and her father John died near Constantinople in 1871. Living at 32 Rue Qasr-el-Nil, Léon and Mary decided to start a family and two daughters, Beatrice and Edith, appeared in quick succession but tragically died as infants. Their son and only surviving child, Maurice, was born in 1895; another daughter Marie-Ghislaine, who was born in 1889, died aged one. Although Adrian remembered that his step-mother 'appeared very pretty . . . full of rigorous ideas accentuated by a strong will and a violent temper',[17] she was far more a governess than the warm maternal figure the little boy had been so arbitrarily deprived of.

Peter Fleming, who served with Carton de Wiart in Norway and China in the Second World War and knew him well, empathized in the biography he started writing in the 1960s that Carton de Wiart

> adjusted himself to a situation which few children (and still fewer only children) are called upon to face: a situation in which they lack not only a mother's love

and care but any clue to her identity. It is an experience which can hardly fail to leave its mark, especially when the child has no brothers or sisters and few playmates. De Wiart [*sic*], when he grew up, set a higher value on solitude and had far less fear of loneliness than is at all common among active, full-blooded men, and I suspect a cocoon of self-sufficiency into which he was always ready to retire was first woven during his waif-like childhood.[18]

Léon had one great advantage in Cairo for he had direct access to the King of Belgium's investment affairs through his cousin Edmond, Chevalier Carton de Wiart. Four years his senior, he was the Chef de Cabinet of Leopold II and later Grand Marshal to King Baudouin and a Director of La Société Générale de Belgique. His other cousin Henri Carton de Wiart became Minister of Justice in 1911 and then prime minister after the First World War. Such close family connections were invaluable for winning business. Léon's role would have been to prepare companies for listing on Stock Exchanges, legally sign off their prospectus and then often help to refinance them through rights issues or mergers with other corporations.

It would have been in this context that he applied to become a Student of Gray's Inn in 1903[19] at the age of forty-nine. Described as Doctor of Law (Brussels), advocate of the Belgian Bar and the Bar of the Mixed Tribunals,[20] Examiner in International Law at the Khedival Government School of Law in Egypt, he was introduced by Edmund Dicey CB, at the time Treasurer of the Inn but best known as a foreign affairs and leader writer for the *Daily Telegraph*. The two men had probably met in Egypt when Dicey was writing *The Story of the Khedivate* (1902), a follow up to his *England and Egypt* (1881). Léon was called to the bar in 1908 and continued to appear in the London law register until his death in 1915.

Living in Cairo with his father and step-mother, Adrian added street Arabic to his mother tongue, French, and the family lingua franca of English. It was a relatively carefree childhood with pony riding at home and holidays by the sea at Ramleh although as he later wrote, 'it was a life too lonely and formal to be truly happy'.[21] On reaching his eleventh birthday, he was despatched to England to the Oratory, a small Roman Catholic public school in the Birmingham suburb of Edgbaston that had been established in 1859 by Cardinal Newman, the champion of English Roman Catholicism. By this time, his father's cousin Maurice was secretary to Cardinal Bourne, the head of the Roman Catholic Church in England. Holidays were usually spent staying with school friends in England or in Belgium with his cousins at Hastière-pas-delà, a sleepy town on the banks of the Meuse where his uncle Constant lived in a rambling country house. Here there were fish in the river, wild boar and roe deer in the woods; and cliffs, caves and waterfalls to explore in the densely forested hills of the Ardennes.

Despite his fluency in English, Carton de Wiart's classmates viewed him as a foreigner which made his life at an English public school far from easy. In addition to the irksome regime of 'fagging', he was regarded with typical xenophobic suspicion and it was only when he began to excel at games that he found acceptance with his peer group and his confidence grew. Ending his school days as Captain of the School and of cricket, football and tennis, he went up to Balliol in January 1899 after passing the Competitive Entrance Exam. A dry comment in his Balliol obituary[22] suggested that 'surely this extraordinary buccaneer must have come up to the college as a result of Sligger's[23] links with European and aristocratic Catholicism'. Dating back to 1263, Balliol College had nurtured the English upper classes over the centuries with a preponderance of Old Etonian students.[24] Clever, athletic and moderately wealthy, Carton de Wiart erred on the side of a life of leisure and sport, failing – or 'ploughing' to use Oxford slang – his Law Preliminary first-time round. The authorities took a lenient line and allowed him to return for the start of the October term on 9 October.

Coincidentally, Paul Kruger, the President of the South African Republic, had issued an ultimatum the same day, giving the British government forty-eight hours to withdraw all its troops from the borders of the Transvaal and the Orange Free State, failing which they would go to war with Britain. The British government rejected the ultimatum and war was duly declared.

The Second Boer War, as it became known, was the termination of the struggle left unresolved in the ten-week dispute of 1880–1 between Great Britain and the descendants of the original Dutch settlers who had landed in the Cape in 1652. Motivated by trying to constrain European empire-building competition in Africa and, as always, with an eye on the bottom line as the profits from the diamond and gold fields gushed like inexhaustible fountains, the British government embarked on the first modern media war with Fleet Street as the hub of the Imperial spin machine.

The *causus belli* revolved around the refusal of the Boers to grant Burgership to the thousands of *uitlanders* or British foreign workers who had flocked to the area to work in the mining industry in the frenzied search for more and more precious metals and stones. This was construed by the British as a barefaced attempt to treat them as second-class citizens with no political rights. This time round hostilities were preceded by a barrage of propaganda. London newspapers[25] painted a dire picture of the flight of the uitlanders, inciting their readers to clamour for war. *The Times* led the charge, describing how 'refugees . . . tell stories on all hands of outrage and insult . . . by the Boers, who are behaving like semi-savages'.[26] An eyewitness reported in the *East London Standard* how fifty Boers thrashed British train passengers with 'leathern *sjamboks*'. Portrayed as vicious, inhuman and backward, the Boers were demonized to such an extent that a collective moral outrage gripped Britain. As the principal cheerleader, *The Times* opined gleefully in September 1900 that 'the war, more than any other in modern times, was and is a popular war'.

As 18,000 Boers crossed the frontier of Natal at daybreak on 12 October 1899, Carton de Wiart headed for the recruiting office. The temptation to enlist rather than continue his studies was irresistible and from that moment he knew 'once and for all that war was in my blood'.[27] It was to be a life-changing decision which he probably would not have made if his father had been in England to encourage him to take his studies seriously with the prospect of a rosy legal career beckoning. Or maybe, as Peter Fleming suggested, his mother's 'wilder blood' ran in his veins;[28] here was the Adyghe warrior from the Circassian mountains throwing off his undergraduate robes.

There were however several problems to be overcome, none of which proved insurmountable to the determined young warrior. He was Belgian by nationality, underage and therefore ineligible to join the British Army. This was solved by passing himself off as British and enlisting under a false age and name in the pandemonium of the recruiting office. No. 13010 Trooper Carton duly reported for duty to 51st Company, 19th Battalion (Paget's Horse) of the Imperial Yeomanry, a volunteer force created on 2 January 1900 by the British Army for service in South Africa.

Its founder, George Paget, was the son of a British general; he had also joined the Army, fighting in the Russo-Turkish War of 1877–8 and the Greco-Turkish War of 1897, as well as the Zulu War in 1879. A portly figure who frequented the dining and smoking rooms of Pall Mall, Paget recruited 500 officers and men, most of whom had been regular soldiers. Paget's Horse wore a badge made up of the letters *PH* which provided a source of mirth for London wags, who suggested that it stood for 'Piccadilly Heroes' or more commonly for 'Perfectly Harmless'.

Trooper Carton's company together with the 52nd and 68th Companies departed for South Africa on the troopship *Tagus* on 16 March 1900 with the 73rd Company following on 31 March on the *Delphic*.[29] The battalion arrived in Cape Town in April and was sent to the nearby Maitland Camp where it spent many weeks waiting for the arrival of its horses. For Carton de Wiart, the experience of going off to war had been one of drudgery from start to finish, mainly spent cleaning latrines and swabbing the sick from the mess decks on the troopship followed by weeks of cleaning stables, fetching food and forage, striking tents and other routine tasks[30] with no sight of the enemy or swish of a passing bullet. When the company finally arrived at the Orange River with the prospect of clashing with the enemy, he developed a fever and was sent to hospital where he 'felt my ignominy as a soldier was complete'.[31]

Discharged from hospital earlier than expected, the young trooper attached himself to a local corps that happened to be in the area of Douglas and set off with them to cross the Vaal River in full view of some Boer riflemen. He was shot twice, first in the stomach and then in the groin. When later asked how many Boers were engaged in the action, he replied: 'Not many but the few there were very good shots'.[32] He was not the first to be hit by a Boer marksman with a Martini-Henry or Mauser rifle. When General Redvers Buller recommended Captain Congreve of the Rifle Brigade for a VC, he remarked that 'some idea of the nature of fire may be gathered from the fact that Captain Congreve was shot through the leg, through the toe of his boot, grazed on the elbow and the shoulder, and his horse shot in three places'.[33] Carton de Wiart could consider himself lucky.

Back in the hospital which he had just left, his identity was soon rumbled, his father notified, and he was sent home to England to be invalided out of the Army on 22 October. The drums of war which had beat so loudly a few months before were muffled as he arrived back, 'bereft of glory',[34] to face Léon who had returned to England that year to apply for British nationality.[35] Reconciliation between father and son was immediate, paternal forgiveness warmly granted and soon Carton de Wiart found himself back at Balliol reading law. Although he had many college friends including the bedazzling Raymond Asquith,[36] the irrepressible roof-climbing Aubrey Herbert and the future Himalayan mountaineer Charlie Meade, having tasting the thrill of action albeit it briefly, he could not settle down and when the Christmas term ended, he went to Cairo to ask his father to let him take up the profession of arms as a career. Reluctant to quash his son's ambition which had been expressed with great passion and resigned to the fact that one less lawyer in the family was not the end of its illustrious legal tradition, he gave in. Before long, Carton de Wiart was on his way back to South Africa in search of the action and glory which had so far eluded him.

2

Peacetime soldiering and marriage

With a healthy bank balance after a generous replenishment by Léon, Carton de Wiart bade his farewells in England and sailed for South Africa, this time in a first-class cabin on a Union Castle liner rather than a troopship. No longer serving in the British Army, he had a cunning plan to re-enlist, this time with the Colonial Corps as a trooper in the Imperial Light Horse. His rationale was that this ploy would avoid the necessity of a year's training which the Regular Army would put him through as a matter of course.

In his year-long absence, the nature of the war in South Africa had dramatically changed. By September 1900, the British had taken control of both Boer Republics, except for the northern part of Transvaal, but they found it impossible, even with 250,000 troops, to police the area in its entirety. The Boers had responded by adopting guerrilla warfare tactics, avoiding pitched battles and using their local knowledge and resources to harass the occupying forces for that is how they regarded the British. Organized into commandos, they proved formidable irregular fighters.

The British were therefore forced to revise their tactics, concentrating on restricting the freedom of movement of the Boer commandos and depriving them of local support. William St John Brodrick, the Secretary of State for War, and Lieutenant General Lord Kitchener, General Officer Commanding (GOC) British Forces in South Africa,[1] came up with a strategy to build over 8,000 fortified blockhouses at key points along the railway lines that provided the vital lines of communication. These in turn were linked by barbed wire fences to break down the vast *veld* into smaller areas which were then subjected to cordon and sweep operations by columns of infantry and mounted cut-off parties.

Another British response was to deny the guerrillas supplies and shelter. Draconian tactics were employed, destroying everything that could give sustenance to the Boer guerrillas. As British troops swept the countryside, they systematically destroyed crops, burned homesteads and farms, thus creating a tidal wave of refugees – both Boer and African men, women, children – whom they interned in 'camps of refuge', later called concentration camps.

On arrival in Cape Town in January 1901, after passing a demanding riding test, Carton de Wiart succeeded in enlisting in the 2nd Imperial Light Horse as a trooper. He found his companions to be of 'a very indifferent type'[2] and two of his tent mates 'most unsavoury specimens'.[3] The much higher rates of pay tended to attract fly-by-night chancers intent on enriching themselves rather than selflessly fighting for Queen and Empire.

Despite the change of tactics to adapt to a more static form of war, VCs[4] for the Imperial Light Horse kept coming. At the Battle of Tygerkloof in December 1901, Surgeon Captain Tommy Crean won a VC when he attended the wounds of two soldiers and a fellow officer under heavy enemy fire 'after he himself had been wounded, and only desisted when he was hit a second time, and as it was first thought, mortally wounded'.[5] However, for Carton de Wiart like most other soldiers, life seemed 'to consist of trekking from one end of the country to the other, without aim or object',[6] all the while the enemy remaining elusive. When an opportunity arose to single-handedly cut a barbed wire obstacle covered by Boer sharpshooters, it was promptly quashed by his colonel who told him not to be a damned fool.[7] His Record of Services states that he was severely wounded in the knee at Bethlehem in August 1901 and then 'slightly wounded in the face and hands' at Harrismith in September,[8] he did not mention either occasion in his memoirs.

Within a few weeks, his commanding officer, Lieutenant Colonel Charles Briggs,[9] who was on secondment from the King's Dragoon Guards, selected him for a commission and on 14 September 1901, Carton de Wiart was gazetted a Second Lieutenant in the 4th (Royal Irish) Dragoon Guards,[10] a famous cavalry regiment in the British Army first raised in 1685 as the Earl of Arran's Regiment of Cuirassiers. It had been renamed as the 4th (Royal Irish) Dragoon Guards in 1788 and served in both the Peninsular and Crimean wars with distinction.[11] Its last active service tour had been in 1882 in Egypt at Tel le Kebir where it took part in the rout of Urabi Pasha's revolt.

He sailed home in September from South Africa and joined the Regiment at Rawalpindi in India in March 1902 by way of Cairo where he visited his father. After a musketry course[12] at Changla Gali in the Murree Hills, he was sent with the advance party to their change of station at Muttra ('Mathura') in the Agra district in north-west India. With no polo ground or fox hunting, he and his fellow cavalry officers turned to pig-sticking, a sport which involved killing a wild boar with a spear while riding at full speed over blind country. Lieutenant

Colonel W. A. Tilney of the 17th Lancers found it exhilarating: 'Pig-sticking is a grand rush of a few minutes with every thought concentrated on the pig, and none for your own or your horse's safety. The horse must look after himself and you.'[13] Philip Woodruff extolled in the *Men who Ruled India* that a good pigsticker 'must have the same qualities — the power of quick but cool judgement, a stout heart, a controlled but fiery ardour and determination not to be beaten — that are needed in the crisis of a riot, or for that matter for a battle…in fact good pigstickers were good officers.'[14]

The 4th Dragoon Guards were officered by an eclectic group of young men. His contemporaries included Old Etonians Harry Gurney and Bobby Oppenheim, Old Harrovians 'Butcha' Hornby and Henry Sewell, and Bob Ogilby who was soon to transfer to the Life Guards. Gurney had had a colourful career to date, joining as a trooper and gunner in the Rhodesia Light Horse during the Matabele campaign, then serving with the Egyptian Coast Guard under the Khedive from 1898-99 with the exotic sounding rank of *Saghalagashi* or in plain English adjutant. Another great friend of Carton de Wiart was Bobby Oppenheim, the great-grandson of Salomon Oppenheim, the founder of the Sa. Oppenheim jr. & Cie banking empire. Bobby had originally joined the Scots Guards but had become disenchanted with regimental soldiering in London and sought a transfer to India.

When the order came for the regiment to embark for Cape Colony in South Africa in 1904, Carton de Wiart was relieved: 'India for me was a glittering sham coated with dust and I hoped I should never see her again.'[15] By now the war was by now over and after taking over from the 16th Lancers in Middelburg, the newly promoted Lieutenant Carton de Wiart was given six months home leave in October which he spent in Cairo with his father and step-mother. Bob Ogilby came to stay and the two young officers drove around in an Oldsmobile with a phaeton body, one of the first such cars in Egypt.

It was during this leave in January 1905 that he met 18-year-old Princess Freiderike 'Rikki' Fugger von Babenhausen, the eldest child of the Fifth Furst Fugger von Babenhausen, Chamberlain to the Emperor Franz Joseph I of Austria, and his wife Fürstin 'Nora' née zu Hohenlohe-Bartenstein und Jagstberg. One of the great characters in the twilight years of Austro-Hungary, Nora had been brought up in Hradec Králové in Bohemia by her mother Rosa, a member of the Sternberg family, who had moved there after her husband Prince Karl had been 'seized with a deep melancholia from which he could never be cured.'[16] When Karl died aged forty, Nora's grandfather Count Jaroslaw von Sternberg put Neděliště Castle at Rosa's disposal; in winter she would move to Prague where

Count Jaroslaw had a house in Radetzky Square and when spring came, she would decamp to his apartments in the Prater in Vienna. When he died in 1874, Rosa and her three children[17] moved to a small estate at Bílé Poličany to the north of Hradec Králové which he had thoughtfully bought for his daughter; as was her custom, she continued to winter in Vienna. When Nora was seventeen, Rosa married a widower, General Leopold Prince de Croÿ-Dülmen, whose distinguished family had been members of the Imperial Diet since 1486. Now living in No.10 Schönburgstrasse in Vienna which her mother had commissioned the architect Viktor Rumpelmayer to design in 1880, and with the help of her well connected step-father, the youthful *salonière* Nora knew everyone and if she did not, she made it her business to.

Love was in the air for Nora when her cousin Prince 'Cary' Karl Fugger von Babenhausen, adhering to the rarefied rules of Austro-Hungarian social etiquette, declared his intentions towards her as serious after dancing two cotillions with her in the same season. Despite a brief lapse when he became infatuated with the precocious 16-year-old Baroness Mary Vetsera who was later to die in tragic circumstances with Crown Prince Rudolf at Mayerling,[18] they went on to announce their engagement. However, as an officer in the k.u.k. Leibgardereitereskadron (The Emperor's Lifeguards) he was not permitted to marry so he was posted to another cavalry regiment, the 9th Hussars *Graf Nádasdy*. He managed to gamble away what little money he had on the first night with his new regiment including his entire monthly allowance from his father, so consequently on the day of his wedding in March 1887 he was penniless. That did not stop the newlyweds honeymooning in Klagenfurt, Venice and Nice, where he managed to lose his monthly allowance again, this time in the casino at Monte Carlo.

Born in 1887, Rikki had been brought up in Austro-Hungary where Prince Cary was stationed, first at Sopron (Ödenburg)[19] with the 9th Hussars and then at Szombathely (Steinamanger) with the 11th Hussars. Her mother's frenetic social life and addiction to *tritsch-tratsch*, the Viennese passion for gossip, revolved around the court in Vienna – a two-hour carriage drive from their married quarter – and so her peripatetic childhood followed the social season when the family rented castles like the eighteenth-century Schloss Hunyadi at Maria-Enzersdorf and villas such as Graf de la Fontaine und d'Harnoncourt-Unverzagt's in the Prater, all within easy range of the city centre. When she was eight, her mother rented a villa in Hietzing on the edge of the fashionable Schönbrunner Schlosspark and started to introduce her children to the Imperial family and their courtiers. These were the days when Vienna 'was a city of beauty, of song, of music, of the dance and of joyfulness, the city of art and distinction . . . which did not have its equal in all this wide world – the Vienna which had grown to the height of its glory under the benevolent sceptre of the wise Emperor Franz Joseph'.[20] Whenever she could, Nora would also visit Berlin, Paris and London though it is not clear from her diaries whether her daughters accompanied her.

Prince Cary led the life of a typical well-to-do aristocratic Austro-Hungarian army officer, when, apart from manoeuvres, there was little to do other than gamble, ride and shoot, not unlike his English Edwardian counterparts. He certainly had little opportunity to rise to high rank if he had wanted to for there were no wars to fight. Under the direction of the Emperor's nephew, Archduke Albrecht, Duke of Teschen, the army had stagnated for years since 'his power was that of the bureaucrat, not the fighting soldier, and his thirty years of command over the peacetime Habsburg Army made it a flabby instrument of war'.[21]

The Fugger family originated in Swabia and after acquiring the rights over the City of Augsburg in the fourteenth century, later became nobles of the Holy Roman Empire. In 1803 Rikki's paternal line became Princes of the Empire, when Babenhausen was raised to the status of a principality of the Holy Roman Empire. Their power – and the reason for their fame – lay in the fact that they had been bankers to the Habsburgs since the sixteenth century. Few of Europe's ruling families have been able to advance without external financial assistance for their armies and plans for expansion. The Habsburgs were no exception and over the centuries they leant heavily on the willingness of the Fuggers to lend them money when needed, usually at attractive rates of interest and often secured against the assets of the Imperial gold and silver mines.

If the status of European nobility can be measured by their homes, the Fugger Schloss at Babenhausen in Bavaria is modest compared to the iconic Hohenzollern castle at Bisingen but it is nevertheless an impressive building going back to the early sixteenth century. In Augsburg, the Fuggerhäuser on Maximilianstrasse is one of if not the largest town house in Germany and the Schloss Wellenburg outside of the city is a substantial country house even though it is the smallest of the Fugger zu Babenhausen homes. Rikki's mother's family seat was at Barockschloss Bartenstein, the thirteenth-century residence of the Princes zu Hohenlohe-Bartenstein in Württenberg.

After the family had called off Rikki's short engagement to Graaf Willem van Aldenburg Bentinck, 7th Count Bentinck, on account of his Protestant faith,[22]

Princess Nora took her to Cairo to cheer her up. She had high hopes for her daughter and in her memoirs, she recalled that

> we made the acquaintance of a number of interesting persons. Among them was the family of the Duke of Connaught (the third son of Queen Victoria) . . . we celebrated with them the engagement of the charming Princess Margaret to the Crown (Gustav Adolf) Prince of Sweden. We were also present at a brilliant soirée given by Lord Cromer in connection with this engagement. At one of the many fêtes we made the acquaintance of Captain Adrian Carton de Wiart.[23]

Between the endless round of parties, they managed to climb to the top of the pyramid of Cheops with two Arab guides pulling Nora up by the arms, while a third one pushed her from behind.

Returning from leave, Carton de Wiart found South Africa a strikingly different place from the war-torn country where he had soldiered in 1899 and 1901. The war had finished at the end of May 1902 when the terms of surrender were signed in Pretoria. Lord Milner, who had led the diplomatic effort to bring hostilities to an end, then began the Herculean task of the reconstruction of the ravaged countryside and reconciliation with a disgruntled population smarting from what they saw as a colonial occupation. It was far from easy as the pressing need to address issues such as repatriation of the Boers, land settlement, education, justice, policing and infrastructure was exacerbated by an economic depression. At the heart of his programme was the plan to provide the Transvaal with a system of representative government, a half-way house between Crown Colony administration and self-government and in order to do that it was essential to treat the British and the Boers as equal partners.

Suffering from ill health difficulties, Milner left Pretoria in April 1905 and his successor the Earl of Selbourne, a former First Lord of the Admiralty, took over in May with the brief to implement Milner's plan through a gradual transition. Under pressure from the new Liberal government in London which had approved his Memorandum of 7 January 1907 outlining the advantages of union, the process of self-government was accelerated and by June 1907 the Orange River Colony had been given it. Key to the success was Selbourne's relations with the Botha government in reconciling the Dutch and British communities.

It was around this time that Carton de Wiart was appointed Orderly Officer or *'galloper'* to Brigadier General Thomas Hickman, GOC Middelburg District, and in the course of his duties, he met General Sir Henry Hildyard, the C-in-C South Africa, who invited him to come to Pretoria as one of his ADCs, the other being his son Reggie.[24] Based at Robert's Heights, the GOC and the Governor

General of South Africa worked hand in hand and for the first time Carton de Wiart was able to observe the synergies between politics and the military. He moved in the same social circle as 'the Kindergarten', the nickname for a dynamic group of young men whom Milner had recruited to implement his policy. Their ranks included John Buchan, an Oxford contemporary of de Wiart and a future Governor General of Canada; Philip Kerr, later (as Lord Lothian) Ambassador to Washington; Geoffrey Dawson, future editor of *The Times*; Lionel Curtis, nominated for a Nobel Peace Prize in 1947; and Patrick Duncan, the first South African citizen to be appointed Governor General after independence.

When not travelling with the GOC in his train, there was plenty of opportunity for him to play polo, ride in hurdle races and relax in the Rand Club in Johannesburg. He became a great friend of Muriel Marjoribanks, the wife of Captain Dudley Marjoribanks[25] of the Royal Horse Guards who had been posted to South Africa in 1905 to work for Lord Selbourne as his Military Secretary. The Marjoribanks family had amassed a fortune in the nineteenth century through their control of Coutts Bank and the Meux Brewery Company and entered politics as Liberal MPs. Dudley's father, the second Lord Tweedmouth, was the First Lord of the Admiralty in Sir Henry Campbell-Bannerman's 1905 Liberal government; his mother, Lady Fanny Spencer-Churchill, was Winston Churchill's aunt. Added to these connections, Muriel's father, St John Broderick, was Secretary of State for War. Muriel became devoted to Carton de Wiart and was at his bedside in London on many occasions when he was later hospitalized.[26]

His life as an ADC revolved as much as around Sir Henry's social as well as his military life. Carton de Wiart enjoyed dining out on an anecdote of the time:

> Lady Hildyard was a most charming hostess but an inveterate gambler, and South Africa with its fortunes won and lost overnight was a dangerous centre for the unstable. One day she came to me in great distress. She had gambled and lost an enormous sum, practically all Sir Henry's capital, and what should she do? I advised her to confess at once. All Sir Henry said was: 'Never mind, my dear, I might have done much worse myself.'
>
> I was always a reluctant card player, but bridge was considered an essential part of an ADC's equipment. One night Lady Hildyard who was my partner, had committed what I considered to be several enormities and as she got up to leave the room at the end of our game, I shook my fist after her retreating back. Sir Henry entered the room at that unfortunate moment, and I thought I was for home. Instead, he turned to Major Winwood the military secretary and said: De Wiart's a very patient man, isn't he?'[27]

In 1906 he returned to England for an operation on an old wound and spent his sick leave in Vienna where he found the Viennese 'as gay and unmaterialistic as the French are witty and grasping'.[28] Although Princess Nora and Rikki had returned to Cairo in 1906, it was probably in Vienna that he met up again with Princess Rikki who had become besotted with him, much to her parent's alarm. Princess Nora's elder sister Mary had fallen in love with Albert von Lonyay, a Lieutenant of Hussars, who had duly proposed to her. Despite the fact that the Lonyays were one of Hungary's oldest families, her mother Princess Rosa was horrified – 'a nobody – a First Lieutenant – and a Protestant in the bargain – no money – *voilà tout*! How could he have had the effrontery to ask for the hand of a princess Hohenlohe?'[29] Mary held her ground and was banished to the village church 'bare of ornaments and without taste' where, in front of a few curious peasants, she married her beloved Albert.

Like his father, Carton de Wiart had applied for naturalization and became a British citizen on 25 April 1907.[30] General Hildyard's retirement in 1908 coincided with the move of the 4th (Royal Irish) Dragoon Guards to Preston Barracks near Brighton. After disembarking at Southampton from SS *Morea* on 19 September, Carton de Wiart set off for Austria where Princess Rikki, by now his fiancée, awaited him. Lady Tweedmouth told Peter Fleming in 1964 that they had become engaged in Egypt – it was announced in *The Times* on 16 October just eleven days before the wedding – and that the marriage was backed by both families.[31] Rikki's sister Princess Hanau gave Fleming another version, namely that her father had been against the marriage from the beginning as Carton de Wiart had no money and secondly his mother was 'from India'.[32] Baroness Houtart, the daughter of Henry Carton de Wiart, confirmed[33] to Fleming that Prince Fugger von Babenhausen had been against the marriage but settled 1 million Belgian Francs on his daughter's future husband.[34]

The marriage took place on 27 October 1908,[35] Rikki's 21st birthday. The wedding held at St Stephen's Cathedral in Vienna[36] was officiated over by the Cardinal of Austria, Johannes Baptist Katschthaler, and the Carton de Wiart family was represented by Baron Edmund Carton de Wiart.[37] The Fuggers von Babenhausen must have been disappointment by Rikki's choice but at least their other children fared better socially. Her sister Sylvia married the Graf Freidrich zu Münster-Derneburg whose mother was the daughter of the 12th Earl of Kinnoull; her brother Georg to Grafin Elizabeth von Plessen from the wealthy aristocratic Mecklenburg family; her sister Maria to Furst Heinrich von Hanau Graf von Schaumburg with their magnificent Hořovice castle; and her brother

Leopold to Grafin Vera Czernin von und zu Chudenitz, a member of the richest and most influential family in Western Bohemia.

The newlyweds rented a large villa called San Remo in Hove next to Brighton where his regiment was stationed. Within three years they had two daughters: Anita born on 21 July 1909 at Schloss Babenhausen in Bavaria and Maria-Eleanora ('Ria') born on 26 September 1911 at the Fuggerhäuser in Augsburg. In the 1911 census, Carton de Wiart is shown as living in Hove with Rikki and Anita aged one; Rikki's sister Sylvia (aged eighteen) is registered as a visitor. The live-in household staff of eight servants included a butler, footman and a lady's maid from Bohemia. They then moved to the Elms in Rottingdean, a former home of Rudyard Kipling. Meanwhile, his peacetime Army career slowly progressed with an Intelligence course in 1909 and promotion to Captain the following year. A key member of the regimental polo team, he took part in the Inter-Regimental Tournament at Roehampton in July 1911.

Every summer they would travel in some style to Schloss Wellenburg outside Augsburg, but Princess Hanau remembered that money was always short, and that Princess Nora helped financially. According to her, Carton de Wiart disliked Germans so never spoke their language in public but, out shooting, the game keepers said he spoke it quite well.[38] It was when he was shooting one day with Count Franz von Colloredo-Mannsfeld at Sierndorf Castle that Carton de Wiart met Colonel Bob Sandeman, the Colonel of the Royal Gloucestershire Hussars, an English yeomanry regiment, who offered him the job of adjutant.[39] 'Loath as I was to soldier in England, I knew the life of a yeomanry adjutant was an enviable lot and renownedly [*sic*] pleasant both militarily and socially, and Gloucestershire the heart of good hunting country.'[40] Not surprisingly the regiment had adopted an old hunting song, 'D'ye ken John Peel', as its regimental march in 1890.

The decision to be seconded to the Royal Gloucestershire Hussars in the sleepy English countryside appears somewhat out of character for the dashing young Carton de Wiart who, to date, had relished his personal freedom, craving excitement above all else. In hindsight, this appears a complicated personal juggling act, motivated by a desire to reconcile his predilection for risk with the mundane domesticity of married life with young children and the limitations of humdrum peacetime soldiering in Edwardian England. How long would it take him to drop the tumblers and fall off his unicycle?

A-hunting we will go

Captain Carton de Wiart arrived to take up his new post as adjutant of the Royal Gloucestershire Hussars at the Barracks in Gloucester on 1 January 1912. Rikki and their two young daughters were staying in Germany with her mother Nora, whose routine had been somewhat disrupted by the death of her father-in-law in 1906. Schloss Babenhausen in Bavaria had passed to Prince Cary on the proviso that he agreed to live there for six months a year, which meant that Nora had to uproot herself from Viennese society and move to Ulm where she found 'neither taste nor comfort in the castles (she) was to occupy in the future'. With her customary energy, she set about 'turning the extensive castle of 80 rooms which was rather incompletely furnished into a handsome and comfortable home'.[1]

Yeomanry regiments had originally been raised in the 1790s to defend England against a Napoleonic invasion. Once that threat had passed, their role changed to one of policing and several were deployed to put down the Swing riots that broke out in the 1830s around the country in protest at farm mechanization. The Royal Gloucestershire Hussars, officered by landowners and manned by tenant farmers or employees from large estates, could trace its origins back to 1795 although it was only in 1847 that it adopted its current name.

On the outbreak of the Second Boer War in 1899, the War Office created the Imperial Yeomanry to reinforce the Regular Army, and the existing Yeomanry Cavalry regiments were asked to provide volunteers. Here was a chance for Thomas Hardy's Puddletown Volunteers and Dorset yeomanry 'to be put in front'. The Royal Gloucestershire Hussars contributed a squadron of men, around half of whom were existing members, the remainder being recruited in October when they enlisted for service in South Africa. On 28 February 1900, under the command of Captain William Playne, the 128-strong squadron left for Liverpool to board the *Cymric* for Africa. They were designated the 3rd Company of the 1st Battalion Yeomanry Cavalry.

As mounted rifles rather than cavalry, they saw their first action on 5 May at Thaba Nchu. More actions followed, including at Transfontein, Elands River and

Harrismith. On their return to England in July 1901, the men of the 1st Battalion were absorbed back into their parent regiments, and the Royal Gloucestershire Hussars was duly awarded its first battle honour, 'South Africa 1900–01'. They had lost three men in action and an officer and seven men had died from illness and disease.

In April 1901, the domestic Yeomanry Cavalry was renamed the Imperial Yeomanry and reorganized into regiments of 593 all ranks, grouped as before into four squadrons but with the addition of a machine-gun section. When the Territorial and Reserve Forces Act 1907 came into effect, all volunteer forces, including the yeomanry, were bundled into the Territorial Force. The Royal Gloucestershire Hussars conducted its first annual training under the new scheme in the summer of 1909, when, as part of the 1st South Midland Mounted Brigade which included the Warwickshire and Worcestershire Yeomanry, together with the 1st South Western Mounted Brigade (the Wiltshire, North Somerset, Hampshire and Dorset Yeomanry), it assembled on Salisbury Plain for exercises. What a glorious sight it must have been as over 3,500 men and 3,000 horses pitched camp on the grassy downs of Wiltshire, a scene reminiscent of the early nineteenth century.

With the squadrons dispersed in Gloucester, Bristol, Newport and Stroud, the duties of the adjutant encompassed several tasks, predominantly manning, horses, training and discipline. As the personal staff officer to the commanding officer, Lieutenant Colonel Bob Sandeman, a good working relationship between the two men was key to an efficient and happy regiment. With a revised establishment of 25 officers and 417 other ranks (ORs) together with 430 horses, Carton de Wiart ran his office from the Hohenlohe-Bartenstein house in Vienna once the summer training season had come to an end and 'had all the papers sent out to him to sign and return . . . occasionally . . . resorting to the expense of a wire'.[2] As soon as the hunting season started, he brought his family back to England, initially renting a flat in Cirencester and then a house at Brinkworth to the south of Cirencester. With the Badminton Hunt covering nearly two-thirds of the county, it was apt that the Honorary Colonel of the Regiment was the Duke of Beaufort, 'a model of a Master who hunts his own hounds'.[3] Weighing in at some twenty stone, his Grace took to the field with four horses – one to ride to the meet, one for the hunt and two in reserve. Famous for riding enormous mounts, he rarely jumped a fence as he had mastered the art of opening a gate with his crop in double quick time. In a field patronized by senior soldiers of the day such as Major General Jumbo Wilson, then Director of Military Operations, and Major Edward Ellington who later became Marshal of the Royal Air Force, Carton de Wiart was in his element as a fine horseman on the hunting field, a skilled polo player on the Big Field ground at Cirencester and a fearless steeplechaser, keeping two chasers in training, one of which came second in the Grand Military Gold Cup at Sandown. Rikki would occasionally be summoned to a social event; in June 1912 they both went to the Yeomanry Ball at Cirencester's Corn Hall, one of the highlights of the county's social calendar.

The following year, a similar pattern of activities came around with annual training on Salisbury Plain in May; one day, all the troops on the plain were assembled to watch an aeroplane from the Royal Flying Corps fly past for the first time. After escorting King George V round the Royal Agricultural Show at Bristol, the regiment gathered in July near Gloucester for tactical exercises. For the British Territorial Force, these halcyon months spent often at leisure with the Empire at its apogee turned out to be the calm before the worst military conflict in history.

Frank Fox, the Regiment's historian,[4] wrote

> the year 1914, up to the declaration of war against Germany, was singularly quiet for the soldier, but it was hardly a happy quietness. The kingdom was tossed and vexed by many unhappy dissensions. In Ireland civil war was threatened. In England serious labour strikes, the 'Suffragette' disturbances, and an unexampled bitterness in party political strife, seemed seriously to threaten social order. The general vexation and dejection of the public mind had naturally its reflection in the defence forces. As the clouds of the Great War began to gather few were fully confident that their country could meet the coming crisis with resolution and dignity.

On 3 January 1914, Carton de Wiart received a letter from his father in Cairo with news of a financial disaster. In his memoires, he writes that Léon owing to a 'slump' and 'over-trust in his fellow men'[5] had lost all his money. The result was that he was unable to continue his allowance to his elder son which led Carton de Wiart to the conclusion that 'he could not afford to soldier in England'. So he decided to 'sever his ties, begin a new life and possibly see active service abroad'.

Admittedly Egypt was going through a period of negative growth for there had been a slowdown in the agricultural sector which was the engine of the country's economy and real per capita GDP fell by 1.70 per cent over the period 1912–20. However, this does not amount to a mini-Wall Street Crash of 1929. As in all markets, not every investment in Egypt was copper bottomed. Some like Le Sociétè des Tramways d'Alexandre faltered when the railway and tram financier

Simon Philippart was sentenced to two years in prison for fraud in 1900; and a real estate company, the Koubbeh Garden Company, failed in the 1920s but the majority of the forty-four Belgo-Egyptian enterprises continued to prosper.

There had indeed been a financial crisis in Egypt but that was six years earlier in 1908 due to the ripple effect of the Panic of 1907 in the US markets. Léon appears to have weathered it without difficulties although the demand for new Belgo-Egyptian listings decreased[6] from nineteen between 1905 and 1907 to seven between 1908 and 1912. With an inside knowledge of all the companies he had worked with,[7] it would have been unusual and entirely out of character if he had lost all his money through gambling on the Stock Markets or making ill-judged loans. He was far from destitute for in early 1915 he was lunching with Sultan Hussein Kamel[8] as an honoured member of the Belgian community in Cairo. He was so well regarded that there is still a street in Heliopolis named after him.

However, if Léon really did have to stop his allowance, surely Carton de Wiart could have asked his wife for her immensely wealthy and respectable family to support him in his elite cavalry regiment rather than see him leave it for a less fashionable one or an obscure overseas posting. It was not to be the case. After annual training at Patcham outside Brighton in May,[9] he transferred to the Somaliland Camel Corps, and on 23 July sailed for Africa, once more in search of excitement. Soldiering in Somaliland certainly had its attractions as it was known to be dangerous: no fewer than six VCs had been awarded for gallantry there since 1902.[10]

Peter Fleming concluded that the clue to this precipitous decision lay in Carton de Wiart's autobiography when he wrote,

> momentarily my father's disaster gave me a shock and I wondered how I shall acclimatize myself to poverty. My second reaction found me almost glad, for it opened out the whole wide world again to me; it meant I could not afford to soldier in England, could sever my ties, begin a new life and possibly see active service abroad.[11]

The ties that he looked forward to severing were the ties that bound him to Rikki. His marriage had not broken up for she adored him, but it had foundered. As Fleming put it, 'only chivalry masked the indifference he felt for his charming, silly wife. Divorce, a far graver step in those days . . . was in any case out of the question for Catholics'.[12]

Whatever his intentions may have been, Carton de Wiart's approaching Somaliland adventure suddenly looked ill-timed and, from the point of view of his family, ill-considered. In the context of the impending conflict in Europe, its military significance was irrelevant. However, there was to be no turning back.

Twelve days after Carton de Wiart sailed for Africa, at 7 pm on 4 August, the Royal Gloucestershire Hussars were mobilized[13] and on 15 April 1915 sailed for Egypt on board the SS *Minneapolis*, disembarking at Alexandria on 24 April and making camp on Chatby Beach. On 11 August, they received orders to embark for Gallipoli and after landing at Suvla Bay they were brigaded in 1st South Midland Brigade as part of the British 2nd Mounted Division. On return to Egypt, they took part in many of the battles that formed the Sinai and Palestine Campaigns, primarily as part of the Imperial Mounted Division. Losses due to enemy action but mainly sickness were considerable, amounting to 11 officers and 130 ORs, many of whom had served with Carton de Wiart.

Carton de Wiart's father and step-mother were in Cairo when war broke out, but his extended family were all in Belgium and most would remain there for the duration of the war. After the German invasion in August 1914, the country was placed under the control of a German military government and much of it subjected to martial law. When evidence of atrocities by German soldiers against the civilian population began to emerge such as the massacre of nearly 700 people at Dinant, it was Carton de Wiart's cousin Fr Maurice Carton de Wiart,[14] the Diocesan Treasurer of Westminster Cathedral, who drew attention to them through the diary of one of his nurses which he arranged to have published. He himself, together with a surgeon, had led one of the first parties of nurses[15] to Belgium, to Hastière-par-delà, the home of the Carton de Wiart family on the edge of the Ardennes. When the Saxon Third Army reached the town, a reign of terror followed. On 23 August, they shot the town doctor who had cared for casualties from both sides and another eighteen civilians. The church was desecrated. At one point, the nursing party itself was threatened and it was only through the intervention of Fr Maurice's friend, Countess Marie-Charlotte-Ghislaine de Villegas de Saint-Pierre of the Red Cross in Brussels, that they were permitted to leave. When they returned to London, the bullet-ridden Red Cross flag used during their expedition could be seen flying over the heights of Dollis Hill.[16]

Maurice's brothers, Count Henri de Wiart and Baron Edmund de Wiart, both served their country with merit. Count Henri went with the government-in-exile to Sainte-Adresse outside Le Havre; and Edmund enlisted, aged almost forty-year-old, as a private soldier in the 2nd Carabinieri, and was sent to Antwerp. On retirement at the statutory age of forty, Charles de Broqueville, Minister of War, sent him to London to represent the Belgian government on Herbert

Hoover's Commission for Relief in Belgium (CRB).[17] At the same time, he was appointed financial delegate to the British government. In this double role and as a friend of both the financier Emile Francqui who had started *Comité Central de Secours et d'Alimentation* (Central Relief and Food Committee), the Ministers at Sainte-Adresse and Herbert Hoover, he made an important contribution towards maintaining the credibility of the government-in-exile which in reality did not govern enemy-occupied Belgium. He was also the Secretary General of the Official Committee designated by the British government for take care of the 250,000 Belgian refugees in the UK; under his responsibility, more than 10 million francs were advanced to them by the National Bank of Belgium.[18]

As for Rikki, six years of marriage had taken a course which she had never envisioned as a 21-year-old bride as she walked down the aisle of St Stefan's Cathedral in Vienna with the handsome young man she loved so passionately. Now subject to the Aliens Restriction Act of 1914, she found herself stranded in England with two small daughters[19] and without her husband who was hundreds of miles away in remote north east Africa. Her mother Princess Nora remained in Germany where she lost her youngest daughter, six-year-old Helene, in the winter of 1915 and her mother Rosa in 1918 after 'a stroke of apoplexy' in Klagenfurt.[20] Baroness Houtart[21] told Peter Fleming that when they met in Brighton in 1917, Rikki grumbled about her 'enemy wartime' status, while all the time having photographs of her father and brothers in German full dress uniform on the piano and a huge gilt inkstand on the bureau which was a wedding present from the Kaiser. She was never 'English' – it was an astute yet obvious comment for how on earth could she have been anything other than the daughter of a proud and distinguished German aristocratic family.[22] Her brother George, at one point a prospective husband for the Kaiser's pretty daughter Princess Viktoria Luise, fought for the Kaiser's Army with distinction, and her other brother, Leopold, volunteered to serve as an observer with Die Fliegertruppe (the Imperial German Flying Corps) and was decorated on several occasions. How difficult it must have been for her throughout the First World War.

Part II

Somaliland 1914

4

To war with the Mad Mullah

The contrast to the rolling countryside of Gloucestershire could not have been more marked. In his 1923 history of the Somaliland war, Douglas Jardine paints a vivid picture of the country:

> Bereft of all vegetation but a few scattered thorn-bushes bristling like hedgehogs, it is destitute of wealth and forbidding in aspect. The fine burning sand is driven by rainless storms into innumerable drifts. All the world seems ablaze; and it is but seldom that a cloud obstructs the pitiless sun. From this desert of surpassing desolation, the traveller gradually ascends the passes of the foothills through country that is almost as inhospitable, known as the Guban i.e. burnt. Bare bituminous boulders flank deep and sandy river-beds bestrewn with rocks. Then undulating plains covered with coarse grass and intersected by broad sand-rivers are crossed, until the main mountain range (Golis) is reached. Here, at 4,000 to 6,000 feet above sea level, the climate is invigorating and comparatively equable. . . . From the Golis one passes to the vast undulating plateau that slopes very gradually southwards to the Webbi Shebeli. Here you find almost every variety of scenery. Mountains like the Bur Dab range, that suddenly and unexpectedly rise straight out of the plain; large strips of rolling open pasture-land with grass that stands as high as a man's waist; great areas of dense bush; and only occasionally barren desert devoid of vegetation. . . . The land is a land of war. Its pastures have been watered with the blood of brave men; its barren rocks have witnessed many a savage battle.[1]

Early in 1885 Great Britain had concluded separate 'protective treaties' with all the Somali tribes, adding some 68,000 square miles to Her Majesty's African Empire. 'Protective' meant safeguarding British commercial interests. Responsibility for this important littoral on the main sea route to India was given to the Government of India but on 1 October 1898, owing to Somaliland's proximity to Italian-controlled Abyssinia, and with a view to the development of the resources of the interior, it was transferred to the Foreign Office. At the time, hopes of peaceful and prosperous development in the Somaliland

Protectorate ran high but the following year they were dashed by a young Somali called Mohammed bin Abdullah Hassan, 'a tall, wiry, dynamic man with a little goatee beard',[2] who soon became known to the world as the Mad Mullah.

At first, there was no evidence that Mohammed had any intention of leading a political movement with the object of driving the British out. On the contrary, he appeared to have been 'an earnest seeker after the truth, a staunch believer in the Q'oran [sic] as propounded by his superiors at Mecca, possessed of a special aptitude for learning the tenets and dogmas of the Mohammedan faith'.[3] He gained few adherents among the comparatively sophisticated inhabitants of Berbera and he soon retreated to the interior, where he set up his headquarters near Kirrit, his mother's home when he was a child.

However, after a frosty exchange of letters between the Mullah and the Vice-Consular Court at Berbera in March 1899, the consul-general in a despatch to the Marquess of Salisbury stated he was no longer in any doubt that he was organizing a rebellion. On 30 July, the consul-general informed the Foreign Office that 'reports from the Dolbahanta (tribe), apparently on good authority, are to the effect that the Mullah has gone off his head. It is said that he fired twice at his nephew, killing his horse, and that he was only prevented from doing further damage by being seized by his followers.'[4] From this time forward he was known to the British public as the Mad Mullah and to the traders of Berbera as *wadal wal*, 'idiot' or 'lunatic'.

The consul-general proved right and in August 1899, with a force of 5,000 men, of whom 1,500 were mounted and 200 armed with modern rifles, the Mullah arrived at Burao, an important communications centre less than a hundred miles from Berbera. He immediately declared himself to be the expected Mahdi and proclaimed a holy war against the infidels. According to the British, his followers styled themselves Dervishes whom no bullets could harm, and all Somalis who had not joined him were denounced as Kaffirs or infidels and ordered to acknowledge his authority.

Faced with an impending insurrection, in November 1900 Lieutenant Colonel Eric Swayne[5] was sent to Somaliland to take command of an expedition to neutralize the Mullah. His first task on arrival was to raise and train a levy of 1,500 Somalis to replace the 2nd Battalion King's African Rifles, who were being withdrawn for service in Ashanti. The Dervishes were now estimated at some 5,000 men, mostly mounted on horses, with some 600 rifles; the tribes whose loyalty towards the British would be doubtful if the expedition failed, were thought to possess some 60,000 spearmen.

In the first encounter, the British prevailed and the Mullah's forces suffered some 1,200 killed and wounded with 800 prisoners captured. However, by October 1901 the Mullah had reassembled his scattered forces and had advanced against the Dolbahanta well within British territory. His Majesty's government decided to launch a second expedition and Lieutenant Colonel Swayne was again appointed to command it. By now the Mullah's force had swollen to some 12,000, of whom 10,000 were said to be mounted and no less than 1,000 carried rifles. By the end of second expedition, despite the British inflicting heavy casualties on the rebels, the Mad Mullah was still at large, prompting the Cabinet to proceed with a third Somaliland expedition, this time working with the Italians in Abyssinia to prevent the Mullah's retreat over the border.

With the acquiescence of the Foreign Office, military and financial control of the expedition was handed over to the War Office. A force of nearly 4,000 men drawn from many different corners of the Empire assembled for a campaign as Jardine put it,

> against an inscrutable enemy, whose range of movements extended from Cape Guardafui to the equator, from the sea into Abyssinia, who offered no target for attack, no city, no fort, no land, and no possessions save those of others which, if lost, could be replaced as easily as they had been acquired. In short, there was no tangible military objective, but only an outlaw who would know how to fight when odds were in his favour and how to scuttle across waterless and barren deserts when the odds seemed against him.[6]

In early July 1902, the third expedition returned to camp nursing losses of 213 killed (including 13 British officers) and 60 wounded. Meanwhile the elusive Mullah remained at large. A fourth even larger expedition mounted in October killed an estimate 2,030 Dervishes at a cost of 3 British Officers and 5 British ORs killed and 10 British Officers and 18 British ORs wounded. Both in terms of blood and treasure, by April 1905 no less than £2,420,000 had been spent on the four expeditions – at a time when the Treasury was still reeling from the massive incremental cost of the Boer War – the British strategy was deeply flawed.

In a House of Commons debate on 30 April 1903, the Liberal MP James Bryce saw

> the Mullah, as a religious fanatic . . . something between a Trappist and a teetotaller. He obtained an enormous influence over his followers by preaching a jehad [sic] against the infidels. There were two courses open to the Government when, three or four years ago, the power of the Mullah began to grow, and one of these was a strictly defensive policy. He was said to be mad, but there had never

been a case of madness having so much method. . . . The officers of our forces, as usual, desired a forward policy; and the Government seemed to have been led to enter upon expeditions which had the effect of incensing the Mullah and quickening his appetite for war.

In the same debate, Lloyd George wondered 'if the Mullah was mad, what was the War Office? It would really be interesting to have the Mullah's opinion of both the War Office and the Foreign Office'.

It came as a relief when news came of a meeting between Commendatore Pestalozza, the representative of the Italian government, and the Mullah. An Anglo-Italian agreement known as the Pestalozza or Illig Agreement was drawn up and signed by all parties on 5 March 1905. There was now a considerable body of opinion in Westminster that any further expenditure in maintaining an indefinite and costly defensive campaign against the Dervishes was unacceptable. In March 1910, John Dillon the Irish MP reminded the House[7] that

> I made a suggestion, at least ten years ago, that this gentleman (the Mullah) ought to be offered, say £2,000 *per* year, and then he would keep quiet. I do not really know that he has been doing any harm when let alone. I am perfectly certain that for a modest sum he would become entirely friendly to the British Government. And observe the saving it would be supposing you paid this gentleman, as is the custom of the Government in India to pay along the frontier subsidies to tribes as long as they kept quiet, whereas you have spent £4,000,000 and many lives in chasing him, and for what purpose I never could find out.

In the same debate, the normally pugnacious Winston Churchill, Home Secretary at the time, admitted he had concluded that 'during the last ten or eleven years (when) we have been interfering and meddling in the internal affairs of Somaliland we have not been able to give any real security or tranquillity to the country'.

Far from bringing peace to the Protectorate, by arming the tribes for the ostensible use for self-defence against the Mad Mullah, the Illig Agreement ushered in an era of internecine warfare between them for many saw it as an opportunity to pay off old scores and to revive ancient feuds. This fratricidal strife extended to civil war between rival combinations of the same tribe. Spotting an opportunity to exploit the widespread disorder which was only sporadically policed by a small force of Camel Constabulary, in January 1913 the Mullah moved to Tale, where, with the help of Arab masons from the Yemen, he constructed a huge stone fortress with walls 14 feet thick at the base and about 6 feet at the top, covered by fire from several other forts 50–60 foot high.

Within these fortifications there were wells; and, inside the encircling walls, there was ample space for livestock and stone granaries for millet. Smaller forts were erected in other districts. It was a dramatic change of tactics from guerrilla warfare to one of static defence

It was not long before the Mullah's Dervishes clashed with the Constabulary; and on 9 August, in an action lasting a little over five hours, a pitched battle took place at Dul Madoba. By the time the 2,000 Dervish riflemen left, 395 of their men lay dead on the battlefield and scores more wounded. Of the 109 Camel Constabulary, who had left Burao on the previous day, thirty-five were killed, seventeen were seriously wounded, and twenty-four deserted. The survivors in the *zariba* at the end of the action consisted of Mr Cecil Dunn, Captain Gerald Summers (wounded in three places); twenty-three men, some of whom were slightly wounded but fit for further action; and the seventeen seriously wounded. The head of the Camel Constabulary, thirty-year-old Political Officer, Richard Conyngham Corfield, had been killed within the first hour. In the course of this single engagement, the Camel Constabulary had been eliminated as an effective fighting force. No wonder the British press headlines read "HORRIBLE DISASTER TO OUR TROOPS IN SOMALI-LAND".

Further embarrassment followed when a small force of Dervishes descended on Berbera in March 1914, causing widespread panic and bringing into question the very viability of the British administration. It spelt the end of the Camel Constabulary who were reorganized on military lines and styled the Somaliland Camel Corps. This new force, commanded by Lieutenant Colonel Tom Cubitt of the Royal Horse Artillery, comprised 18 British officers and 500 Somali rank and file, 2 companies being mounted on camels and the third on ponies. In addition, there was the Somaliland Indian Contingent, 400 strong, recruited from picked men in the Indian Army, of whom 150 were mounted on camels and attached to the Somaliland Camel Corps. There was also a temporary 400 strong garrison of Indian infantry.

Competition for places had been keen for as Churchill had sensed before the Boer War, 'the little titbits of fighting . . . distributed by luck or favour, were fiercely scrambled for throughout the British Army'.[8] It was this desire to see action, to savour the taste of battle that motivated the applicants for there was no garrison to relieve, no rich territorial prize to win, no civilian hostages to rescue or foreign power to deter. The only reward was a grudging recognition among peers for derring-do in far off uncomfortable places and a guaranteed campaign medal.

The primary function of the new Camel Corps was to enable the friendly tribes to avail themselves of their grazing grounds and water without molestation by the Mullah. The objects in view in Somaliland were defined in the House of Lords on 13 April 1914 by Lord Emmott, then Under Secretary of State for the Colonies, as being 'to keep order in the West and to prevent the further advance of the Mullah in the East'.

After his success at Dul Madoba, the Mullah decided to extend his influence into the rich grazing grounds of the Ain Valley. It was an excellent base from which to carry out raids in all directions and in no time at all he had erected forts around Shimber Beris as strongholds for his men to control the local tribes. It was clearly the first duty of the reorganized Camel Corps to capture Shimber Berris and release the Ain Valley from Dervish domination.

This was the situation when Carton de Wiart arrived in Somaliland in August and made his way up to Burao. For him, the Mad Mullah 'was a godsend to officers with an urge to fight and a shaky or non-existent bank account'.[9] His fellow officers 'were all short of cash, a fact quite unnoticeable in Somaliland which was about the one and only place on earth where one could not use it'. He instantly took to Tom Cubitt whose leadership qualities,[10] including his 'unrivalled flow of language', he found admirable and soon befriended fellow officers Captain Paddy Howard, Captain John Hornby (brother of Butcha) and Captain Alistair 'Boomer' Colquhoun.

By November, after a period of intensive training, the Corps was ready to launch its attack on Shimber Beris. Accordingly, on 17 November, Colonel Cubitt and his 2 staff officers, Major Summers and Major 'Pug' Ismay,[11] left Burao[12] with a self-contained mounted column of 14 officers and 520 rank and file. The neighbourhood of Shimber Berris was reached two days later without the Dervishes being aware that the column had even left. Cubitt's target was a group of six two-storied stone blockhouses, each garrisoned by up to fifty Dervishes.

Carton de Wiart gave a swashbuckling account of the assault:

> At last the word came to attack and we charged over the intervening ground (and) achieved the blockhouse without a casualty. Then, and only then, I realized what a tough proposition this blockhouse was going to be. The only entrance was a door, bit to get to that door we had to jump three feet to the thresh-hold which was covered by loopholes above it. I was in my shirtsleeves and the first shot fired at me passed through my rolled-up sleeve and did no damage (but) the blast blew me backwards and I wondered what to do next. Some of our men were being hit and the wounds were bad as the bullets were heavy and soft. . . . By this time I was seething with excitement. I got a glancing blow in my eye but

I was too wound up to stop – I had to go on trying to get in. The next hit was to my elbow, and I plucked a large but not too damaging splinter from it. By the following shot split my ear, and as the doctor was standing conveniently near, he stitched it up there and then. . . patched up and still wound up, I tried to storm the blockhouse but a ricochet from a bullet went through the same damaged eye. We were so near the Dervishes that I could touch their rifle with my stick which was only a couple of feet long.[13]

Pug Ismay[14] remembered joining Carton de Wiart in a hollow about eighty yards from the fort:

He had a bandage over his left eye, but I had no idea that he had already lost the sight of it and was in great pain. He said that the rifleman in the gallery was still a menace but that any amount of lead had been pumped into the fort and there could not be many survivors. He proposed that a couple of machine-guns should concentrate on the gallery for a full two minutes, and that the five British officers on the spot should then try and rush the door. Everyone thought this was a good idea. The five of us lined up, and the two machine-guns opened fire on the gallery. Chunks of masonry at once began to fall, and it looked like it might collapse at any moment. The seconds sped by. We kept an eye on our watches, and when the two minutes were up, we raced forward in silence. Carton de Wiart, on my right, was immediately hit in the arm and the ear, but did not check his stride. Symons, on my left, was the first to reach the door, but a bullet through the head sent him reeling backwards. Lawrence,[15] on the left of the line, was hit in the arm. It was clear – so far as anything could be clear in that melée – that the gallery was still intact.

Carton de Wiart had indeed been lucky compared to poor Captain Symons who had died on the spot. Despite the machine-gun fire brought to bear on the fort, it refused to surrender so Cubitt ordered a withdrawal at 3 pm after a firefight lasting nearly five hours, his main concern being to get the wounded back to Burao for treatment. It took another five hours to reach their camp at Little Bohotle. For Carton de Wiart, 'it had all been the most exhilarating fun and the pace too hot for anyone to have had any other sensation but thrill, primitive and devouring. By the time I got back to camp I was in bad shape, my eye very painful, and I was practically blind'.[16]

The Times ran a story on 1 December 1914 titled 'Somaliland Success – Destruction of a Dervish stronghold – Camel Constabulary engaged' and in the copy referred to Lieutenant Carton de Wiart having been 'severely wounded'. Sent on a camel down to Berbera on the coast some eighty miles away, Carton de Wiart was evacuated to a hospital in Aden and then by a P&O steamer to Egypt where an ophthalmic specialist advised him that his eye needed to be removed immediately.

Back at Shimber Berris, Cubitt's expedition had called up an old 7-pounder gun to evict the Dervish defenders and then returned to Burao on 25 November. In the absence of any explosives, the forts had proved to be indestructible to the firepower available to the Camel Corps and so in February 1915 Cubitt returned with some Pioneers who systematically demolished the forts with guncotton charges.[17] However, since it was not the government's policy to hold captured ground, the Mullah and his forces were soon back in residence. It would be another six years before the campaign finally finished when the Mullah's fort at Medishe was bombed by the fledgling RAF, forcing him to flee to Italian Somaliland where he died aged sixty-four from influenza.[18] 'A huge, fat nightmare of a man, so corpulent that he could no longer sit cross-legged, he had defied the British for twenty-one years and none of them had ever set eyes on him.'[19] Such was the longevity of his rebellion that no less than six clasps were issued for the African General Service Medal – Somaliland 1901, Somaliland 1902–4, Jidballi (10 January 1904), Somaliland 1908–10, Shimber Berris 1914–15, and Somaliland 1920.

As to whether he was mad, Pug Ismay gave him the benefit of the doubt in a report written in 1919: 'the Mullah's position has demanded military genius, administrative ability and diplomatic skill. History has shown how effectively he has met these demands.'[20] Peter Fleming was harsher, summing him up as 'a provocateur, not a prophet, a glib paranoiac better qualified to prey on superstitious fears that to arouse immortal longings'.[21]

After a nightmare journey to England when 'physically and morally the world was black and I was sick at heart',[22] Carton de Wiart was admitted to Sir Doulas Shield's twenty-bed hospital at 17 Park Lane. An Australian surgeon Shield, like Carton de Wiart, was a veteran of the South Africa War. A former member of Sir William Clarke's half-battery of Victorian Horse,[23] he had enlisted in 1902 for service in South Africa with the 6th Battalion Australian Commonwealth Horse but arrived too late to see action. In 1911 Shields was asked by the widow of the Melbourne financier Benjamin Fink[24] to attend her only son who was gravely ill. He was unable to save him but a grateful Mrs Fink bought a mansion at 17 Park Lane in London, which she converted into the Harold Fink Memorial Hospital, and asked Shields to move to London to run it.[25] When Carton de Wiart was admitted, although still funded by Mrs Catherine Fink it had been renamed as the Hospital for Wounded Officers, and as surgeon-in-chief, Shield operated on over 1,500 officers during the war years.

The ophthalmic surgeon to the King Edward VII Hospital of Officers, Sir Arnold Lawson, confirmed the verdict of the Cairo eye specialist and removed Carton de Wiart's left eye on 3 January 1915. In the process he found a sizeable piece of metal behind the eyeball although it is not recorded whether a newly introduced electro-magnet was used. After a month he was discharged and given sick leave before appearing before a medical board. Taken aback that Carton de Wiart was intent on going to fight in France, they suggested that if he wore a glass eyeball, the chances of him passing fit for general service would commensurably improve. Ironically, it had been a nineteenth-century German oculist Friedrich Müller-Uri who had pioneered a new form of glass called cryolite which was widely used by all armies. Taking them at their word, he duly appeared at the next board with a glass eye and they stuck to their side of the bargain and passed him.

As he came out of the Queen Alexandra Hospital at Millbank, he hailed a taxi, climbed into it and after throwing the glass eyeball out of the window,[26] covered the empty eye socket with a black patch. He was now ready to take on the Kaiser's Army.

Part III

The First World War 1915–18

In Flanders fields

In February 1915, Carton de Wiart embarked at Southampton to join his old regiment, the 4th (Royal Irish) Dragoon Guards, as a squadron leader at Mont des Cats within sound of the guns at Ypres. The regiment had been in France since August 1914 and had almost immediately been deployed as a reconnaissance force on the border with Belgium. In the Retreat from Mons, Regimental Drummer Edward Thomas is reputed to have fired the first British shots of the war and Carton de Wiart's friend 'Butcha' Hornby had the distinction on 22 August of being the first English soldier to kill a German Kuirassier, using a cavalry sword as his weapon of choice.[1] The battles of the Marne and the Aisne soon followed, then the war of manoeuvre stalled, and the opposing forces dug in around Ypres. In early 1915, the regiment had converted to the infantry role and had done several tours in front-lines trenches, always returning to their mounts back in reserve.

By the time he arrived, the Second Battle of Ypres was getting underway. Sent up to the line, Carton de Wiart experienced for the first time two of the most terrible weapons of the Western Front, heavy artillery and gas. His second-in-command was blown to pieces when standing next to him as they observed the enemy's fires. Late on 9 May, the regiment was ordered to relieve some infantry holding the front line on the Zonnebeke road and made its way up the road to rendezvous with a staff officer who would guide them in from there.[2] Walking in the pitch black with the adjutant, Captain Alex Gallaher, alongside the commanding officer, Colonel Arthur Solly-Flood, Carton de Wiart's party bumped into a group of Germans. Within seconds they had opened fire 'at two or three yards range' and Carton de Wiart found himself sprawled on the ground with his left hand shattered by two rifle bullets, 'a gory mess'.[3] After picking himself up, he staggered back down the road with his hand wrapped in a scarf as the Germans continued to fire at him. As if that was not enough, the adjutant who was also heading back mistook him for a German and took a pot shot at him. Fortunately, he missed and someone then recognized his voice; his groom and three other troopers appeared out of the darkness and carried him to the Field Dressing Station at Potijze Chateau where a doctor examined his hand. All the palm had been shot away and most of his wrist had been peppered with bits of his wristwatch. When the doctor refused to amputate the two fingers which were hanging off like chipolatas, Carton de Wiart pulled them off himself.

Meanwhile the regiment had spent the remaining hours of the night digging in enough to repel a German attack at dawn the next day. Under direct observation and about 200 yards from the enemy, they then spent the rest of the day motionless in their unfinished positions until relieved at midnight by the East Surreys. Every runner who attempted to move between Regimental Headquarters and the squadrons had been hit.[4]

By way of military hospitals at Hazebrouck and Boulogne, Carton de Wiart found himself back in 17 Park Lane, seriously ill and exhausted from pain. His recovery was to take months and despite the efforts of the doctors to save his hand, it was finally amputated in December. It would have been of some consolation to him when his DSO for 'distinguished service in the Field, in connection with the successful operations against Dervish forces at Shimber Berris, Somaliland, during the months of November 1914' was gazetted on 14 May 1915.[5]

While he was hospitalized, his father Léon died in Cairo; with Adrian in London and her son Maurice away, Mary was left on her own to wind up her husband's estate. On 9 June 1915, *The Times* reported 'his death will leave Cairo the poorer for a great pleader and an attractive and interesting personality'.[6] The *Globe* described him as 'one of the principal members of the European colony in Egypt and among the leading lawyers of Cairo whose services were frequently utilized by members of the Khedival family . . . a very great authority on Egyptian affairs, and his advice was often sought by the British authorities, including Lord Cromer'.[7] Although Léon had taken British nationality in 1900, he had continued to act as if he was still Belgian and played a large part in Belgo-Egyptian affairs as an active member of the 'Cercle belge' and of the 'Sociètè belge de bienfaisance du Caire' right up to the end of his life.[8] Carton de Wiart had last seen his father on his way back from Somaliland and noted that 'his brain had begun to fail and that the end could not be far off. Although I had been prepared for his death it did not lessen the blow, for he was my only real tie in the world, the one solid piece of background and well as the most kind and generous of fathers'.[9]

Managing once more to bluff his way through the Medical Board by regaling them with stories of how he adept he had become at fishing and shooting with just one hand, he rejoined his regiment near Boulogne on 20 February 1916. At least he was £500 better off (£250[10] for the loss of a hand on top of £250 for an eye) and a disability pension of £100 per year.

Major General Tom Bridges, whom Carton de Wiart had soldiered with in South Africa, was now commanding 19th Division[11] and had asked him when he visited him in hospital whether he would like a job with him. This request had a tonic effect on him and true to his word, Bridge's offer materialized with a posting order in March as second-in-command to Lieutenant Colonel Monty Hill of the 7th (Service) Battalion, Loyal North Lancashire Regiment, which formed part of Kitchener's New Second Army. 'The Preston Pals' as the battalion was known had all signed up on the same day in September 1914 following an appeal by Cyril Cartmell, son of the town's mayor. They went shoulder-to-shoulder with their mates and, after parading before crowds of well-wishers in the Flag Market, they marched down to the railway station ready to go to war. Once basic training had been completed, the battalion disembarked at Boulogne in July 1915 and after concentrating in the St Omer area, went into action at Pietre in a diversionary attack in support of the Battle of Loos. When Carton de Wiart arrived, they were in a quiet sector of the line at Neuve Chapelle but were taken out of the line in early May and sent to Amiens to prepare for the Battle of the Somme. A stickler for physical fitness, Carton de Wiart immediately took charge of physical training (PT) and soon the battalion including officers was on parade at 6.30 am every day for vigorous physical exercises.

With the Somme offensive imminent, Bridges needed his best officers in charge of the assaulting infantry to spearhead the attack. Officer losses in the regular infantry had been very severe and few with any experience were available. So, after being given carte blanche by General Sir Hubert Gough,[12] Bridges cherrypicked 'a gallant band of cavaliers' from the Cavalry[13] and extracted Tom Cubitt from the Gunners as a brigade commander.[14] From his time in Somaliland, Carton de Wiart understood and sympathized with the infantryman who 'endured danger, hourly and daily, until it became monotonous; discomfort, noise, long spells of the line, fatigues and carrying parties; and he was dog-tired and looked it...He had little to cheer him but his own unfailing spirit and superb sense of humour'.[15]

Being highly regarded, on 15 June 1916 Carton de Wiart was duly elevated and became acting commanding officer of the 8th Battalion Gloucester Regiment, part of 57th Infantry Brigade. A week later he was promoted to Lieutenant Colonel and formally took command.[16] For fighting soldiers, command of a cavalry regiment or infantry battalion is the highlight of their career and where they make their name for selection to higher command. Carton de Wiart was in his element even more so as, according to the adjutant Captain Walter Parkes who had arrived around the same time, 'the regiment was at that time somewhat in the Doldrums (with) a Commanding Officer of doubtful quality'.[17] The commander of 57th Infantry Brigade, Brigadier General George 'Ma' Jeffreys, made a lasting impression on Carton de Wiart for, as a former officer in the Grenadier Guards, he insisted on the highest standards of discipline, turnout and skill at arms.

Within days of his taking over at Rainneville, the battalion was subjected to strenuous sessions of PT at 6.30 am each morning followed by route marches, practice bayonet fighting and company tactical exercises. Carton de Wiart made a point of getting to know the platoon commanders and as many non-commissioned officers (NCOs) and men as he could in the short time he had before the Somme offensive opened. Well acquainted with the men of Gloucestershire from his yeomanry days, his arrival 'gave . . . a fantastic boost to its morale which was never lost. . . . His influence over the men from Gloucester was immense and there was never any doubt – as we shall see – that they would have followed him anywhere'.[18] On 27 June, the battalion moved to Franvillers Wood and then to the Corps reserve line at Millencourt.[19] The British Army was about to launch its massive attack on the German defences behind the River Somme, 'an unappealing river, marshy and meandering but the countryside that surrounds it appears fondly familiar to an English eye, rising and falling in long, green swells and hollows reminiscent of Salisbury Plain'.[20] The rationale behind the offensive was to relief the pressure on the French Army at Verdun which had been fighting for its very survival since February. If Verdun fell, the theory went, so would Paris and then all of France.

The British plan was for Lieutenant General Sir Henry Rawlinson's Fourth Army to capture the Thiepval-Combles massif north of the river while the French launched a simultaneous attack to the south. The first obstacle that had to be overcome was the heavily fortified German position in the small village of La Boisselle which dominated two valleys through which British troops would have to advance.[21] At 7.28 am on 1 July an enormous mine was detonated under the German strongpoint at Schwabenhöhe (Swabian Height) just south of La Boisselle, signalling the start of the assault by 34th Division. Despite the size and fury of the mine detonation, the advance stalled for the German defences enjoyed mutual support from flanking defences that other parts of the initial advance had failed to overcome, including the village itself. Now it was the turn of Bridge's 19th Division. On 3 July at 1.30 am the Gloucesters moved up in support of 8th Battalion Staffordshire Regiment. Soon the situation reverted to chaos as the Staffordshires mistakenly began to withdraw. Carton de Wiart and other officers got out of the trench and reasserted control, enabling the battalion to reach its start line; the sight of their commanding officer standing on top of the trench in full view of the enemy armed with nothing more than his stick, calmly giving directions to platoon commanders, was inspirational to the men.[22] The Gloucesters attacked at 3.15 am in the half-light of sunrise.

In his book *The First World War*, John Keegan summarizes the objective:

> To the naked eye, viewed from our trenches before the battle started, the village . . . appeared but a mass of bricks and mortar. Yet below ground all was different. The Germans during the two years they had held that position had constructed vast dugouts and shelters often as much as thirty feet down. These were connected, one with another, by passages proof against the heaviest shells that could be hurled against them. Thus, while to all outward appearances La Boisselle was a rubble heap giving little or no protection against an attacking force, it was in fact a terribly strong position in which a small garrison of brave determined men – as indeed the Germans were – who had lived there for more than a year and knew every hole and corner of the place were able to offer a stout resistance for a considerable time and to cause heavy casualties to any attacking force.[23]

Once on the objective, the British faced a maze of trenches and deep dugouts that could only be cleared by hand-to-hand fighting and bombing parties. Enemy snipers would pop up, fire and disappear back into the warren of passages. Carton de Wiart wrote, 'La Boisselle was a truly bloody scene. The casualties had been appalling; there were dead everywhere, not a house standing, and the ground as flattened as if the very soul had been blasted out of the earth and turned into a void.'[24] Officers attempted to coordinate the bombing attacks but in doing so exposed themselves to enemy snipers and soon casualties mounted. At 6 pm Bridges came up to the line and, with two of his commanding officers killed and two wounded, put all the British troops in the village under Carton de Wiart's command. All night, exhausted and still in contact with the enemy, Carton de Wiart and his men remained on the objective and by 8.10 am on 4 June he was able to report that it had been secured. Twenty minutes later the Germans mounted a series of ferocious counter-attacks and by midday it was touch and go if the position could be held for much longer.

The troops of 57th Brigade were strung out along the line of a hedge from where Carton de Wiart personally conducted the battle, pulling safety pins out of Mills bombs (No.5 hand grenades) with his teeth and chucking them at the enemy with his one good arm. This was not as simple as it might appear to be for the pulling ring was attached to a split pin designed to be pulled out by the thrower's left hand using considerable force. Unless Carton de Wiart had straightened out the split with his right hand (or got someone else to do so), it would have been impossible to extract with his teeth. With a seven second fuse, he would also have had to keep his head down for, on explosion, the base plug had been known to fell the thrower. Despite being subjected to heavy shelling, under his inspiring leadership the British line held firm and by late afternoon the village had been recaptured. The Gloucesters, who had moved to the support line at Ryecroft Street at 9 am that morning, were now moved up to La Boiselle to occupy the enemy dugouts. The following morning, they held the support line all day under heavy shelling until on the night of 5/6 June Carton de Wiart was able to withdraw his battalion along the Pozieres-Albert road; and by 2.30 am they arrived in Albert where for the first time in five days and nights they were able to sleep. The cost in lives and injuries for the battalion was grim: 6 officers had been killed, 14 wounded and 282 ORs killed, missing or wounded. The total British casualty list for the four-day battle for La Boisselle, an area not much larger than Trafalgar Square, was 3,500 and 'speaks of the desperate nature of the three days' continuous struggle. It was a real "dog fight", a soldier's battle, and the Germans never fought like that again'.[25]

However, Caton de Wiart was delighted with the performance of his men.

> The effect on the battalion of this successful attack was quite extraordinary and their already high morale rose still higher; one felt that they could never admit defeat. They had every reason to be pleased with themselves, for if they had not pushed through to their objective when the leading battalion gave up, the advance of the whole of that sector of the front would have been jeopardized.[26]

General Bridges came to thank the battalion before they moved to Millencourt for the next ten days. Reinforced with drafts totalling 250, daily training resumed with early morning PT, drill, bayonet practice and route marches.

His adjutant Walter Parkes gives an insight into Carton de Wiart's style of leadership, noting that

> he had in ordinary conversation . . . a gentle manner and speech not in the least of the kind so often associated with spectacular bravery but his one remaining eye was as keen as a hawk's and when really annoyed a flow of language of this world. . . . He always had a word for everyone and never forgot a man who had been under his command.[27]

At 9 pm on 20 July, the battalion moved into the old German Line close to Bazentine-Le-Petit to take part in a night attack on the German switch line running through High Wood. After relieving 10th Worcestershires in the front line at 9.30 pm on 22 July, together with the 10th Royal Warwickshires and the 7th South Lancashires, the battalion advanced. Carton de Wiart had already made an inauspicious start for on his way up to the line the day before one of his surviving officers was killed alongside him. While heading for the start line, he suddenly found himself 'flat on my face, with the sensation that the whole of the back of my head had been blown off'. After spending the next few hours in a shell hole with shells bursting all around, his batman managed to get him to the Dressing Station. Here he heard the bad news that the attack had failed. The War Diary reads – '1am. Attack failed our casualties being one officer killed, five wounded, eight missing including the CO. Lt Col de Wiart [*sic*] gunshot wound in the neck. 186 casualties among other ranks.'[28] Of the eight new officers he had received on the afternoon before the attack, not one came back alive.[29]

For his heroism at La Boiselle and the intense fighting which followed, Tom Bridges recommended Carton de Wiart for a VC:

> For most conspicuous bravery, coolness and determination during severe operations of a prolonged nature. It was owing in a great measure to his dauntless courage and inspiring example that a serious reverse was averted. He displayed the utmost energy and courage in forcing our attack home. After three other battalion Commanders had become casualties, he controlled their commands, and ensured that the ground won was maintained at all costs. He frequently exposed himself in the organisation of positions and of supplies, passing unflinchingly through fire barrage of the most intense nature. His gallantry was inspiring to all.

Now back in his old room at 17 Park Lane under the care of Shields, Carton de Wiart was told that his skull was intact and that the bullet had miraculously gone straight through the back of his head without touching a vital part. After just three weeks leave, he rejoined his battalion on 12 September. In his absence, it had been involved in another bloody engagement at Bazentine on 30 July when eight officers had been killed, three wounded and three missing with ORs casualties of 160 killed, missing or wounded. Major Lord A. G. Thynne,[30] who had taken over temporary command from de Wiart on 24 July, had been wounded in the leg and replaced by Major C. H. Harding.

The 8th Gloucesters were back in the line on 16 September and when they came out eleven days later, they paraded with the rest of the brigade at Borre before General Sir Herbert Plumer, GOC 2 Army, who presented Carton de Wiart with the ribbon for his VC which had been gazetted on 9 September. Three weeks of training followed and on 18 October the battalion took over the old German front line dugouts to the north of Ovillers from which they went forward and relieved the 8th North Staffordshires in the Stuff Redoubt. The following day the Redoubt was heavily shelled, wounding two officers; and the next morning at 8.15 am Carton de Wiart was wounded in the ankle by shell fire. At midday the battalion was relieved by 6th Wiltshires and left the line. It had been an expensive static three days in the line with one officer killed and two wounded with sixteen ORs killed and forty-seven wounded.

Yet again, Carton de Wiart was on his way back to 17 Park Lane. Sent on sick leave, his VC was presented to him at Buckingham Palace by the King on 29 November. It must have been a sombre occasion for seven[31] posthumous VCs were presented by the King that day to the parents of sons who had been killed in action. While still on sick leave, he met up with General Bridges who was in London on leave. The witty society beauty Lady Cynthia Asquith recalled going to tea with the Bridges and 'with them – great excitement – was the hero of the war, Carton de Wiart. He is wonderful undisfigured by his Nelson wounds – loss of eye and arm – and I rather fell in love with him. Very good looking, with great distinction – hands and gentle languid manner – certainly most attractive.'[32]

After a brief spell as commanding officer of 8th North Staffordshires in the line at Hebuterne, on 11 January 1917, on the recommendation of General Sir Hubert Gough,[33] Carton de Wiart took over command of 12th Brigade which formed part of the British 4th Division. His rise from major to brigadier general in just under two years was nothing less that astonishing, even by the standards of the First World War. It was a ringing endorsement of his leadership, competence and fearless personal example in battle. He had been an outstanding success as a commander of an infantry battalion: his superior officers knew they could rely on him to carry out their orders whatever the difficulties; and his men, in their turn, knew that he would be alongside them in the heat of battle. If anyone would be the last man standing, it would be him. Even when wounded, he soon reappeared. Such was his aura of invincibility which inspired ordinary men to excel themselves.

A lucky and not so lucky brigadier

In moving from a battalion to a brigade, Carton de Wiart had left the world of 'units' where there exists a familiarity between all ranks, whether at platoon, company or battalion level[1] to a new military stratum of 'formations' where interpersonal discourse is restricted by necessity to that of one between commanders, both above, sideways and below. For Carton de Wiart, at the top of the tree was General Edmund Allenby, GOC Third Army.[2] Below him was the GOC XVII Corps, Lieutenant General Sir Charles Fergusson,[3] and next level down[4] was 4th Division under Major General Billy Lambton.[5] The other brigade commanders in the Division were Brigadier General Aubrey Pritchard of 10th Infantry Brigade and Brigadier General Ralph Berners of 11th Infantry Brigade. They had all heard about the one-eyed, one-armed VC and several knew him of old.

Carton de Wiart's new command, 12th Brigade, moved from Sailly Laurette to Bouchavesnes on the eastern edge of the Somme salient on 24 January 1917 to position itself to relief 11th Infantry Brigade in the line. The brigade 'bayonet' strength on paper was:

1st Battalion King's Own (Lancaster) Regiment (33 Officers and 906 OR) commanded by Lieutenant Colonel O.C. Borrett, DSO

2nd Battalion Lancashire Fusiliers (40 Officers and 728 OR) commanded by Lieutenant Colonel C.J. Griffin, DSO

2nd Battalion Duke of Wellington's Regiment (39 Officers and 909 OR) commanded by Lieutenant Colonel A.G. Horsfall

2nd Battalion Essex Regiment (31 Officers and 1162 OR) commanded by Lieutenant Colonel S.G. Mullock[6]

12th Brigade Machine Gun Company (11 Officers and 180 OR)

12th Brigade Trench Mortar Battery (3 Officers and 71 OR)

Brigade Headquarters was a relatively small affair with a senior staff officer known as the Brigade Major, in this case Captain James Fison MC[7] of the Suffolk Regiment, and a junior staff officer known as the Staff Captain, Captain A. J. Trousdell MC of the Royal Irish Fusiliers. The brigade had its own machine-gun company and trench mortar battery which Carton de Wiart could allocate as he saw fit. In total, he notionally had over 4,100 officers and men under command. The reality was somewhat different as the numbers waxed and waned, with casualties, leave and divisional administrative tasks all eating into the 'bayonet strength'. There would be moments when manning levels, reduced by heavy casualties after major engagements, were perilously low while commanders waited for battlefield replacements to arrive.

Infantry brigades held a frontage of the first line trenches for periods of between a week and ten days until relieved by another brigade. Within the brigade a typical deployment was one battalion in the front line, with the other two in reserve, about two to three miles back. Rotated every forty-eight hours, the forward battalion had several sections deployed as outposts in the front trench with two companies manning strong points behind them. The third company was in reserve to act as a counter-attacking force and the fourth company was resting. Two brigades of a division would be deployed forward with the third brigade in reserve.

After a quiet spell, Carton de Wiart handed over to 11th Infantry Brigade and on 17 February the Brigade log notes that 'Brigade HQ opens at Chateau Suzanne',[8] a seventeenth-century château lived in by the Estourmel family. For the next six weeks, Carton de Wiart and his staff prepared the brigade for the forthcoming Battle of Arras when the 9th and 4th Divisions of XVII Corps had been warned to attack the German positions north of the River Scarp as part of a diversionary attack by the British in support of a major French offensive down the Aisne valley.

Following heavy losses on the Somme, the Germans had taken the decision to shorten their lines. Over the last nine months, the German army had built a formidable new defensive position called 'The Hindenburg Line' and by 18 March they had completed their withdrawal behind this line. This created serious complications for British planners on the eve of the offensive. For the French, the problem was even more acute, as their forthcoming attack was intended as a breakout from a salient that no longer existed. However, General Nivelle decided to proceed. The British were to begin their operations a few days before those of the French, the intention being that the German reserves would be transferred north to counter the attack around Arras. With these reserves committed to battle, the much larger French force would punch through or 'rupture' the German lines to the south and roll up the German army unopposed from the rear. This was to be the knockout blow on the Western Front, and Nivelle had boasted that his offensive would end the war.[9]

In early April, the Brigade moved to Y Huts, 1,000 yards east of Etrun. The weather was atrocious, 'rain alternating with snow and sleet, the temperatures relentlessly low; wet and shelling had turned the chalky surface of the attack zone into gluey mud, everywhere ankle-deep, in places deeper'.[10] The following day, the Brigade log notes that 'Carton de Wiart slightly wounded but remained on duty'.[11] In fact, his ear had been ripped by a piece of shell fragment: Major Jock Evetts of 26th Highland Brigade remembered him passing by 'with his head bandaged up and his steel helmet perched on top of it'.[12] Excitement was mounting as Zero Hour was announced for 5.30 am on 9 April. At 4.30 am, the Brigade took up positions in the open near St Nicholas and waited. Not a shot was to be heard thanks to the British artillery bombardment and by 3.45 pm that afternoon Carton de Wiart's Brigade had captured the German trench system west of Fampoux 'with no difficulty'.[13] In the process they took 230 prisoners and captured several howitzers, trench mortars and machine guns. Their losses were 14 officers and 153 ORs. That night it was bitterly cold with biting wind and snow.

By morning, the Germans had regrouped and the following night launched two counter-attacks which were both repulsed. The next day, 11 April, the Brigade was ordered to make a night attack which stalled due to German MG fire. It was a costly engagement with casualties of 10 officers and 290 ORs with only 40 prisoners taken. By the time they came out of the line on 12 April, the Brigade had incurred another ninety-four ORs casualties and the loss of Lieutenant Colonel Sidney Mullock, Commanding Officer of 2nd Battalion Essex Regiment, who was killed when returning from a commanding officers' conference at Fampoux.[14]

Captain Colin Gubbins, later head of the Special Operations Executive in the Second World War,[15] recalled Carton de Wiart's method of planning an attack:

> I was sent to his headquarters as a liaison officer and joined him in the dug-out. . . .When the divisional orders for the next day's attack reached him – long and voluminous – he read these through twice, questioned me on one or two gunner matters, then deliberately tore up the orders and sent for his battalion commanders; a ten-minute conference; a few clear verbal orders from him; and it was all over. He could not abide what he called 'bumph war'.[16]

Such an ostensibly cavalier approach could be construed as irresponsible, yet there is no evidence to suggest that his brigade or its battalions were ever compromised. Indeed, his own brigade written orders were a model of clarity and brevity. Behind the stylish insouciance lay a first rate brain, one that had passed the Balliol open examination.

In the Brigade's Account of Operation[17] for 9–12 April, Carton de Wiart did not hesitate to state the facts as he saw them:

> April 9th, 10am The 9th Division instead of sending on their attacking troops for Athies and the Brown Line according to schedule time, kept them back and the result was that this Brigade was hung up in the open and lost some 150 men from Artillery fire.
>
> April 9th 4.15pm. The attack on Fampoux was much hampered by the fire of our own heavy artillery.
>
> April 11th. The artillery barrage was very feeble and quite failed to keep the (enemy) MG fire down.

In a separate report dated 15 April, Carton de Wiart drew attention to 'Points to be noted'.

> For practically the whole time the Brigade was in the front line it was shot at by our own heavy artillery and I consider it of the utmost importance that the heavy artillery should have an FOO (Forward Observation Officer) up in the front and in touch with Brigade and battalion commanders. Liaison between Brigade and heavy artillery is really non-existent at present and it is a most unsatisfactory state of affairs for the Infantry.
>
> Excellent reports of the Fuse 100 had been received and troops were told that they could rely on the wire being cut but there was only one small lane out on the Brigade front and most of the wire was absolutely untouched.
>
> Liaison between the Cavalry and infantry is another point that wants attention. There was certainly a great chance for the Cavalry after the capture of the 4th line system – had some Cavalry been near at hand – and in touch with the Brigade.
>
> Another point I should like to bring forward is this – at present infantry are under the impression that their stay in the line depends on the amount of casualties they have. As a matter of fact, casualties, unless exceptionally heavy, do not affect the troops much. Physical exhaustion is what demoralizes them and if they knew that once their objective was secured, they would be relieved within a reasonable time, say 48 hours, it would be of the greatest benefit to the men. . .
>
> Telephone communication forward from Brigade HQ was better than I have seen it before but behind Brigade HQ it was never satisfactory.

In country like this which we are operating in now, Machine Guns should certainly be pushed right forward as soon as the objective is secured. The Battalions did this with the Machine Guns allotted to them – and achieved most excellent results.[18]

After a week refitting, the Brigade moved to Montenescourt, then Manin, Le Cauroy and Liencourt from where Carton de Wiart went on leave after handing over to Lieutenant Colonel Borrett.[19] By now the great French advance had disintegrated; 29,000 French soldiers had been killed and over 100,000 casualties sustained. Nivelle had been removed and replaced by Pétain. In the British sector of the line, losses had amounted to some 20,000 men; and by 23 April, attrition had set in with the opposing armies ensconced in their trenches and fortifications for months to come.

On 2 May, Borrett received orders to attack the German position at the Chemical Works. This had been the scene of bitter fighting in April when the 4th South African Infantry and 2nd Battalion Seaforth Highlanders had been virtually annihilated. At 3.45 am on 3 May the Brigade advanced under a creeping barrage. Over the next 6 days the battle raged between the German defenders and the attacking British; and by the time the Brigade was relieved on 9 May, it had lost 6 officers killed, 13 wounded and 25 missing and OR 68 killed, 402 wounded and 621 missing. By any yardstick, it was a dreadful carnage.

There was to be no respite for the Brigade was ordered back into the attack on 11 May but this time it captured the chemical works and the Roeux cemetery. When they were finally relieved, the Brigade marched to Penin where it was inspected by Lieutenant General Edmund Allenby, the architect of the Battle of Arras. By now it only had 68 officers and 1,968 ORs[20] including reinforcements compared to its January roll of 157 officers and 3,956 ORs.

Carton de Wiart had returned from leave in time to write up the Account of Operations.[21] Like many of his peer group of young brigade commanders who realized they now had a voice within the army hierarchy, his post-operational reports did not shy from criticism nor was he reticent about suggesting improvements to the prevailing tactical doctrine.

The reasons for the failure of the attack of this Brigade on the Chemical Works on 3 May 3 is, in my opinion, due to the fact that the time allowed for the capture of the works was not sufficient, and to the hour at which it took place.

It has been said that the failure was due to the buildings not having been properly 'mopped up', but 'moppers up' are useless in an objective of this sort, for the few seconds that must elapse between the first wave going through the buildings and the 'moppers up' entering them, just give the enemy time to man his emplacements. He then shoots down most of the 'moppers up' and rear waves of the attack and can then turn his attention of the leading wave if that has not already been dealt with by the enemy supports.

The only satisfactory way of tackling an objective like this is for the attacking troops to get a footing in the village and move on, doing their own 'mopping up' as they go along.

The village ought to be the only point attacked for attacks on the flanks invariably get broken up from the fire of the village or strongpoint.

The cases of La Boisselle, Ovillers and High Wood on the Somme were very similar to this. When these places were merely objectives in a big attack, they not only failed to be taken themselves, but the attack on the flanks failed with very heavy losses.

Likewise, if a barrage passes quickly over a place like the Chemical Works, the troops who have now got accustomed to following the barrage, neglect the fighting in the houses for fear of getting too far behind the barrage.

The barrage should get them into the village and then form a protective barrage beyond it while they clear it up.

The heavy artillery preparation on the days preceding the attack was not satisfactory owing to the absence of liaison between them and the infantry, but this was remedied before the second attack.

In June, the Brigade moved to Penin to the north-west of Arras to continue training with welcome diversions provided by the Divisional Horse Show and the Brigade Rifle Meeting. By 11 June, they were back in the line at Arras where they remained for the next eight days under sporadic artillery fire. It had become a war of attrition with each side taking around ten casualties every day. Out of the line they became the Divisional reserve which meant supplying daily working parties for a raft of mundane duties. Although out of harm's way, they were glad to go back into the line on 28 June. Carton de Wiart returned to England on leave after delegating command to Borrett.[22] When he returned on 13 July, they were in the process of handing over once more to 11th Infantry Brigade and moved to Logan Camp to refit and train. Both June and July had been quiet months by the standards of the day. That was about to change.

On 9 August, a major raid was mounted by the Brigade. From 6.30 am British guns started their barrage against the German lines; and at 7.45 am the raiding party of 9 officers and 222 ORs[23] set off. Met by heavy enemy machine-gun fire and a hail storm of rifle grenades, it lost momentum and stalled; throughout the day and night, the wounded and 'missing' made their way back in dribs and drabs to their own lines. Of the nine officers who set off, eight were killed, missing or wounded and for ORs, the comparative figure was eight-two. The Brigade remained in the line until 16 August, during which time it carried out an aggressive night patrol programme to gather intelligence.

In his report to 4th Division,[24] Carton de Wiart was blunt about the reasons for the failure.

> in the first place, the fact that the raid was attempted in daylight. The troops had to cross about 200 yards of open ground in full view of the enemy and there was practically no chance of this being done (covertly) in the daylight. Heavy machine gun fire was brought to bear on the troops as soon as they were seen, and we suffered very heavy casualties as the men still tried to go on and a few did reach the German wire and were killed there . . . I cannot speak too highly of the conduct of the officers and men taking part in the raid; they went on in spite of the heavy fire, and it was to this cause that I attribute the heavy casualties.

He was also critical of the support arms, taking the artillery to task for their weak barrage and the Royal Flying Corps (RFC) whose work was 'certainly not satisfactory from the Infantry point of view'.

Back in the line on 31 August, the Brigade took over the Pelves sector. The front was quiet with occasional shelling by both sides, including gas. When it came out of the line on 7 September, casualties had been remarkably light with only three officers wounded (one by gas) and five ORs killed with nine wounded (four by gas). Training resumed in the Blaireville area and then the Brigade moved to St Sixte for another week's training before moving to the support area to relieve 61th Infantry Division in the line. This was its entrée to the Third Battle of Ypres, later to become known as the Battle of Passchendaele. Described as

> one of the dreariest landscapes in Western Europe, a sodden plain of wide, unfenced fields pasture and plough intermixed, overlying a water table that floods on excavation more than a few spadefuls deep . . . of long unimpeded fields of view . . .leading in all directions to distant, hazy horizons which promise nothing but the region's copious and frequent rainfall.[25]

Flanders was a familiar ground for the British who had been fighting over it since the First Battle of Ypres in 1914 and the Second Battle in April 1915.

The British had wanted to attack in the Flanders area in 1916 but had conceded to French wishes to launch a joint assault on the Somme. But in 1917, after the Arras offensive which had brought such early success for the British, General Sir Douglas Haig planned to launch a major attack in the Ypres Salient and, unlike Nivelle's advance which had ground to a halt in May, force the breakthrough

that he believed would win the war. In a major decisive action to break through
the German defences, he aimed to capture the high ground surrounding Ypres,
including the Passchendaele ridge, through a series of smaller battles. This attack,
working with the French, would culminate in the conquest of the Belgian coast
and would alleviate the growing threat of the German submarines operating
from Belgian ports.

Haig's plan called for a preliminary attack on the Messines Ridge (north
of Armentières) in order to straighten out the Ypres Salient on its southern flank
and to attract German reserves. This was executed on 7 June by the Second
Army, under General Sir Herbert Plumer. A strictly limited attack, made with
siege-warfare methods and based on preparations begun a year before, it proved
an almost complete success within its limits. It owed much to the surprise effect
of nineteen huge mines that were fired simultaneously.

In the early hours of the morning on 31 July, Haig's offensive began and after
more than 3,000 guns had poured 4.5 million shells on the German defences,
the infantry assault went in. But to his surprise and contrary to everything he
had told the Cabinet back in London, far from capitulating, the German army
fought well and Allied gains were not as large as expected. Then it began to
rain and the explosion of millions of shells merely turned the battlefield into a
swampy pulverized mire dotted with water-filled craters deep enough to drown
a man or a horse, all made worse by the churned-up graves of soldiers killed in
earlier fighting.

By the time Carton de Wiart's Brigade arrived there on 29 September,
thousands of soldiers on opposing sides had attacked and counterattacked across
sodden, porridge-like mud in a bare landscape almost devoid of buildings or
natural cover, all under a relentless deluge of exploding shells and flying shrapnel
and a raging torrent of machine-gun fire. Carton de Wiart took command of
the Langemarck sector and immediately sent patrols out to ascertain which
trenches were occupied by the enemy and, if possible, to snatch prisoners for
unit identification. Although hampered by bright moonlight, all returned with
valuable information of enemy dispositions.[26]

Augmented with the Household Battalion,[27] the Royal Naval Battalion and 1st
Battalion the Rifle Brigade, 12th Brigade now fielded seven battalions including
the 2nd West Riding Regiment which had replaced the 2nd Duke of Wellingtons.
Although on paper regimental numbers looked impressive, by the time leave,
hospitalized cases, working parties, reinforcements held at the Division Training
Battalion, the actual front line number shown in brackets were remarkably small:
for example, 1st Bn King's Own Regiment 38 officers and 928 ORs (21 and 308);

2nd Bn Lancashire Fusiliers 38 officers and 924 ORs (22 and 370); 2nd Bn Duke of Wellingtons 41 officers and 894 ORs (17 and 434). The weather conditions were appalling. It had been raining for weeks and from 4 to 9 October over 30 mm of rain fell. Much of the ground had become an impenetrable swamp.

Despite the appalling conditions of the battlefield and the concerns of his commanders, Haig believed the Germans were ready to give up at any moment and thus was determined to press on regardless of casualties across a seven-mile front to capture the Passchendaele ridge. Part of General Gough's Fifth Army, after moving up in torrential rain on 9 October 4th Division attacked over an 800-yard front at 5.30 am with 12th Brigade in the lead.[28] The creeping artillery barrage was moving 100 yards every eight minutes but much of it was ineffective due to the muddy conditions which smothered high explosive (HE) shell detonations. Early in the advance, Lieutenant Colonel Horsfall was killed; and by 12.30 pm it was clear than the attack had ground to a halt. In his headquarters, Carton de Wiart received reports by pigeons, runners and aircraft drops of the positions of his battalions and their casualties, some accurate, others not. There was little a brigade commander could do in these circumstances other than to deploy his reserve and wait for the outcome. By 6 pm the Division consolidated its line and that night both sides remained inactive, recovering from the day's onslaught. Two of the Brigade's battalions, 2nd Lancashire Fusiliers and 2nd Duke of Wellingtons, had been so badly mauled that they were taken out of the line.[29]

The Household Battalion went back into action at Poelcappelle against a strongpoint of pillboxes and a blockhouse marked on the map as Requette Farm where fighting had been going on since 9 October. The farm was briefly taken but then lost as the remnants of the battalion fell back under its last three remaining officers, all of whom had started the day in the support companies. The battalion was utterly exhausted and not a single NCO above the rank of Corporal remained unwounded. The reckoning was the loss of over 400 casualties for a temporary advance of 600 yards over a swamp pockmarked by gaping shell holes. The battalion went back into rest at Arras where it received its final draft of 400 reinforcements from Windsor.

The action at Poelcappelle marked the beginning of the main Battle of Passchendaele which opened on 12 October. 12th Brigade was to lead 4th Division's attack with a composite force of its two remaining two battalions and two from the 10th Brigade. In all, two lead battalions with a battalion each in support and reserve were to take the first objective about 200 yards forward, then pivoting on the right to the final objective another 300 yards forward at Water

House. The ground had been soaked again by overnight rain – in de Wiart's words, 'a vast sea of malignant mud and water'[30] – and the advance by the right-hand battalion was stopped at Requette Farm by determined German resistance and massed machine-gun fire, during which contact with the neighbouring battalion of the 18th (Eastern) Division was lost. The advance of the left-hand battalion faced less opposition and by 6.20 am had crossed the Poelcappelle – le Cinq Chemins road, captured Memling and Senegal farms and contacted the 17th (Northern) Division. After the capture of Requette Farm by the right-hand battalion, more German machine-gun fire was received from the Brewery and Helles House, which stopped the attack on the right flank. Requette Farm was lost to a German counter-attack around noon, and attempts by reinforcements to retake the farm were abandoned as darkness fell. The Brigade extended a defensive flank on the right to maintain contact with the 18th (Eastern) Division. The new front line curved back through Besace Farm to west of Helles House, south-west of Requette Farm, north of Poelcappelle.[31]

On 13 October, the attack was halted until weather conditions improved and the Brigade subsequently withdrew. Ten officers and 380 ORs were either dead, wounded or missing. After a further stint in the line, they were relieved by 102nd Brigade and sent to Arras for a week of refitting and training before relieving 11th Brigade in the line at Monchy de Preux on 8/9 November. Activity was relatively low key with the exception of an enemy trench mortar gas attack which wounded fourteen men. Three night-raids were mounted, two by 2nd Bn Lancashire Fusiliers and one by the King's Own which managed to bring back one prisoner but at a cost of an officer and six ORs missing from the twenty-seven strong raiding party.[32]

It was during the day of 23 November, when in the middle of a heavy enemy barrage, Carton de Wiart was visiting the front line trenches prior to being relieved by 11th Brigade[33] that 'within a few yards of Battalion HQ, . . . I thought someone had hit me, and putting my hand on my hip I found I was bleeding profusely'.[34] He was carried to the nearest Dressing Station and then evacuated to hospital where he was immediately operated on. Coming to some hours later, he asked for the staff to ring through to Divisional HQ to find out what the Brigade's losses had been. The answer came back none other than him!

Yet again, he was back in 17 Park Lane, this time for Christmas and the New Year. After three months, he was passed fit again and on 7 April 1918 assumed command of the 105th Infantry Brigade, 38th (Welsh) Division, in the Toutencourt, Senlis, Bouzincourt, and Martinsart sectors to the northeast of Albert.[35] On 21 March, the Germans had launched Operation MICHAEL. This attack, which became the opening salvo of their Spring Offensive, aimed to deliver a single, decisive, war winning blow. The Germans intended to strike the southern British flank, to separate the British and French armies and then move north to engage the bulk of the British forces in France in a *vernichtungsschlacht* (battle of annihilation). The aim was to inflict such a defeat upon the British armies that the country would abandon the war, which in turn would force the French to sue for peace. After the first ten days of the German offensive, the casualties suffered by the 2nd and the 47th (London) Divisions were such that the 38th Division was ordered south to take up positions near Albert to relieve the two formations.

The division was kept in reserve near Albert until the night of 11/12 April, when it relieved the 12th (Eastern) Division. The Germans had captured high ground near Bouzincourt and Aveluy, overlooking the British lines. The division was ordered to retake it to gain observation positions overlooking the German positions in the Ancre valley while at the same time to deny the Germans the ability to observe the British lines. Over the next two days, 105th Infantry Brigade relieved 115th Infantry Brigade in the Toutencourt Sector and went into the line at Senlis. Under command, Carton de Wiart had 4th North Staffordshire Regiment, 15th Cheshire Regiment, 15th Sherwood Foresters and 18th Lancashire Fusiliers. Throughout their tour, the Brigade was heavily shelled; in one day alone over 500 enemy shells fell on Bouzincourt and another 200 HE and gas shells the same night.

On 20 April, an entry in the Brigade log reads, 'Brigadier General Carton de Wiart wounded in left leg while reconnoitring in Martinsart.'[36] He was indeed seriously wounded, nearly losing his left leg, and was out of action for the next six months. He returned in time to see the end of the war. Eight days after the Armistice was signed on 11 November, Carton de Wiart assumed command of 113th Brigade in the 38th Division. On 27 November he assumed temporary command of 38th Division.[37]

In his memoirs, Carton de Wiart famously wrote,

> Frankly I had enjoyed the war; it had given me many bad moments, lots of good ones, plenty of excitement, and with everything found for us. . . . Far and away the most interesting and important lesson that I learned was on man. War is a great leveller; it shows the man as he really is, not as he would like to be, nor as he would like you to think he is. It shows him stripped, with his greatness mixed with his pathetic fears and weaknesses, and though there were disappointments they were more than cancelled out by pleasant surprises of the little men who, suddenly, became larger than life.[38]

Given that he had never been to Sandhurst or to the Staff College, Carton de Wiart's Great War record was all the more remarkable. He only arrived in France in February 1915, at the time a substantive one-eyed captain, where his first command was a cavalry squadron in the infantry role. Having lost his left hand, he went on to command two infantry battalions, win a VC, then command three brigades and ended the war as a divisional commander, in the process being wounded five more times. In all, since his first tour in South Africa, he had been hit by gunfire or shrapnel thirteen times, resulting in eleven wounds. He was, in the true sense of the word, indestructible.

Carton de Wiart made light of his wounds but, in reality, the physical trauma and pain would have been considerable. He had made the long journey of evacuation back to 'Blighty' no less than five times. It started at the Regimental Aid Post just behind the front line and meandered by way of horse drawn cart, motorized ambulance, train or barge past a Casualty Clearing Station to a Base Hospital in one of the French channel ports and then continued by hospital ship to Kent and train to London. Pain relief varied from pure ether to morphine; anaesthetics were delivered by gas, either alcohol or ethyl chloride mixed with chloroform and ether. Thanks to exceptional medical care and his extraordinary will to live, he survived but would stoically live with pain – at times intense – for the rest of his life.

Part IV

Poland 1919–23

A tall order

The Polish brief

After the Armistice of November 1918, the Allied peacemakers began to converge on Paris with their entourages of diplomats, soldiers and special advisers. Much to Carton de Wiart's surprise, the War Office nominated him to be second-in-command to General Louis Botha, the former South African prime minister, who had been selected as the British military delegate on the Inter-Allied Commission to Poland.

> My geography being a little shaky, I had only a hazy idea as to the whereabouts of Poland, but I knew it was somewhere near Russia and that the Bolsheviks were fighting there. I could not think of any adequate reason why I had been chosen for this inviting job, and I accepted it with alacrity before anyone had time to change his mind. Then I proceeded to find out all I could about the situation there.[1]

First stop was Paris.

A convenient start point for the modern history of Poland is 1569 when the Kingdom of Poland and the Grand Duchy of Lithuania joined forces to form the Polish-Lithuanian Commonwealth. For the next two centuries it was the largest and most populous country in Europe and, at its zenith, bordered on Brandenburg, the Habsburg Empire (Silesia and Hungary to the west and south west), the Ottoman Empire to the south (Moldova) and Muscovy to the east and north. Surrounded by meddling neighbours and riven with internal dissent, by the end of the eighteenth century it had been devoured, partitioned by Russia, Austria and Prussia. As a country, Poland had ceased to exist.

In the Napoleonic Wars, the Polish state had been restored by the victorious French as the Grand Duchy of Warsaw and become a dependency of France. Then at the Congress of Vienna in 1815 when the victors of the war against Napoleon – Russia, Austria, Great Britain and Prussia – redrew the map of

Central Europe, a new Kingdom of Poland, known as the Congress Kingdom, emerged. Even smaller than the Grand Duchy, although nominally independent with its own government, in reality it was effectively part of Russia for the Tsar was its hereditary king. The only exception was Kraków which became an independent Polish city state albeit under the protection of Russia, Prussia and Austria. Following the revolutions of 1848, the Habsburgs absorbed Kraków into their Galician province and once again there was no vestige left of an independent Poland.

During the First World War, the Central Powers of Germany and Austria-Hungary captured most of Russian-owned Poland and in November 1916 they announced their intention to establish a fully independent Polish state which more or less replicated the 1815 Kingdom of Poland, but this time as a puppet state of Germany, not Russia. When the peace treaty between the Central Powers and Bolshevik Russia was signed in February 1918, both Lithuania, the Baltic States (Latvia and Estonia) and the Ukraine were accorded the status of independent states, the former effectively satellites of Germany with German Dukes enthroned, the latter split between a Ukrainian National Republic in the east and a Ukrainian crownland in eastern Galicia and Bukovina. Tellingly, Poland was not discussed as it was still within the control of White Russians and therefore not under the jurisdiction of the Bolshevik government.

Eight months later, when the armies of the Central Powers had finally disintegrated, the fate of Poland moved centre stage. With the collapse of the Austro-Hungarian Empire, apart from Poland, five new states had emerged in Central and Eastern Europe: a dismembered Austria shorn of its 800 years of Habsburg rule, a shrunken Hungary, the newly created Czechoslovakia, the fledgling Ukrainian Republic divided into eastern and western halves, and the new Kingdom of Yugoslavia, territorially aloof to the south. A sixth new state – Poland – had been promised by President Wilson but it existed only on paper with an unelected government-in-exile in Paris.

When these succession states started fighting among themselves and with Communist revolutions erupting in Munich and Berlin while others simmered away in Budapest and Kosice, Western Europe ponderously prepared for the Peace Conference at Versailles, 'a nest of golden dreams, a mist of memories, a seed-plot of hopes, a storehouse of time's menaces'.[2] As the historian Norman Davies succinctly puts it, 'in the latter stages of the First World, Eastern Europe fell to pieces'.[3] With an insecure Bolshevik Russia beset by civil war on its eastern borders and a bitter and slighted Germany to the west, the future of Poland now rested with the four Western allies – France, Great Britain, the United States and Italy.

Britain had tabled its support for a new independent Polish state at the Versailles Declaration on 3 June 1918; and by the time the Paris Peace Conference opened, the British delegation had a concrete set of proposals. Central to their plan was a homogenous Polish state capable of resisting pressure from both of its avaricious neighbours Russia and Germany and with access to the sea at Neufahrwasser rather than Danzig. The official in charge, Sir Esme Howard,[4] who had been summoned to the Foreign Office on 13 November and told he was to be the Peace Conference's senior official for 'the Baltic Provinces, Russia, Poland, Ukraine, Caucasus & c',[5] had already sent a team into Poland to accompany the famous composer and politician Jan Paderewski on his return from New York in December 1918. Consisting of Colonel Harry Wade, the British Military Attaché in Copenhagen, Richard Kimens,[6] a former Polish-speaking Consul in Warsaw and Rowland Kenney of the Secret Service Bureau, the team kept Howard abreast of the political and military landscape throughout January.

At the Inter-Allied Conversation in Paris on 23 January 1919, the British prime minister Lloyd George drew attention to 'the great difficulties of the present Polish situation', specifically that while the Poles were begging for guns, rifles, ammunition and even troops to defend themselves against the Bolsheviks, none of the Allies were prepared to contribute troops. The real difficulty, as he saw it, was that 'the Poles were giving the appearance of an attempt to forestall the decisions of the Peace Conference by seizing territory whose rightful possession could fairly be said to be a disputed question'.[7]

It was therefore agreed that a Commission consisting of one soldier and one diplomat from each of the Allied Great Powers should be sent to Poland to investigate and report. On behalf of the British Empire Delegation, he put forward the names of General Louis Botha and Sir Esme Howard, at the time Ambassador to Sweden.[8] Botha had been the Union of South Africa's first president after the Boer War and was seen as a conciliatory figure capable of broking ceasefires between the various warring parties for, at the time, Poland was at war with the Germans, the Russian Bolsheviks, the Ukrainians, the Czechs and the Lithuanians.

The day before, Lloyd George had offered Howard the job of British delegate to a conference set up by President Wilson between the representatives of all the competing factions in Russia and Allied delegates at a neutral venue on the island of Prinkipo off Constantinople, ostensibly to arrange a peace treaty. With his knowledge of the Bolshevik leaders, Howard sensed a political elephant trap and turned it down. 'I told him frankly that if his object was to come to terms with the Bolsheviks, he had better take another man and said I thought that anything done to confirm in power Lenin . . . was too dangerous a policy for me to wish to see carried into effect.'[9] It turned out to be a good call as the French dug their heels in, and the White Russians were reluctant to attend.

The Inter-Allied Commission as it was styled quickly assembled in Paris. The Americans nominated Major General Frank Kernan, the Secretary of the American Commission to Negotiate Peace, and Dr Robert Lord; the French[10] General Henri Niessel and Joseph Noulens (the former French Ambassador in St. Petersburg) and the Italians General Giovanni Romei Longhena and Giulio Montagna. The concept was that they would be the eyes and ears for the Paris-based Commission on Polish Affairs headed by the experienced French diplomat M. Jules Cambon who was assisted by Sir Willie Tyrell,[11] Dr Isaiah Bowman (USA), Marchese Pietro della Torretta (Italy) and M. Otchiai (Japan). The Secretary to the British Commissioner was the formidably bright Lieutenant Colonel Frank Kisch, CBE, DSO, on secondment from Military Intelligence, who was later to play a key role in evaluating the intelligence sent by de Wiart from Poland.

In many respects, Howard was the architect behind the Commission on Polish Affairs. On 5 February he had written to Lord Hardinge, the Permanent Under Secretary at the Foreign Office, pointing out 'the utmost gravity' of the position in Poland.

> Unless the Associated Governments can very quickly come to the help of the Polish government with the necessary supplies of arms, ammunition, food and raw materials there is really a serious danger that the Polish political organization, such as it is, may fall to pieces and make the work of building up an independent Poland one of extreme difficulty for some time to come.[12]

He was particularly concerned about Germany who

> is clearly, by all means in her power, whether by assisting the Bolshevik, or by anti-Polish propaganda, or by egging on the Ukrainian, or by Bolshevik propaganda in Poland itself, doing every she can to destroy the Polish Government, and in this way making impossible the establishment of an independent Polish State . . . the whole object of Germany would appear to be to re-establish a coterminous frontier between herself and Russia.[13]

Only too aware of the tardiness of the Peace Conference to respond, he suggested 'an Inter-Allied Committee for dealing exclusively with Polish affairs to which the recommendations of the Commission in Warsaw should be immediately submitted which would . . . submit matters of higher policy at once to the Principal Delegates'.[14] It was to prove to be a smart move that put Poland to the fore. Whether the actors would stick to the Paris script was altogether another matter.

Around the same time,[15] the Inter-Allied Teschen Commission was established to stop the Polish-Czech War which had erupted on 23 January and to fix the respective frontiers between the two countries. At the heart of the issue were the great coalmines and industrial plants of the former Habsburg Duchy of Teschen ('Cieszyn') in Eastern Silesia. The British member was Lieutenant Colonel B. J. B. Coulson who had commanded the 7/8th the King's Own Scottish Borderers at Loos in 1915. Little did he know there was to be no quick fix.

Due to leave on 9 February, General Louis Botha was suddenly taken ill and as a last minute substitute, the War Office nominated Carton de Wiart who was already in Paris to replace him. His letter of appointment from the British Delegation in Paris read:

> I have to inform you that you have been appointed British Military Delegate on the Inter-Allied Commission which is about to proceed to Poland for the purpose of investigating existing conditions in that country and reporting thereon to the representatives of the Allied and Associated Governments at the Peace Conference, and if possible, taking such steps as may be necessary to bring about a cessation of hostilities between Poland and neighbouring countries.[16]

Howard noted in his diary, 'General Carton de Wiart, VC, said to be "the bravest man in the British Army", who has thirteen wound stripes and has lost a hand, a foot and an eye, comes to Warsaw with us. He seems a first rate fellow . . . a splendid man and withal the most modest of men.' In another entry, he mused that 'Carton de Wiart was, I think, mainly interested in the Polish problem from the military point of view, because it offered him the chance of hearing bullets whizzing about his head once again, a chance of which he freely availed himself on the Eastern frontiers of Poland'.[17] However, he rued the loss of Botha for 'he carried much weight with Mr Lloyd George, which neither Carton de Wiart nor I could be said to do'.

In harness with Howard and the rest of the Mission, Carton de Wiart set off by train for Warsaw via Switzerland, Prague and Vienna. After a brief meeting with President Masaryk in Prague Castle which resulted in little clarification of the unfolding situation in Poland other than he assured them the Czechs would keep to the terms of the Paris Pact for Teschen, they continued their journey by train, stopping at each large town for M. Noulens to give a short speech. Howard remembered that 'people at these stations looked very anaemic, ragged and poor'.[18] On 12 February, four days after leaving Paris, the Mission arrived in Warsaw and was met by Jan Paderewski, the Minister of Foreign Affairs.

Noulens sent an upbeat message to Paris: 'The Commission was enthusiastically received in Czech territory, and the population turned out to sing National Anthems in their honour. At Prague had an interview with M. Masaryk and examined him the Clauses of the arrangements regarding Teschen. At Warsaw was received by M. Paderewski who made an enthusiastic speech'.[19]

Carton de Wiart and Howard were given an apartment leased by Baron Taube[20] in a house belonging to Prince Czartoryski. Baron Mikhail Alexandrovich Taube, a Russian international lawyer and historian, came from the old Swedish-German 'von Taube' family, one of the branches of Baltic Barons in the service of the Russian throne. Howard would have known him in Finland when Taube was Foreign Minister of the short-lived Trepov government before he moved to Sweden when Howard was ambassador there. Two young Poles were attached to the Mission, Birmingham economics graduate Jan Ciechanowski[21] and Downside-educated Count Jerzy Potocki[22] under the watchful eye of Captain Clement Levenson-Gower,[23] who was the British delegation's general factotum. Both Howard and Carton de Wiart were immediately made members of the Klub Myśliwski (the Hunting Club), the hub of intrigue and political gossip in Warsaw.

Esme Howard was seventeen years older than Carton de Wiart and had spent the early part of his life in the Diplomatic Service, first in Ireland, then Rome and Berlin. In 1890, aged twenty-seven, he left the service 'out of boredom'[24] and travelled widely including a stint prospecting for gold in South Africa and setting up a rubber plantation in Tobago. A talented linguist fluent in ten languages, Howard was also a passionate social reformer and developed his own Economic Credo, the centrepiece being a partnership between the state, business and the Trade Unions. Like Carton de Wiart, he joined the Imperial Yeomanry and went to South Africa to fight in the Second Boer War, fortunately returning home unscathed. Gravitating back to the world of diplomacy, he was sent to Crete, Washington, Vienna, Budapest, Switzerland and finally to Stockholm where he spent the entirety of the First World War.

Already in Warsaw, Colonel Harry Wade, the British Military Attaché in Copenhagen, who had been sent there as a member of Howard's British Delegation to Paderewski, had intercepted Captain Tommy Johnson of Military Intelligence on his way back to England[25] and despatched him to Lwów to report to General Tadeusz Rozwadowski with the aim of stopping the fighting between Polish and Ukrainian forces.

The day after their arrival, they went to meet the Chief of State, General Josef Piłsudski, a man 'with deep-set eyes of searching penetration, heavy brows and a drooping moustache which was peculiarly characteristic'.[26] Carton de Wiart made an instant friend of the General which was to stand him in good stead throughout his tour. The two had much in common for both were men of action although their backgrounds could not have been more different.

Born in 1867 to a noble Roman Catholic family near the village of Zułów, at that time part of the Russian Empire, from his youth Piłsudski had been an ardent Polish nationalist. As Howard pointed out, 'at his school in Wilno lessons were in Russian, teachers were Russian, prayers were said in Russian, history was in Russian, and his language – the Polish language – was treated as the tongue of traitors and punished as such.'[27] Aged twenty, the Tsarist authorities arrested him on a trumped up charge of plotting to assassinate Tsar Alexander III and sentenced him to five years' exile in Siberia. On his release in 1892 – his nationalistic ardour ignited rather than dowsed – he joined the revolutionary Polish Socialist Party (PPS) in Wilno and became an underground organizer, or in modern parlance a terrorist. Two years later, after the arrest of Jan Strozecki, the editor of *Robotnik*, the illegal newspaper of the PPS in Russian-controlled territories, he took over as its editor.

The first edition had been printed in London, a hotbed of left-wing Polish revolutionaries out of reach of the Russian authorities, and when, using a false identity, he moved to London for six months in 1896 – his visit coincided with the Congress of the Second International – Piłsudski found lodgings with fellow PPS activist Leon Wasilewski[28] in Leytonstone and with Bolesław Jędrzejowski, the secretary of the PPS Foreign Committee. As well as continuing to edit *Robotnik*, he printed a pamphlet *In Remembrance of May*[29] for distribution throughout Europe. He left England with fond memories of Speakers' Corner and Soho street markets and with colloquial English language skills[30] and, according to Jędrzejowski, he had also read some famous military textbooks in English.[31]

During this period, almost all political parties in Russian Poland and Lithuania adopted a conciliatory position towards the Tsar in the expectation of some form of limited autonomy; the alternative, incorporation within the Kaiser's increasingly assertive 'New Course' Germany, was unpalatable. Not so Piłsudski: his PPS was prepared to fight for Polish independence and to resort to violence to achieve that goal. On the outbreak of the Russo-Japanese War in the summer of 1904, he travelled to Tokyo to assist the Japanese government by starting a guerrilla war in Poland to serve as a distraction. He also offered to supply Japan with intelligence and proposed the creation of a Polish Legion from

Polish conscripts in the Russian Army who had been captured by the Japanese. He came away with funding for weapons and ammunition although his hosts declined his Legion proposal.

On his return, Piłsudski formed a paramilitary unit[32] and in March 1905, just as the Russian Revolution gathered momentum, they started a campaign to assassinate Russian police officers. In April, he ordered the PPS to launch a general strike: it involved some 400,000 workers and lasted 2 months until it was broken up by the Russian authorities. In June, Piłsudski sent his paramilitaries to join the workers' uprising in the city of Łódź. By the end of the year, he was calling for all Polish workers to rise up. It went unheeded as unemployment and repression began to sap the ardour of his fellow countrymen.

Anticipating a coming European war, Piłsudski was more determined than ever to establish an independent Poland and to do so he needed an army. With the connivance of the authorities in Vienna, he founded a military school in Kraków for the training of paramilitary units which he subsequently transformed into an 'Association for Active Struggle' whose main purpose was to train officers and NCOs for a future Polish Army. By 1914, his nascent army totalled some 12,000 men. Now aligned with the Central Powers and using a fictitious 'National Government in Warsaw' as his authority, Piłsudski sent his forces across the border into an area the Russian Army had evacuated in the hope of breaking through to Warsaw and sparking a nation-wide revolution. When this proved unacceptable to Vienna, he established the Polish Legions, taking personal command of their First Brigade. In July 1916, after the Battle of Kostiuchnówka when the Legions delayed a Russian offensive at a cost of over 2,000 casualties, Piłsudski demanded that the Central Powers issue a guarantee of independence for Poland. Hoping to increase the number of Polish troops that could be sent to the Eastern Front, thereby freeing German forces for France, on 5 November 1916 the Powers proclaimed the independence of Poland by recognizing the Regency Kingdom of Poland.[33] Piłsudski's 1914 dictum, 'only the sword now carries any weight in the balance for the destiny of a nation' had proved correct.

Piłsudski agreed to serve in the newly created Regency government as Minister of War but as the fortunes of the Central Powers went into decline, he became increasingly strident in his demands that his men should no longer be used as 'German colonial troops'. When he ordered his soldiers not to swear an oath of loyalty to the German-controlled *Polnische Wehrmacht* in which the Legions had been embedded, he was promptly arrested and imprisoned in the Prussian fortress at Magdeburg. The Polish units were disbanded, and the men were incorporated into the Austro-Hungarian army.

On 8 November 1918, three days before the Armistice, Piłsudski was released by the Germans and despatched by train to Warsaw on the understanding that he would not act against German interests. Three day later, he was appointed Commander-in Chief of Polish forces by the Regency Council and was entrusted with creating a national government for the newly independent country. His first act was to proclaim an independent Polish state; and on 22 November he officially received the title of Provisional Chief of State. It had been an extraordinary journey for this self-taught Austro-Hungarian general and former 'polemicist, publisher of clandestine newspapers, political agitator, bank-robber, terrorist and urban guerrilla leader'[34] who had been imprisoned twice by the Russians and once by the Germans.

True to his agreement with the Germans, he negotiated the evacuation of the German garrison from Warsaw and of other German troops from the 'Ober Ost' authority.[35] Over 55,000 German soldiers peacefully departed Poland, leaving their weapons to the Poles. Well aware that Polish territory was vulnerable to attack from several quarters, he now set about organizing an army out of Polish veterans from the German, Russian and Austrian armies. However, Piłsudski and the first Polish government were distrusted in the West because he had co-operated with the Central Powers in 1914 to 1917 and because the Regency governments of Daszyński and Jędrzej Moraczewski were seen as primarily socialist. None of them was minded to send arms or munitions to the maverick Polish general.

The problem was that there were in fact two Polish governments, one in Warsaw and the other known as the National Committee in Paris, the latter headed by Piłsudski's long-time nationalist rival, Roman Dmowski. Much the same age, Dmowski had grown up in Warsaw and he too was arrested by the Tsarist authorities for organizing a street demonstration in celebration of the 100th anniversary of the 1791 Polish Constitution. His crime was deemed lesser and, after five months in Warsaw Prison, he was exiled to Latvia for a year.

Always opposed to violence, when he had been approached by Japanese intelligence during the Russo-Japanese War, he had managed to persuade them that Piłsudski's proposal to create a second front in Poland was unrealistic and it was duly dropped. He next clashed with Piłsudski in the anti-Russian uprising in Łódź when his National Democratic Party supporters exchanged shots with the PPS. Despite the vicious crackdown in 1906 by the Russian police when over 2,000 people were killed and over 1,000 death warrants handed down in Warsaw, Dmowski continued to preach non-violence, advocating the pen rather than the sword. His pro-Russian and anti-German stance endeared him to the Triple

Entente and in 1917 he created a Polish National Committee in Paris, in effect a government-in-exile which the French immediately recognized, followed by the British and Americans the next year.

Two governments in one country are problematical for any state; and as Howard noted, 'the Piłsudski Government was looked on with suspicion and even hostility by the Polish National Committee in Paris which had been accepted by the Allied and Associated Governments as the official representative and mouthpiece of the Polish people.'[36]

Given the mutual dislike and opposing views of the two men, there was a real chance of civil war in Poland. Indeed, on 5 January 1919, two of Dmowski's aristocratic supporters attempted to stage a coup against Piłsudski. It was the charismatic and passionate Polish patriot Jan Paderewski who came to the rescue with a compromise for he saw that both men needed each other. Although Piłsudski had taken charge of Poland, he needed Dmowski to arrange for the Allies to provide arms and ammunition for his army; and Dmowski, although his National Committee had been recognized by the Allies, needed to get back to Poland if he was to have any domestic political credibility, for a Polish government-in-exile was meaningless to the man on the street in Warsaw. Therefore, it was agreed that Paderewski and Dmowski would be the official representatives of the Polish government at the Paris Peace Conference and Piłsudski the provisional President of Poland in Warsaw. In January 1919, Paderewski became Prime Minister of Poland and Foreign Minister of the new government, which now received official recognition in the West.

However, this was not the end of the problem of Polish independence by any means for it was Dmowski with his pro-Russian sentiment and aversion to armed force who put forward proposals for Poland's boundaries at the Paris Peace Conference. His vision was that of an ethnically and religiously homogeneous Polish kingdom in which the citizens would speak Polish and be of the Roman Catholic faith, so his proposed borders incorporated most of East Prussia, Posen and parts of Silesia, all of which had a significant and, in some cases, a majority German population, and in the east they encompassed all of Lithuania except the very north, most of Belarus, West Volhynia and Podolia (Ukraine) and all of Galicia. These territories were mostly populated by Lithuanians, Belarussians and Ukrainians. In Dmowski's book, everyone would be part of the Polish national state.

Piłsudski differed. He envisaged recreating the historical multi-ethnic Polish-Lithuanian Commonwealth that had existed from the sixteenth century to the end of the eighteenth in the form of an *Intermarium*, a 'Between-Seas' multinational federation or *Międzymorze*, extending across territories lying between the Baltic, Black and Adriatic Seas. These would include the Baltic States (Lithuania, Latvia, Estonia), Finland, Belarus, Ukraine, Hungary, Romania, Yugoslavia and Czechoslovakia. Piłsudski believed in a wide definition of Polish citizenship in which peoples of different languages, cultures and faiths were to be united by a common loyalty to a Federal Polish state, not unlike a version of the British Commonwealth.

His other geopolitical vision, Prometheism, proposed the dismemberment of the Russian Empire and the divestment of its territorial acquisitions. In a 1904 memorandum to the Japanese when he proposed opening a second front, he declared:

> Poland's strength and importance among the constituent parts of the Russian state embolden us to set ourselves the political goal of breaking up the Russian state into its main constituents and emancipating the countries that have been forcibly incorporated into that empire. We regard this not only as the fulfilment of our country's cultural strivings for independent existence, but also as a guarantee of that existence, since a Russia divested of her conquests will be sufficiently weakened that she will cease to be a formidable and dangerous neighbor.[37]

Dmowski regarded Piłsudski's views as alarming nonsense and felt that the presence of large number of ethnic minorities would undermine the security of the Polish state. However, from his vantage point in Paris all he could see was the Peace Conference, whereas Piłsudski was engaged on the ground in Poland, dealing on a day-to-day basis with the tussle for control of Wilno and the rest of central Lithuania and the dangerous antics of the Ukrainian population in Galicia who pronounced it part of the Western Ukrainian National Republic, a claim that triggered a war which was to last until the summer of 1919. As to the former Russian occupied lands, it was not to be until March 1921 that the border question was finally resolved at the Treaty of Riga.

It was into these mine-strewn political fields where the seeds of chaos watered by nationalism and ideology were fast sprouting that Carton de Wiart was catapulted as Head of the British Military Mission (BMM). It was a landscape populated by politicians and soldiers of all persuasions and nationalities and as treacherous as the mud-filled craters of Passchendaele. He was to be tested to the extreme on more than one occasion.

A finger on the Polish pulse

Two traits were to bedevil Carton de Wiart throughout his tour: first, the reservations of the British government about Piłsudski's nation-building agenda, and secondly, the stance of the French who regarded any assistance to Poland from other Allied countries as meddling in their sphere of influence. Against this background, the resources and thus the activities of the military element of the British Delegation to the Inter-Allied Commission to Poland were constrained by other more important initiatives emanating from London and Paris. From the start, it was a poor relation to the larger British Missions: Major General Poole[1] at Archangel and Murmansk[2] (along with Major General Maynard's[3] SYREN Force); Major General Knox[4] with Admiral Kolchak in Siberia; Major General Holman[5] with General Denikin in the Ukraine; General Sir Hubert Gough[6] in Finland and the Baltic States; and Brigadier General Burt[7] in Latvia and Lithuania.

The original establishment for Carton de Wiart's Mission had been threadbare – one brigadier-general, one General Staff Officer (GSO) Grade 2, one attached officer, one clerk and two men.[8] In picking his staff, Carton de Wiart was fortunate in being able to secure the services of Major King as his GSO1 and Captain Maule, his former adjutant,[9] as his GSO 2. Both were exceptionally competent and resilient officers. Major Paris RE who had just been repatriated from internment in Germany was also recruited. Lieutenant Commander H. B. Rawlins[10] came on board as the Naval representative. The financial officer of the British element of the Inter-Allied Mission, Captain Garnon-Williams, had been given an imprest account of £3,000 by HM Treasury, approximately £87,000,[11] a fraction of the budget allocated to the Baltic and Russia Missions.

Poland was in a terrible condition when the Mission arrived. German, Austro-Hungarian and Russian armies had been crossing it in both directions for nearly four years, draining the country's resources which resulted in shortages of fuel and foodstuffs. Herbert Hoover leading the American Relief Administration calculated that parts of the country had been subjected to no fewer than seven invasions and retreats by different armies. Deserters, refugees and Displaced Persons brought crime and disease into the cities where worthless currencies were in circulation. Typhus epidemics occurred yearly. Industry was at a standstill and farmers and their horses struggled to cultivate ground that had not been turned over for four years. Not surprisingly, the 1919 harvest failed. Doctor Vernon Kellogg of the American Relief Administration reported that 'We see very few children playing in the streets of Warsaw. Why were they not playing? The answer was simple and sufficient: the children of Warsaw were not strong enough to play in the streets. . . . Their weak little bodies were bones clothed with skin, but not muscles. They simply could not play'.[12]

The Polish Army as a legal entity was non-existent but that did not stop the Poles sending their shopping list to Paris, including 220,000 infantry rifles with bayonets and 'a necessary quantity of aeroplanes, motor cars . . . armoured trains, field kitchens, explosives, carts, horses, saddles, tents, rugs, uniforms, petrol, oils'.[13] Major General Sir William Thwaites, the Director of Military Intelligence, advised the Foreign Office that 'the urgency of delivering arms to the Poles with a view to enabling them to organize their defence against the Bolsheviks appears to outweigh the necessity of obtaining guarantees (in respect of the territorial wishes of the Peace Conference).'[14]

Carton de Wiart took his cue from this and on 19 February signalled Paris that he had 'informed Polish government that steps are being taken to supply them with German rifles, ammunition and equipment. . . . Polish troops fighting Bolsheviks on East Front have no ammunition and it is difficult to explain failure to provide it, especially as Czechs have ample equipment from Allied sources'.[15] He explained how

> a voluntary army (was) being raised in Poland[16] for defence against Bolsheviks. . . . Such an army is being formed under the auspices of the Polish General Staff, organized and commanded by General Wacław Iwaszkiewicz-Rudoszánski. Polish government has voted sum towards its equipment and further funds have been raised by landowners. Has been approached by Count Ladislas Puslowski[17] as to possibility of purchasing arms and ammunition in England. Urges that in view of serious menace of Bolsheviks, His Majesty's Government should assist formation of army as much as possible.

This did not go down well with Lieutenant Colonel Frank Kisch[18] in the British delegation in Paris for Colonel Harry Wade[19] had already told him that it was being raised to defend Lithuania and 'the Lithuanians don't wish to be defended by Polish troops – this is not difficult to understand'. The British Delegation in

Paris endorsed this view and wondered whether it was a matter of 'annexation rather than defence'. Deftly sidestepping the request, both officers recommended that the Polish Purchasing Commission in Paris worked directly to the War Office through the Polish representative in London.[20]

There was definitely something amiss going on and in a despatch dated 3 March, the Director of Military Intelligence noted that

> while Polish authorities ARE CONTANTLY URGING [*sic*] Allies to assist them resist Bolshevik threat to Poland the greater part of their forces are concentrated in Eastern Galicia facing the Ruthenes and in Cracow-Teschen area facing the Czecho-Slovaks . . . you should impress on Polish authorities importance of concentrating their military resources on defence of Poland against Bolsheviks invasion if the danger they refer to is real. Present distribution of Polish forces, apart from leaving the eastern frontier relatively undefended, does not strengthen Polish arguments in favour of Allied assistance.[21]

As Norman Davies observes,

> in the chaos prevailing in the first few weeks of 1919, it is hard to believe that anyone in Soviet Russia or in the new Republic of Poland should have deliberately courted a major, foreign war. Soviet Russia had barely survived its second winter of blockade and mass starvation. Lenin's writ ran only in a restricted area of Central Russia, walled in on all sides by powerful enemies who denied all access to the outside world. Even if the Bolshevik leaders had wanted to attack their western neighbours, they would have been physically incapable of doing so.[22]

Carton de Wiart later remarked in his memoir, 'I was finding out fast that in Poland there is always a political crisis on tap'.[23] He would also discover that the views put forward by Lewis Namier[24] of the Foreign Office's Political Intelligence Department 'were bitterly opposed to a strong and independent Poland'.[25] Another British diplomat, Ted Carr, who had initially been in favour of recognizing Poland and its claim to Danzig, fell out with the Polish delegation and vehemently opposed Polish expansion into areas formerly occupied by Germany.

An armed tussle between Polish and Ukrainian nationalists in Lwów had been going on since the end of October 1918 when the Ukrainian nationalist Captain Vitovsky and his 'Sich riflemen' had staged a coup against the Austrian government of Eastern Galicia– some say with their connivance[26] – and declared an independent West Ukrainian National Republic. It was the result of years of political friction between Poles and Ukrainians; both had their own ethnic and cultural identities, and both saw themselves as legitimate claimants to the

Eastern lands of the Austrian province, the Poles the more so as it had been historically part of the Polish lands.[27]

Matters came to a head when Piłsudski sent reinforcements to the increasingly beleaguered Poles in the city and by late November it was firmly in Polish hands. A battle for Przemyśl, the main strategic rail hub between Lwów and Eastern Galicia, followed when the Poles once more prevailed. But all was to change when Major General Mykhailo Omelianovych-Pavlenko, a highly decorated Russian officer, took charge of the motley collection of Ukrainian forces and turned them into a semblance of a well-organized army.

With Lwów now surrounded by his forces, Pavlenko planned his assault but the Poles got wind of his plans and despatched a large relief force which successfully fought its way into the city. A stalemate ensued until, with a greatly enlarged army totalling nearly 60,000 men, the Ukrainians launched a new offensive in February to capture the Przemyśl – Lwów salient. It started well but to Pavlenko's irritation General Barthélemy's Mission requested a ceasefire to enable the Commission to travel to Lwów to arrange a ceasefire.[28]

On 6 February 1919, after arriving in Lwów with General Longhena and General Barthélemy, the Italian and French representatives 'without having heard one shot fired or seen even the flicker of an enemy's hind quarters',[29] Carton de Wiart found the city surrounded by the Ukrainian army who fortunately were doing little other than the occasional 'light shelling to show they were at war'. Making their way to his headquarters the next day, the Mission reached an agreement with Pavlenko and Symon Petliura, the Chairman of the Ukrainian Directorate and Chief of Military Forces, to send a delegation to Lwów to discuss peace terms. Carton de Wiart and General Barthélemy negotiated up an armistice while they delineated a line to which the Ukrainians could withdraw but the whole exercise proved a waste of time, not surprisingly since the terms would have given Poland a third of Eastern Galicia. After calling the Ukrainian Mission 'un tas de cochons', he left for Warsaw with his staff. On the journey back, they came under machine-gun fire and two Polish officers who had hitched a lift with them were killed.[30]

Fighting resumed and on 22 March the Peace Conference again asked for a ceasefire so they could re-open negotiations. The Ukrainian Army now numbered 126,000 men against a Polish army of 156,000. Gratuitous and at times bitter politicking followed in Paris with Lloyd George and Foch pushing different agendas and no agreement was reached between the warring parties. Then, as so often happened in those chaotic days, alarm bells rang in Paris when Béla Kun's Hungarian Red armies appeared in Slovakia and news came that the

Bolsheviks had contacted the Poles in Volhynia, the area of Ukraine to the east of Galicia. Suddenly the occupation of East Galicia became a strategic necessity and on 25 June the Supreme Council authorized Poland to occupy all of Eastern Galicia and establish a civil government.

With its capital Wilno now the centre of the 'Litbel' Soviet Socialist Republic, Lithuania was another hot spot in early 1919 and on 4 March, Carton de Wiart sent the Foreign Secretary, Arthur Balfour, a long report about a meeting he had had with Piłsudski about Lithuania. The crux was that Piłsudski favoured an autonomous Lithuanian state which would be part of a Polish Federation. As he himself came from Wilno, this was indeed an informed view. However, if the Lithuanians disagreed and stayed with the Letts, that could also be an acceptable outcome providing they dropped their claim to Wilno. They had also discussed the border regions and the likely preference of the indigenous Russian population.[31]

Arriving back in Warsaw on 6 March, Carton de Wiart discovered that the rest of the Allied Mission had gone to Posen, the capital of the Province of Posnania which had been recently returned to Poland by Germany under the Paris Peace Agreement. He immediately set off to join them but found that the plethora of conferences, dinners and dances were not his favourite events and it was a relief when he was summoned to Paris to report to Lloyd George and Field Marshal Sir Henry Wilson.

On the way to Paris, he read the Interim Report of the British Economic Mission to Poland in which the author Lieutenant Colonel R.J. McAlpine identified industrial unemployment as 'in some ways Poland's gravest problem. In my opinion, based on a study of local conditions and also on experience of similar conditions in Russia in 1917, the problem brooks no delay'. Arriving in Paris on 9 March, Carton de Wiart presented his own report to Lloyd George and Wilson. Over dinner he raised the Polish request that a senior Allied officer, naturally French as Poland was in the French sphere, should be sent to Warsaw to act as Chief of Staff to Piłsudski. Wilson took him to see Maréchal Foch the next day who was unable to agree to Paderewski's choice of General Henri Gouraud, one of France's most successful generals and the liberator of Strasbourg where he had successfully evicted the recently installed Alsace-Lorraine Soviet Republic. Instead, Foch appointed General Paul Henrys. In Carton de Wiart's opinion, Henrys was 'a failure in Poland' and let the side down by allowing his 1,500 officers to 'indulge themselves in easy and pleasant living, not at all conducive to successful military training'.

It was during this period that the Irish artist Sir William Orpen arrived in Paris at the invitation of the British government to record the Peace Conference on canvas. Like Jean-Baptiste Isabey at the Congress of Vienna a hundred years before who had supplemented Talleyrand's official commission by painting many of the notable attendees in his Viennese atelier, Orpen set up his studio in the Astoria Hotel on the Champs d'Elysée and started painting the great and the good – President Wilson and Prime Minister Lloyd George, Generals Botha and Smuts, and Admirals Wemyss and Beatty. Towards the end of the Peace Conference, he chanced upon Carton de Wiart: 'The warrior, General Carton de Wiart, VC, came to sit: a man who loved war. What a happy nature! He told me he never suffered any pain from all his wounds except once – mental pain – when he temporarily lost the sight of his other eye, and he thought he might be blind for life. A joyous man, so quiet, so calm, so utterly unaffected'.[32] Along with Augustus John's portrait of Colonel T.E. Lawrence in his Arab robes,[33] Orpen's painting of Carton de Wiart remains one of the most enduring images of all the politicians and generals[34] who posed during those heady days in post-war Paris.

Carton de Wiart returned to Poland on 14 March and two weeks later the Inter-Allied Mission withdrew back to Paris where it wound down. Under the wing of the Acting British Commissioner Richard Kimens,[35] Carton de Wiart's team waited until the Military Mission to Poland Bill passed its final reading in London. As Major King put it, 'we are really here before our time but by calling ourselves Representatives of the British Army, everyone is content provided we don't interfere in non-military matters'.[36]

At the end of March, Howard, Carton de Wiart and their ADC Jan Ciechanowski went down to Kraków where they stayed with Count Franciszek Potocki and his wife at their beautiful Pałac Potockich on Rynek 20. The Potockis had lost their great mansion at Peczara and its famous vineyards near Winnica in the fighting between the Ukrainians and the Polish. For Howard, it was his last weekend in Poland as he was now on his way back to England. His partnership with Carton de Wiart had been remarkable for its cordiality and shared perspectives.

On 8 April, the Military representatives of the Inter-Allied Commission submitted their nine-page report on Military Questions. It was a hard-hitting critique of the performance of the Peace Conference. In regard to Posnania, they found that 'the moral authority of the Entente is diminished as a result of this disturbed situation. The Poles are astonished that the Great Powers, who were able to achieve victory and impose an armistice, should be powerless to cause the enemy (Germany) to carry out its clauses'. As for Eastern Galicia, 'there, as in Posnania, the results obtained by the Allies are not calculated to increase the moral prestige of the Entente'. They ended their report with a request that 'help should be given to Poland (a) because all necessaries are lacking in that country (b) because her geographical position is such that it would be possible, with her co-operation, to separate Germany from Hungary and Russia, and to isolate the most dangerous sources of Bolshevism'.[37] The wisdom and first-hand knowledge of these senior soldiers fell on deaf British ears, but the French were listening.

Carton de Wiart returned to Poland from Paris and by 13 April had compiled an extensive report to Kisch. He had visited the newly formed 1st Polish Division at Jablona which had 'a great dearth of instructors' with 7,000 men 'still in mufti, at least 5% with no boots.' He had then gone to see Major Campbell-Krook, his representative in Posen, where he found the sub-commission 'leading a very pleasant social life in (the city) they have never yet left. Colonel Marquet is very vain and very careful of his position as President'.[38] From then on, Marquet was in his sights and Major General Thwaites, the DMI, delivered a stinging request to Sir Maurice Hankey, Secretary to the Cabinet and one of the few men to have the ear of Lloyd George, asking him to have the Posen Sub-Commission abolished in view of the fact that the Noullens Commission had already been dissolved and 'it is preposterous that Carton de Wiart's authority over his representative at Posen should be restricted by the French'.[39]

The problem was that the French carried far greater weight in Polish military affairs than the British. Since June 1917, they had provided barracks, training and equipment for a volunteer Polish Army made up of Poles who had served in the French Army, former POWs of Austrian-Hungarian and German armies (nearly 35,000) held in France and Italy, and Polish emigrants from the United States, Canada and Brazil (23,300). Instructed by French officers, in 1918 the Blue Army as it became known owing to the colour of its French uniforms, had fought as part of General Gourand's 4th French Army in the Champagne sector. By an agreement of 28 September 1918, it was recognized by the Triple Entente member countries as the official army of Dmowski's government and in October General Josef Haller, a former officer in the Austro-Hungarian army, was appointed its commander. An ardent Catholic and patriot like many of his contemporaries, he had started off with the Habsburg Army, then defected to the Russians with his regiment, then fought against the Bolsheviks before finally escaping to France.

Piłsudski had at first prevaricated about allowing the Blue Army into Poland for he feared that Dmowski would use it to unseat him. However, once Paderewski had made him Head of State with Dmowski's consent, he urged the Allies to send it post haste to Poland. There were only two ways it could travel, either by sea to Danzig or overland to Warsaw. Both options were vetoed by the Germans until finally an agreement was reached for it to be transported in sealed trains. By March 1919 the Blue Army numbering some 60,000 well-armed veterans including elements of the Bayonne Legion of the Légion Étrangère, began to arrive and three regiments of infantry were immediately deployed to the Ukraine theatre. The arrival of the Blue Army was to transform the credibility of the fledgling national army. From July onwards, General Henrys and his 1,500 strong[40] Military Mission were given the training mandate and all instruction was based on French Army manuals and procedures.

Britain had played no part in this timely transfusion of military power to Piłsudski's scant resources. The British Military Mission remained a small fact gathering team which fed information to Paris. In his first report to Lieutenant Colonel Kisch of 24 March 1919, Carton de Wiart recounted his experiences of a visit to Brześć Litewski.

> I went and had a look at the country East of this place as far as Slonim which is still their infantry front. As far as Byelostok[41] [sic], conditions are normal and one sees a good number of people on the road and in the villages, and the land is cultivated when not too marshy. Byelostok is normal too, and though food is not plentiful, there is enough from what I saw.
>
> East of Byelostok conditions are very bad, every village is deserted, and all the land is lying fallow. It really is dreadful, for miles and miles one sees nothing in the way of life at all, and though the soil is not rich, it must have produced very fair crops before the war. There are a lot of forests too, and they seem alright [sic] placed.
>
> At Volkovisk, General Szeptycki[42] has his headquarters and there are a few inhabitants there beside the troops…This general was Chief of the Staff until a few weeks ago, and seems a capable energetic man, much above the average. He accompanied us to Slonim where he is making a bridgehead.
>
> On 10 March the Bolsheviks tried to capture Slonim, and when Szeptycki took command he at once pushed out the cavalry and advanced some 40 kms without any trouble; as his front is one of 150 kms and he has 5,000 rifles, two cavalry regiments and ten canon, you get the Bolshevik military form at a glance!
>
> The Bolsheviks have one division opposite him with Headquarters at Minsk, and another in reserve behind that one, both indifferent he tells me, and they must be all that.
>
> The Germans at Grodno have told Szeptycki they are going to evacuate it shortly, and they will hand it over to his troops. There is one Lithuanian regiment in the town and they have told him they will not oppose his entry but he is not sure the rest of the Lithuanian army will be in the same frame of mind and I

should not be surprised if there was trouble with them unless we can step in at the right moment and smooth things down but I cannot get good information, and I have no one I can send at present.

Slonim is very much knocked about and there are very few people in it. The Russians in their retreat took everyone with them from the towns and villages and very few have come back. I gather that thousands and thousands died on the road.

The troops I saw gave a very good impression, they are a well grown crowd and have a splendid spirit though they are very badly clothed and equipped. A great number of them are just boys, but all of them very keen and full of fight.

…From Slonim we went to Brześć Litewski via Rujani and Prujani…A great part of Brześć Litewski was destroyed by the Russians in their retreat too, and it is in a miserable condition with very few inhabitants. General Listowski[43] has his headquarters here but I did not see him. His front has been heavily attacked on the 21st, the Bolsheviks having tried to force the canal to bare Szeptycki's right flank but they failed.

From Brześć Litewski, we went to Byela and here again conditions begin to improve, and we came back via Syedlets.

All the roads we went by were good, but they will not remain so for long if there is any heavy traffic along them. But as they cannot have been touched since the war, they are really wonderful and those that go through the marshes represent some extraordinary work in the road making line.

…From all this you will gather that I do not anticipate military trouble from the Bolsheviks on this front for the time being and that with a little help and much work in the organization line, this front should be secure. But the economic conditions are appalling, however that does not concern us though I hope you will point out this fact to those interested.

Rather than waiting for desultory decisions to be forthcoming from Paris, the Poles took matters into their own hands. Piłsudski arrived at the Lithuanian front on 15 April 1919 and after driving the Red Army from Wilno on the 21st, took the salute at a victory parade in the city. The occupying Bolshevik army was sent packing and fell back on Minsk. For Lenin, the situation looked dire. The Soviet II Army, chased out of Estonia in February, now waited in the suburbs of St Petersburg for an assault by the British-backed General Yudenich. The Soviet VII Army which had seized control of Latvia in January had likewise been evicted and was desperately fighting for its survival. The XII Army, the conqueror of Kiev in February, was being hard pressed by the British-sponsored General Denikin, and in Siberia Admiral Kolchak also sponsored by the British was poised to cross the Urals with his forces. As Norman Davies puts it 'The Soviets were clenched in an iron fist of which the Western front was no more than a knuckle of the smallest finger'.[44]

With his high-level contacts, Carton de Wiart was able to provide timely and accurate intelligence to both the Foreign and War Offices. On 9 May, he informed Balfour that 'General Haller's army undoubtedly intended for Eastern Galician campaign. Cannot ascertain when operations are to begin but expect it must be very soon. Plan is…Eastern Galicia and make it autonomous. Personally, I am putting no pressure to prevent this for fear of not being able to obtain any more information'.[45]

On 11 May, Carton de Wiart wrote to Major General Thwaites at the War Office in London[46] that:

I am sure that Haller will attack the country South East of Lemberg[47] [*sic*], though he will not touch the town and he can then say he has no troops in it . . . I saw Haller on 8th, he very carefully avoided the subject of where his army was to go, but on my expressing the opinion that the Ruthenes would destroy the oilfields, he said 'I have taken all possible precautions against that'. And as he also went to Lemberg to bury a mother-in-law or see her grave, I think the plan of campaign is clear . . . I had a long interview with Piłsudski a few days ago, he talked chiefly of the capture of Vilnius . . . The Poles propose to push in as far as the Berisina[48] [*sic*], and Minsk can be expected to fall within the next few days. They do not propose to attack northwards at present as Piłsudski is very nervous of the Germans around Kovno, and I have noticed a very marked feeling of nervousness on his part with regard to what the Germans may do on all the Polish frontiers. He did not have this six weeks ago, and as he is very good at getting information, it is worth noting.

He ended his letter with a warning.

'I would humbly suggest that by far the best policy would be to let the Poles clear Lithuania and Eastern Galicia of Bolsheviks, provided they make a declaration that no annexation is contemplated and that they behave reasonably towards the populations of these countries. I am afraid any other policy would only cause a great deal of bad feeling and would not stop the proposed attacks, but only make them more bitter'.

He followed this with another telegram to Balfour on 14 May,[49]

in my opinion military preparations are too advanced and public feeling too strong to stop operations on the Ukrainian front from here (Warsaw). You must either immediately conclude Armistice in Paris or let operations continue by obtaining declaration from the Polish government that no annexation of Eastern Galicia is contemplated. Any other course of action would lead to very grave situation here. As no guarantee with respect to Haller's army was obtained before it left France and in view of French policy which our influence here is not strong enough to oppose at present, I feel the latter course would give better result.

Carton de Wiart was correct about the Polish attack on the Ukraine which he confirmed in a telegram of 16 May.[50] On 17 May, in another despatch to Major General Thwaites in London, he made the observation that 'Paris moves much too slowly to keep pace with the ever changing situation in these parts'. This indeed was the nub of the problem. In the south, the Polish campaign against the Ukrainians in Volhynia ended in May but the much larger conflict in Eastern Galicia with the Western Ukrainian Republic which centred over the control of Lwów and the adjacent oil fields was only resolved in July. The result not unexpectedly meant that the new burgeoning Polish State now had a 500 mile border with Soviet Russia which many thought could only lead to an all-out war. Realizing the clock was ticking, Piłsudski made a bold move to seize Minsk, a major transport hub in the Eastern borderlands, and by using his cavalry as an arm of manoeuvre interdicted the Bolshevik lines of communication. On 8 August Minsk fell and for the next nine months the Soviet armies sat behind the Dvina and Berezina rivers, glaring at the upstart Poles.

It had been a stellar nine months for Piłsudski, both militarily and politically. He had dared and he had won. Wilno, Lwów and Minsk were firmly under Polish control, the Posnan issue had been resolved in his favour and with an army of 540,000 men and another 170,000 conscripts in training, he was now in a position to talk to the Bolsheviks *pari pasu*. He was well advised to since if either Denikin or Kolchak, both traditional Russian nationalists, emerged as the leader of a new quasi-Tsarist Russia, what guarantee was there that they would be well disposed towards Polish territorial integrity? Consequently, emissaries were despatched to Moscow in July.

The Treaty of Versailles was signed on 28 June and ten days later, Howard took his family to Scotland for a well-deserved summer holiday. On 24 July he was appointed Ambassador in Madrid, a promotion in Foreign Office terms but personally he felt that, somehow, he had failed Poland and the Peace Conference. After investing mind, body, and soul into the peace process from Day One, he realized he personally had achieved little and felt he had been cheated. His diary for 1 July reads: 'My part has had little to do with the Peace Conference. None of the Russian problems have been solved and I have been put out of the Polish Commission on account of my supposed ultra-Polish tendencies. No one sees that Poland and the Baltic Provinces are the keys to the whole situation in Eastern Europe'.[51]

In truth he had been upstaged by Prime Minister Lloyd George who thought he was God's chosen architect of a new world order. Few agreed and as the perspicacious Irish journalist Dr Emile Dillon opined,

> opportunism is an essential element of statecraft, which is the art of the possible. But there is a line beyond which it becomes shiftiness, and it would be rash to assert that Mr. Lloyd George is careful to keep on the right side of it. At the Conference his conduct appeared to careful observers to be traced mainly by outside influences, and as these were various and changing the result was a zigzag. One day he would lay down a certain proposition as a dogma not to be modified, and before the week was out, he would advance the contrary proposition and maintain that with equal warmth and doubtless with equal conviction. Guided by no sound knowledge and devoid of the ballast of principle, he was tossed and driven hither and thither like a wreck on the ocean.[52]

In his autobiography, *Theatre of Life, life seen from the stalls 1905-36*, Howard looks back on his time in Poland and points to the conundrum of Lloyd George who:

> Was so obsessed with making peace with Soviet Russia that it mattered nothing to him what progress the Communist ideas might make in Eastern Europe and he was willing to allow all new neighbouring states to fall into the Soviet net provided he could get the temporary respite he needed. He apparently never understood what those who knew something of Russian conditions fully realised, namely that Marxism, like a new religion, had its fanatical adherents who now believed they could sweep the world as Mohammedanism did in the centuries after the prophet's death, not by force of persuasion but by conquest. That at least was the intention of Trotsky. It nearly succeeded because Lloyd George would not support a policy of helping the new countries of Eastern Europe against the Soviet attacks and also, I may say, because our Military delegation, dominated by Field Marshal Wilson, distrusted the powers of these new states to defend themselves against Russia, whether Imperial or Soviet, and put their faith in the White Russian leaders (and) supported them with arms and munitions which would have been valuable if given to Poles, Estonians, Letts, Lithuanians and Finns.

During a visit to Paris in September, Carton de Wiart was approached by his half-brother Maurice to help extricate him from a legal wrangle he was having with the Army. Fifteen years younger than Adrian, Maurice had gone to Eton and, on the outbreak of war, joined the 6th Battalion Lancashire Fusiliers. In 1915 he transferred Welsh Guards in France. Placed on the retired list in 1916 having been found 'permanently unfit for service' after suffering 'shell shock', in November 1918 he had returned to Egypt where his widowed mother still lived and was employed as ADC to General Sir Arthur Money, Chief Administrator of Occupied Territory Administration.

When that appointment came to an end, Maurice thought he was a free agent and signed a six-month contract at the Polish Legation in London to fight with Polish Army. On 5 September, he travelled to Paris with a 1,000 Francs[53] advance in his pocket en route for Warsaw. Much to his surprise, he then received a letter from the War Office instructing him to report for duty in Egypt. Protesting that he was no longer serving with the British Army, he was placed under arrest by the Military Police and ordered back to England. Learning that his famous half-brother was in town, he arranged to meet him and asked for his assistance in clearing the matter up. Carton de Wiart was unsympathetic and told him that he was not in a position to help. Maurice had no option other than to return to London where he was attached to the Grenadier Guards in the Tower of London under 'open arrest'. Charged with disobeying a lawful order, he was severely reprimanded and discharged.[54]

Attention in London and Paris was now focused on the Civil War in Russia which was entering a decisive phase. The British-backed White armies of Admiral Kolchak in Siberia and General Denikin in South Russia advanced resolutely towards Moscow. In the north-west General Yudevitch attacked Petrograd. The interventionist faction in Paris expected Poland to march on Moscow in collaboration with Denikin. It was a fantasy, aided by an offer from Paderewski in September to send a 500,000 man army into Russia providing that the Allies covered its £1,000,000 a day cost. The Americans were honest enough to say they were not ready to find the money; the French postulated that such an invasion would rally all Russians to the Bolsheviks; and the British declared that they would be in breach of their obligations to act only on the authority of the Great Powers. When Carton de Wiart was summoned back to give his view to the War Office, he had lunch with Winston Churchill, still Secretary of State for War, and relayed Piłsudski's opinion that Denikin's chances of getting to Moscow were slim.

However, by October, Denikin's army was only 300 kms from Moscow. He was looking forward to spending Christmas in the capital. Ignoring Carton de Wiart's intelligence, Churchill informed the cabinet that the Bolsheviks would soon be finished. Unknown to Churchill, the Bolsheviks and Piłsudski had begun talks on 11 October and by early November, they had agreed on an exchange of military and civilian prisoners. The reason why the Russians had offered the

Poles a secret deal was to buy time to get their own army organized for a counter-attack against Denikin and thereby allowed Trotsky to move 43,000 troops away from the Polish front.

Seemingly unaware of the depth of the ideological gap between Piłsudski's Prometeism and Denikin's nationalistic White Russians, Churchill sent General Briggs to Warsaw to persuade Piłsudski to join Denikin in his advance against the Bolsheviks. 'During the interview', wrote Carton de Wiart, 'I could see that Piłsudski was not in the least impressed by what Briggs was telling him, and when Briggs left Piłsudski said that Denikin would fail to get to Moscow, and worse still, that he would soon be back in the Black Sea'.[55] On 15 November, Denikin was indeed defeated at Kastorskaya and Kursk fell soon after. By early December, the Bolsheviks were in Kharkov and Denikin's army headed south in a disorderly retreat.

Around this time what can only be described as the Sorry Affair of the Greatcoats and Boots started. Messrs Cope, Williams and Pearl of Holborn had agreed to sell the Poles 600,000 greatcoats and 200,000 pairs of boots at an agreed price but would not sign a contract until they were certain that the goods could be delivered without hindrance. The Polish government undertook to make best efforts to ship the goods to Danzig, but they hoped the British government could use their offices in Berlin with the German government to allow the goods to be consigned via Illowo and Mlava. The Foreign Office retorted that while they were 'ready to examine whole question (of support for Polish Army) in a friendly spirit…(they) should not assent to any recommendations in which main responsibility for transporting or bearing cost of transportation should be placed on His Majesty's Government'.[56] Even when Sir Horace Rumbold, the British Ambassador in Warsaw, advised in November that 'General Carton de Wiart who has just returned from Wilno confirms that many Polish soldiers at the front are without boots and greatcoats . . . cold is intense',[57] they did not relent. Even more injurious was the decision of the Supreme War Council in Paris to renege on an undertaking they made in October to give the Polish Army 10,000 rifles, 1,400 machine guns and 18 million rounds of small arms ammunition, all of German pattern. Instead, they were diverted to the Letts in consequence of a Russian-German attack on Riga.[58]

Encouraging telegrams to Denikin were soon to be the only help Churchill was able to provide. Lloyd George's policy of terminating aid to the Whites was confirmed in the Inter-Allied Conference held in London 11–13 December. The French prime minister, Clemenceau, sided with Lloyd George on this question and preferred the idea of forming a *cordon sanitaire* or a barrier of independent states to contain the spread of Bolshevism towards Europe. The most important of these buffer states would be Poland, which would also eliminate somewhat the threat of revanchism from Germany that Clemenceau considered more acute than that of Bolshevism. The conference resolved that the Allies would not enter into any further commitments to assist, militarily or financially, the 'anti-Bolshevik elements' in Russia; individual nations would, however, be free to leave their political or military Missions in Russia as long as they wished. The Whites would also still be allowed to purchase war matériel from the Allied countries. The message was clear; Russia would be left to decide her own fate without active intervention of the Allies on the White side of the conflict. This came close to acknowledging the Bolsheviks as the de facto winners of the civil war.

Moreover, the reports from South Russia were most discouraging. The Bolsheviks continued their advance to the south and Denikin was becoming desperate. He even asked Churchill directly to send British troops – 'only one or two army corpses [*sic*]' – to save the Whites from defeat. Churchill continued publicly to advocate the White cause, but he admitted in a personal letter of 31 December 1919 to General Wilson that Denikin's story would soon end. He also instructed General Holman to advise Denikin to start negotiations for a truce with the Bolsheviks as he no longer considered a victory possible.[59]

In Greater Russia, the future of the Whites was equally bleak. General Nikolai Yudevitch's army had retreated back into Estonia having failed to take Petrograd in November; Irkutsk fell on 24 December; in early January 1920, Admiral Kolchak, who had resigned as the Supreme Ruler of Russia, was detained by the Czech Legion and handed over to a Bolshevik Military Committee; and General Knox's Siberian Military Mission sailed home from Vladivostok on Boxing Day. Lloyd George was delighted for he had always advocated that the best way of dealing with the Bolsheviks was through trade and mutual advancement in commerce and industry.

While his public life was closely followed by *The Times*, Carton de Wiart's private life in Poland in 1919 was a topic of conversation in Viennese salons where gossips talked of an affair with Princess Olga Radziwiłł, the wife of Prince Léon Radziwiłł. Born in St Petersburg in 1886, she was the younger daughter of Baron Johann von Simolin-Wettberg zu Brickenhof,[60] the head of the Baltic branch of the Simolins, an old merchant family from Turku which had once been the largest city in Finland and briefly the capital of the new Russian Grand Principality of Finland in 1809. Olga had married Prince Leon in 1911 in Saint Petersburg and their first child Prince Anton was born the following year. In

January 1920, a second son, Prince Jerzy Mikolaj, was born and 'expected to have a black patch'.[61] Billy Cavendish-Bentinck,[62] who had spent over two years as Third Secretary at the British Legation in Warsaw in the early 1920s, told his biographer Patrick Howarth that at that time 'I knew Carton quite well. I was very fond of him. He had great success with women'.[63] In conversation with Peter Fleming in 1964, he remembered how 'Adrian first walked out with Olga R, who had a baby'. He added that her son Prince Jerzy was by then working in Italy[64] and looked very much like de Wiart.[65]

The year ended on a low for Anglo-Polish relations. The Great Powers had resolved to dispose of East Galicia from Austro-Hungary with the British making noises that it could go to Russia or even Czechoslovakia. This suggestion so incensed the Poles that they showed their displeasure by refusing to dance after dinner at a ball hosted by Sir Horace Rumbold at his residence just before Christmas. De Wiart, who in September had tried but failed to persuade Lloyd George that East Galicia should go to Poland,[66] was asked by a flustered Lady Rumbold to find out what was the matter. The explanation was simple. How could the Poles dance when the British were taking East Galicia away from them? An incandescent Carton de Wiart told them that they would have been better advised not to accept the invitation in the first place and one account relates that, 'white with fury', he suggested to Lady Rumbold 'I should throw the whole lot out of the house if I were you'.[67]

Tempers now began to fray; voices were raised and soon a Pro-British Pole challenged an Anti-British Pole to a duel. Carton de Wiart accepted to be his first second and General Baron Mannerheim, the dashing former Regent of Finland, the other. When the two officers called on their principal's opponent the next day, they found he had left post haste for Vienna. In hindsight, it was a most fortunate outcome for a duel provoked at the Ambassador's residence, irrespective of the outcome, would have been a diplomatic disaster. Temporarily cold-shouldered by the members of the Klub Myśliwiski, Carton de Wiart waited for the affair to die down while 'Sir Horrid Grumbles' as he was affectionately known soothed ruffled Polish egos.

Game, set and match to Piłsudski

At the beginning of 1920, the British government was trying to extricate itself from its failed gamble in Russia. On 10 January there were still 394 officers and 1,529 other ranks serving with the British Military Mission with General Denikin, including 93 officers and 291 other ranks of the Royal Air Force. The scale of Churchill's bet dwarfed British aid to Poland; Britain had supplied enough war matériel to equip fully an army of 250,000 men, far more than Denikin was ever able to muster.[1] In all, at least £100 million was spent on Denikin's army, according to Churchill's figures.[2] All this was of little comfort to the Poles who were still waiting in the icy grip of winter for their British boots and greatcoats.

In Poland, the New Year started ominously with both Warsaw and Moscow preparing for war. By April, Piłsudski was ready to make his move; all Polish officers had been withdrawn from training and sent to the front and the armies ordered to take up forward positions. However, before he could give the final go-ahead, he needed to counter the threat of being caught in a Russian pincer movement from the south east and north east. His solution was to create an independent Ukrainian state allied to Poland which would in effect half the land border between Russia and Poland, allowing him to concentrate his forces in the north. However, although his choice of Symon Petliura, Carton de Wiart's bête noir from Spring 1919, made political sense as he was willing to join a greater Polish federation, militarily it was risky for, to date, he had proved to be a loser on the battlefield. Nevertheless, on 21 April, an agreement was signed between both parties with Petliura recognized by Poland as the supreme authority of the Ukrainian People's Republic. Included in the agreement were arrangements of borders, cultural rights and, importantly, a mutually beneficial trade package.

Four days later, Piłsudski opened his offensive and by 3 May a party of Polish Hussars had penetrated into the outskirts of Kiev. By the 7th it was in Polish hands and over 30,000 prisoners taken along with significant quantities of war material. An unexpected hiatus followed with Petliura failing to make any progress in organizing an administration while the Polish Army marked time on the River Dnieper awaiting the arrival of the feared First Red Cavalry Army or *Konarmiya*. Commanded by former Tsarist NCO Semyon Budyonny and composed of Cossacks, partisans and freebooting bandits, this maverick formation had left Kuban in the eastern Crimea seven weeks earlier and over the course of a thirty-day march had covered 750 miles. A Polish cavalry officer described how 'this swarm of horsemen would raise gigantic dust-clouds on the horizon, blotting out everything for miles around and giving the impression of a great, fast-moving and fantastic force pouring into every available space, and finally kindle a feeling of utter impotence in the enemy ranks.'[3]

In many ways the inheritor of Napoleonic tactics and forerunner of the 1939 Blitzkrieg variation, Budyonny's cavalry could bring its whole might to bear at one point on the enemy in quick time and exploit success which is exactly what it did on 5 June when all four divisions attacked the Polish 13th Infantry Division. By 10 June the Poles were forced to evacuate Kiev. Consequently, Poland was threatened by a Russian invasion on two fronts rather than one, although thanks to an orderly withdrawal by General Śmigły-Rydz, they managed to extract most of their men and equipment.

In pre-empting the Soviet offensive by attacking the Russian armies in the Ukraine, Piłsudski had given the Bolsheviks a perfect opportunity to play the victim of an unprovoked assault. Members of Parliament pressed the government on whether it was providing military assistance to Poland, given that Piłsudski was acting outside of the terms of the Paris Agreement. The answer from Churchill was no. This was more a statement of fact rather than policy for on 1 May the Danish steamer *Neptune*, laden with munitions and equipment for Poland, had been accidentally rammed on the river at Gravesend and towed ashore where she beached. Two weeks later a British cargo ship, the *Jolly George*,[4] was being loaded in the London docks with munitions for Poland. When the dockers got wind of its destination, they alerted Ernie Bevan, General Secretary of the Dockers' Union, who promised his support if they took strike action. The coal heavers refused to refuel the ship and its cargo never left the East India Dock. Thanks to Piłsudski, the 'Hands off Russia' campaign was up and running.

Carton de Wiart decided to see for himself how events were progressing and together with Lieutenant Commander Bernard Rawlins and his batman James, he went down on the train to Grodno on the Neman River where there was heavy fighting between General Mokrzecki's Polish Battle Group and Gai Bzhishkyan's III Bolshevik Kavkor (Cavalry Corps). Setting off to the front by car, they soon spied some Cossacks on the road ahead. For once discretion was the better part of valour and Carton de Wiart retired back to the station where he persuaded the station master to attach his personal carriage, a smart *wagon lit* which Rawlins had managed to purloin in Hungary, to the end of a refugee train 'of great length and infinite variety' pulled by two engines. Once the train had left the station and reached a sedate top speed of 8 mph, the Cossacks began to take pot shots at it, but these made little impression. Soon a pair of light field guns opened up and a round smashed into Carton de Wiart's coach causing the carriage to drop on its wheels. Realizing they were now sitting ducks, the party scampered out of its carriage and ran alongside the length of the train looking for a safer berth. As they clambered on to a bogey truck, Carton de Wiart's single good hand slipped and he fell by the tracks. Up in a flash – although it seemed to him an eternity – he ran up to the crawling train and leapt aboard. The damaged coach was now acting as an anchor on the whole train and making the enemy artillery's job a lot easier, so it was cast off and its fate consigned to the Cossacks.[5] They reached Warsaw without further incident. On 7 July, *The Times* reported that

> General Adrian Carton de Wiart the British Military attaché, who was on a visit to Rodno [*sic*] . . . had a narrow escape from being captured. A shell hit his car, which was the last car on the last train leaving Rodno. The General who is a VC, one-armed and one-eyed, ran some hundreds of yards under fire and only just succeeded in clambering into a goods wagon.[6]

The legend of his indestructibility lived on.

Among his many escapades in Poland, flying incidents and accidents featured regularly. On a visit to see General Gough and Brigadier General Burt in Riga, he was flown up by a French pilot who was forced to keep low to avoid bad weather. Passing over a German position, Carton de Wiart noticed a rifleman take a pot shot at him and after landing discovered a fresh bullet hole six inches away from his seat. Returning in the same plane, the pilot had to make a forced landing due to engine trouble, luckily finding a gap in the sea of forests beneath them. After tinkering with the engine, the pilot took off again only to make another forced landing. Carton de Wiart set off to find help and eventually ended up in the back of a country cart with a Lithuanian military escort for a thirty-five mile journey to the nearest railway station where he took a train to Kowno.

In July 1920, Lieutenant Commander Kenworthy MP asked Winston Churchill in the House of Commons 'whether General Carton de Wiart obtained permission from the War Office to take part in the demonstration flight to Kieff [*sic*] in a Bristol aeroplane on behalf of a Polish syndicate; and whether it is considered part of General Wiart's duties to take part in demonstrations of this kind?'[7] Churchill replied that 'there is no objection to a British officer taking an aeroplane flight; in fact, although not forming part of his duties, the interest displayed by General Carton de Wiart in the enterprise appears commendable'. This story had appeared in the British press for, in another forced landing, the plane had turned turtle, leaving Carton de Wiart trapped upside down in his seat after the cargo of provisions had jammed him in.

On the northeast front, a dynamic young former Tsarist officer, 27-year-old Mikhail Tukhachevsky, had arrived in Smolensk in May and started to cautiously probe the Polish lines. By June, for the first time in its uncertain existence, the Bolshevik government could marshal all its forces at one place at one point in time. With nearly 5 million men under arms and with 800,000 'bayonets', it stood ready to attack Poland. The offensive opened on 4 July, Wilno fell ten days later, and Grodno succumbed on 24 July. The next day, Tukhachevsky ordered his men to occupy Warsaw by 12 August at the latest. By the end of the second week of August, the Red Army stood on the banks of the Vistula.

The Allied governments in Paris looked on aghast for all the while they had been assuming that Poland was going to invade Russia. For Lloyd George, whose policy of trading with the Bolsheviks rather than military intervention had been accepted by the Peace Conference albeit grudgingly by some states, this was a matter of acute embarrassment.

Carton de Wiart was not surprised since he had always thought that Warsaw would be seriously threatened by the Bolsheviks as he was doubtful about the ability of the Polish Army to stop a determined advance. He had seen at first hand its weakness as an amalgam of different elements – Russian, German, Austrian – all trained on different lines and armed with different weapons. At command level, he had also witnessed the friction between competing officers which did not bode well for a unified command structure. He asked the British Ambassador Sir Horace Rumbold if he would support his views, but he politely declined. It was only when the French General Joseph Barthélemy encouraged him to get in touch directly with the War Office that he spoke his mind to Major General Thwaites who was still Director of Military Intelligence.

Saddled with the original Allied guarantees of Polish independence, Lloyd George told the House of Commons on 21 July that 'we British cannot disinterest ourselves in the fate of Poland. . . . It is to the British interest . . . that Poland should not be wiped out. It would be fatal to the peace of Europe and the consequences would be disastrous beyond measure'.[8] His response and that of other Allied leaders was to launch a new Inter-Allied Mission under the banker Viscount D'Abernon[9] with the redoubtable Sir Maurice Hankey as the prime minister's personal representative. Lieutenant General Sir Percy Radcliffe[10] (Director of Military Operations) was nominated by the Army Council as the military representative. The French appointed M. Jean Jules Jusserand (the French Ambassador to Washington and a confidant of President Wilson) and General Maxime Weygand, Maréchal Foch's Chief of Staff.

When they reached Poland, brimming with ideas of imposing a political reshuffle to rein in the Poles while at the same time appeasing Russia, Sir Horace Rumbold told them in no uncertain terms that if Piłsudski went, there would be a revolution and whatever the outcome it would be a good deal worse that the status quo. Effectively the Mission was obsolescent from the moment it arrived for by the time their train drew into Warsaw station, the Bolsheviks were only 130 miles from the city. Piłsudski asked Weygand how many divisions he had brought with him, fully knowing that the answer was none. When Weygand asked Carton de Wiart for his opinion, the stark reply was that nothing could halt the Polish retreat until they reached Warsaw where they would probably be able to whip up enough national fervour to defend it.[11] Such frankness prompted D'Abernon to characterized Carton de Wiart 'a man of marked independence of judgment'.[12] In his daily meetings with Piłsudski, Carton de Wiart observed that he was unusually fatalistic and was invoking the name of the Almighty to save the city like long-ago Byzantine Emperors when the walls of Constantinople were invested by Avars or Ottomans.

As Norman Davies says, 'in the last analysis the fate of Lloyd George as leader of the Allied powers and perhaps as British Prime Minister (now) rested in the hands of the people he had done everything to discourage, the hands of Polish soldiers still manning the defences of beleaguered Warsaw'.[13] Paris could only sit and watch as the battle for Warsaw began when Brześć fell and the Russians crossed the River Bug. On 6 August, the Polish Supreme Command redistributed the Polish armies to three fronts rather than two. The implementation of this Herculean and hazardous order strained every sinew in the Polish Army, but it was successfully carried out, enabling the defensive battle to be fought on separate sectors of the front line – the Vistula bridgehead, the Wikra, the Wieprz and the Russian frontier to the southeast.

The same day, D'Abernon telegraphed Lord Curzon urging him to despatch a Franco-British expeditionary force of at least 20,000 men. Meanwhile, Lloyd George was busy with his own initiative to arrange an armistice between the two belligerents and was talking to the Russian delegation of Leonid Krassin, the Soviet Trade Commissar, and Lev Kamenev, Trotsky's brother-in-law, in London. Both parties were urged by Britain and the Entente to meet at Minsk on 11 August to begin ceasefire negotiations. Yet on 10 August, Lloyd George heaped compliments on the Poles, telling the House that:

> They 'are a brave people – there is no braver people in Europe: they have always made fine soldiers, and some of the greatest military achievements in Europe stand to their credit – but they have got their difficulties . . . they have been suddenly called upon . . . to undertake the functions of nationhood in the most perilous position you could place them in. There are enemies behind them, enemies in front of them, difficulties to the south and difficulties to the north; great hatred towards them, some of them traditional, some of them racial, some of them religious – furious, savage hatreds surging around them, and they are a nation with no frontier which is a defensible one. There is no nation in the world placed in such a position of jeopardy by Providence as Poland. She struggled for centuries; she fell; she was torn to pieces; but here was a resurrection of Poland and she was starting a new life'.

Then, in a thinly disguised attack on Piłsudski laced with condescension, he continued, 'but it was a new life without training, without discipline, with none of her leaders trained either in government or in war. Of course, she has made blunders. They were the blunders of irresponsibility . . . theirs were the mistakes of inexperience; the mistakes of a people who had had no chance to learn how to govern'. The implication was clear; the Allied powers knew best what to do next. He ended by announcing that:

> we are sending no allied troops to Poland. . . . We have made that clear to Poland, and it is essential we should make it clear to this country. It would not be necessary if the Polish resources were thoroughly organised and well directed. I wish to make it clear that this is all on the assumption that the Minsk Conference fails and fails not because of any obstinacy on the part of Poland and not because Poland refuses to accept terms which we think, under the circumstances, are as good as she has any right to expect. It is on the assumption that the Bolshevik Government imposes conditions which are inconsistent with national freedom and are excessive. In that event, the Allies, out of the stores at their disposal, will help to equip the Polish people for their own defence.[14]

By now the Poles had long tired of British posturing and Parliamentary waffle and paid no heed to the various Allied ultimatums orchestrated by Lloyd George in Paris. As Harold Nicolson[15] scathingly put it, the Allies intention 'was to render Poland a European Azerbaijan', a reference to the short-lived Azerbaijan Democratic Republic which had been gobbled up by Soviet Russia in 1920. When they were given twenty-four hours on 10 August to accept Russian peace terms that centred on the so-called Curzon line as the new border and a reduction of the army to 50,000 men, they refused and launched their counter-attack.

At one point, Carton de Wiart took the Ambassador Sir Horace Rumbold and General Radcliffe to the front near Mława, 100 miles north of Warsaw. Travelling by car with Carton de Wiart at the wheel and with the Naval Mission providing a machine-gun escort vehicle, they spotted a Cossack up a telegraph pole, busy cutting the wires while his fellow riders looked on. Unable to resist such a plum target, Carton de Wiart ordered the machine gun to open up and the Cossacks scattered. They soon regrouped and started to return fire from 600 yards while Carton de Wiart with his one arm desperately tried to turn the car around on the narrow road. He was mightily relieved to extract his passengers intact and deliver them safely back to Warsaw. Both appeared to have enjoyed themselves enormously.

His prophesy that the Poles would stage a successful defence of Warsaw proved right when the Bolshevik advance halted fourteen miles from the city. The journalist Curzio Malaparte, who was attached to the Italian Diplomatic Mission, described the mood:[16]

> Warsaw these days looked like a town waiting to be pillaged. The great heat seemed to suffocate all voices and noises. The crowds in the streets were perfectly noiseless. Now and then an endless convoy of trams carrying the wounded would slowly steer through these crowds. The wounded sometimes looked out of the windows shook their fists and swore. A ceaseless hum spread from pavement to pavement, from street to street. A group of Bolshevik prisoners, battered, bent, and limping, with red stars on the front of their uniforms, marched between hedges of mounted Uhlans. The crowd opened in silence to let them pass and immediately closed again. . . . Heavy clouds charged with heat and dust darkened the horizon which vibrated and thundered as though a battering ram had charged it.

On the night of 13 August, Malaparte went to the Hunt Club:

> Among the noblemen and great landowners . . . that night, besides (Prince) Sapieha and Trompczinski,[17] we found some of the most representative members of the Opposition to Piłsudski and Witos. The only foreign Diplomats were Count Oberndorff, the German Minister, the British General Carton de Wiart and the Secretary of the French Legation. Everybody seemed at ease except Sapieha and Oberndorff. Sapieha pretended not to hear the proposals that were being made beside him and occasionally leaned across to say a few words to General Carton de Wiart who was discussing the military position with Count Potocki. That day the Bolshevik troops had advanced considerably in the Radzymin sector, a village about twenty kilometres from Warsaw.

'We will fight to the end,' General Potocki was saying.

'You mean, till tomorrow,' said the British General, smiling.

Count Potocki had left Paris only a few days before but he was already planning to go back as soon as possible, as soon as fortune smiled on Poland again.

'You are all like your famous Dombrovski[18] (sic) who led the Polish legion in Italy in Napoleon's day,' said Carton de Wiart, 'Dombrovski used to say I shall always be ready to die for my country but not to live in it.'

Such were the men and such their ideas. You could hear the rumble of guns in the distance.

The next day Piłsudski launched a daring counter-attack and by 24 August, Tukhachevsky's 100,000-strong Western Front[19] was no more; overstretched, short of men and supplies, his armies were in disarray. One had ceased to exist, two were devastated and two severely damaged. The Soviet invasion had been repulsed by the genius of Piłsudski and his home-grown Polish armies. Although D'Abernon and Jusserand had both sent appeals for military aid, even specifying six infantry and two cavalry divisions, no Allied troops had been forthcoming.

As for Lloyd George, he attributed the defeat of the Bolsheviks to the timely arrival of the Inter-Allied Mission and the brilliance of D'Abernon and Weygand. 'He shared the laurels of a battle which he had done everything in his power to prevent.' As Norman Davies points out, 'in 1920 Lloyd George did not save Poland; Poland saved Lloyd George.'[20] Neither D'Abernon nor Weygand were happy about these insincere tributes; the latter acknowledged in his memoirs that '*la victoire était polonaise, le plan polonaise, l'armée polonaise*'. D'Abernon agreed: 'The credit of designing the plan which led to so great a success, viewed broadly, was due to the Polish initiative' but he qualified this view by saying 'without General Weygand there would probably have been no plan. . . . General Weygand's personal energy in supervising the details and execution, and bringing order and method to the operations of the Polish force, were essential to success. Without them the plan may well have failed.'[21] It was not the end of the war. Fighting continued around Zamosc in late August where for the first time Budyonny's Konarmya was badly battered as were the Polish Uhlans whose suicidal courage defied belief.

Lieutenant General Sir Percy Radcliffe submitted a glowing report about Carton de Wiart and his men:

I wish to bring to notice the excellent work done throughout the operations – starting from the opening of the Campaign in the spring – by General Carton de Wiart and his officers, who spent the whole of their time in the front line obtaining valuable information which could be obtained in no other way, and by their soldierly bearing and cheerful camaraderie affording much needed encouragement to the Polish troops. The heroic figure of General de Wiart in particular was sufficient to inspire confidence the moment he appeared on the scene, and this gallant officer contributed greatly towards maintaining British prestige at a time when for other reasons it had sadly diminished.[22]

The days of the Mission were now more or less over. Carton de Wiart wrote to the Director of Military Intelligence on 25 August submitting the names of Major Mockett, Lieutenant Commander Rawlings and Captain Maule for awards and Majors King, Campbell-Krook and Grant along with Captain Hamilton and Lieutenant Garnon-Williams for Mentions in Despatches. Typically, he also asked whether he could recommend Commander Wharton, Lieutenant Commander Gore-Brown and Lieutenant Buchanan of the Naval Mission for Mentions. Mockett and Rawlings both received OBEs and Maule an MBE.

Asked to put forward the names of Polish officers, he recommended Piłsudski for a GCMG; Haller for a KCB; Rozwadowski, Sosnkowsk, Śmigły-Rydz and Sikorski for CBs; and Wolikowski, Krajowski, Pik, Konarzewski and Jung for CMGs.[23] The War Office passed these on to the Foreign Office.

For his exceptional service in Poland, in September the Secretary of State for War recommended him for a KBE.[24] Even though General Sir Richard Haking,[25] Commander of the Allied Contingent in Danzig, had written to the CIGS that Carton de Wiart 'is the only man there (in Warsaw) who Piłsudski really pays attention to and no doubt you will see what can be done to give him some distinction for his work',[26] both recommendations produced a bureaucratic and unsympathetic response from the Military Secretary, Philip Chetwode:[27]

> I have discussed this question with the CIGS (Field Marshal Sir Henry Wilson) and he agrees with me that to give this officer a Knighthood for these services might be dangerous. He is a Brevet Colonel of 27 July 1920 only, this promotion having been conferred automatically on his appointment as ADC to the King; he is second senior Major in the 4th Dragoon Guards, and his name is under consideration for command of a Regiment. He already holds the CB, CMG and DSO and I suggest that to appoint him to a fourth Order would not be agreeable to His Majesty if it can be avoided.

Winston Churchill sent a testy reply in October:

> I think Carton de Wiart ought certainly to be made a KBE for all his work in Poland this year, for the risks he has run and for the admirable reports he has

presented. I certainly consider he is the sort of man who ought to be a Knight on account of his own extraordinary personality. There are only one or two alive like him, and if you look down the list of KBEs (civil and military) you will find one or two who have received the accolade for lesser claims.

Neither Carton de Wiart, Piłsudski nor any other Polish officer received an award from an ungracious British government. The French gave Piłsudski the Grande Croix de Legion d'Honneur and the Médaille Militaire; the Italians were equally gracious, awarding him a Knight Grand Cross of the Military Order of Savoy and the Knight Grand Cross of the Order of Saint Maurice and St Lazarus.

On 20 September, the last act of the Russo-Polish war opened with a titanic clash between Piłsudski and Tukhachevsky at Niemen. The Poles prevailed and after twenty months of war hostilities finally ceased on 16 October. At the Treaty of Riga in March the following year, Piłsudski doubled the area suggested by Curzon at the instigation of Lloyd George and raised his country's population to 27 million. Lord Curzon, the Foreign Secretary, remained dismissive of Poland's triumph. For him, through the prism of the international mandate the victors of the Great War had awarded themselves, Poland had behaved reprehensibly and deserved the stigma of a reprobate member of the world community. The irony was that if Poland had slavishly adhered to every out-of-date instruction emanating from Paris, the chances of her survival would have been non-existent. If the Red armies had prevailed and captured Warsaw, they would have most likely have surged on into Germany, Hungary and Czechoslovakia.

Carton de Wiart had been a witness at first hand of what Harold Nicolson described as 'the imprecisions of British post-war diplomacy',[28] best illustrated by the failure to provide promised support when the Russians crossed Curzon's 'red line'. His soldier's intuition, his belief in Piłsudski's leadership and military competence and the highly efficient informal intelligence organization he had created since the day of his arrival in February 1919 all combined to validate his sound judgement. Rumbold's replacement, William Max-Müller, noted that in the summer of 1920 'the two foreigners whose advice carried the greatest weight were Sir Horace Rumbold and General Carton de Wiart'.[29]

By the beginning of 1921, the remit of the British Military Mission had been reduced commensurately after the Treaty of Riga was signed but many territorial issues remained outstanding. Although Galicia and Volhynia in Western Ukraine had been ceded to Poland, the status of Eastern Galicia remained unresolved with Lloyd George insisting on its autonomy. There was still underlying friction on the border with the Ukrainian Soviet Socialist Republic in the east and the eastern frontier had yet to be recognized by the Allied powers. In the north, relations with Lithuania remained hostile and tense; since 1918, the ownership of Wilno had changed hands twice. In July 1921, Poles clashed with Germans in Upper Silesia, triggering the return of British troops to help French forces occupy the area. The British Mission ticked over, allowing time for leave; Carton de Wiart was spotted in Beaulieu-sur-Mer near Monaco by *The Tatler* magazine's correspondent and featured in its Riviera letter.[30]

The brain child of Lloyd George, the Genoa conference in April 1922 was billed as a forum for 'the reconstruction of economic Europe, devastated and broken into fragments by the desolating agency of war'[31] to which both Russia and Germany would be invited as equal partners. Among the many disparate issue on the agenda were Polish 'matters outstanding'. To the consternation of the British, Germany and Russia signed a separate bilateral agreement at Rapallo twenty miles to the east of Genoa in which each renounced all territorial and financial claims against the other and agreed to normalize their diplomatic relations and to 'co-operate in a spirit of mutual goodwill in meeting the economic needs of both countries'.

The whole raison d'être of the conference evaporated overnight and the result was to crystalize opinion against the British prime minister; Genoa was seen as 'a parody of summit diplomacy at its worst'[32] and by October, his coalition government had collapsed and he was gone but not before his ill-considered support of the Greek invasion of Asia Minor had gone disastrously wrong. Suddenly Poland was back in favour and in September the British government invited General Władysław Sikorski, by now the Chief of the Polish General Staff, to meet with Field Marshal Earl Cavan, the CIGS, in London. The tone of the meeting was friendly with both men looking forward to improved relations on the military side, recognizing that they had been stifled to date by divergent foreign policies. The British still lagged a long way behind the French who had signed a political and military alliance with Poland in February 1921[33] which included sending troops to Poland if it was attacked by Germany or weapons and military advisers if attacked by Soviet Russia.

In early 1923, Carton de Wiart was asked by the British legation to go to Wilno and file a report for the League of Nations on the Polish-Lithuanian position there, for heavy fighting was rumoured to be raging. In particular, Lithuanian 'volunteers' had invaded the Memel in the Polish Kłajpeda region which had been under French administration since 1920. Taking Major Grant and a Polish intelligence officer with him, Carton de Wiart set off by train through the mid-winter landscape. When they reached a blown-up bridge, they detrained and went by sledge to the nearest Polish headquarters where they were given directions to the fighting. This time by car, they headed off and soon came across a sentry on duty outside a house. Initially mistaking him for a Pole, they soon realized he was a Lithuanian and after a frantic mêlée, when most of the guard turned out and let off their rifles, an officer invited them into the house.[34]

Given that it was 20° below freezing, the party accepted and after meeting with a succession of senior officers, Carton de Wiart was told that he was to go by car to Lithuanian Headquarters at Kovno. Insisting that his two officers come with him and that the British Minister be informed without delay about their detention, Caton de Wiart next met the Lithuanian Foreign Minister who questioned him about his activities. Explaining that he had crossed into Lithuania entirely by accident and that furthermore he had no wish to stay, he was released and, after turning down the offer of an apology by the Lithuanian prime minister, he returned to Poland via Konigsberg and Danzig. When he got back, he was shown 'a most touching and flattering obituary notice written in memoriam and published by the Wolff Agency in Berlin'.[35]

This was to be his last adventure in Poland. In summing up his contribution, Norman Davies writes that

> the role of the Allied Military Mission is full of contradiction. The British Mission in Warsaw was hugely embarrassed by the Cabinet's refusal to send the supplies requested. It degenerated into a source of military intelligence on Russia to the War Office. Its chief, General Adrian de Wiart VC was a wasted asset. This indestructible warrior . . . possessed all the qualities designed to appeal to the Polish officers among whom he was sent. He was wealthy, aristocratic, cosmopolitan, Catholic, heroic and indefatigably foolhardy.[36]

However, there is another dimension to the intelligence gathering activities of the Mission. Although the nature of the intelligence was military – the movement of troops, battlefield reports, orders of battle and other military matters – its application was to provide guidance and direction to assist Allied politicians, not military commanders, in their decision making. By accurately charting the progress of Piłsudski as he set about creating a nation state of his own design rather than the one envisaged by the Great Powers in Paris and by forecasting with uncanny accuracy the likely outcome of his campaigns, Carton de Wiart's British Mission delivered a priceless flow of timely high-grade political intelligence.

In a draft despatch to London, Sir William Max-Müller, head of the British delegation in Warsaw, tried to ice an indigestible cake:

While Mr Lloyd George was Prime Minister, the average Pole, no matter to what political party he was attached, had a fixed idea that British policy was hostile to Poland, and that Lloyd George himself suffered from a peculiar dislike of the Polish character. I have on many occasions attempted to combat this view by pointing out it was ridiculous to imagine that British statesmen, in considering the main line of their country's foreign policy, would be influenced by any particular friendship or hostility towards Poland and that neither individuals nor political parties in England could be labelled as either pro- or anti-Polish. The very fact that a large body of opinion in Poland has got such ideas into their heads proved that they failed to appreciate the causes of past misunderstandings nor did they yet grasp the ordinary British view about Poland in particular or Europe in general.[37]

Herein lies the nub: 'The French have grown accustomed to consider their own position in this country as a privileged one. The tradition of friendship between the two countries is long standing and in 1920 during the Bolshevik invasion French assistance was of a practical character.'[38] Clearly, the British had no misgivings about their abject failure to arm the Poles, preferring to characterize them as intransigents who had flouted the wishes of the Peace Conference.

In April 1923, Carton de Wiart was detailed to oversee the visit of Field Marshal Earl Cavan to Poland in May, a tall order for it would follow on from a much trumpeted ten-day triumphal visit by France's Maréchal Foch, the principal French signatory to the 1921 Franco-Polish Alliance. On 3 May, Carton de Wiart witnessed the arrival of Foch and his staff in Warsaw when they were greeted by Prime Minister General Sikorski and Marshal Piłsudski and the hectic schedule which followed – the unveiling of two prestigious monuments, one to Count Josef Poniatowski, the other to Napoleon Bonaparte, military parades, gala dinners and receptions and awards to Foch of the honorary title of Marszałek Polski, the Grand Cross of the War Order of Virtuti Militari, an Honorary doctorate from Warsaw University and Honorary Polish citizenship. On the surface, the visit had been a glittering success but behind the scenes the French agenda had stalled; discussions with Piłsudski about the organization of the Polish Army to facilitate a combined French-Polish advance on Berlin in the event of war turned testy for, while the French understandably saw Germany as the threat, the Poles protested they faced both Germany and Russia.[39] Such was his irritation that Foch had been heard to mutter, 'it would be a good thing to replace him with a professional general'.[40]

On 16 May, Cavan, his wife and his Personal Assistant, Captain Freddy Beaumont-Nesbitt of the Grenadier Guards,[41] arrived in Kraków from Vienna and after attending some field manoeuvres left for Warsaw,[42] where they were met at the station by Marshal Piłsudski and a Guard of Honour. It was almost the equivalent to the Foch visit for the following day Cavan spent the morning in talks with Piłsudski and General Kazimierz Sosnkowski, the Minister of War, and then had lunch at the Belvedere Palace with President Wojciechowski. That evening Prime Minister Sikorski hosted a dinner and dance in his honour at the Royal Warsaw Castle which most of the Cabinet attended as well as senior representatives of all the other Allied powers. The following day, Cavan visited the School of Signalling, inspected an aviation camp and toured the War Museum. That evening there was another dinner and dance, this time at the Legation attended by Piłsudski, the Prime Minister, the Minister of Foreign Affairs, and the Minister of War. His last day was spent 'off duty' with some sightseeing, lunch with Carton de Wiart's friend Countess Joseph Potocka, an afternoon at the races, and an evening ballet at the Opera House.

Sir William Max-Müller expressed surprise at the scale of the success of the visit.

> I must confess that I was myself astonished at the excitement caused in all circles by the prospect of the visit and also at the scale of preparations made by the Polish government and military authorities to render it both instructive and enjoyable . . . he (Cavan) was himself overwhelmed with the courtesies, attention, friendliness and boundless hospitality with which he and Lady Cavan met at the hands of every Pole, official or privately.[43]

De Wiart must have been delighted by the respect Cavan was held in by the senior Polish officers who practiced the same profession of arms. Cavan's reputation as an able and courageous commander on the Western Front and then Italy would have preceded him through the good offices of Carton de Wiart, among others.

The Mission now came to an end and its work taken over by Lieutenant Colonel Emilius Clayton RA, who had been the Military Attaché in Warsaw since 1920. During the four years he spent in Poland, Carton de Wiart had made the transition from that of an inspirational and legendary battlefield commander to one of a consummate diplomat, mixing in the highest political echelons and earning the confidence of world leaders. Trust in the world of politics is rare but Piłsudski and his generals endowed Carton de Wiart with theirs and he cherished it above all else. In his usual understated way, he summed up his time in Poland by declaring 'our military mission had had a most interesting and happy time. We had assisted at the birth of the new Poland, and had seen a nation emerge alive, strong and kicking. The joy of the Poles was infectious, and we shared their feelings'.[44]

The war he had witnessed in Poland had been markedly different from that on the Western Front where industrialized nations had clashed on a hitherto unknown scale, inflicting appalling casualties on one another. The Polish-Russian war of 1920 was almost redolent of an eighteenth-century campaign with armies living off the land as they advanced or retreated. Soldiers were underfed, ill-equipped, often without boots and their uniforms in rags; medical care for the wounded was primitive or non-existent. On the battlefield, scant regard was paid to the First Geneva Convention, particularly by Budyonny's Konarmiya which massacred captured soldiers and civilians alike as it rampaged across the countryside. On top of this noxious fusion between a vicious civil war and an international armed conflict lay a bloody blanket of murderous excesses of nationalism and clashing ideologies: the Bolshevik armies made short work of 'enemies of the people' like priests and landowners, the large Jewish communities in the borderlands were regularly attacked and decimated, looting and desecration of churches and country houses became commonplace. Although he had only been an observer, all this was a far cry from Carton de Wiart's youthful quest for glory in South Africa and Somaliland and the ordered world of the British Army in France. Yet he was far from repelled by his experiences; indeed, the exact opposite reaction set in and he determined to return.

Part V

Polesie 1923–39

The missing years

Self-exile to the Pripet marshes

On his return to England in 1923, substantive Colonel Carton de Wiart resigned his commission and was transferred to the Regular Army Reserve of Officers with the honorary rank of Major General.[1] It marked an acrimonious end to his remarkable career in the British Army for despite his entreaties to Field Marshal Lord Cavan in December 1922 followed by a testy correspondence with fellow cavalry officer Lieutenant General Sir William Peyton,[2] the Military Secretary at the War Office, bemoaning the apparent bias to promote staff officers rather than fighting soldiers, he failed to secure command of a brigade in England.[3] The War Office did eventually verbally offer him the 2nd Cavalry Brigade stationed at Sialkot in the Punjab but he turned it down for India held few charms for him.

By now estranged from Rikki, he decided to sell his house in Onslow Square in South Kensington and all its furniture. No longer in the Army and with his daughters, fourteen-year-old Anita and twelve-year-old Ria, living with their mother in Sussex, there was no reason to stay in England, even less so when he received an invitation to visit Poland from his former ADC, Prince Karol Radziwiłł who had inherited the 150,000 hectare estate at Mánkiewicze (Stolin)[4] in the Polesie region from his brother, Prince Stanisław Radziwiłł, who had been killed fighting the Bolsheviks during the Kiev campaign in 1920. Little had changed in this part of Poland, once described as 'a land of exuberant fancy. A remarkable autumnal stillness is peculiar to its sea of marsh, a stillness not disturbed even by the humming of a gnat and only broken now and then by the gentle rustling of the rushes'.[5]

One of Poland's oldest and most distinguished '*szlachta*'[6] families along with the Czartoryski, Lubomirski, Potocki, Sapieha, Tarnowski and Zamoyski among others, the Radziwiłłs were both Princes of the Holy Roman Empire and 'Ancient' Princes of the Polish-Lithuanian Commonwealth.[7] Over the centuries, the family produced cardinals, chancellors, generals, senators and, through marriage, a queen of Poland. Although many of their estates were in Eastern Poland (today's Belarus and Ukraine), in the nineteenth century the family based themselves in Berlin where they had established close links with the Prussian Court after Prince Antoni Radziwiłł had married the niece of King Frederick the Great. In was here, in the magnificent Radziwiłł Palace on Wilhelmstrasse,[8] that Prince Karol was born in 1885, the son of Prince Jerzy who died at the early age of fifty-four after a life of over-exuberance.

After school in Warsaw, he studied agriculture at a university in Kraków and then joined the Russian Army in 1914 where he served as a squadron commander with the Putawy Legion, a regiment created by the Polish National Committee to fight alongside the Tsar's soldiers. Later in the war, he was with the 1st (Krechowieki) Uhlans and the adjutant to General Jozef Dowbor-Músnicki who had been given the job of creating the Greater Polish army after November 1918. When fighting broke out in Eastern Galicia and Volhynia, Karol joined the 12th Podolan Uhlans and took part in the great cavalry battle of Komarów where Budyonny's 1st Cavalry Army was comprehensively defeated. Karol had certainly lived up to the traditions of the knights of the Kingdom of Poland and the Vistula Uhlans, 'the Picadors from Hell' in the Peninsular War.

When he was a student at Agricultural College, Karol married his Izabella Radziwiłł, whom Wacław Lednicki described as 'fantastically beautiful'.[9] Their only child, a daughter 'Balala', was born in 1915. Izabella supported her husband throughout the First World War, working in a field hospital near Kiev and then becoming Chairwoman of the Committee for Assistances to Soldiers of the 12th Podolan Ulhans – in effect, this meant she funded the sabres ('*Radziwiłłowska*') of the entire regiment and some uniforms to boot. After 1921, she became President of the Society for the Development of Eastern Territories with headquarters in Stolin. Her good works and charitable activities resulted in the award of a Dame Grand Cross of Honour and Devotion of the order of St John of Jerusalem (Maltese) in 1927, and in 1929 a Dame Grand Cross of Justice of the Order of St Lazarus of Jerusalem.

After meeting up in Warsaw, Prince Karol and Carton de Wiart travelled by train to Łuniniec to the east of Pinsk, where they were collected by country carts 'which bumped us the thirty miles to his newly inherited property at Mánkiewicze'.[10] Situated on the 155,000 hectare Dawidgródeck estate[11] which had been in the Radziwiłł family since the sixteenth century, the Neo-Baroque house had been built relatively recently in 1904 next to a fifty-hectare park on the banks of the Horyń River designed by his mother Maria Radziwiłłowa some twenty years earlier. The house itself was in a shocking condition having been used by occupying troops; all the furniture and contents, including the priceless library and engravings from Nieświeski Castle, had been destroyed. However, for Carton de Wiart, nothing could detract from the surrounding landscape with its 'wild flat beauty all its own, with limitless forests, lakes and rivers stretching into the distance. It was the home of every variety of wildfowl, and obviously a sportsman's idea of paradise'.[12] He fell in love at first sight with this countryside of vast swamps and wide inundated lands with its pine forests and infinite variety of broad-leaved woods – oak, birch, ash, hornbeam, beeches, maple, lime and many others – and it must have been a comedown to return to England still at a loose end.

Some months later, Prince Karol contacted him and told him he had found a house on the estate previously lived in by a head forester within a few miles of the Russian frontier which might suit him and so Carton de Wiart returned to Poland to view it. Fifteen miles[13] from Mánkiewicze, which was still in the process of renovation, the Prostyń estate[14] could only be approached by water and it took a whole day, with four men paddling the boat down the River Lwą, to reach the small island on which the wooden house stood. This was the definitive moment when he decided to stay put, a choice that would separate him from his family and friends through sheer distance for years to come.

In his memoirs, Carton de Wiart give few clues as to the rationale behind his decision other than 'I found what was for me the perfect life, with everything I had desired since I was a small boy'.[15] From an objective standpoint, he had been more or less continuously in action throughout the Great War apart from time in hospital recovering from a plethora of wounds. The following four years in Poland had also been stressful in that he spent his time travelling around an amoeba-like warzone characterized by unpredictable events, humanitarian disasters and atrocities. Although he chirpily told Sir William Orpen in 1919 that 'he never suffered any pain from all his wounds', there is plenty of hearsay evidence which suggests he did, much as he would have liked to defy medical science. So it may well have been that cumulatively he was suffering from 'despondency' as depression was often referred to in those days and just as he had done as a small boy to escape the strictures of his step-mother, he retreated into a world of his own.

Many years later in a letter dated 1 November 1944 to his daughter Ria, Carton de Wiart wrote:

> As to your mother coming to see me . . . when I was home, I thought it over and could see no good coming of it. When I went to Poland and found it habitable,

I asked her to come out – but she preferred Vienna which I quite understood; but as far as I was concerned it finished my married life. I have no feeling against her whatsoever. I never should have married as I always hated married life. Nor did I try to make the best of it. She is not to blame in any way . . . that is briefly the story.[16]

At the time Rikki and their daughters must have felt abandoned.

To Carton de Wiart's embarrassment, Prince Karol refused to accept any rent, a state of affairs he managed to compensate by building a house for staff and making other improvements over time. Prostyn was to be his home for the next sixteen years and the Radziwiłłs his adopted family. He loved the feudal splendour of the great Polish landlords in their palatial homes with their legion of servants and found their way of life, vivacity and hospitality enchanting. 'This then was the world I was choosing to live in, and I realized my luck in having such an opportunity.'[17] Billy Cavendish-Bentinck wondered whether he had not transferred his affections from one female member of the Radziwiłł family (Olga) to another (Izabella).[18] In his memoirs, the writer Wacław Lednicki described him as 'being deeply attached to Princess Radziwiłł'.[19]

News then reached Carton de Wiart that his step-mother had had a stroke in Cairo where she had continued to reside after the death of Léon in 1915. It may be that his step-brother Maurice was also there as he had returned to Cairo after his discharge from the Army in 1920. Carton de Wiart set off to settle her affairs and rehouse her in England. The day he arrived saw the murder of the Sirdar, Sir Lee Stack, and he witnessed the 'majesty and dignity' of the High Commissioner, Lord Allenby, driving through the streets with an escort of 16th Lancers. Installed in the exotic Mena House Hotel at the foot of the Pyramids, he often rode out with Allenby when they discussed the Great War and he also touched base with General Sir Richard Hakins,[20] Commander British Troops Egypt, at one point offering his services to him if fighting broke out. Having made the necessary arrangements for his step-mother[21] to move to Stone Gap Bungalow in Broadstairs, Carton de Wiart returned to Poland where Prince Karol was now in residence in his refurbished mansion at Mánkiewicze.

He was overjoyed to be back.

Prostyń gave me a wonderful welcome, and I dropped into its life as easily as into a deep armchair . . . it was a lonely spot but I never felt the loneliness for the countryside had so much to give, everything in fact I had ever wanted, plenty of sport, lovely wild country and the sense of remoteness. The peace and quietude could be felt; the singing of a nightingale was a rude interruption. For the first time in my life, I had found a place where I could get away from people, for much as I like them, I do not like to feel encircled by them.[22]

A pattern to Carton de Wiart's life soon established itself with his former soldier servant, Holmes, looking after him, an excellent Polish cook in the kitchen and his old groom, Matthews, in charge of the riding horses at Mánkiewicze. When Holmes decided to return to England, he replaced him with another former soldier servant, James. He found a new hobby, farming, and cultivated enough land to cater for the needs of the household until the winter closed in when supplies were brought in by sledges across the snow-covered frozen lakes and rivers. He remembered his first journey by sledge at night from Mánkiewicze to Prostyń, 'the country all white with snow with the trees standing like ghostly sentinels, the sledge drawn by horses with their bells jingling. Suddenly the road was lit by outriders carrying flaming torches and turning the whole countryside into a shimmering fairyland.'[23]

The estate provided two German keepers who lived in their own cottages except when bandits were about when they wisely moved into the servants' house. De Wiart shot nearly every day when he was at Prostyń, a ritual which followed the seasons. In the early spring, the main activity centred on stalking capercaillies ('*głuszec*') in the forests at dawn which proved to be more difficult that it sounded as the cock birds, despite their giveaway clicking noises, were extraordinarily difficult to see and alert to the slightest sound or movement. It was only when they were singing their love-song that a film closed over their ears and for a matter of seconds they could not hear approaching danger; in fact, so complete was the sound blackout, that if the first shot missed, there was time for a second one.[24] In June, pigeons were in season and in July duck and solitary snipe[25] shooting began. By the end of August, mallard shooting started 'in real earnest and on a very big scale.'[26]

Camped out in small sheds (*budans*) or sometimes staying in hunting lodges, the shooting party would be up by 1 am or 2 am and make their way to hides which had been prepared around the *saads*, large stretches of water where duck congregated as river levels dropped in the summer. Once the ducks had started flighting in the semi-darkness of early dawn, shooting would begin and last for three or four hours. If Carton de Wiart was shooting on his own, he would set off in a long canoe-like boat with one keeper, the other following with the call-ducks in another boat, and once they had reached the shooting ground, they would camouflage the boats by hiding them in the long rushes. The female call-ducks were encouraged to start quacking to attract the drakes but if they were having an 'off' day, the keepers would imitate the calls instead.

Arthur Sutherland, a wartime acquaintance of Carton de Wiart, came to stay with him and the Radziwiłłs in April 1927. A keen shot himself, he found 'shooting not too easy from a low boat' but was impressed by 'the keepers calling perfectly: all the different ducks come to the various calls'. On one occasion, a fellow guest Count Jan Szołdrski shot his toe off with a .410 and had to return to Mánkiewicze and was operated on that night by a surgeon from Pinsk. Meanwhile, 'Adrian and I went on and flighted woodcock in the evening'; he could hear the male birds coming towards him 'making a snoring noise'. After bagging 13 woodcock and 119 duck, Sutherland returned home, enthusing about his fortnight on the Pripet river where the 'duck shooting . . . is the best in Europe', and 'the exceptional kindness' offered by the Radziwiłłs.[27]

Autumn shooting also encompassed driven hazel-grouse in the narrow rides in the forests and walking up blackcock ('*cietrzew*'). By the first week of December, bird life on the marshes had vanished and hunters turned their attention to wolves and wild boar. At Mánkiewicze, some 700 beaters were deployed for the boar hunt and the only time Carton de Wiart joined the shoot there he saw over 147 boar killed. It did not appeal to him. The best moments at Prostyn for him were 'those evening flights when I waited alone, not far from my house, and felt the quiescent stillness of the coming night full of a tired magic, bringing the bustle of the day to a peaceful close'.[28] Come late December, he would return to England for three months and frequent his old haunts in St James's.

Prince Karol's passion[29] was to restore the dwindling elk population which had been decimated first during the war and then by rampant 'Revolutionary' poaching of 'free food'. Of a once huge herd, there were only seven left. By 1931, it had risen to 140 as a result of his management which included sending guards to live in the forests for up to a month to monitor and count the animals. Based at his hunting lodge at Hołow nad Lwą, he himself would spend weeks at a time 'chatting with elk', visiting the lekking grounds and overseeing the network of footbridges and observation towers built to access the swamps and impenetrable marshes of the Polesie wilderness. He would often go out on his own to stalk and to his great satisfaction, in 1937 he won a prize at the International Hunting Exhibition in Berlin for the fourth best Polish elk. The keepers quipped that 'the Kniaź had shot a Kniaź'.

In 1926, Marshal Piłsudski, now the Minister of Military Affairs, came to the great Radziwiłł castle at Nieśwież to confer the Order of the 'Virtuti Militari' on the tomb of Prince Stanisław Radziwiłł, his former adjutant, who had been killed by a shell fired from an armoured train during a Red army counter-attack on Kiev according to the *Boston Globe*.[30] Piłsudski remembered it differently, writing to his wife Alexandra that

> one of my aide de camps, Count Radziwiłł, has been killed. You know how much I liked him personally, and I valued him too as a good officer on whom I could always rely. He was killed at Malin, that one place we were unsuccessful. He fell back wounded and when our squadrons drew back the Bolsheviks despatched all the wounded without mercy. We found him after we had counter-attacked pierced all over with bayonet wounds.[31]

It was a momentous occasion with most of the major aristocratic landowning families and leaders of industry and commerce invited by Prince Karol on parade as a gesture of support to the Marshal after he had orchestrated the overthrow of the elected government of President Stanisław Wojciechowski and Prime Minister Wincenty Witos. The coup of 14 May[32] had been Piłsudski's response to the growing concern about the rapprochement between Germany and Russia in April and Germany and France the previous year. When rampant inflation and widespread corruption were added to the sense of impending isolation and perceived abandonment by its former Allies, the Marshal feared for the very existence of the Poland he had created out of the ashes of the First World War. Carton de Wiart almost certainly would have been an honoured guest.

When he died ten years later, the Marshal's death was widely reported in Britain. On 12 May 1935, thousands lined the rain-swept streets of Warsaw and then Kraków to pay their respects to the man who had given them their country back. *Gaumont British News*'s opening title read 'Death of Dictator-Hero', neatly encapsulating the enigma of the controversial Marshal. After abruptly announcing 'Polish dictator dead' on 12 May, *The Times* explored this further:

> The daring and romantic qualities of his character and career have no doubt been exaggerated by his followers, just as the reverse side has been blackened by his enemies, but he was a great soldier and capable statesman. Seldom did any one arouse at the same time and among his own countrymen such bitter hatred and such unswerving loyalty and veneration. To his supporters he was always the wise father of his people, shaping their political doctrines for the best and never sparing himself in his country's cause. To his detractors he was an inveterate and unscrupulous conspirator, with a criminal record behind him, who sacrificed Poland's welfare to his own ambition for personal power. The truth lies nearer the first of these two estimates. Piłsudski rendered his country

great services. When the time came for it to reunite, he did for it what no other man could have done.[33]

From the moment he first met him in Warsaw in February 1919, Carton de Wiart had rated him highly, indeed in *Happy Odyssey* he wrote, 'since those days it has been my destiny to meet many of the great men of the world, but Piłsudski ranks high among them – in fact, for political sense, almost at the top.' They had quickly developed a firm friendship based on openness and trust which had survived the bruising vicissitudes of British foreign policy towards Poland. There is no record as to whether Carton de Wiart attended the state funeral in Kraków; Britain was represented by Field Marshal Earl Cavan, France by Marshal Pétain and Germany by General Göring. Viktor Chernov, a founder the Social Revolutionary Party in Russia, had watched the progress of Piłsudski from exile in New York and observed that 'the biographers of Pilsudski say in his later phase he had no friends, only admirers – and a mass of enemies acquired from the ranks of his former friends'. Carton de Wiart would certainly have considered himself an exception.[34]

Despite living in Polesie for nearly sixteen years, Carton de Wiart left no diaries or scrapbooks, so only a feint picture merges of his life there. A 1929 fragment[35] of a film by the Polish amateur cinematographer Zofia Chomętowska shows her friend, the Italian writer Aurora Beniamino, Balala Radziwiłł and Carton de Wiart swimming in a lake, the latter seen diving off the end of a jetty and then, clad in a long bath robe, arranging bottles on the water's edge to cool them down. In the 1930s, the artist and writer Henryk Uziembło[36] described meeting Carton de Wiart on a journey he made down the River Lwą and noted 'the luxuries that the British warrior has made for himself: sofas, ottomans, paintings – Fałat landscapes,[37] Wojciech Kossak's horses.[38] The kitchen, with a smoky chimney, shines with a suit of brass saucepans and roasting pans.'[39] The only thing that Uziembło didn't like was the sight of dead birds of prey – 'hawks spread out on the fence, eagles and magpies, ripped open, with guts on top.'

While relishing his new and uncharacteristic solitary existence for a man of his stature, visitors were still welcome. In 1925, his daughter Maria came to see him[40] and, around the same time, his friend the MP for Wells, Lieutenant Colonel Anthony Muirhead,[41] stayed at Prostyń. One unexpected visitor was the merchant banker Rex Benson[42] who was on his way back from Russia. An old Balliol man, they may well have first met in 17 Park Lane for Rex had been seriously wounded in his right arm and had to have numerous operations to regain its use. They certainly knew one another from the Paris Peace Conference when he had been with Field Marshal Sir Henry Wilson and the British Military Mission before being despatched to Russia by Lloyd George to open up trade links with the Bolshevik government. Given a large cargo of tea among other basic commodities, he arrived in Batumi without possessing a word of Russian. After his Russian-speaking companion, Tommy Carr, was arrested, he travelled across country to Moscow on his own where he proceeded to sell £10,000 of goods, hiding the payment in banknotes inside his boots. He was searched at the Russian–Polish frontier but, fortunately, was not asked to remove his boots. The Bank of England duly honoured the bundle of notes without question, even though they appeared somewhat worn and full of holes.[43] As a key figure in the interwar Secret Intelligence Service (SIS), Benson's visit to Prostyń was possibly more than just social.

Freddy Beaumont-Nesbitt, who had accompanied Filed Marshal Cavan to Warsaw on his 1923 visit, came out to Prostyń to shoot duck and recounted to his family how if one of the guns had to cross a ditch, it was the duty of the nearest beater to lie down and form a bridge so the shooter could cross with reasonably dry feet – for which he received a small tip. The great thing all the beaters longed for was to be shot by one of the guns, when they would be suitably rewarded by Prince Karol in gold.[44]

One mysterious visitor to Mánkiewicze in 1931[45] was Lady Elizabeth Lafone,[46] eldest daughter of 6th Earl of Stafford, who had married Michael Lafone, a 'bad hat' member of the Happy Valley set in Kenya, described by James Fox in *White Mischief* as 'a fierce womanizer with an eyeglass'. She divorced him in 1931, taking her three-year-old son Julian[47] with her.

Paul Lourie, a Jewish plywood and veneer industrialist, recalled visiting Mánkiewicze[48] in 1938:

> I accepted an invitation from Prince Karol Radziwiłł to visit his estates on which were some of our most important timber sources. . . . I took the train to the tiny railway depot near the Russian border. A princely sleigh awaited me and took me on a ride of several hours, through primeval forests and swamps to the castle. Here they enjoyed the good life, with liveried servants, silk tapestries, antique furniture and thick carpets – an intriguing contrast to the world outside. This was where the prince lived. The princess, a cousin of the last Spanish king, Alphonso XIII, was rarely there, preferring Paris. The prince's companions were his elderly, unmarried daughter,[49] an old gentleman who was said to be Tsar Alexander II's illegitimate son, and a one-armed, one-eyed English general, Carton de Wiart . . . there for the hunt.

While he was away in Poland, family life continued back in England and Germany. On 4 November 1933, his elder daughter, 24-year-old Anita married

Walter Thompson, a young scientist. Her mother, Rikki, gave her away at the wedding at St Michael and All Angels Church in Thursley; her sister Ria was a bridesmaid. Her choice to renounce Roman Catholicism caused a lasting rift with Carton de Wiart who could not accept it. The same year, Rikki's brother, Prince George Fugger von Babenhausen, died suddenly, aged forty-five.

Always a great admirer of the British, often hunting in England before the war, many remembered him as the winner of the International Class for officers' chargers at Olympia in 1912, 'dressed in the magnificent uniform of his regiment and mounted on his black charger, alone in the crowded arena, winning for his country this coveted trophy'. A *Times* correspondent recalled that

> since the War Prince Fugger had been very keen on polo and had made many friends of English officers and others playing at Vienna and Budapest. During the last four years he had organized with Herr Weininger the polo season at Bannacker, where those who have taken part will ever remember his kindness and hospitality. Just twenty-four hours before his death he was playing polo as cheerful and happy as he always was when among his friends and his ponies, which were the joy of his life.[50]

Parted from her mother – her father had died in Klagenfurt in 1925 – and her brother Leopold and her two sisters who all lived in Central Europe, and with her husband living 1,000 miles away in the Polish-Russian borderlands, Rikki now found herself socially alone in England and although she attended events such as Lord Monk Bretton's funeral in Sussex in 1933[51] and the Carmarthen Show with the Dynvors in 1937, she increasingly looked to Vienna as her real home although the family home at No.10 Schönburgstrasse had been sold long ago in 1919.[52] Her sister-in-law, Vera née Czernin, had divorced her brother Leopold in 1936 and two years later married the former Austrian Federal Chancellor Kurt Schuschnigg,[53] who was at the time imprisoned by the National Socialists. Her sister Sylvia's marriage to Graf Freidrich zu Münster-Derneburg remained unconsummated. On a brighter note, in 1934, Anita gave birth on 21 August to Deidre, Rikki's first grandchild.

In 1936, Prince Karol's daughter, Balala Radziwiłł, whom Carton de Wiart had known since she was eight years old, reached her twenty-first birthday and announced her engagement to Prince Edmund Ferdynand Radziwiłł. Born in 1906 in Berlin the oldest child of Janusz Franciszek Radziwiłł[54] and Anna Lubomirska, after graduating from high school in 1926, Edmund had studied law at the University of Poznań and then went on to read law and history at Oxford. After coming down, he returned to Poland and did his military service in the Cadet School of Cavalry in Grudziądz. From 1933 he helped his father in the administration of family's huge estate at Ołyka[55] and became involved in societal and political activities. After their marriage, the couple settled at Ołyka where he ran a stable of purebred English Thoroughbred horses, opened a dairy co-operative, and Izabella founded a kindergarten.

The following year, Maria 'Ria' Carton de Wiart married Roger Walker of Duncton,[56] Surrey. In *The Times* announcement of 27 July 1937, her address was given as Allington Farm, Lewes; Rikki was styled in the announcement as 'of Poland and Vienna'. The day before Carton de Wiart had written to Ria to put her off coming to Mánkiewicze on account of 'the awful drought . . . no duck at all . . . getting about next to impossible'.[57] Walker had been married before and this caused some consternation with Carton de Wiart on the grounds of incompatibility of divorce with Roman Catholic doctrine. At the wedding on 11 November, it was Rikki who gave her away; Carton de Wiart was in England at the time but recuperating in hospital in London after an operation.[58] In August 1938, Ria gave birth to Roger, Carton de Wiart's second grandchild. The family had moved into a large 1850s house called The Street in Heath Carnock in Lancashire where her husband worked for the old established family leather business, William Walker and Sons Ltd, the famous Bolton tannery firm. In the 1939 *Register*, Rikki was also shown living there as 'incapacitated', a reference to her arthritis, together with a nurse, housemaid and cook.[59]

As the war clouds once more began to stack up over Europe, after returning from his annual winter visit to England in 1938/39,[60] Carton de Wiart wrote to Field Marshal Lord Gort VC, the CIGS, asking to be employed in the event of war. His answer was 'evasive, indefinite and altogether disheartening'.[61] So he remained in Poland, keeping in touch with friends and old colleagues such as Pug Ismay to whom he wrote from Mánkiewicze in May 1939:

> I have thought a lot about you these last three weeks. You must be having a hell of a time.
>
> Here the people have been wonderfully calm and determined – but how long they will resist the provocation that is going on is another matter. 'Staying' is not their strong suit.
>
> I felt anxious some time ago, when people at home seemed to think that Danzig was not worth fighting about. After all, it doesn't represent a place now, but a principle and I wonder if these same people were prepared to return Gibraltar to the Spanish and even perhaps to give Liverpool to the Irish?
>
> However, the PM's speech at the Albert Hall did a lot of good.[62]

I remember when we (last) met we agreed that Hitler had not as yet made a single *geste de reprochement* and as far as we know he hasn't done so yet.

As a matter of fact I don't believe there will be any much change as long as he thinks we are looking for excuses to keep the peace; but I am sure there will be a change if he thinks we are looking for an excuse to make war.

We were taught how to deal with a bully at school, and he is the most perfect specimen of that breed yet produced.

If – a damn big one – things calm down, you had better come here for two or three weeks and have a real rest. The shooting starts 15 July and though it looks like a bad year, you will have a real rest and some sport.

As it turned out, in June he finally received instructions to report to the War Office in London.

What happened to his generous hosts, the Radziwiłłs of Mánkiewicze, during and after the Second World War? In 1939, 53-year-old Karol was mobilized and reported to the cavalry centre in Łuków. From there he was posted to the General Staff in Brześć, and later to the Independent Operational Group 'Polesie', based at Pinsk under command of Brigadier Franciszek Kleeberg. After engaging the Germans at Brześć and Kobryń, Group Polesie retreated towards the Romanian border with the rest of the Polish army but after losing contact with Army Headquarters, Kleeberg decided to try and relieve Warsaw. He managed to capture Dęblin and see off Soviet attacks in the Świętokrzyskie Mountains but then came up against General Gustav von Wietersheim's XIV Motorized Corps at Kock in early October. After a dogged defence over five days during which he inflicted considerable casualties on the attacking Germans, Kleeberg and his encircled troops surrendered having run out of ammunition and food.

Along with the remainder of Group 'Polesie', Karol was captured at Kock but managed to escape, and after obtaining an Italian visa, made his way to Italy, then to France where he rejoined the Polish army. When his unit was disbanded, he travelled to London where he continued to serve in the Polish army and became an inspector for the management of the Army. In 1947, with Poland now behind the Iron Curtain, he emigrated to South Africa and started a poultry farm. Twenty years later, with his wife Izabella, he returned to Poland where he died on 24 October 1968 in Warsaw and was buried in the family tomb in the Wilanów cemetery.

Carton de Wiart's Prostyń hunting friend, Count Jan Szołdrski z Szóldr, was executed by the Germans on 23 October 1939. The Holocaust Research Project records that 'Count Szołdrski, a landowner at Gołębin, had a smile on his lips as he came to the place of execution in the Kościan marketplace. The Germans thought he was sneering at them, so they beat him up until he was unable to stand'.[63]

There remains the inevitable speculation that Carton de Wiart with his strong links to the War Office Directorate of Military Intelligence had some quasi-official intelligence role in his long sojourn in Polesie. He himself wrote that 'the Russians, and in fact a great many of the Poles too,[64] imagined I lived in Prostyń for the purpose of spying. But no one has ever informed me what I was going to spy on in a desolate marsh inhabited by birds and beasts'.[65] Unquestionably the nearby border with Russia was extremely porous and in the early 1920s the Polish government created the Korpus Ochrony Progranicza (KOP), a border force to defend specifically the eastern border against Soviet incursions and gangs of armed poachers. Polesie had its own brigade organized into three battalions each with its own area. Together with the Directorate of State Forests which had been established at the same time, Prince Karol was integrally involved in their activities in order to safeguard the wildlife on his vast sporting estate. In these circumstances, it would have been most surprising if Carton de Wiart had not kept his ear to the ground.

Part VI

Poland 1939

Prelude to the Second World War

Blitzkreig in Poland

After digesting the Sudetenland in October 1938, Hitler announced that it was his last territorial demand in Europe. The Poles had used the crisis to prise the city of Bogumin in Teschen from the Czechoslovaks, an action that had backfired diplomatically. In his address to the House of Commons on 28 September 1938, Prime Minister Chamberlain had spelt out that, while Britain fully appreciated the interest of the Polish government in its minority population in Czechoslovakia, he hoped 'they would do nothing in the present delicate situation to extend the scope of the present crisis'.[1] His words went unheeded and, for many people in both Britain and France, Poland looked like a willing accomplice of Germany.

In early 1939, after Hitler increased his rhetoric about incorporating the Free City of Danzig into the Reich, alarm bells finally began to ring in Warsaw. Foreign Minister Józef Beck's trust in Hitler was fast evaporating and when German troops marched into Prague in March, expunging the freedom of a nation born only twenty-one years before, the Poles woke up to the enormity of the threat they were facing. Czechoslovakia had now been comprehensively dismembered by Hitler's creation of an independent Slovak state beholden to Germany on Poland's southern border. Shortly after, the Lithuanians caved in to an ultimatum from Berlin and allowed Hitler to occupy the industrial city and port of Klaipeda (Memel) on the Baltic Sea to the east of Danzig, an act of aggression that triggered a secret Polish mobilization. Furthermore, the Romanians had signed a German-Romanian Treaty for the Development of Economic Relations on 23 March 1939 which in effect established German control over most aspects of the Romanian economy, including the all-important oil fields.

Already compromised by the charade of the 'Peace in our time' Munich agreement, Chamberlain told the House of Commons that should Poland be attacked by Germany, the British government would 'lend the Polish government all support in their power . . . in the event of any action which clearly threatened Polish independence'.[2] It was a hollow offer, pounced on by Lloyd George who said in an echo of the past that Britain 'could not send a single battalion to Poland' in the event of war.[3] More promises kept coming. France and Poland signed the Kasprzycki-Gamelin convention in May, with the former undertaking to bomb Germany in the event of a German invasion of Poland and mount a land assault within three days of mobilization followed by 'a bold relief offensive'. In July, General Ironside[4] promised the Polish foreign minister '100 bomber aircraft of the newest type' and a batch of Hawker Hurricane fighters.

The best construction that can be put on these 'guarantees' is to see them as a trip wire or line in the sand beyond which Germany could only advance at the risk of an all-out European war. A sense of dèja-vu now pervaded the familiar landscape of post-1918 Poland, made even more alarming by the news of the Nazi-Soviet Pact on 23 August. Suddenly even the most optimistic Pole could see the spectre of his country being partitioned by these historic enemies; the sense of security provided by the Polish-Soviet Non-Aggression pact of July 1932 and the German-Polish Non-Aggression Pact of January 1934 dissolved like melting ice.

Carton de Wiart was living at Prostyń, somewhat down on his luck as his overtures to Field Marshal Lord Gort, the CIGS, to employ him as the war clouds gathered had been brushed off. He had been at a dinner for General Sir Edmund Ironside hosted by the Military Attaché at his apartment in Warsaw in July. Ironside noted he was in good form and 'he told me that they hadn't had any proper winter or snow for three years and that the whole country was dried up. Unless they had rain, the German could go anywhere in his mechanical vehicles. He was praying for rain in case of war.'[5]

Later that month, he was abruptly summoned to report to the War Office where his old friend Major General Freddy Beaumont-Nesbitt, now Director of Military Intelligence, asked him to head up the reconstituted No.4 British Military Mission to Poland. The two men had met in Poland twice before when Beaumont-Nesbitt had accompanied Viscount D'Alberon in 1920 and later stayed with de Wiart at Prostyń.[6]

The brief was threefold:

1. The first duty of the British Mission to Poland will be to ensure that the programme of co-operation of the Polish Army in the combined plan as

agreed in the Staff conversations is carried out. This will be in accordance with separate instructions issued by M.O.1.

2.   In view of the difficulties of rendering direct military support by the British Armed Forces to the Poles, the question of inspiring confidence is of the greatest importance and every opportunity for the exertion of personal influence of members of the British Mission must be exploited.

3.   It will be the duty of the British Mission to keep the War Office fully informed of the military situation in Poland and in the zone of operations of the Polish Army.

After collecting his uniform, Carton de Wiart returned to Poland to await further orders.

> At lunch time on 22 August, I had shot sixty snipe, and was sitting smoking my pipe and hoping to get my century, when my hopes were interrupted by the arrival of a man with an urgent message for me to ring Warsaw. I hurried to the telephone at Mánkiewicze, got through to the number, and found it was the British Ambassador telling me to come at once.[7]

Packing his uniform and a few necessities, he set off for the embassy, leaving his lodge at Prostyń in the care of his household staff.

Arriving in Warsaw, he realized the outbreak of war was not a question of weeks away but of days. Although the Agreement of Mutual Assistance between the United Kingdom and Poland had been signed on 25 August with promises of mutual military assistance between the two countries if either was attacked by some 'European country', the city palpably throbbed with fear amplified by the sound of troops passing through it on horseback or in vehicles. In the public parks gangs of labourers dug slit trenches for primitive air raid shelters. Carton de Wiart's first call was on Marshal Edward Śmigły-Rydz, the Commander-in-Chief of the Polish Armed Forces, an officer he knew from the post-war period and held in little regard 'for his capabilities . . . were never fitted for the responsibilities which were thrust on him'.[8] He immediately took issue with the Marshal's strategy of fighting a defensive battle on the western border as the countryside favoured the attacker and there were no obstacles to hinder his advance for the drought had reduced river levels to a trickle. The Marshal exclaimed that if he retired even a few miles, he would be accused of abandoning hundreds of thousands of Polish citizens and so he had to stand and fight whatever the consequences. Appalled by this attitude of 'putting heroics before reason', Carton de Wiart then tried to persuade him to move the Polish fleet out of the Baltic. This time he succeeded in shifting his objections and under Operation PEKING, a number of Polish naval vessels later reached Britain.[9]

At 4.45 am on 1 September, *Fall Weiss*, the German invasion of Poland, commenced. That night, Carton de Wiart wrote in the wake of the bombing of Warsaw, 'with the first deliberate bombing of civilian, I saw the very face of war change – bereft of romance, its glory shorn, no longer the soldier setting forth into battle, but the women and children buried underneath it.'[10] His tone had markedly changed from his earlier verdict that 'frankly I had enjoyed the war' when he summarized his experiences in the First World War. As a front line soldier, it was understandable that he had overlooked the German bombing raids against Britain that had killed and injured nearly 5,000 civilians between 1914 and 1918.

While Carton de Wiart had been making his way to Warsaw, a group of MIR[11] officers assembled at the War Office in London with orders to leave immediately for Poland. MIR had started life in March 1936 as General Staff [Research], a small section consisting of one major and a secretary which reported directly to the Director of Military Operations and Intelligence. Its first incumbent came up with the idea of the Army Education Corps, the second examined military medicine[12] but by 1938 their successor, Major Jo Holland of the Royal Engineers, had a more warlike agenda. With a charter to 'research into problems of tactics and organization . . . in order to collect new ideas on these subjects' and a modus operandi 'to go where they like, talk to whom they like but be kept from files, correspondence and telephone calls',[13] Holland tasked his section to research the subject of guerrilla warfare.

After extensive study of the Boer War, the Russian Revolution, the Irish Troubles, the Spanish Civil War, and the Sino-Japanese War, in the early part of 1939 the section, now known as MIR, advanced the proposition that guerrilla warfare and other allied activities would prove to be an important feature of the impending war. With this in mind, Major General Beaumont-Nesbitt hand-picked Lieutenant Colonel Colin Gubbins (RA), Major Tommy Davies (formerly of Courtaulds and now with the Grenadier Guards), and captains Alan Brown (Royal Tank Corps), Peter Wilkinson (Royal Fusiliers) and H. J. 'Boy' Lloyd-Johnes (RA) to join Carton de Wiart. Already the author of *The Art of Guerrilla Warfare* and *Partisans' Leader handbook*, the energetic Gubbins had already done the rounds in Warsaw, Bucharest and Riga to brief the Military Attachés on guerrilla warfare.[14] Brown and Wilkinson had both been in Czechoslovakia as military intelligence officers with the British Legation.

Gubbins's team crossed over to France and, after picking up Major Hugh Curteis of the Highland Light Infantry in Marseilles, sailed for Alexandria which they reached on 31 August. From there they made their way to Athens in three flying-boats and on touching down in Piraeus harbour were greeted with the news that the Germans had invaded Poland that morning. The flying-boats were immediately ordered back to Egypt but the ever-resourceful Gubbins persuaded the Polish Minister in Athens to fly them to Warsaw in two LOT Lockheed Super Electras[15] which were staging in Athens. These took them via Salonika to Cernăuți in north-eastern Romania where the Polish Consul-General rose to the occasion and chartered four taxis to take them across the border to Kolomija from where they could catch a train to Lwów.[16]

Peter Wilkinson recalled that their

> progress was slow, often interrupted by the farm carts bringing in the last of the harvest, while the balconies of the houses in the villages we drove through were heavy with ripening maize cobs. The peasants waved and the children shouted as we drove past for we were clearly persons of importance. I was intoxicated, as much by the delicious local wine which we had had at luncheon as by the richness of the scene, its golden colour and its auras of happiness and contentment so soon to be destroyed.[17]

They finally reached Warsaw as dusk was falling on 5 September in time to hear that Great Britain and France had been at war with Germany for the past forty-eight hours and the Polish Corridor and Pomerania lost.

Carton de Wiart was waiting for them at the embassy. With him were three additions to the Mission: the military attaché Lieutenant Colonel Roly Sword of the 4th Hussars; Harold 'Perks' Perkins, a British businessman from Galicia who had been co-opted to join the Mission; and Major John Shelley,[18] the SIS Passport Control Officer at the embassy. Shelley had had a most unusual career to date. After serving with the King's Own (Royal Lancaster Regiment) in France and Belgium until September 1915, he had joined the Royal Flying Corps as a Balloon Officer and was posted to the Egyptian Expeditionary Force where he was employed with the Egyptian Army until 1924, during which time he spent two years on his own gaining intelligence in the southern part of the Sudan. On return to England, he transferred to the Grenadier Guards and then worked with the Shanghai Defence Force as an Intelligence Officer. In 1933 he became the first head of the SIS Station in Jerusalem where he remained until replaced in 1936. In 1939 he went to Poland as the SIS representative and at the age of fifty-one married a Polish girl thirty years his junior.

No sooner had he arrived than Major Tommy Davies was ordered by Carton de Wiart to return to London with the diplomatic bag and a personal report to Beaumont-Nesbitt. As Wilkinson recalled, 'no telegram could possibly convey' the seriousness of the situation.[19] It was a good choice for Davies, with an extensive contact list of his own, was highly respected as an intelligence officer by both the War Office and SIS. The first message that Carton de Wiart wanted to ram home was that the 'situation was extremely serious. . . . German complete supremacy in the air had neutralised the Polish counter-attacks . . . the Germans were using medium bombing aircraft to break up Polish formations . . . furthermore there was complete superiority on the part of the Germans as regards mechanised forces'. From this followed a strong request for support, firstly fighters to ward off attacks by medium bombers on military targets, towns and factories and then to deter reconnaissance aircraft from locating concentrations of Polish troops behind the front line; secondly for light machine guns and small arms ammunition (SAA) 'which should be forwarded without delay so that they could reach the country before the frontiers were completely cut off'. Finally, in his typical straight-talking vein, Carton de Wiart wished to point out that 'the delay of 48 hours of the British declaration of war had caused the greatest mistrust of our intentions and this will continue to exist until positive action is taken by the British'.[20]

As to the dropping of pamphlets by British bombers on Germany, 'this had caused considerable concern in Poland as they see no useful purpose and they feel we are not serious in our intentions and are simply waiting until Poland is overrun when we shall agree some kind of peace'.[21] He elaborated on this topic in *Happy Odyssey*, 'England could give no help at all but made matters worse by inflicting on us the perfectly useless, and extremely irritating, leaflet raids which had no physical effect on the Germans[22] and no moral effect on us. We were crying out for bombs, not bits of idealistic paper.'[23]

The next day, 6 September, news came that the Polish GHQ and General Staff had left the capital for Brześć Litewski, so the Mission, by now fifty-strong, loaded its baggage onto three trucks and set off that evening in pursuit. It was a taste of just how difficult it was going to be to keep abreast of developments on the front line. For Carton de Wiart, 'it was my first sight of that slowly moving mass of heartrending humanity, pushing and pedalling their incongruous forms of transport, clutching their children and pitiful bundles, and trudging no one knew where.'[24]

Carton de Wiart's car was an American Pontiac which Wilkinson had bought in Warsaw with some of the Mission's gold sovereigns as no transport had been provided by the Poles. As it hurtled down the long straight roads, a German Fieseler Storch reconnaissance plane materialized in the rear view mirror and started to fire its machine gun. The driver immediately looked for cover and spotted a large tree on the side of the road someway ahead. As he started to slow down, Carton de Wiart prodded him with his cane and, having ascertaining that this was the first time he had been under fire, told him to his foot down and drive on. It turned out that the Pontiac was faster than the Fieseler Storch![25]

That night they reached Łuków, a village sixty miles southeast of Warsaw. The Mission report notes that 'previously, except for stray incidents, targets for air bombardment had been of a military nature'.[26] On 7 September, however, the open town of Łuków was bombed indiscriminately with explosive and incendiary bombs, with considerable loss of life; one of the victims was Mrs Shelley, the young Polish bride of Major Shelley, the Passport Control Officer.

Gubbins meanwhile had met with the Deputy Chief of Staff who was ensconced in the eighteenth-century Vauban fortress at Brześć who told him that the Army was withdrawing to the Vistula-San line. He confirmed that 'German air action had been so effective that the mobilisation and concentration of the remaining ten divisions of the Polish Army was being rendered impossible'.[27] Gubbins who had returned to Łuków that night set out to Litewski the next day only to learn that the Poles were now withdrawing to the River Bug and that it was unlikely that they could hold the Vistula line. The half-hearted attack by the French on the Saarland that day had little impact on events in Poland. When General Stanisław Burhardt-Bukacki, the Polish military envoy to France, read the text of General Gamelin's message to Marhal Śmigły-Rydz stating that half of his divisions were in contact with the enemy, and that French advances had forced the Wehrmacht to withdraw at least six divisions from Poland, he told the Marshal, 'Please don't believe a single word in the dispatch.'[28] Ironside later remarked that 'the French had lied to the Poles in saying they going to attack. There is no idea of it'.[29]

That night the Mission moved to Włodawa which was nearer to the Polish GHQ and installed themselves in the Adampol home of Count Zamoyski, a friend of Carton de Wiart. 'The Zamoyskis offered meals and baths to members of the mission whom they treated as though they were weekend guests. It was a real home from home; even the dogs were addressed in English.'[30] Here Gubbins compiled an aide memoire for the CGS.[31]

1. The Germans have gone beyond the strict limits of military fairness.
    They have attacked and destroyed factories in the middle of towns, power

stations etc. The evidence of this is unimpeachable and we are therefore presumably free to take the gloves off to this extent.

2. There is a hope, but not more than a hope, that the Polish line will be stabilized on a north and south line through Lublin.

3. But the chances of this line holding are remote unless we can at least hearten the Poles to the extent of promising to do our utmost to supply them with aircraft, light machine guns and ammunition. We appreciate that from a military point of view anything we can send may never reach the Poles and, in any case, may not have much material effect. But the moral [sic] effect will be very considerable. So far as aircraft is concerned, a consignment of fourteen absolutely modern fighters (Hurricanes) and nine Battles,[32] together with 6,000 tons of bombs and 2¾ million rounds of small arms ammunition should now be nearing Constanza. In addition, a further consignment of twenty-nine Battles is to be despatched as soon as shipping is available. Two ships will be available at Ellesmere Port on 12 September but sailing dates are not known.

NB. It is also suggested that the Foreign Office ought to take up at once with the Ministry in Bucharest the question of prompt transit of all the aircraft now on their way and of the consignment that is to leave next week with all despatch.

At a conference on the evening of 9 September, Marshal Śmigły-Rydz who had arrived at Brześć Litewski from Warsaw announced he was going to fall back on the Pinsk-Brześć – Deblin line. This meant that half of Poland had effectively been ceded to the enemy. Carton de Wiart impressed on him the necessity of establishing a firm line on the Vistula and San rivers covering Lwów and Lublin in order to maintain communications with Romania and that in the event of further retirement that line had to be maintained. Śmigły-Rydz reiterated that 'he was absolutely determined whatever happened to fight to the very end on Polish soil, however small the area he held might be'.[33]

In London, Major General Mieczysław Norwid-Neugebauer, the head of the Polish Military Mission in London, sent General Ironside a memo asking him to send Poland '100 complete equipped pursuit planes' and suggested that the best way to get them there was send over pilots from Poland who could then fly them from France over German territory.[34] The British by this stage had no intention of sending either troops, tanks or aircraft to assist the Poles as they had abruptly realized that they themselves were in for the long haul in containing and ultimately defeating Germany.

On the night of 11/12 September Polish GHQ moved to Włodzimierz. Peter Wilkinson remembered Carton de Wiart whimsically suggesting that they all retired to Prostyń where in the depths of the Pripet marshes they could survive more or less indefinitely far out of reach of the Germans.[35] The idea was quickly dropped as the imperative was to stay in touch with the Polish General Staff, so the BMM re-established itself at Tarnopol where they managed to find accommodation in the Dunin-Borkowski's country house at Strusów some ten miles from the town which was crowded with refugees.

Carton de Wiart went to see the Marshal who was in a more hopeful mood that he could establish a line on the Vistula and San rivers and urged Carton de Wiart to ask the RAF to attack targets in the west to relieve pressure. Back at Mission HQ, Roly Sword and Hugh Curteis arrived back from Lwów where Carton de Wiart had sent them to speak to General Sosnkowski, GOC of the Southern Army, with the news that the Germans were well to the east of the River San and thus a profoundly serious threat to the Polish left flank had developed.[36]

At 3 am on 13 September, Gubbins, Davidson and Wilkinson set out for the village of Krzemienica where the British embassy staff had pitched camp. Gubbins and Group Captain Davidson went to Lwów the next day to find that the Germans had reached the outskirts of the city and were trying to force an entry. Only the skilful defence of General Władysław Langner prevented them while women and children built barricades in the streets. That night Polish GHQ once more moved, this time to Mlynów near Dubnor. A planned withdrawal had become an unplanned retreat and when Gubbins and Davidson met with Deputy Chief of Staff at Mlynów on 14 September, it was clear to them that communications had broken down and that 'the situation was obviously desperate and only by desperate measures might something still be saved'.[37] The new line ran from the Romanian to the Hungarian borders which indicated that 'the Marshal and the Polish General Staff realised that defeat was staring them in the face, and only by some dramatic retirement could possibly some part of their harassed forces break contact with and escape from the German armies which threatened their destruction.' Colonel Smoleński, the Director of Intelligence, told them that a German column was heading their way and that 'this was the end of the line'.

Meanwhile in London, Norwid-Neugebauer again appealed to Ironside having received a negative answer to his memo of 10 September, emphasizing that 'the main cause of our retreat is once again the overwhelming majority of the German aviation.'[38] He reminded him that

> during my last visit you assured me that all assistance, namely material supplies required by the Polish forces should be given by the British forces . . . and yet we are facing the fact of the refusal of an action by the powerful Allied Aviation, as well as the refusal of assistance which could be granted by the British Air Force in replacing with their aircraft our losses.'

On the morning of 15 September, the Mission moved to Kosów near Kołomyja where Polish GHQ and the Marshal had now congregated. Carton de Wiart sent Gubbins and Wilkinson to see them and to impress on them the utmost important of protecting the Stanisławów–Cernăuţi railway which was now Poland's only lifeline to the outside world. Later that day, Roly Sword spoke to the Chief of Staff who referred to the 'terror which the unrestricted German bombardment of open towns was attempting to achieve . . . these wanton attacks were reducing the population to a state of desperation.'[39]

The next morning, on 17 September, the Red armies attacked from the east; at 6 am Soviet T-26 tanks started rolling across the sparsely defended 1,400 kilometres eastern border of Poland and 'with that there came to an end all organized resistance to this double invasion of Polish territory.'[40] Carton de Wiart saw Marshal Śmigły-Rydz that evening and asked him what his probable movements were as these would determine those of the Mission. The Marshal replied that he was awaiting eventualities but wanted the Mission to move to Kuty on the Romanian border. Carton de Wiart returned to Mission HQ at Kosów but at 8.30 pm Prince Paul Sapieha, the ADC to General Władysław Langner, arrived with a message from the Marshal saying he was about to cross the Czeremosz River at Kuty into Romania and telling Carton de Wiart to do likewise. 'Our mission now being useless, we packed up and set off by car for the frontier, fifteen miles way.'[41] Prince Sapieha, who aged thirty-nine was 'the oldest Second Lieutenant in the Polish Army', had previously managed to send his American wife and their two small children to Romania after their family home and farm at Rawa Ruska had been bombed by the Germans.[42]

The Mission's main party had already left and at 9.30 pm, the rear party, comprised of about a dozen people in a small convoy of cars, set off from Kosów and inched their way south through a shuffling mass of refugees and retreating Polish soldiers all making their way towards the 400-metre wooden bridge at

Kuty. Forty miles northeast, thousands more refugees headed for the bridge over the Dniester at the summer resort of Zaleszczyki, caught between the advancing armies of the Germans from the west and the Russians from the east. Before the Mission reached the Romanian border post at Vijniţa, they decided to change into civilian clothes except for Carton de Wiart who insisted on wearing his uniform.

> Fortunately, it began to drizzle and he was persuaded to put on a raincoat and remove his general's hat. However, he was in a truculent mood and after crossing, at the first Romanian checkpoint he remarked loudly to everyone within earshot 'There are only three sorts of Romanians: they are either pimps, pederasts or violinists and bloody few are violinists'. He then repeated this observation in French for the benefit of the sentry who saluted in blank incomprehension and waved us through.[43]

All members of the Mission were accounted for except Major Curteis and Lieutenant Rowton who were attached to General Dembiński's Headquarters near Syryj and crossed into Hungary later. The Romanians were nervous about their latest arrivals for although still a neutral country, the government and its maverick head of state, King Carol II, were only too aware of the vulnerability of their country's geographic position if it should come to rely on military help from far-off France and Britain for Hitler had made it clear that unrestricted access to the Romanian oil fields was non-negotiable. Furthermore, the terms of the 1927 Polish-Romanian Treaty of Alliance did not extend to foreign Military Missions. After a terse interval with the Romanian Border Protection Force, the Mission split into two parties: Carton de Wiart and Sword with their Polish liaison officer Captain Dąbrowski headed for Bucharest via Bacău while Gubbins, Davidson and Wilkinson set off to Cernăuţi where they rendezvoused with MIR's Captain Richard O'Brien McNabb who had driven up from Bucharest to meet them. With a briefcase full of banknotes to pay off the variety of officials they would meet on their way, passing by Romanian 'soldiers in threadbare uniforms and straw sandals . . . oxen pulled their fields guns',[44] McNabb delivered the Mission safely to Bucharest. Junior members of the Mission who stayed in the Athenée Palace Hotel were greeted on their first morning by the gory sight of the bodies of Iron Guards legionnaires strung up outside the Royal Palace across the square. They were greatly relieved to be sent to Constanţa on the Black Sea where Denis Wright[45] of Gallahers Tobacco successfully outbid a German attempt to intern them in an auction with the Romanian authorities.[46]

On reaching the city, Carton de Wiart immediately touched base with the British Minister Sir Rex Hoare who set about exfiltrating him as soon as possible for he was clearly an embarrassment to his hosts now that Britain was at war with Germany. Although there is no evidence that he had a mandate for making mischief in Romania, Olivia Manning in *The Great Fortune* portrays an uncanny likeness to him in the character of Commander Sheppy, 'an absurd naval officer with one arm and an eye-patch braying like an ass about his sabotage plans'. Sheppy is a cruel caricature of Carton de Wiart.[47]

Issued with a new passport, Carton de Wiart boarded the Simplon-Orient Express to Paris with Gubbins and the service Attachés, telling all within ear shot that he was travelling *incognito*. In Paris he lunched at the Ritz with Colonel William Fraser, an old friend who was the Military Attaché there, before flying to London where he went straight to the War Office to report to General Ironside.

> I was met with the remark: 'Well! Your Poles haven't done much.' I felt that the remark was premature and replied: 'Let us see what others will do, sir.' No one who had not been there could imagine what the Poles were up against. The Germans had prepared for this war for years, and it was the world's first experience of the power of mechanised force used on a gigantic scale. It was the armed might of Germany against the weight of human bodies, and if heroism could have saved the Poles their story would have been a different one. At that particular moment, I did not think it was for us or any other allied nation to deny them praise.[48]

Now living at 14 Pall Mall,[49] he gave King George VI a 'first-hand account of recent events in Poland'[50] and made several more visits to the War Office to hammer home the lessons learnt about German strategy and tactics.[51] Most officers received his findings with 'various degrees of scepticism, since it seemed inconceivable that the German panzer tactics could succeed against such a sophisticated defence as the Maginot Line'.[52] Lord Halifax saw him at the Foreign Office and the Prime Minister Neville Chamberlain invited him to dinner with Lord Hankey, the newly appointed Minister without Portfolio, whose son Robert had been First Minister in Warsaw and come out with the British Military Mission. When the question of the effectiveness of the leaflet drops was raised, de Wiart did not mince his words.

With his previous experiences in Poland and his understanding of the fragility of the new Polish State, Carton de Wiart was sanguine in his analysis, characterizing it as 'a struggle . . . between on the one hand a country of enormous industrial capacity and ruthless energy directed towards one end, war, and on the other a country of limited resources and wealth, gallant but poor, still handicapped by the tragic history of the last 160 years'. In his view it was not a question of if Poland capitulated but of how long she could hold out.

As for the Mission, there had been no opportunity to carry out all the War Office's instructions.

> The Polish army fought to the last gasp; my actions in this sphere were confined to pressing the Polish General Staff to adopt a sound strategy. It only remained for me to keep the War Office fully informed of the military situation in Poland, and to study the strategical and tactical lessons of the fighting; this I was able to do by the efforts of my staff and my signal personnel.[53]

Ever attentive to ensuring that those under his command received due recognition, in his report he highlighted the services of Gubbins, Sword, Wilkinson, Perkins, Methven, Green and five Royal Signallers. He also drew attention to Captain Wharton RN, Group Captain Davidson RAF, and Captain McNabb of MIR in Romania.

Although the life span of the Mission turned out to be less than three weeks, Carton de Wiart's calm and confident leadership throughout the hectic, dangerous and mostly chaotic days of the German and the Russian invasions had not only allowed his team to collect and send timely and accurate intelligence back to London but also ensured the safe passage to Romania of members of the embassy and their families and other service personnel. His own efforts to mentor the Polish General Staff and in particular Marshal Edward Śmigły-Ridz who he knew lacked confidence and the skills of a successful general may not have produced the desired results but it was not for lack of persistence or effort on his part. He received no recognition from his own government, but the Poles were more appreciative, bestowing the *Krzyz Walecznych* (the Polish Cross of Valour) on him together with Gubbins, Shelley, Sword, Lloyd-Johnes and Davidson which HM The King granted them the right to wear on their uniforms.[54] He was invited to a dinner on 11 October at the Polish Embassy to meet the Foreign Minister August Zaleski which was attended by Lord Halifax, the Foreign Secretary, and Sir John Simon among others and again on 15 November to welcome General Władysław Sikorski, the Polish prime minister in exile and newly appointed Commander-in-Chief, an altogether larger affair with the British Chiefs of Staff present as well as Winston Churchill and other government ministers.[55]

On a personal level, the invasion of Poland had brought Carton de Wiart's life in Polesie to an abrupt end. Most of the contents of his house at Prostyń including his paintings and precious Purdey shotguns were sent for safekeeping to the National Art Gallery in Minsk which was later burnt down by the Germans in 1941. Both his soldier servant James and his groom Matthews were captured and interned by the Russians in September 1939 and repatriated to England in 1940. The wooden house and outbuildings at Prostyń vanished without trace.[56]

The British were long on words. Winston Churchill told the House of Commons on 3 September that

> We are fighting to save the whole world from the pestilence of Nazi tyranny and in defence of all that is most sacred to man. This is no war for domination or imperial aggrandizement or material gain; no war to shut any country out of its sunlight and means of progress. It is a war, viewed in its inherent quality, to establish, on impregnable rocks, the rights of the individual, and it is a war to establish and revive the stature of man.[57]

Such eloquence could not disguise the fact that Britain had been in no position to come to the assistance of Poland in the first place. None of the 111 British aircraft purchased by Poland were available to take part in operations and a £60 million pound loan had been watered down to £8 million.

In the same debate, Willie Gallacher, the fiery Scottish MP, questioned Chamberlain's reliance on 'admirable restraint'.

> The Government of Poland, said the Prime Minister, had shown admirable restraint, and he hoped and was sure that they would continue to do so. Why should the Polish Government show admirable restraint? This is exactly what we were told about the Government of Czecho-Slovakia. The Prime Minister at that Box a year ago said that the Government of Czecho-Slovakia were showing admirable restraint. Why is it that it is always those who are being attacked who have to show admirable restraint and that we allow the aggressors to go on from one stage to another?

Sadly, dropping leaflets neither constituted encouragement nor stopped aggression. At 4 pm on 6 October, General Kleeberg and his valiant Group 'Polesie' were the last Polish soldiers to surrender. In the space of five weeks, the Wehrmacht had defeated the fourth largest European army, ousted the government of the Second Polish Republic, and appropriated nearly 200,000 square hectares as German territory. As to the Russian invasion, no formal protest was lodged by the British government; and in the *Sunday Express*[58] Lloyd George praised the Soviet leadership for 'liberating their kinsmen from the Polish yolk'. The fact that their T-26 tanks were modeled on the Vickers 6-tonne Light Tank manufactured under license in Russia was a classic example of the former prime minister's foreign policy rooted first and foremost in trade.

Figure 1 Rue Qasr-el Nil, Cairo. (Image of postcard *c*.1900).

Figure 2 Hastières pas Delà, Belgium. (Courtesy of Sir Adrian Carton de Wiart's family).

A YOUTHFUL LOOKING CARTON DE WIART, THIRD FROM LEFT AT REAR, IN MUTTRA, INDIA, 1902. LT HORNBY. WHO WAS TO DRAW THE FIRST BLOOD IN 1914, IS SEATED FRONT LEFT.

Figure 3 Officers of 4th Dragoon Guards in India 1902. (4th/7th Dragoon Guards Regimental Museum).

Figure 4 Lieutenant Carton de Wiart, 4th Dragoon Guards. (Courtesy of Sir Adrian Carton de Wiart's family).

Figure 5 De Wiart and Rikki at Hove *c.*1910. (Courtesy of Sir Adrian Carton de Wiart's family).

Figure 6 Troops approaching Shimber Beris. (TNA WO106/272 Crown Copyright).

Figure 7 De Wiart on leave with his daughters *c*.1916. (Courtesy of Sir Adrian Carton de Wiart's family).

Figure 8 De Wiart on leave with his daughters *c*.1916. (Courtesy of Sir Adrian Carton de Wiart's family).

Figure 9 Anita, Rikki and Ria 1920. (Courtesy of Sir Adrian Carton de Wiart's family).

Figure 10 Inter-Allied Mission 1919. (Courtesy of Anthony Loyd).

Figure 11 De Wiart with Max-Müller *c.* 1923. (Bibliotheque Nationale Francais).

Figure 12 Prince Karol Radziwiłł. (Włodzimierz Puchalski).

Figure 13 De Wiart at Prostyń *c.* 1927. (Courtesy of the Sutherland family).

Figure 14 The house at Prostyń. (Courtesy of the Sutherland family).

Figure 15 The river at Prostyń. (Courtesy of the Sutherland family).

Figure 16 De Wiart with members of the Friends' Ambulance Unit on their return from Norway 1940. (Getty Images).

Figure 17 Vincigliata, Fiesole, Italy. (Wikipedia Commons).

Figure 18 SEXTANT Conference Cairo. Front row, from left: Chiang Kai-Shek, Franklin Delano Roosevelt, Winston Churchill, and Chiang's wife, Soong Mei Ling. Back row: Shang Chen, Liu Wei, Brehon Burke Somervell, Joseph Stilwell, Henry H. Arnold, Sir John Dill, Lord Mountbatten, and Carton de Wiart. (Bridgeman Images).

Figure 19 Generalissimo, Mountbatten, T.V. Soong, Lt Gen Browning and de Wiart. (IWM SE 3547).

Figure 20 Fishing with Joan on the River Lee. (Courtesy of the Sutherland family).

Figure 21 Joan at Aghinagh House. (Courtesy of the Baron Houtart family).

Part VII

Norway 1940

A gallant fiasco

On his return from Poland, Carton de Wiart 'retired to hospital for some treatment'[1] and began to fret about his future. The spectre of yet more medical boards and an inkling that he had his detractors in high places in the War Office haunted him and it was with relief when on 29 November General Ironside gave him the 61st Division in Oxford, a second line Territorial Army division formed as the duplicate of the 48th (South Midland) Division.[2]

The division's area stretched from Birmingham to Portsmouth and from Cheltenham to Reading, some of it familiar to Carton de Wiart from his days as adjutant of the Royal Gloucestershire Hussars. This was the time of the Phoney War where the French Army and the British Expeditionary Force deployed to the west of the impregnable Maginot Line and waited. Composed of militiamen who had been called up in September, the division was grouped in three brigades, all consisting of underequipped and partially trained battalions of county regiments.

Losing no time, Carton de Wiart toured his command and began to come to grips with the immensity of the scale of training required to bring the division to anything like a state of combat readiness. Fitness, marksmanship and minor tactics training programmes were all hampered by a lack of instructors, but this was no different to the experiences of the other TA Divisions. It was of some comfort to him that 'with the rest of the world I put great faith in the French Army and believed it to be of formidable strength and most modern equipment'.[3] In the spring of 1940, all was to change.

In the early hours of 8 April 1940, the German Kreigsmarine put to sea from its Baltic ports and headed north. Operation WESERÜBUNG, the German invasion of Denmark and Norway, had begun. By the following evening, though far from entrenched, German troops had landed in Horten, Arendal, Kristiansand, Bergen, Egersund, Trondheim and Narvik. German command in Norway reported to Berlin that the occupation of Norway had been accomplished. The

British and French, long aware of the importance of Swedish iron ore exports to Germany from the Norwegian port of Narvik, had drawn up a number of plans, all of which depended on the consent of the Norwegian government which was still neutral. The plan finally adopted comprised laying two minefields to close the passage south of Narvik and the despatch of an Allied military force to occupy the port and secure the railway up to the Swedish border. This would be augmented by landings at Trondheim and Bergen and a raid on Stavanger.

Although the minefields were successfully laid by the Royal Navy on the morning of 8 April, the news that the German fleet had put to sea with the invasion forces radically altered the picture. Over the next twenty-four hours during which there were scattered engagements between the opposing naval forces, it became clear that the Germans had simultaneously captured the four biggest towns in Norway: Oslo, Bergen, Trondheim and Narvik. In haste, Britain and France sent a counter force to retake Narvik. No sooner had AVONFORCE, consisting of 24th Guards Brigade and 146th Infantry Brigade, sailed from Scapa Flow on 12 April, it became apparent that the recapture of Trondheim was of greater political and strategic importance for if the Germans remained ensconced in the Trondheim area, they could dominate the coast line to the north and south with their naval and air forces. So an Anglo-French seaborne landing in the Trondheim area and a direct attack by the Navy on the city – Operation HAMMER – replaced Narvik as the priority.

When HAMMER was deemed too hazardous on account of German air superiority, the final plan adopted by the War Cabinet involved two landings some 300 kilometres apart, one at Namsos to the north of Trondheim (MAURICEFORCE) and the other at Åndalsnes to the west (SICKLEFORCE). By quickly expanding these bridgeheads, a pincer movement would enable a defensive front to be established along the roads and railways and thus halt the German advance from Oslo. After landing at Molde and Åndalsnes, SICKLEFORCE was tasked with the capture of Dombass sixty miles south and then to advance to Trondheim; to the north, MAURICEFORCE was to disembark at Namsos and then make its way south towards Trondheim where it would meet up with SICKLEFORCE.

Consequently, on 14 April, 148th Brigade which had been earmarked for Namsos was diverted by Churchill to Åndalsnes; and 146th Brigade on passage to Narvik was rerouted to Namsos. General Ironside protested, pointing out that if half the Narvik force was removed, the Narvik operation would be jeopardized. Either abandon Narvik altogether, he argued, or at most, invest it. He was overruled.[4]

From the start, the Secretary of the Chiefs of Staff Committee, General Pug Ismay, was not confident:

Amphibious operations require highly trained personnel, a great variety of technical equipment, a detailed knowledge of the points at which the landings are to take place, accurate information about enemy strengths and dispositions, and, perhaps above all, meticulous planning and preparation. In the case of the projected Norwegian expeditions, none of these requirements could be fulfilled.[5]

As the tempo quickened, the War Office frantically searched for a commander for MAURICEFORCE who was available at short notice and when he received a call in the middle of the night to report to Whitehall, it dawned on Carton de Wiart that 'the reason might be Norway, especially as I had never been there and knew nothing about it'.[6] Appointed commander of the North Western Norwegian Expeditionary Force on 12 April, he handed over command of the 61st Division and with a skeleton staff from his Divisional headquarters including Colonel Bulger Duke (his Assistant Adjutant and Quartermaster General), he prepared to leave for Norway. His ADC Captain Neville Ford was away for the weekend, so he took Captain Elliot, one of his Brigade Majors, with him instead.

His instructions[7] from General Ironside were broad-brush, reflecting the constant changes in plans. The object of the Anglo-French expedition was 'to provide encouragement for the Norwegian Government' by forming a rallying point for it and its armed forces and to establish a base for any subsequent operations in Scandinavia. Specifically, he was to secure the Trondheim area and its road and rail network after making an unopposed landing in Namsos. So far, so good but it all depended on the ability of the Navy to clear the fjords of German warships and on the arrival of troops and stores in the right place at the right time.

The British elements in Carton de Wiart's MAURICEFORCE consisted[8] of 146th Infantry Brigade commanded by Brigadier C. G. Phillips with three infantry battalions – 1/4th Battalion, The Lincolnshire Regiment; The Hallamshire Battalion, The York and Lancaster Regiment; 1/4th Battalion, The King's Own Yorkshire Light Infantry (KOYLI) – and an RE field company. Of the two Field Ambulances promised only one arrived. The two anti-aircraft (AA) batteries[9] were never fully operational. The French element, commanded by Général Sylvestre-Gérard Audet, comprised Général de Brigade Béthouart's 5th Demi Brigade Chasseurs Alpines – 13th Battalion including 31 Ski Reconnaissance Company; 53rd Battalion; 67th Battalion – and a section of engineers, an AA Battery and an anti-tank Company.

For the War Office's clandestine unit MIR, with which Carton de Wiart had worked closely in Poland the previous year, events in Norway offered a chance to deploy their hand-picked teams[10] and MAURICEFORCE was given Military Mission No. 10. Commanded by the well-known travel writer, Captain Peter Fleming of the Grenadier Guards, the Mission consisted of Polar explorer Captain Martin Lindsay, 2nd Lieutenant Jack Scott-Harston, 2nd Lieutenant Gordon O'Brien Hitching,[11] and Sergeants Berriff and Bryant of the Royal Signals. Taking off in a Sunderland flying boat from Shetland on 13 April, after the rear gunner had scared off two tailing German aircrafts, the Mission arrived over Namsos to reconnoitre the area ahead of the arrival of the main force.[12] Fleming wrote in his diary of their dramatic arrival:

> Suddenly swinging around a bend, we saw Namsos ahead of us: a little huddle of coloured wooden houses crouched between the mountains and the water. In a few seconds we were circling over it...There was our objective: so near and yet so far, like a toy in a shop window. Smoke rose from its chimneys; trampled snow lay in its streets. A ginger cat walked meditatively down one of them. But apart from the cat there was no sign of life at all . . . No.10 Military Mission had been ordered, less than 48 hours ago in Whitehall, to find out who was in occupation of Namsos. Here it was, hovering over the place like a kestrel over a rickyard, and for all it knew, Namsos might have been occupied by the Tibetans.[13]

Once they had landed, the Mission was able to confirm naval reports from the previous day that the area was clear of German forces but, after setting up their HQ in the Grand Hotel with the help of Captain Edds RM who had been landed the night before by destroyer with his party of Marines to verify the landing conditions, Fleming's party were unable to contact the destroyers due to a fault on their wireless (W/T) set.[14] It was only early on 15 April that Fleming managed to get a signal through to the Admiralty:

> Locals co-operative. Namsos reconnoitred daily by enemy aircraft. Both Namsos and Bangsund being snow covered, partially evacuated and very small, offer no concealment for considerable force. Local deployment impossible owing to four feet snow before proceeding on sparsely wooded country. Some motor transport (MT) available, no detail yet, rolling stock on single track railway. Southbound movement of any force much larger than one battalion must be slow and conspicuous from air. Namsos at present short of fresh water. Meeting de Wiart dawn 15 April.[15]

Carton de Wiart, who had been delayed by a blizzard, arrived by flying boat on the afternoon of 15 April only to be greeted by a flight of German Ju88s. The

Sunderland pilot manoeuvred his aircraft at high speed over the water of the fjord to present as hard a target as he could to the marauding German aircraft and it was only after an hour and a half that the destroyer HMS *Somali* was able to send a boat to collect him. His ADC, Captain Elliott, had been wounded in the attack and had to return to Scotland in the flying boat, leaving the general without a personal staff officer.

> On board I found Colonel Peter Fleming and Captain Martin Lindsay, and whoever may have been responsible for sending them I thank him now, for there and then I appropriated them and a better pair never existed. Colonel Peter Fleming from being adventurer and writer turned himself in general factotum number one and was the epitome of [Gilbert and Sullivan's]:
>
> *Oh, I am a cook and a Captain bold,*
> *And the Mate of the Nancy brig*
> *And a Bo'sun tight, and a Midshipmite,*
> *And the crew of the Captain's gig!*
>
> Captain Martin Lindsay, explorer and traveller, picked up the bits where Peter Fleming left off, and between them they were my idea of perfect staff officers, dispensing entirely with paper.[16]

At 10 pm HMS *Somali* put into Namsos under cover of darkness and Carton de Wiart called a conference on board. It was clear to everyone that German air activity posed a serious threat to the imminent landings and they concluded that landing troops in daylight directly from troopships was out of the question and that men and stores would have to be transported by destroyer from the fjord at Lillesjona where they were currently anchored. Setting off in HMS *Somali* later that night, in a signal to London dated 16 April at 1.25 am, Carton de Wiart told the CIGS, General Sir Edmund Ironside:

> Arrived Namsos 4.40pm but could not board destroyer until 6.15pm owing to number enemy aircraft. There is no possibility of landing troops from troopships here on account of enemy air activity. A landing will have to be carried out at night by destroyer. I hope to land two or three battalions on night 16/17 April. Marines will be relieved by then. On night 17/18 April I will land remaining battalion of brigades. 740 enemy are at present at STODALEN and I hope to have fuller information tomorrow. I hope to attack enemy on 21 April. Chief difficulty at present is enemy air policy. We have no planes here at all. Enemy have been very active and have shadowed destroyer all day and made three raids here. My impression is that they suspect an attempt to land troops as enemy aircraft have been much more active today than yesterday. Concealment of

troops by day is very difficult. There is little cover and still a great deal of snow. However, if it is essential to advance, the sooner it is done the better. I cannot at present judge situation at Trondheim, but it will be essential that strong action should be taken as regards enemy air activity when I attack. If there is to be a naval attack at Trondheim and it is successful, General Audet should attack as soon as possible after it. If you could inform me of date of this attack it would help decide definite date of my attack.[17]

By midday on 16 April, most of the Hallams and Lincolns at Lillesjona had been transferred to Tribal Class destroyers which set off at full speed for Namsos while under air attack. Carton de Wiart had transferred to HMS *Alfridi* in Lillesjona and had returned on it to Namsos, remaining on board that night so he could signal London. Landing inexperienced troops at night in snow and ice conditions and offloading their stores at the same time proved a time-consuming operation and at times chaotic but there was no choice. Brigadier Phillips, who had been on the lead vessel when his brigade was diverted at sea, finally arrived on HMS *Ardent* on 17 April to take command. With Lillesjona still under air attack, the Navy decided to risk bringing a troopship into Namsos with the rest of the brigade and successfully disembarked them the next night. By 18 April, all of 146th Brigade had assembled at Namsos and, after obliterating traces of its landing, began to make its way slowly south, moving only at night in line with Carton de Wiart's orders.

By now on the cruiser HMS *Cairo*, Carton de Wiart took stock. The picture was far from rosy. The men were mostly poorly trained Territorials; indeed, some had hardly fired their .303 rifles, let alone a Bren gun. Nearly all of them were untested, their officers showing 'little experience in handling men'.[18] The War Office was well aware of this for General Ironside wrote in his diary on 2 April 1941, 'nobody has dared to say that the Territorial Army is virtually untrained after seven months of training. It is untrained, and we don't seem to have made a very good show of it. There is a lack of leadership all through'.[19] He reiterated his concern on 12 April when he noted that 'our great handicap is that we have such untrained troops with which to deal. Presumably the Germans have not sent their worst troops to these ports'.[20] With enemy air superiority, movement was restricted to the three hours of darkness with radio silence imposed for much of the time. Furthermore, with deep snow on either side of the main road, it was impossible to move across country without snowshoes or skis. One battalion had left its mortars behind and the other's mortar platoon was only partially trained. Add to that the absence of any artillery and anti-aircraft guns and MAURICEFORCE was left with no heavy indirect fire or air defence weapons.

No motor transport had been unloaded which meant that Carton de Wiart and his staff had to rely on local civilian drivers and their private cars. As to supplies, a considerable amount had either been left in the UK or been misrouted in the constant change of unloading tables like the 170 tons that had been returned to Britain on SS *The Empress* troop ship.

Much of the credit for the trouble-free landing should go to Fleming for Lieutenant Atwater RN had told Colonel Holland in London that the Navy reckoned that 'Fleming's (and his team) presence in Namsos had made it possible for him to cut communications with the rest of the country and had thus given the Navy three days security for landing British and French troops with their stores before the Germans started bombing them'.[21] Fleming had gone ahead on 16 April with Sergeant Bryant to see the Norwegian Generalmajor Laurantzon at his HQ at Kvam. Before leaving, he signalled the Admiralty: 'Reliably reported railway bridge south of Verdal demolished, road bridge still intact 14 April. Confirmed some light troops landed at Trondheim . . . Thawing but cross-country movements off. Inadvisable without skis for probably three weeks. Note: Heavy W/T screening and long distance caused delay in reception.'

After being briefed on the disposition and capabilities of the Norwegian forces in the area, Fleming concluded that with low ammunition states and no artillery the Norwegians would not be able to make any significant contribution to taking on the advancing Germans. Instead, he asked Laurantzon to deploy his ski-troops as a harassing force and sent his own signallers with their W/T sets back to Norwegian HQ the next day to assist with communications. They managed to establish a voice link over thirty kilometres and a morse link over forty kilometres, but the overall signals environment was very patchy; at one point by Lake Snaasa, they were down to a one-mile range.

Led by HMS *Cairo*, a second wave of Allied troops, 5th Demi Brigade of the French Chasseurs Alpine, disembarked at Namsos at 2.30 am on 20 April. Carton de Wiart came ashore by whaler and headed for his headquarters. Unaware of the cat and mouse game being played by the British with the Germans, the French engaged some enemy aircraft the next morning thereby revealing their whereabouts. This triggered a devastating bombing raid lasting from 10 am to 4.30 pm which turned the town centre of wooden houses into an inferno, disrupting water and electricity supplies and destroying a large part of the French stores and ammunition. It would be unfair to pin all the blame on the French as it later transpired that the Germans had intercepted British signals and furthermore that the Reuters news agency had announced on 19 April that British soldiers had landed at Namsos.[22]

Well equipped for winter warfare, the French rapidly dispersed outside the town and 'took to the rocks like rabbits'. Standing in the open, beneath a hailstorm of bombs, Carton de Wiart 'fished in his pocket for his cigarette case, took a cigarette out of it and lit it – no easy task for a man with one arm – and muttered: "Damn Frogs – they're all the same. One bang and they're off!"[23] For No. 10 Military Mission it had been a disaster: 'Our sets destroyed in Grand Hotel. Civilian telephone exchange destroyed. Bang went remaining skeleton communications inland.'[24] With no airstrip in the area and no aircraft carrier immediately available, Carton de Wiart saw 'little chance of carrying out decisive, or indeed, any operations'

It transpired that the Chasseurs Alpine had landed without much of their mountain warfare equipment, particularly their mules whose load carrying capability allowed them to move off road. The convoy carrying their artillery, ammunition, mules, and motor transport was still in Brest. Their ski binding straps were missing as well, which meant that, without cross-country capabilities, Carton de Wiart found them 'completely useless'[25] for the job in hand.

That night, as HMS *Nubian* steamed up Namsos fjord, its skipper Lieutenant Commander Lampard observed from a distance 'a red glare in the sky which was realised to be a big fire'. When the town came into view, 'the sight was remarkable. The whole place was a mass of flames from end to end and the glare on the snow of the surrounding mountains produced an unforgettable spectacle.'[26] Carton de Wiart came on board and counselled that with the destruction of the storehouses and most of the infrastructure at Namsos, further landings of stores would be unadvisable given the level of German air activity. He signalled London, 'Enemy aircraft have almost completely destroyed Namsos. . . . At present impossible to land more men or materials . . . I see little chance of carrying out decisive or, indeed, any operations, unless enemy air activity is considerably restricted.'[27]

The next morning, Carton de Wiart set off to scrounge some rations for his staff while Peter Fleming was busy shovelling snow into a saucepan to make tea:

> I watched him saunter down the steep hill towards the quay as the church-bells rang and the first air raid of the day was unleashed. A conspicuous figure in his red hat . . . he maintained an even pace down the centre of the gutted street. Machine-guns clattered; smoke drifted from burning buildings; the Heinkels were flying so low that the bombs had no time to whistle before they burst. Carton de Wiart paid not the slightest attention. From safe bivouacs in the wooded heights around Namsos hundreds of men were watching him – French infantry, British base personnel, all in some degree shaken by their recent

ordeals, all (at a guess) becoming a little more war-worthy as they followed his lackadaisical progress. The Luftwaffe went home with empty bomb-racks. The General returned with some delicious sardines. His single eye surveyed my preparations for breakfast. Devastation was all around us. 'Better get rid of those eggshells somewhere', he said. 'Don't want the place in a mess'.[28]

Brigadier Phillips's brigade reached Verdalsora and Steinkjaer/Vist on the afternoon of 18 April, the former only forty miles from Trondheim and was well positioned to launch a coordinated attack with SICKLEFORCE and the Royal Navy. Carton de Wiart visited them at Steinkjær on 20 April and also met with the Norwegian colonels Getz and Wettre. He explained his plan to them but left them out of his Order of Battle for Generalmajor Laurantzon, the district commander of the Trondheim region, had told Fleming on 17 April that his Norwegian troops were low on ammunition and had no artillery. Phillips had also come away from an earlier meeting with Getz who had just taken over the Trondheim area with the impression that the Norwegian troops were mainly inexperienced militia with scant training and were short of officers.[29] Like the British, they too had no air support or heavy weapons and furthermore were short of rifles and ammunition.[30] So it was hardly surprising that Carton de Wiart did not include them in his plan to recapture Trondheim other than allocate them some flank protection tasks.

Back in Namsos, another group of French troops had arrived on SS *Ville d'Alger* transport vessel, but Carton de Wiart ordered her out to sea as he was adamant that the risks were too great and that conditions ashore after the last crippling raid remained too chaotic. The principal British sea transport officer had been killed and his Number Two wounded. The next day he reluctantly changed his mind and the French troops were brought ashore by the escorts as she was too large to moor alongside the wooden jetty. The result was that she departed without landing her heavy stores including skis, mules, anti-tank guns and an anti-aircraft battery. The same night a smaller British freighter had managed to get alongside the jetty but only managed to unload a small part of her cargo of ammunition, petrol and 300 vehicles. She returned the following two nights to complete unloading. Fortunately, heavy snowfall prevented German air activity during the daylight hours.

For Phillips and his brigade, the waiting was over. In the early morning of 21 April, the bridge at Verdalsora was attacked by 200 German troops and at 6 am a further 400 Gebirgsjägers (Mountain troops) landed at Kirkenesvaag to the west of Steinkjær. Intense air activity hampered any movement by the

British and Norwegian troops on the ground and by midday Steinkjær was ablaze. Initially Phillips rushed his companies like firefighters to deal with the German incursions, but it soon became clear that his poorly equipped and untested Territorials were no match for the Gebirgsjägers and the Polish campaign veterans they were up against. 'Time and again when coming under fire, the Landser spread out, climbed the hills on skis, dragging sledge-borne machine guns into commanding positions that outflanked their opponents. The use of snowshoes and skis and their ability to move through the snowy terrain with relative ease repeatedly frustrated the British defences.'[31] The arrival in Beitstadfjorden of the German destroyer *Paul Jacobi* with her five 5-inch guns made the British position untenable as she fired at will at opportunity targets. Limited to rifles, Bren guns and 2-inch mortars, they retired north out of reach of the German naval guns, some of 1/4 Lincolns chased across the snow bound terrain by crack German ski-troops. That evening the Germans landed at Steinkjær which had been reduced to a charred empty shell after non-stop air and naval bombardment.

The withdrawal of 146th Brigade had been carried out 'under very adverse conditions in many cases by mountain tracks in thick snow – the Lincolns and KOYLI losing most of their Bren guns, thick clothing and reserve stores and ammunition'.[32] The Territorials had risen to the occasion – the KOYLIs completed a fifty-eight mile march in forty-two hours[33] winding their way along snowbound forest tracks at night.[34] Others had encountered much tougher going. The company commander of C Company Lincolns recalled,

> for four and a half hours we stumbled up the mountain, the snow getting deeper, until at the top we were struggling in snow almost up to our waists. We had as a guide my compass and the huge fire in Steinkjær. At 3am when we were practically exhausted…we found a barn into which we all clambered and fell asleep. We had travelled only one and a half miles.[35]

Morale was understandably low when Corporal Lane and his retreating company met Carton de Wiart:

> We fell in outside and set off on the roads again and marching down the road in charge of a small column of men was the general in charge of the Namsos operation . . . no other than General Carton de Wiart, the one armed Victoria Cross holder. He gave us a pep talk and his manner seemed to give the lads a boost. By now the news hawks were around following the column. They were taking pictures . . . of a retreating army, but I don't think they got many pictures that day because the old general showed he'd lost none of his fire. . . . He was

carrying an officer cane under the armpit of his missing arm and he removed it and took a swipe at those with cameras, knocked them to the ground and trampled on them. He was a right fiery old bugger, but everyone laughed like hell at this action. Some of the things he said to those reporters . . . turned the air blue. After a long march, the general led us to some building that turned out to be a dairy. There he got permission for us to bed down overnight while he went off. We never saw him again.[36]

In a signal to London timed at 8.29 pm on 22 April, Carton de Wiart gave his frank assessment of the situation confronting MAURICEFORCE.

Have seen Phillips [commander of 146th Brigade] who has situation in hand. The battalion from Verdal area is retiring. The three companies at Vist are in touch with a strong force of Germans and will attempt retiring tonight to Steinkjær area. Steinkjær has been bombed and completely destroyed. Our men cannot fight off-road owing to deep snow, this does not handicap the enemy who is using snow shoes. I have ordered Phillips to retire by the Steinkjær-Namsos road but when enemy discover this move everything on this road will be destroyed and in this weather it will put a very heavy physical strain on the men. I had hoped that by pushing Phillip's brigade south as far as I did, and if a heavy raid on Trondheim had taken place, I might have made a dash for Trondheim but now I clearly cannot do this and I must try and extricate Phillips. When his brigade gets back to Namsos they will find no accommodation, no water, no facilities, and the bridge may not be standing. Troops in Verdal sector shelled by destroyer today 22 April. I should be grateful if you would let me know what your policy will now be. I much regret to give you such a gloomy view of situation but it is a true one.[37]

General Ironside understood this and wrote in his diary on 19 April that 'at this junction the situation might still have been saved and Trondheim might still have been captured if the third move, to which both these operations were subsidiary and on whose success their usefulness entirely depended, had been immediately executed, namely the direct assault from the sea'.[38]

To the south and west, SICKLEFORCE had had more than its fair share of problems. Early on, the command structure was beset with bad luck. Major General 'Boots' Hotblack[39] received his instructions as commander of SICKLEFORCE on 17 April. That evening, he was found unconscious at the bottom of the Duke of York's steps off the Mall and was taken to Millbank hospital. He was replaced by acting Major General Horatio Berney-Ficklin[40] but on 19 April, Berney-Ficklin was injured when his plane crashed at Kirkwall in the Orkneys and once more a replacement had to be found, this time acting

Lieutenant General Bernard Paget[41] who finally arrived on the ground at Åndalnes on 25 April, just days before the end of the campaign.

The first elements of SICKLEFORCE to land – 148th Brigade commanded by Brigadier Harold Morgan[42] – had made their way to Dombaas from where they were sent to the Gudbrandsdal valley and placed under Norwegian command. Composed of 1,000 men from Territorial battalions with just two officers having previous active service experience, the brigade soon found itself in action at Balbergkampland. Under constant air attack, short of sleep and without food for long periods, the Territorials doggedly held the bridge at Tretten to allow the Norwegians time to regroup. By 9.30 pm on 23 April, by now reduced to 9 junior officers and 300 men, the brigade withdrew to Heidal. It was another forty-eight hours before General Paget and Brigadier Arthur Kent-Lemon's 15th Infantry Brigade arrived at Åndalsnes. Far from delivering a knockout blow on Trondheim, 'his task was to extricate his force along a narrow valley-route which the enemy might at any time outflank, through a base which lay already in ruins, under conditions imposing a severe strain upon British, much more upon Norwegian, morale.'[43]

Over the next four days, the MAURICEFORCE line stabilized as for some reason the Germans had halted their advance a few kilometres to the northwest of Steinkjær. The Norwegian 3rd Dragoons withdrew on the right flank, blocking roads and blowing bridges as they went, and then met up with the 1st Battalion of 14th Norwegian Infantry Regiment. The Norwegian line of the right flank now held. Poor weather and a lull in German air activity had enabled a second group of French troops to land with all their stores and equipment and by 25 April the whole of MAURICEFORCE had finally disembarked. General Audet went up to the front line and met Colonel Getz on the evening of 26 April, the same day that Wing Commander Maxton and his airfield recce party arrived to search for suitable landing grounds near Namsos. For the first time, a sense of optimism prevailed as the combined British-French-Norwegian force of some 8,000 now considerably outnumbered its Germans opponents. Carton de Wiart, who had moved his headquarters to a farmhouse at Spillum to be nearer the front, conferred with them the next day and plans for a counter-attack were agreed.

However, the underlying situation remained grave. Being a seasoned campaigner, Carton de Wiart sensed that London had no inkling as to what was actually happening on the ground and despatched Fleming in a flying boat back to England to report on the seriousness of the situation. On arrival, he was greeted with some surprise for *The Daily Sketch*, acting on information from Stockholm[44] that he had been killed in a bombing raid on the Grand Hotel in Namsos, had run the headline 'Author Killed in Norway', with a picture of Fleming and his wife Celia underneath and a short obituary. After delivering Carton de Wiart's despatches to the War Office, Fleming had a breakfast meeting with Churchill, then still First Lord of the Admiralty, who impressed him as a politician who 'knew how, and how not, to wage a war'.[45]

On his return two days later, Fleming told Carton de Wiart that 'you can really do what you like, for they don't know what they want done'.[46] Shortly after, on 27 April, much to Carton de Wiart's irritation, a complete divisional staff turned up who 'took up a lot of unavailable space . . . (with) not much for them to do'[47] apart from what Fleming, Lindsay and Major Rohan Delacombe[48] were already doing. Exasperated by their sudden appearance, he mused that 'I felt that soon we would be all staff and no war'. With them came a Royal Marine howitzer battery, a Field Ambulance, a dock labour company, rifles and ammunition for the Norwegians and other stores.[49] Owing to the fact that the jetty was piled high with French equipment and there was still a French ship tied up alongside, only the Divisional Headquarters party and some of the howitzers were unloaded. There was no ammunition for the howitzers.

The situation was by now unsustainable. Ship to shore communications relied on signal lamps manned by Fleming's two Royal Signallers. The Allied campaign to recapture Trondheim and stem the German advance had ignominiously ground to a halt and was in reverse. The two expeditions were too far apart to mutually support each other and without air cover both were exposed to enemy aircraft at every point along their lines of communications. Late on 27 April, Carton de Wiart received a signal from Lieutenant General Massy,[50] to whom the CIGS had given direct control of operations on 22 April, to begin the evacuation of his 6,000 strong force, prioritizing the rescue of men over that of equipment. Inexplicably, despite incessant air attacks on the port and shipping, troops and equipment were still being landed at Namsos including 166 Battery of 56 Regiment RA. When Rear Admiral Vivian arrived at Namsos on HMS *Carlisle*, he found the sloop HMS *Bittern* and three Anti-submarine trawlers either sunk or on fire. Carton de Wiart agreed with his decision to take the remaining trawlers and warships to sea during daylight hours to conserve them for the evacuation.

The responsibility for the evacuation of MAURICEFORCE fell to Vice Admiral Cunningham of the 1st Cruiser Squadron and he left Scapa Flow on 29 April with three cruisers, five destroyers and three French transports. During their passage they were joined by four more destroyers, giving them the capacity to take off Carton de Wiart's estimate of 5,700 men. The plan was to use the nights of 1 and 2 May to extract MAURICEFORCE but thick fog made navigation too hazardous and forced Cunningham to head back to open waters. A daring attempt by Captain Lord Louis Mountbatten on HMS *Kelly* and three other destroyers to enter the fjord failed when they were spotted by a German reconnaissance aircraft at 5 am on 2 May and despite using the fog as cover to hide in, one of them, HMS *Maori*, was damaged by a bomb.

Cunningham after conferring with his officers decided that the evacuation had to be completed in a single night. It was their last chance. The 2nd Demi Brigade and 146th Infantry Brigade had withdrawn together and by 2 May were dug in along the perimeter of the Namsos bridgehead. French ski patrols were still in contact with the enemy; and a party of the Hallams with their commanding officer covered the demolition charges at the bridge over the Namsfjorden at Bangsund. The French were to board first followed by the British. The evacuation started at 10.30 pm and at 1 am the sound of an explosion heralded the demolition of the bridge at Bangsund.

> At 1.30am the translucent twilight over the hills around the harbour became brighter, full daylight was fast approaching, the Hallams had still not arrived and the Admiral was most anxious to get the convoy away. Another day at Namsos for the Rear Guard seemed a certainty. The Bofors had been kept back for such an eventuality. Then suddenly the situation changed. Company after company arrived at the quay and were rushed onto the transports and destroyers, and the Bofors Battery was called in. Except for a small rear guard, the evacuation was complete by 1.50am.[51]

By 3.15 am on 3 May, with over 5,400 safely boarded, Cunningham's convoy was underway. The last ship to cast off was the destroyer HMS *Alfridi* which Carton de Wiart had been planning to embark on when he discovered his baggage had been sent to the cruiser HMS *York*, so he boarded her instead. It was another twist of luck for the Luftwaffe found the convoy at daybreak and subjected it to attacks throughout the day. HMS *Alfridi* was sunk by Stukas at 2 pm that afternoon; fifty-two members of her crew were lost, thirteen soldiers of the Yorks and Lancs and the thirty crew who had been rescued from the French destroyer *Bison*. The convoy finally dropped anchor at Scapa Flow on 5 May,[52] Carton de Wiart's sixtieth birthday and exactly eighteen days since they had first sailed. The next day, Namsos fell to the Germans without a shot being fired. Four days later, Chamberlain resigned as prime minister, the government fell and Churchill emerged as leader of a wartime coalition.

Well aware that they had to keep the Norwegians out of the loop for security reasons, both General Audet and Carton de Wiart wrote personal letters to

Colonel Getz which were delivered to him at 11 pm on 2 May. Carton de Wiart's was subsequently published in the *Svenska Dagbladet* and read:

> It is with great grief that I now inform you that we must evacuate this district and each of us feels it deeply. We leave some material here – we hope you will come and take care of it – and we are convinced it will be of great use for you and your brave corps. As to ourselves, we hope to be allowed to return here and help you successfully to end your campaign.[53]

Getz, deeply upset by being kept in the dark about the Allied withdrawal, realized that any meaning resistance was now fruitless and signed an armistice with the Germans on 5 May.

In their short time together in Norway, Fleming and Carton de Wiart became firm friends as well as comrades in arms. That friendship continued in the latter stages of the war when the two men were together in Chongqing in China and was celebrated by Fleming in a witty article called 'Beau Sabreur'.[54] Carton de Wiart held a candle to the memory of Fleming in Norway and late in 1944 was heard to tell Mountbatten, 'I can't think what you want with this bloody great staff. I only had Peter Fleming in Norway and was never bothered with bumf at all.'[55]

General Ironside had travelled up to Scotland to meet the returning troops and took Carton de Wiart to lunch at the New Club in Edinburgh along with two French generals and the GOC Scotland. Apart from welcoming their safe return, there was little to celebrate as press reports indicated that the Germans had taken Mosjoen. Out of touch with Gubbins, the CIGS could only speculate as to what was happening and retired that night, 'very upset at the thought of our incompetence. We are not a machine fitted to make war upon a scale of improvisation. You cannot do that against the Germans.'[56]

A few hours after Carton de Wiart arrived back in London, Admiral Sir Roger Keyes MP paid him a visit. A Nelsonian figure who had served with distinction in the Boxer rebellion in China and throughout the First World War culminating in his leadership of the raids on the German submarine pens in Zeebrugge and Ostend, it was Keyes who had been the architect of the idea of a naval raid on Trondheim and had sold it to Churchill as First Lord of the Admiralty and then to the Chiefs of Staff. What they failed to buy into was his core concept to send capital ships into the Trondheim fjord to dominate the battle. Carton de Wiart had no grudge to bear against the Navy but pointed out that its non-appearance at Trondheim 'knocked out all idea of attacking the town'.

Well briefed by Carton de Wiart, when Keyes entered the chamber of the House on 7 May in full uniform, he was able to say with conviction:

> When I realised how badly things were going later, and saw another Gallipoli looming ahead, I never ceased importuning the Admiralty and the War Cabinet to let me take all responsibility and organise and lead the attack. It was not the fault of the officers and men for whom I speak that the naval co-operation, on which the General commanding the Namsos Force depended, was not provided, and without which the whole operation was doomed to failure. At a moment when the General was confident of success and was advancing from Steinkjaer along the only road to Trondheim in the hope of finding British ships to assist him and harass the enemy with their gunfire, instead he found two German destroyers, which opened fire on his flank, transported troops and landed them behind his advanced guard which they captured or destroyed, thus defeating the whole expedition. It is a shocking story of ineptitude, which I assure the House ought never to have been allowed to happen. If prompt steps had been taken immediately and carried out with energy and speed, even after the first check occurred at Steinkjaer, the situation could have been retrieved by immediate naval action. Since, as the Prime Minister has pointed out, the possession of Trondheim and its aerodrome at Vaernes was so important strategically, almost any effort was justified even if it involved some naval risks and sacrifices. I do not believe that the loss would have been anything like those which we have suffered in the whole evacuation of the troops from Namsos.[57]

It took Leo Amery MP to succinctly sum up the Norwegian campaign in the same debate: 'It is a bad story, a story of lack of prevision and of preparation, a story of indecision, slowness and fear of taking risks.'

In his report on the Norwegian campaign, Lieutenant General Massy put on record

> the services rendered by Major General B. C. T. Paget, for the skill with which he conducted operations on the southern front from the time he took command until the final evacuation. Major General A. Carton de Wiart proved that he still possesses the energy and dash for which he has always been famous. Brigadier C. G. Phillips proved by his handling of his Brigade during the difficult days of Steinkjaer, that he is a commander of marked ability. Brigadier Morgan gave abundant evidence of the capacity for making decisions which is so essential in a commander. Brigadier Kent-Lemon proved himself a skilful and determined leader.[58]

In his report on the Operations in the Namsos Area,[59] Carton de Wiart gave a withering summary 'of the numerous other errors and omissions which contributed to the failure of the expedition apart from any question of enemy action'. In his usual outspoken way, he wrote: 'Finally, I am forced to the sad conclusion that not only had the lessons we had learnt so dearly at Gallipoli, Salonika and Mesopotamia been forgotten but we now make even more basic mistakes of a most elementary nature.'

Norway had been a poisoned chalice from Day One. Caught by surprise by the speed of the German invasion and by the inherent weakness of Norway which had underinvested in defence by preferring to adopt neutrality as a safe haven,[60] the Anglo-French response never had any chance of success. In many ways a rehearsal of Dunkirk, it was little less than a small miracle than Carton de Wiart and the Royal Navy managed to extricate MAURICEFORCE with only a handful killed and wounded. On a top-down analysis, Gordon Corrigan is withering in his verdict of the campaign:

> There are many examples of Britain's long military history where muddle, indecision and mismanagement have led to defeat and disaster, but for a campaign that demonstrates gross incompetence at the very top of government, and spinelessness by the War Office and the Admiralty for putting up with it, it is difficult to find a better example than Norway in 1940.[61]

General Sir David Fraser, himself a veteran of the Northwest Europe campaign, takes a bottom-up view:

> The Germans were trained to go forward, to find ways round, to climb to higher ground where it could be done, to infiltrate positions, to keep up the offensive, as a matter of instinct and basic training as much as a response to orders. German tactical ability, at every level and particularly the most junior was here experienced for the first time – and the discipline which harnessed that ability and directed the whole. The experience shocked the British Army.[62]

After his experiences in Poland, Carton de Wiart was the one man who was not shocked. On a lighter note, he would have received a warm welcome from his fellow members at White's Club on his return. Noting that Evelyn Waugh knew de Wiart 'slightly but enough, as a fellow member of White's Club',[63] Christopher Sykes in his biography of Waugh identified him as a contributor to the fictional character of Brigadier Ben Ritchie-Hook, the one-eyed irascible warmonger in command of Hazardous Offensive Operations in *Men at Arms*, who glared out at the Halberdier subalterns 'balefully with a single, terrible eye. It was black as the brows above it, this eye, black as the patch which hung on the other side of the lean skew nose'.

For portrait painters, de Wiart provided the perfect subject for a *grand blessé* hero and Cathleen Mann (the Marchioness of Queensbury)[64] entered her recently commissioned painting of him for the Royal Academy Summer Exhibition of 1940. It found favour with the Hanging Committee and was exhibited in Gallery No.3 along with Kenneth Green's portrait of Major General Paget. Billed by the *Illustrated London News* as 'Carton de Wiart of Namsos'[65] and featured on the front cover of *Tatler and Bystander*, the painting perfectly captured the indestructible officer so revered and loved by the British public. No wonder *The Yorkshire Post* correspondent noted, 'there was always a large crowd opposite the portrait of Major General Carton de Wiart.'[66]

Part VIII

Italy 1941–3

A reluctant guest of Mussolini

On his return to duty on 14 May, Carton de Wiart took back command of the 61st Division from Major General Edmund Schreiber[1] who had been caretaking it during Operation HAMMER. Invasion rumours began to circulate and the idea that German paratroopers assisted by the Irish Republican Army (IRA) would land in Ireland took hold. It later transpired that in early 1940 the IRA Acting Chief of Staff, Stephen Hayes, had indeed drawn up Plan KATHLEEN for an amphibious assault in the Londonderry area by 50,000 German troops and sent it by a courier to Germany.[2] The Abwehr dismissed it as amateurish. Such was the level of concern that on 20 June, the War Office ordered the Division to Northern Ireland. Carton de Wiart himself 'never believed the Germans had any intention of invading Ireland' but was very grateful 'for any reason that sent us there, for it was an ideal training ground for troops and the division improved enormously from the moment of (its) arrival'.[3] Now responsible for the defence of the whole of Northern Ireland including Belfast, Divisional Headquarters based itself in Ballymena with its units scattered across the six counties, mainly Antrim, Derry and Tyrone. Beach landing sites were identified, obstacles and pill boxes erected, and defensive positions dug and camouflaged. Brigades and battalions practiced counter-attacks on paratroop landings and coastal raiders, all the time chivvied along by Carton de Wiart who drove from unit to unit to follow the progress of training. Captain John Figges[4] who was the Divisional Intelligence Officer/GSO 3 Operations remembered him as 'a magnificent man . . . courageous . . . troops would follow him . . . brave as a lion, charming man'.[5] There were of course welcome diversions like fishing and shooting.

His first GOC in Northern Ireland was Major General Hubert Huddleston[6] and, like Carton de Wiart, a veteran of the South African War and the 1914–18 War in France. The two got on splendidly but, in July, Huddleston, who had only been there for a few months, was suddenly sent to the Sudan as Governor General. His replacement was Lieutenant General Sir Henry Pownall[7] who had been Field Marshal Gort's Chief of Staff at Dunkirk. Although he had served in France and Belgium in the First World War and then on the North West Frontier where he won a bar to his DSO, Pownall's great strength was his ability as a staff officer and he had spent much of the 1930s in senior positions in the War Office. A stickler for detail who played by the book, he was not prepared to go against the decision of the Military Secretary to retire Carton de Wiart on grounds of age when he reached his sixty-first birthday. Despite his protestations, Carton de Wiart had to relinquish his command and left disconsolate, wondering what on earth he should do with himself. At least he had the satisfaction of having taken over as the Colonel of the 4/7th Royal Dragoon Guards from Major General Solly-Flood, his former commanding officer at Ypres, who had retired in March 1941.

On 5 April, he received another one of those urgent messages from the War Office to report immediately. His luck seemed to be holding. This time 'the offer was a real prize, for it was to go to Yugoslavia and form the British Military Mission.'[8] There were then second thoughts about the feasibility of a Mission; and on 8 April the Chiefs of Staff Committee minuted that he would be 'an observer liaison officer and not part of an inter-service mission'.[9] Four days later, the War Office sent a signal to General Sir Archibald Wavell in Cairo that

> General Carton De Wiart has been officially appointed head of Mission to Yugoslavia but his duties for the present are those of Liaison for you and for War Office. He will be responsible to you and you will settle his relations with British HQ Greece and issue his instructions. Instructions should make it clear that he is to keep in close touch with Yugoslav operations, policy and requests for assistance, repeating relevant reports to War Office.[10]

Since its formation in 1918 as the Kingdom of Serbs, Croats and Slovenes, Yugoslavia as it became known in 1929 had struggled to maintain its unity as a nation state for its old ethnic divisions based on language, geography and history lay simmering beneath the surface. Its king, Alexander I, was assassinated on a visit to France in 1934 by a member of IMRO[11] working in league with the breakaway Croatian Ustaše party; his 'crime' was to try and centralize the country. Sensing this structural weakness, Italy and Germany actively started to have designs on its dismemberment, confident that the original sponsors – the United States, France and Great Britain – had no appetite to prevent them. Croatia was the first to break out, securing autonomous status as a Banovina[12] in 1939, an outcome that infuriated the Serbs. On 25 March 1941, Prince Paul, the regent, felt he had little choice other than to sign up to the September

1940 'defensive' Tripartite Agreement between Germany, Italy and Japan; after all, Hungary, Romania, Slovakia and Bulgaria had already signed it. With the connivance of the British ambassador Ronald Campbell and engineered by the Special Operations Executive (SOE) and SIS, the Yugoslav Army led by General Dušan Simović staged a coup two days later, giving full powers to the English educated seventeen-year-old King Peter. In Belgrade, crowds took to the streets waving Union Jacks and Tricolors. The Joint Intelligence Sub-Committee wrote an upbeat Intelligence Appreciation of Possible Action by Yugoslavia, reporting that 'the new Yugoslav Prime Minister has indicated that the policy of himself and the Army will be entirely pro-British'.[13]

However, at this stage no discussions about joint strategy or military operations had been held and when the British proposed to send the Foreign Secretary Anthony Eden and the Chief of the Imperial General Staff, General Sir John Dill, to Belgrade, Simović initially agreed, only to change his mind[14] just inviting Dill. The CIGS arrived incognito in plain clothes on the evening of 1 April and left for Athens the next morning. Just what he hoped to achieve is unclear for to date Britain had been unable to equip any of the Balkan states with arms or establish any sort of economic or financial leverage to compete with the Germans.

In a 4 April signal[15] to Lieutenant General Sir Robert Haining,[16] the VCIGS in London, Dill revealed that 'the final result of Belgrade visit was disappointing in many ways, but it was impossible to get Simović to sign any sort of agreement. Nevertheless, I was impressed with offensive spirit of Yugo-Slav leaders who will fight if Yugo-Slavia is attacked or if Germany attacks Salonica.' On a less confident note, he reported that 'Yugo-Slavs forces are not yet ready for war and Simović wants to gain time to complete mobilisation and concentration. For internal political reasons he cannot take the first step but must await German move'.

Dill suggested that

> strong liaison will probably be needed in Yugo-Slavia at very short notice. Nobody could of course go until German attack brings Yugo-Slav into war, but personnel should be ready and as near as possible. Have discussed with Wavell and Wilson and suggest Carton de Wiart to lead with George Davy[17] as his Number Two. Wavell has promised to make Davy available.

At 5.12 am on Orthodox Easter Sunday, 6 April 1941, German, Italian and Hungarian troops invaded Yugoslavia. The Bulgarians soon followed. Carton de Wiart no longer had to 'bear the idea of being out of the war'.[18]

Originally a Sunderland flying boat had been tasked to take him, together with his ADC Captain Arthur Fitzgerald[19] and his soldier servant James, to the Middle East but it never materialized, so instead a Wellington from 99 Squadron 3 Group at Newmarket was put as his disposal. Limited to taking only one passenger, Fitzgerald and James were told to follow by cruiser. As he climbed into the Wellington bomber, the AOC of the area, Sir John Baldwin,[20] told him that he had sent ninety-four Wellingtons to the Middle East and all but one had arrived safely. After landing safely in Malta, by now reassured by Baldwin's statistic, he had lunch with General Scobell[21] and then after dining with the Governor, General Dobbie,[22] took off late that night to fly to Cairo where he was due to report to General Wavell.

Falling asleep with his earphones on, two hours later he was woken by the pilot broadcasting an SOS to the crew warning them to prepare for a crash landing as first one, then both engines failed. The Wellington managed to land upright on the sea and the crew and their VIP passenger clambered onto the wing as the aircraft was blown towards the shore. When it finally broke into two, there was no alternative other than to swim for the shore about half a mile away. Taking in hand a crew member with a broken leg, Carton de Wiart set off through the choppy sea and on reaching dry land he was met by a local policeman in Italian service who told him that the British had left the day before. Taken to a friendly local doctor who patched up the crew for most had cuts and bruises and one a broken leg and another a broken arm, Carton de Wiart began to plan their escape when two Italian staff officers turned up and took him off to Bardia. From there he was sent to Benghazi and kept in a small bedroom in a hotel with a guard on the door.

Now he had to come to terms with the fact that he had been taken prisoner, a fate he had never contemplated. 'People who enjoy life seldom have much fear of death and having taken the precaution to squeeze the lemon do not begrudge throwing the rind away. But never, in the innermost recesses of my mind, had I contemplated being taken prisoner . . . . I faced despair.'[23] However, it turned out that he was far from alone as his captors boasted that they also had General O'Connor, General Neame, General Gambier-Perry and several brigadiers 'in the bag'. The following night he was in hospital in Circe and then arrived in Tripoli to be interrogated by Italian military intelligence. After giving his name and rank, de Wiart played the deaf mute until an officer, Captain Camino, took him to the Cavalry Barracks where he was 'treated as an honoured guest'. Now joined by another captured officer Brigadier Edward Todhunter, he was transferred onto a ship in the harbour and several days later on 19 April they sailed for Naples.

From there, under the auspices of an Italian staff officer who had been detailed to look after them, they went by train to Sulmona in the Abruzzi to the east of Rome where Colonel Damiani of the Italian Grenadiers awaited. They were to be his prisoners in the Villa Orsini, a POW camp for senior officers.

The senior British officer was Lieutenant General Sir Philip Neame VC who had been captured with General O'Connor and Brigadier Combe the week before when their car had taken a wrong turning in the desert and driven into a group of Germans. At that time protocol dictated that Afrika Korps had to hand them over to the Italians who had sovereignty over Libya. Another group who, along with Todhunter, had been captured at Mechile by the Germans were Major General Gambier-Perry and Colonel Younghusband. The oldest internees were Air Marshal Boyd and his PA, Flight Lieutenant Leeming, who had made a forced landing in Sicily in 1940.

John Leeming remembered the appearance of Carton de Wiart on 23 April, 'a black patch over one eye . . . an empty sleeve . . . you looked at him and thought immediately of a pirate with a cutlass in his teeth climbing up the side of some old-time merchantman.' He refused to have medical attention, and cursed the Italian doctor who tried to advise him, refusing to be treated as 'a sick man'. The men nicknamed him 'Long John Silver; – a perfect description.'[24]

Life at Sulmona turned out to be unexpectedly pleasant. Colonel Damiani and his English wife were courteous to the extreme given that their 'guests' were prisoners of war (POW). Under the respectful supervision of Lieutenant 'Gussie' Agosto Ricciardi,[25] they were allowed to go shopping, walk in the hills and write as many letters as they liked. Cooked by Sergeant Baxter, food was plentiful and supplemented with rabbits and chickens kept by the prisoners. In charge of this officers' mess behind enemy lines was Sergeant Ronald Bain who managed a posse of batmen to look after the individual officers. Carton de Wiart considered himself fortunate to be well looked after by Prewett, a Royal Gloucestershire Hussar. Philip Neame recalled that Carton de Wiart 'faced captivity in a wonderful way. He was always cheerful and even-tempered, sympathetic, and helpful to everyone. I think he showed less signs than anyone of the stress on nerves and temper imposed by inactivity'.[26]

Like his fellow inmates, Carton de Wiart kept in touch with home and wrote to Anita on 2 June that he had had to write to the bank 'to cut your allowance by half – you must not mind – but this hits me hard financially. I have reduced your mother's by £60 – she will make a fuss but'.[27] Given that POWs continued to be paid by the War Office, this is a somewhat puzzling statement. One possible explanation could be that on retirement he had reverted to his substantive rank of colonel and was not eligible for a Major General's pay as he had not completed thirty days service in his new position as an Acting Major General.

Dick O'Connor and Carton de Wiart soon became firm friends. O'Connor found him

> a remarkable man. He had all the qualities one would have expected from his reputation. Great courage, resolution and integrity, but added to them was a real kindness and understanding of human nature. He was the 'beau ideal' of the soldier or sailor of the late 17th or early 18th centuries. So I can well imagine him in the Indian campaigns of Clive and of Wellington, attacking whatever the odds. At Talavera, Salamanca, and at Waterloo he would have been in his element, and the charge of the Light Brigade he would have taken as a natural sequence in battle. As a sailor he would have had the 'Nelson touch'; 'Close with the enemy whatever the odds'. It would never have occurred to him to do anything else. He was impatient with modern tactics which he found too slow and too complicated. He would never have the patience to wait and build up an 'undefeatable preponderance'. His one idea was to get at the enemy in the shortest possible time. Risks for him existed only to be taken.[28]

Both men had gone through much of the First World War either in or just behind the frontline and had shared the dangers with their troops. Both were excellent horsemen and enjoyed traditional country pursuits. Although O'Connor's formal military education was far more extensive than Carton de Wiart's, they had in common the gift of leadership. The words used by Field Marshal Lord Harding in his address at O'Connor's memorial service in 1981 could have applied to either man: he was 'my ideal of a commander in battle; always approachable and ready to listen, yet firm and decisive and always fair in his judgment of people and events; modest to a degree, shunning the limelight, and embarrassed by praise; calmly resolute and courageously determined'.[29]

All was to change for the VIP prisoners in October when they were transferred to Camp Prigione di Guerra (PG) 12[30] in Florence, acquiring two more inmates in the course of the move, Lieutenant Dan Knox, 6th Earl of Ranfurly, and Lieutenant Victor Smith RNVR. In contrast to the relaxed atmosphere at Sulmona under the light touch of Colonel Damiani, their new quarters at the Castello di Vincigliata in Fiesole seemed more like a traditional prison.

> I thought it was the most horrible looking place I had ever seen. It was a fortress, nothing more or less, perched on the side of a wretched hill, surrounded by ramparts and high walls, bristling with sentries all armed to the teeth. Our hearts, which had risen so high at the idea of leaving Sulmona, sank within us; we were a silent, despondent bunch as we entered this vault of a prison.[31]

Purchased as a ruin in the mid-nineteenth century by the British politician and connoisseur John Temple Leader, the castle had been transformed into an imaginative replica of its medieval heyday by his Italian architect; such was its fame that none other than Queen Victoria had signed the visitors' book on 15 April 1888. The irony of its English heritage was not lost on its new inmates. The Commandant, Captain Francesco, Duke of Montalto, had been educated at Cheltenham College in England, so he spoke perfect English as well as understanding the public school traits of his British captives. However, the daily regime overseen by Colonel Bacci, the area Camp Commanding Officer, was far stricter than Orsini, with roll call twice a day, no privileges, no shopping trips or picnics and certainly no visits to the city's museums. Walks could only be taken in the afternoon and only then under heavy guard. The saving grace of the Castello was that it was large enough for every senior officer to have his own well-furnished room and for lovers of Italian history it offered wonderful views across the city to the Duomo.[32]

Carton de Wiart by now had recovered from his initial gloomy reaction and saw 'the actual move acted as a tremendous impetus and spur to our escape plans. From the moment we arrived . . . we never thought of anything else at all'.[33] Soon the keener escapees devised a punishing physical fitness programme which involved nightly walks up and down the 105 steps to the tower with loads on their backs, culminating in their passing out test of 75 ascents. The first plan conceived was a night escape by four officers – Boyd, O'Connor, Combe and Carton de Wiart. The idea was to wait for a dark and stormy night 'when the Castello would be creaking with ghostly noises',[34] then drop from the ramparts into the moat twenty feet below and scurry past the guardroom. All went well until a spot search caught the plotters out for they had foolishly put their plan on paper. Montalto had been dismissed for being too friendly and overfamiliar with his charges and his successor Captain Tranquille ordered floodlights to be installed around the perimeter. Vincigliata was beginning to look like Colditz. When O'Connor was later caught making a solo run by sliding down the ramparts on a rope, more floodlighting was installed, sentries doubled, and surfeits of barbed wire added to the perimeter defences. Carton de Wiart concluded 'there was only one thing left to us, to go underneath. Immediately we deflected our attention from the great outdoors to the possibilities within'.[35]

After a thorough survey of the castle and its cavernous cellars and complex of tunnels that were found to lead nowhere, the escape committee headed by Neame, a Royal Engineer, decided to dig a tunnel from the deserted chapel behind the dining room to a point underneath the ramparts. It was a daunting project, starting with a ten feet shaft which would lead to a thirty-five feet tunnel, four feet by two feet, dug on a 1:8 downward slope through hard-packed clay and strata of hard rock.[36] The escape party consisted of three pairs: Boyd and Combe; Brigadiers Hargest and Miles; and O'Connor and Carton de Wiart. With only one arm, Carton de Wiart's tunnelling ability was limited, so he took charge of the 'watchers' who provided early warning of sentries and searches. Gambier-Parry, an accomplished amateur artist, took on the task of creating forged documents and the other officers and ORs selflessly played an assortment of roles from staging rival noises to mask the sound of digging to installing electric lights in the tunnel. For seven months, four hours a day, the British POW community chiselled and burrowed their way towards freedom. It was a painstaking process, two foot nine inches being the best ever achieved in one week.

The Carton de Wiart clan in Belgium had been busy trying to arrange his repatriation[37] and had asked the Crown Princess of Italy, a daughter of King Albert of the Belgians, to negotiate on their behalf. She engaged Professor Aldo Castellani, the eminent pathologist and bacteriologist, who had been knighted by the British in 1928 for his services to tropical medicine and who was also the father-in-law of Sir Miles Lampson, the British ambassador to Egypt, to head a Medical Board to review Carton's case. John Leeming takes up the story:

> At last he came downstairs, stamped across the room where most of us were sitting, and flung open the door leading to the little room where the board sat waiting.
> 'Are you the Medical Board?' thundered Carton.
> 'Yes, yes, my General. We . . .'
> 'Well, then, bloody well blank off! Get out! D'hear me! Out with you, the whole blank lot!'
> One of the Board then made a most ill-advised remark. Approaching and putting his hand on Carton's arm, he said, 'Calm yourself, my General, calm yourself.'
> 'Calm myself!' roared Carton. 'Why you blank lot of blank, blank, blanks, . . .'
> Listening in the next room, we cowered under the stop. All of us except Neame: he sat unmoved sewing his tapestry. As he pushed the needle through the canvas he remarked thoughtfully, 'You know, if he talks to them like that, they won't repatriate him . . .'
> As Carton was at that moment expressing a fervent desire to tear the inside out of each member of the Board, Neame's surmise seemed highly probably.[38]

Carton de Wiart remained at Vincigliata and preparations commenced for the night of the escape. O'Connor, who had returned after completing his punishment of a month in solitary confinement in another PG, and Carton de Wiart planned to impersonate peasants from the Tyrol, not an impossible act as O'Connor's Italian had progressed well and he was familiar with the area from his time there in the First World War.

On the evening of 24 March 1943, after waiting for a suitable wet and windy night to cover their escape, conditions seemed perfect. Then the weather suddenly changed and Neame called it off. Disappointment all round ensued but the next night the bad weather returned, and it was back on. Ranfurly, who had replaced Combe, and Neame were first out of the tunnel with O'Connor and Carton de Wiart the last to go. 'As I crawled along that tunnel, I had no nostalgic feelings; I was praying that I might manage all the obstacles in front of me without holding the others back.'[39] As luck would have it, instead of having to climb over a barbed wire fence and then drop on to the road from a considerable height, they walked through a gate which had been unexpectedly left open and were on their way just after 9 pm.[40]

Switzerland lay some 200 miles away to the north and the pair made good progress, walking with their 25 lbs. packs all night and most of the following day along country roads, until they paused for the night in a farm having put thirty-two miles between themselves and the camp. Carton de Wiart's toe after the long march was in a poor state but he bandaged it up and they resumed their long march, this time through more populous countryside with soldiers in evidence everywhere as they approached Bologna. Stopping in villages to beg a bed for the night, they pressed on early each day and apart from being stopped once to show their papers – Carton de Wiart once more played the deaf mute – reached the Po valley. All was well until they were stopped by two Carabinieri on bicycles. After they had scrutinized their papers, the Carabinieri started to chat to O'Connor about Bologna, his hometown on his fake identity papers. As he had never been there in his life, 'we knew the game was up and when we informed our two captors of our (real) identity they nearly embraced us and were so overcome with joy that they insisted we should finish the journey to their HQ in a cart, making a triumphant entry'.[41]

Soon they were on their way back to Florence by train and on arriving at the Castello, were courteously welcomed back by Major Guillaume, the Commandant. They had covered 150 miles by foot over difficult country with heavy loads on their backs in the space of seven days. Of the other escapees, Hargest and Miles made it to Switzerland, Combe was picked up at Milan Central Station and Neame, within a few hundred metres of the Swiss border, was caught in a marshalling yard as he alighted from a goods train.

O'Connor and Carton de Wiart were both sentenced to a month's solitary confinement in their rooms in the castle[42] and they emerged just in time to hear about the fall of Mussolini. Apart from engineering the removal of the obnoxious Commandant Viviani, Guillaume's placement, by writing a disparaging report on him which was 'found' during a search, life became dull as all forms of escape were now out of the question for the guard had doubled and the Castello 'was practically in state of siege'.[43] Then one night in mid-August, the commandant summoned Carton de Wiart and told him he was to go to Rome the next day. No reason was given. Apart from wondering whether he was going to be shot, he remained in the dark until the next morning when he was ushered towards two large cars, the second being for his luggage. Dick O'Connor wrote, 'we all felt like going into mourning – friends and foes alike. Few people have claimed so much admiration and respect. The unconscious influence he exerted over his fellow men, young and old, was unique. He recognised a good man whether he was a friend or foe, nationality made no difference.'[44]

Aware of his new VIP status, all thoughts of death by firing squad vanished and on arrival in Rome, after being billeted in an apartment in a private palazzo, he met with Brigadier General Giacomo Zanussi, the Deputy Chief of Staff. Zanussi asked him to accompany him to England on a visit to discuss POWs and he would be obliged if he could wear plain clothes. Since Carton de Wiart had none, a tailor and shirt maker were immediately produced and the next day Zanussi took him to see General Mario Roatta. He was more direct and told Carton de Wiart that the Italians wanted an armistice and had already sent Brigadier General Giuseppe Castellano[45] to Lisbon to negotiate with the Allies. However, they had had no news from him, so he wished to despatch a second Mission.

Issued with a new Italian passport that stated he had been educated in Algeria, hence his fluent French, he flew with General Zanussi and his interpreter Lieutenant Mario Lanza to Seville and then to Lisbon where on their 'incognito' arrival they hired a taxi and peeled off at their respective embassies. Sir Ronald Campbell, the ambassador, gave Carton de Wiart a frosty reception for his unheralded appearance with General Zanussi had taken him by surprise. He cabled London on 26 August:

MOST SECRET

General Carton De Wiart has turned up in company with another Italian General. They left Rome by air yesterday and arrived in Lisbon this morning.

1. General C. De Wiart was released a few days ago from his prisoner [*sic*] camp, taken to Rome, fitted out with civilian clothes and Italian name

and diplomatic passport and told he was to accompany to Lisbon and if possible to London an Italian general who was empowered to parley armistice terms.

2. Italian General whose name is Zanussi is principal assistant to General Roatta who is Chief of the General Staff in Chief [*sic*] to General Ambennio (Ambrosio) who is Chief of Amy Staff.[46] General Zanussi knows all about General C and General C. De Wiart was told that the dove had been sent out (General C) but as it had not returned another was being despatched (General Z). In point of fact General C must have arrived (barring accidents) a few hours after the departure of General Z.

3. I have told General C. De Wiart in broad terms of the result of General C's visit and unless instructed by you to do so I see no point in receiving General Z as it might introduce unnecessary complications. General De Wiart will so inform General Z at late meeting arranged for tonight in the flat of a member of my staff. General Z will be told to remain here until it is certain that there is no message for him.[47]

Clearly Zanussi was unaware that General Castellano had already met with US General Bedell Smith, the American Chief of Staff at Allied Forces Headquarters (AFHQ); Brigadier Kenneth Strong, the British representative for AFHQ; and SOE's Colonel Roseberry together with Ambassador Campbell and George Kennan, the American Chargé d'Affaires, and that Castellano had left Lisbon by train on 23 August with a W/T set and codes to facilitate Allied negotiations with Marshal Badoglio. The desperation and anxiety of the Italians in sending Zanussi had almost reduced the negotiations to a Whitehall Theatre farce.

After hearing back from the Foreign Office, who instructed him to meet with Zanussi and to show him the comprehensive text of Eisenhower's terms rather that the 'short' military terms shown to Castellano,[48] Campbell instructed Carton de Wiart that Zanussi would have to go and see General Eisenhower in Algiers en route to Rome but Carton de Wiart could return home if he wished. That afternoon he met with Zanussi at the British Embassy and explained what had been decided and offered to return to Italy as a POW to stick to his side of the bargain. Zanussi would have none of it and after staying in the Assistant Military Attaché's flat for the next two days, Carton de Wiart was on a flight to Bristol. Strict security controls were in place when he touched down and he was whisked off to a safe house in Beaconsfield by Brigadier Norman Crockatt,[49] the head of MI5, where he was forbidden to communicate to the outside world. Still enjoying his VIP status, Carton de Wiart felt like the chief character in a

John Buchan thriller that night when he was driven through the blackout to brief Clement Attlee, who was deputizing for Churchill who was in Quebec. The Director of Military Intelligence, Major General Davidson,[50] then debriefed him about Zanussi and told him that the Italian was a bad hat. Somewhat taken aback, Carton de Wiart replied that in the course of their brief acquaintance, he had formed a particularly good opinion of him and that this should go on the record. Days later it turned out that the War Office had given Davidson the wrong file.

Driven back down to Beaconsfield, it was not until the night of 7 September when the armistice became public news that Carton de Wiart was free to surface, and he headed for London's West End where he rented a flat. To his discomfort, he found himself something of a celebrity, a role he loathed, and soon began to fret as to whether he would be employed again. Yugoslavia still beckoned particularly as guerrilla activity had dramatically increased since the spring of 1941. Then, 'into the middle of rapidly advancing boredom came a ray of light. A message from Mr Winston Churchill to come down to Chequers and stay the night'.[51]

Churchill had in fact already welcomed Carton de Wiart back, albeit it indirectly when he mentioned him in his War Situation speech in the House of Commons on 21 September:

> In the interval another Italian general arrived, bringing with him as his credentials no less a person than General Carton de Wiart, V.C., one of our most famous military figures, whom the Italians captured two years ago through a forced landing in the Mediterranean. This second mission, however, did not affect the general course of events, and when General de Wiart [sic] realised this he immediately offered to return to captivity. The Italian officer, however, rejected this proposal, and General Carton de Wiart is now safe and free in this country.[52]

HM The King was also delighted that Carton de Wiart was back and summoned him for an audience at Buckingham Palace on 24 September. The press feted his new freedom with stories in both the national and regional papers; in modern parlance, Carton de Wiart was now a A-list celebrity and one of Britain's best-known soldiers. On 9 December 1943, he was awarded a Mention in Despatches for 'gallant and distinguished service in the field'.[53]

Part IX

China 1943–6

14

A dragon's pool and a tiger's den
The China brief

Driven by General Ismay to Chequers, Carton de Wiart was soon closeted with Churchill in his room and flattered to be offered the position of the prime minister's personal representative to Generalissimo Chiang Kai-shek. It was a typical Churchillian appointment based on his trust in Carton de Wiart's loyalty, shrewdness and integrity, the more so since by Carton de Wiart's own admission, 'China had never figured in my book of reckonings and I imagined it as a long way off, full of whimsical little people with quaint customs who carved lovely little jade ornaments and worshipped their grandmothers.'[1] Over the next three weeks, Carton de Wiart and Major General Herbert Lumsden,[2] whom Churchill had selected as his personal representative to US General Douglas MacArthur of South West Pacific Command, were inducted into the political and military aspects of their respective theatres, 'soaking themselves in the past papers' in a room in the War Office. Both officers were given the rank of Lieutenant General.[3]

There was much to learn. Under the Qing Dynasty, China had been the most powerful nation in the Far East for nearly three centuries (1644–1912) although the Emperor's territorial authority had been challenged in the nineteenth century by the British and other Western powers leading to the so-called unequal treaties and treaty ports. The loss of Korea as a result of the First Sino-Japanese War in 1895 and the humiliating cession of Taiwan to Japan the same year sent a signal of weakness to the European powers. When two German missionaries were murdered in Juye in November 1897, the Kaiser attacked Qingdao, effectively establishing a German colony in Shandong province; the British created a Chinese Regiment to garrison their naval station at Weihaiwei; and the Russians appropriated Port Arthur. The ill-judged decision of the Empress Dowager Cixi to back the Boxer rebellion, a nationalist reaction against the incursions of the Europeans, led to a further weakening of the dynasty and the rise of Japan as the preeminent power in the Far East. After a succession of rebellions, in 1912 six-

year-old Puyi, the twelfth and final Qing emperor, abdicated in favour of Sun
Yat-sen's short-lived Republic of China which was soon usurped by General
Yuan Shi-kai who reintroduced a hereditary monarchy. By 1917, the vast country
had been convulsed by internal power struggles as competing *junfa* or 'warlords'
sought to carve out their political and territorial dominance; the politicians in
Beijing soon became dependent on regional military governors for their support
and political survival.

These seismic internal political shocks constrained China's freedom of
movement when war broke out in Europe in 1914. Unlike Japan, still riding high
on its military reputation after the 1905 Russo-Japanese War, which had joined
the Entente in August 1914 at the invitation of the British and was busy helping
itself to German leased-territories in the Far East including Shandong, China had
declared itself neutral for there were no suitors. By the beginning of 1916 with
British losses continuing to increase on the Western Front, the British Minister
in Beijing, Sir John Jordan, told General Shi-kai that China would be welcome
to join the Entente provided that Japan and the other allies agreed. Given that
the previous year Japan had presented China with the so-called Twenty-One
Demands which if implemented in full would have reduced China to little more
than a Japanese protectorate, it came as no surprise when Japan refused to agree
to Chinese soldiers fighting for the Entente.

Determined to have a seat at the top table and in the hope of recovering
Shandong, Beijing countered with an offer to send voluntary non-combatant
workers to provide a logistical labour force; by late 1916, thousands of Chinese
men, mostly illiterate peasants from Shandong, began arriving in Britain,
France and Russia, 'recruited' under arrangements made by civilian companies
for China was still neutral. By the end of the war, 37,000 had been recruited
by the French and 94,500 by the British; their contribution covered the entire
logistics spectrum from digging support trenches and assembling munitions to
transporting supplies and repairing tanks. When the United States entered the
war in 1917, China officially declared war on the Central Powers to ensure she
had a voice at the eventual peace agreements.

When the invitations for delegates to the Peace Conference in Paris were sent
out in 1918, China fielded five plenipotentiary delegates. Led by Foreign Minister
Lou Tseng-Tsiang, ably assisted by V. K. Wellington Koo, their Ambassador to
Washington, the Chinese demanded that Germany return Shandong province
to them although under the 1898 Convention of Beijing there was no legal
obligation to do so until 1997. Encouraged by President Wilson and his laudable
ideals, Chinese expectations were running high;[4] in an impassioned speech on

28 January 1919, Wellington Koo described Shandong as 'the cradle of Chinese civilization, and, as the birthplace of Confucius and Mencius, "a Holy Land for the Chinese".[5] What he didn't know at the time was that there were no less than six secret treaties which China had signed with Japan, Great Britain, France, Russia and Italy; the two with Japan conferred on Tokyo political and economic rights over Shandong.[6] Once made public, the omission of these treaties undermined confidence in the Chinese advocacy for their cause. When the Treaty of Versailles recognized the legitimacy of the Japanese seizure of Shandong in 1915 and transferred the German concession to Tokyo, Lou Tseng-Tsiang refused to sign. Predictably, a virulent nationalist reaction epitomized by the student-led May Fourth Movement in Beijing swept through China and helped revive the flagging republican revolution. It certainly gave a fillip to the newly formed Chinese Communist Party (CCP) which was quick to cast Western capitalist governments as the bogeymen. The issue was eventually resolved at the Washington Naval Conference in 1922 when, in exchange for naval parity in the Pacific with both Britain and the United States, Japan agreed for Shandong to revert to Chinese control.

Meanwhile in China, the nascent Republic continued to struggle to control the avaricious and increasingly audacious warlords like Zhang Zongchang and Feng Yuxiang as China dissolved in to 'a hodgepodge of nearly independent states'.[7] Exacerbated by the devastating famine in Northern China in the 1920s, the outlook became so dire that the Kuomintang Nationalist Party (KMT) and the CCP joined forces by forming the First United Front which incorporated their armed forces into the National Revolutionary Army, armed and trained by a Soviet Military Mission led by Mikhail Borodin. It was only in the late 1920s, after the death of Sun Yat-sen, that the KMT under Generalissimo Chiang Kai-shek managed to start to reunify the country on his famous 1926 Northern Expedition. Unity proved short lived when the CCP refused to acknowledge Chiang's government in Nanjing, his new capital: in response, the KMT turned on them in 1927 and purged several thousand leftists. The following year, Chiang set off to complete the expedition, this time with 1 million men under arms. However, the real threat was existential.

Tension between Japan and Nationalist China had been growing since the Japanese invasion of Manchuria in 1931 and the subsequent creation of a nominally independent state, Manchukuo, with Puyi, the last monarch of the Qing Dynasty, as its sovereign. At the end of 1932, the Japanese army invaded Rehe Province and annexed it to Manchukuo. Then, in 1935, Japan officially established the East Hebei Autonomous Council, turning the Chinese provinces of Hebei and Chahar into a puppet state. By early 1937 all the areas north, east and west of Beijing were controlled by Japan. Whereas the intentions of Japan were starkly clear to both the CCP and the KMT, their priorities were diametrically different. The CCP needed a war with Japan to escape defeat at the hands of Chiang; the KMT needed to defeat the CCP and solidify their political and military position before they took on the Japanese.

When a clash occurred between Chinese and Japanese troops outside Beijing near the Marco Polo Bridge in July 1937, the looming military confrontation became a reality and the horror of a full-scale twentieth-century air bombardment and ground invasion was unleashed on China, signalling the notional start of the Second World War. A disastrous defeat for the Generalissimo followed at Shanghai in October when he lost over half of his professional officer corps and then a horrified world watched the fall of Nanking in December 1937 with its gruesome mass killings and rape of civilians when an estimated in excess of 100,000 Chinese were massacred.[8]

China still had about 3,820,000 men under arms. Of these, 2,920,000 were formed into 246 divisions classed by the Chinese as 'front-line' troops, plus forty-four 'brigades'. In rear areas there were another seventy divisions and three brigades. Except for the Generalissimo's personal troops, estimated at about thirty divisions, the loyalties of China's troops tended to lie with their war area commanders for the influence of the traditional *junfa* was never far from the surface.

After the departure of Borodin's Russian Military Mission in 1928, Chiang's armies needed not only a new supplier of weapons and munitions but even more a wholescale modernization programme in order to position China as a key player in the balance of power in East Asia. The obvious partner to approach was Germany with whom Sun Yat-sen had previously been in touch as a fellow victim of Versailles; the Germans had modern armaments required by Beijing and the Chinese had huge supplies of raw material for German industry.[9] As early as 1929, German industry acquired 88 per cent of its antimony and 53 per cent of its tungsten through private trade with China.

Banned from sending military advisers abroad, Germany imitated the Chinese labour contracts of the First World War and all its advisers were officers who had resigned and were contracted directly by the Nanking government. The Generalissimo's first German adviser, the charismatic and clever Colonel Max Bauer, grasped Chiang's vision of the need to create a modern military–industrial state and drew up plans accordingly. When Bauer unexpectedly died the following year, his second-in-command Lieutenant Colonel Hermann

Kriebel took over but was soon ousted by Chiang in favour of General Georg Wetzell, a former head of the Reichswehr General Staff. Within a short time, a fully equipped and trained all-arms 'exemplary division' or *Lehrtruppe* had been formed as a seed unit to indoctrinate China's military in the German way of war.

With the rise of Hitler, the role of the Mission came into question as Japan emerged as a potential ally who could be relied upon to open a second front in the East in the event of a German attack on Russia and also to threaten the British Empire in South East Asia and India. Wetzell resigned and was replaced by the seventy-year-old Prussian General Hans von Seeckt who had built up the Reichswehr after Versailles. Observing that the Generalissimo had too many rather that too few troops, in 1935 the ailing general returned to Germany to recover his health, leaving his Chief of Staff, the aristocratic General Alexander von Falkenhausen, in charge of the Mission. This immensely able and experienced officer with a deep knowledge of both Japan and China realized that the prospect of a new Sino-Japanese War looked increasingly likely and did his utmost to maintain trade links and arms exports.[10] It was only in early 1938, that Hitler, under pressure from Japan, recalled the entire Mission and cancelled all trade contracts. Over a hundred former German army officers had rotated through the German Military Mission between 1928 and 1938; they had equipped and trained Chiang's best troops but more importantly, they had given him and his army the confidence to engage Japan on the battlefield.

Having lost his ports and access to the sea to the Japanese, the Generalissimo needed a supply route to the rest of the world, so he ordered a road built from Kunming to Lashio in Burma. The 681-mile road was built by tens of thousands of Chinese labourers in a year and a half and was opened to traffic in mid-1939. Supplies for Chiang's government and troops were shipped by sea to Rangoon, then by rail to Lashio, and finally by road to Kunming. It was aptly called the Burma Road, and it was Nationalist China's main source of supply from the outside world for two and a half years – from mid-1939 to 8 March 1942, the day Rangoon fell to the Japanese.

Throughout the 1930s, the British had been playing it safe in trying to protect their Far East investments and yet not alienate Japan. Steering a middle course through the invasion of Manchuria where British interests were outweighed by her need to maintain cordial relations with Japan, the government despatched its chief economic adviser, Sir Frederick Leith-Ross, to Tokyo in September 1935 with the idea of promoting economic co-operation between the two countries in China. Little resulted from this bold initiative to bring Japan back into the international fold but talks were revived when a Federation of Japanese

Economic Organizations Mission came to London in July 1937 to meet with UK industrialists and bankers. Unfortunately, the Marco Polo bridge incident happened the same week which promptly curtailed discussions.

Despite its major investments and trade flows with China, Britain had to remain on the side-line when it came to military support for the KMT simply because she was in the process of rearming herself and there were no weapons or munitions to spare. However, Britain did allow Hong Kong to be used as the main entry port for shipments of arms to the KMT until this channel was cut by the Japanese capture of Canton on 21 October 1938 and the closure of the Kowloon–Canton railway.

Sir Archibald Clark Kerr, HM Ambassador to China, was under no illusions about the state of affairs in China. Writing to the Foreign Secretary in January 1941, he drew attention to the review of China in 1940 by Sir Arthur Blackburn, the Embassy Counsellor in Chongqing.

> While Japan has been free to draw upon the outside world, China has seen nearly all sources dry up. Of late the Japanese military effort has been almost entirely designed to bring this about. The blocking of the ports of Fukien and Chekiang and of the hinterlands of Hong Kong and Macao, and the seizure of Tonkin have barred routes by which a regular and considerable flow of imports entered China, while the loss of Ichang has dislocated her internal system of distribution. The effect has been to leave China in poor case. Her large armies have been deprived of nearly all of their offensive power and reduced to an inactivity from which they cannot emerge unless by some supreme effort, it may prove impossible to keep them supplied by the Burma Road. Nevertheless, by the sheer weight of numbers, they continue to contain in China very large enemy forces which Japan would now like to set free for use elsewhere.

Financially Britain did its best in 1939. British banks under a Treasury guarantee provided half of a £10 million currency stabilization fund to thwart Japanese attempts to undermine the Chinese currency and replace it with one under their own control. A further £5 million was added to the fund in December 1940 and a £5 million credit for use in the sterling area granted in June 1941. In 1942, the government made available a loan of £50 million. As Sir John Pratt, the Foreign Office's Adviser on Far Eastern Affairs, wrote in *War and Politics in China*,[11] 'this assistance was enough to keep Chinese resistance alive but not enough to enable her to drive the invader from her soil.'

Being less exposed to the imminent threat of Japanese militarism, the American stance towards China had been more overtly supportive in contrast to the British. When hostilities commenced in 1937, President Roosevelt did not invoke the 1937 Neutrality Act on the grounds that neither party had formally declared war. This enabled American supplies to reach the KMT albeit in British 'bottoms'. In two loans in 1939, the American Export-Import Bank lent the Chinese-owned Universal Trading Corporation $45 million, although its use was restricted soley to the purchase of civilian supplies. In June 1940 Chiang Kai-shek's brother-in-law, T. V. Soong, visited the United States to ask for arms and came away with a credit of $25 million.[12]

In November 1940, the Generalissimo sent another Mission under Air Force General Mao Pang-tzo to the United States. With him was the retired American Army Air Corps flier, Captain Claire Chennault. The Mao Mission put in a request to the President's Liaison Committee for 500 combat planes to be flown by American volunteers (AVG). Although the AVG was not supported by lend-lease funds – the Lend-Lease bill was signed off by the President on 11 March 1941 – both the War and Navy Departments extended facilities for recruiting agents and released pilots and crews for service in China's Air Force. When the first volunteers arrived on 28 July, they were sent to the RAF airfield at Toungoo in Burma, with the proviso that the airfield would not be used as a base to attack the Japanese.

Then on 3 July 1941, General Marshall approved the American Military Mission to China (AMMISCA). Its head, Brigadier General John Magruder, was tasked 'to advise and assist the Chinese government in all phases of procurement, transport, and maintenance of materials, equipment, and munitions requisite to the prosecution of its military effort'. Furthermore, he was to 'assist in the training of Chinese personnel in the use and maintenance of materials, equipment, and munitions supplied by the United States' and 'to insure the orderly flow of materials and munitions from lend-lease agencies to the Chinese military forces'. The War Department released its first shipment of ammunition to the Chinese at the end of August 1941 and on 13 September the first group of AMMISCA personnel flew into Chongqing. From the Chinese perspective, the United States was now its 'number one' ally who delivered meaningful military and financial support. Meanwhile the British had sat on the military sidelines and done nothing.

After the Japanese attack on Pearl Harbour in December 1941, the United States saw its main role in China as keeping the country in the war for so long as it stayed in, hundreds of thousands of Japanese soldiers would be tied down on the Chinese mainland instead of being used to fight on other fronts. To that end, the aim was to deliver sufficient equipment, weapons and munitions to build thirty well-equipped and trained Chinese divisions.

In contrast to the Americans, the British had lost face with the Chinese. On 23 December 1941, together with Major General Brett, Chief of the American Air Corps, General Wavell, the British Commander-in-Chief, had gone to Chongqing to see the Generalissimo who offered him his 5th and 6th Armies for the defence of Burma and specifically the vital Burma Road. Wary of the quality of Chinese troops and of the huge administrative tail which would accompany them, Wavell suggested that one division up front and a regiment in reserve would be sufficient with the proviso they were supplied throughout by China. He returned to Rangoon on Christmas Day just as the Japanese were entering Hong Kong, the first of a number of British imperial humiliations that were about to follow.

The Generalissimo later complained to Roosevelt about Wavell's lukewarm response to his offer and in hindsight it was clear that, through no fault of his own, he had misread the politics as the British were out of kilter with the American vision to promote China as 'a Great Power' on the world stage. Relations with Chongqing did not improve when Wavell ordered the appropriation of Lend-Lease supplies sitting on the dockside in Rangoon. As it turned out, both Chinese Armies were eventually involved by default in the defence of Burma but to no avail.

This then was the story of the complex political landscape in China that Carton de Wiart had to digest before heading off to the Far East that autumn. He was fortunate to find an old China hand, Major R. H. Dowler of the Intelligence Corps, as his personal Staff Officer. Together with Lumsden's party, the two officers prepared to leave by air for India on 18 October but not before the Ministry of Information had organized a photographic session with Yousuf Karsh, the world-famous photographer who had arrived in London from Canada on 12 September. Already famous throughout Britain for his 1941 portrait of Winston Churchill in Ottawa – Churchill himself disapproved of it for his cigar had been taken off him for the shoot – Karsh found Carton de Wiart 'one of the most picturesque figures I ever photographed'.[13] His final engagement was to attend the reception in the Dorchester Hotel for the Viceroy-designate and Lady Wavell.

After a four-day delay in Cornwall due to bad weather, they finally reached New Delhi on 30th which 'had sprung up like a mushroom, and although sumptuous'[14] it did not appeal to Carton de Wiart for his old distaste for India had not gone away and he 'disliked the place as much as I had before'.[15] Finding that his house in Chongqing was not yet ready, he had no option other than to mark time in Delhi and so he set off to glean as much information as he could about the progress of the war. Having never met Field Marshal Viscount Wavell apart from a brief encounter in London, the Viceroy's House was his first port of call and the two men established a cordial working relationship that was to stand Carton de Wiart in good stead over the next two years. Visits to General Sir Claude Auchinleck, C-in-C India, and to Major General Orde Wingate, the Chindit leader who was laid up with enteric fever in the Viceroy's House, followed and in the course of his rounds he struck up an enduring friendship with John Keswick of the Jardine Matheson trading conglomerate who had close links to SOE.

Just as he was beginning to get bored waiting in Delhi, Carton de Wiart was ordered to Cairo where the SEXTANT conference between the United States, Britain and China was to be held. During the spring and summer of 1943, President Roosevelt had grown increasingly concerned that China could give up its fight and fall to the continuous Japanese onslaught, so he had proposed the Cairo conference as a means of expressing public confidence in the Republic of China. The conference itself was a stopover on the way to meet the Soviet leader Marshal Joseph Stalin at the EUREKA conference in Tehran.

Since the Generalissimo would be passing through India, Carton de Wiart went down to meet him[16] at the American airbase at Agra but as the plane was delayed, he decided to leave the airfield. Minutes later, the Generalissimo's plane landed so he followed the Chinese party to their hotel and managed to see him. 'I could not help but be tremendously impressed. . . . Although he was a small man, he had a great deal of simple dignity without any form of show, most unusual in dictators, who need an ornate façade to help to build them up to their worshipping publics.'[17]

Peter Fleming who had worked with Carton de Wiart in Norway and was now in New Delhi as Head of D Division, the strategic and tactical deception unit, had met Chiang Kai-shek before the war:

> He came into the room quietly, and stood quite still, looking at us. . . . He was of rather more than average height, and unexpectedly slim. His complexion was dark, the cheek-bones high and prominent, and he had a jutting, forceful lower lip like a Habsburg's. His eyes were the most remarkable thing about him. They were large, handsome and very keen – almost aggressive. His glances had a thrusting and compelling quality which is very rare in China, where eyes are mostly negative and non-committal, if not actually evasive . . . it was obvious that Chiang Kai-shek enjoyed the sound of his own voice far less than most politicians, in China and elsewhere. He was not the usual type of glib and rather impressive propaganda-monger; he did not cultivate salesmanship. . . . Here was a man with a presence, with that something incalculable to him to which the

herd instinctively defers. He was strong and silent by nature, not by artifice. . . .
. He may not be a great statesman, or a very great soldier; events may prove that
the best that can be said of him is that he has been the effective head of the best
government China has had since the revolution...But at any rate Chiang Kai-
shek has something to him. He is a personality in his own right. He is not only
not a mediocrity or a wind-bag, but he could never look like one. That, I think,
entitles him to a certain singularity among modern political leaders.[18]

The next morning, Carton de Wiart returned to Delhi and soon after left
for Cairo where the conference was due to start on 22 November. The
Generalissimo's entourage, which had arrived on the evening of 21st, consisted
of Madame Chiang Kai-shek; General Shang Chen, Chief of the General Office
and the Foreign Affairs Bureau (National Military Council of China); Lieutenant
General Lin Wei, Chief of the Office of Aide-de-Camp to the Generalissimo;
and Major General Chu Shi-ming, Military Attaché Washington. Of the four,
Madame Chiang was by far the most important. The sister-in-law of Sun Yat-
sen, the first President of the Chinese Republic, the US-educated Soong Meiling ('Meiling') had married Chiang in 1927 and acted as his English translator,
secretary and advisor. Very much the power behind the throne, she had worked
closely with the Americans over many years, on one occasion addressing a joint
session of Congress in March 1934. She was ambivalent about the British, whom
she viewed as minor actors on the stage of the war in the Far East and die-hard
imperialists. When W. H. Auden and Christopher Isherwood met her in March
1938, they described her as 'a small, round-faced lady, exquisitely dressed,
vivacious rather than pretty, and possessed of an almost terrifying charm and
poise'.[19]

    After two years as a POW in Italy, Carton de Wiart suddenly found himself
at the top table of world leaders and their advisers. Along with General Sir Alan
Brooke, the CIGS and Chairman of the Chiefs of Staff Committee, Field Marshal
Sir John Dill, the Senior British Representative on the Combined Chiefs of
Staff, and General Sir Pug Ismay, his old colleague from Somaliland who was
principal military advisor to the prime minister, he attended the American–
British Preliminary Meeting on the evening of 22 November; and the next day
the Plenary session in the morning followed by the Combined Chiefs of Staff
that afternoon. As he pithily put it, 'I cannot confess to have profited much from
the experience (but) it did give me an insight into things I knew nothing about.'[20]

    Aside from the American diplomatic rhetoric and schmoozing of the Chiang
Kai-sheks, there was little substance to the Conference which was held in the
Mena House Hotel by the Pyramids. Admiral Lord Louis Mountbatten, the

newly appointed Supreme Allied Commander South East Asia (SACSEA) whom Carton de Wiart had last come across in 1940 as a destroyer captain in Namsos fjord, outlined his plans for an advance on the Arakan front in Burma in the New Year and a concurrent advance on Minthami, Mawlaik and Sittang. He then covered the planned southward thrust by US General Stilwell's Chinese forces from Ledo in February and the role that Major General Wingate's daring new expedition would play in disrupting and confusing the Japanese. He finished with an update on the air supply route over the 'hump' which he hoped would reach 10,000 tons a month. The session then turned to the war at sea and the vague British promise to assemble a formidable fleet in due course in the Indian Ocean which, when used in conjunction with Mountbatten's 'amphibious circus',[21] could prove a game changer. The Generalissimo saw Burma as the key to the whole campaign in the South East Asia and ventured that the Japanese would fight stubbornly and tenaciously to retain their hold on it.[22]

By the evening of Friday 26 November, SEXTANT was over and the American and British delegations prepared to move on to Tehran the next day to meet with Stalin. The statement issued at the end of the SEXTANT conference read:

> The Three Great Allies are fighting this war to restrain and punish the aggression of Japan. They covet no gain for themselves and have no thought of territorial expansion. It is their purpose that Japan shall be stripped of all the islands in the Pacific which she has seized or occupied since the beginning of the first World War in 1914, and that all the territories Japan has stolen from the Chinese, such as Manchuria, Formosa, and The Pescadores, shall be restored to the Republic of China. Japan will also be expelled from all other territories which she has taken by violence and greed. The aforesaid three great powers, mindful of the enslavement of the people of Korea, are determined that in due course Korea shall become free and independent.
>
> With these objects in view the three Allies, in harmony with those of the United Nations at war with Japan, will continue to persevere in the serious and prolonged operations necessary to procure the unconditional surrender of Japan.[23]

Behind the scenes, there had been some useful exchanges of information. The US Joint Staff Planners noted that

> though the Japanese were able to stop the United Nations advance into Burma during the 1942-43 dry season, they probably realise that because of the desire to retain China as an ally and to build up in China for air operations against the Japanese mainland, the United Nations will again carry out offensive operations

this year… However, the Japanese, realising the threat of an Allied advance into Burma, have substantially reinforced that area. The deployment of their forces is generally defensive but the launching of a limited offensive by the Japanese to disrupt Allied plans is a possibility.[24]

Probability would have been a better word.

Carton de Wiart was not the only new face at Cairo for Lord Louis Mountbatten was a recent arrival as well. When he arrived in Delhi to take up his new role of SACSEA on 7 October 1943,[25] mindful of Churchill's directive 'to maintain and broaden our contacts with China', he flew up to Chongqing to meet the Generalissimo on 18/19 October. The creation of SEAC made the command relationships even more complicated than they had been before. Within it there were now three geographic theatres and one operational theatre, representing the interests of three nations and their three military services, all operating in the same area. SEAC was an Anglo-American command which included Burma, Ceylon, Sumatra and Malaya, but not India which was under General Sir Claude Auchinleck's India Command.[26] The Generalissimo's theatre was China. The American administrative theatre, China-Burma-India (CBI), headed by US General Joseph Stilwell, operated across all three geographic areas. It was not subordinate to SEAC.

To make matters even more complicated, the Northern Combat Area Command (NCAC), a joint US and Chinese formation commanded by Stilwell, was based on India Command, and fought in SEAC's area notionally under SEAC command. The US Fourteenth Air Force was based in China, supplied from India, and formally under the command of the Generalissimo. As an exercise in political compromise, this Byzantine command structure was far from perfect. The historian Louis Allen dubbed it 'a Lewis Carroll absurdity'.[27]

Nearly all the inter-Allied military organizations in the Second World War were characterized by personality clashes between commanders and their subordinates and none more so than in South East Asia and China. When he met Stilwell in Cairo, Carton de Wiart found him 'undoubtedly a personality … that of a fighting soldier and no more, and he was an extremely hard man to deal with. He had strong and definite ideas of what he wanted, but no facility for putting them forward'.[28] He wrote to Ismay that 'on the surface he (Stilwell) is all honey, underneath a particularly vile form of vinegar'.[29]

Three years younger than Carton de Wiart, Stilwell had grown up in New York and attended West Point. In the First World War, he had been the US Fourth Corps intelligence officer in France and then went on to do three tours in China, the last as Military Attaché in 1935. Earmarked to plan and lead the Allied

Invasion of North Africa in 1942, on the recommendation of General Marshall he was reassigned by President Roosevelt at short notice to be the Chief of Staff to Chiang Kai-shek; the job also included command of the China-Burma-India theatre and responsibility for all Lend-Lease supplies going into China. After the war, General Marshall recognized that this was 'one of the most difficult' roles given to any US commander.

There was an underlying truth to this in the context of the sheer scale of the Chinese landmass and its almost 1 billion people but Stilwell's arrogance was a hindrance from the beginning. Abrasive, opinionated and scheming, he decided from the first day of his appointment to be confrontational towards the Generalissimo and to be dismissive and derogatory of Chinese military capability and leadership. He told Teddy White of *Time* magazine that 'the trouble in China is simple. We are allied to an ignorant, illiterate, superstitious, peasant son of a bitch'.[30] It was an extraordinary remark by a man who was on his way to be Chief of Staff to the Commander-in-Chief of a foreign army. Carton de Wiart correctly decided to keep his distance, writing to Mountbatten that 'he abuses the Chinese wholeheartedly from the Generalissimo downwards, says he is nothing but a coolie, and should be treated as such. . . .It is ridiculous to think one can treat a man who has risen to the position the Generalissimo has, as if he were a coolie'.[31]

In contrast to Stilwell, Carton de Wiart warmed to General Claire Chennault. A Southerner from Louisiana, Chennault had learnt to fly with the US Army Air Service in the First World War and continued his service after the war until he resigned on account of ill health and general disillusionment with life in the US military. A dedicated aviator, he joined a small group of Americans training Chinese pilots in China and by 1938, the Generalissimo had asked him to train and organize a new Chinese Air Force along American lines. This led to the creation of the AVG of 300 pilots and mechanics funded by the US government which later became known as Chennault's 'Flying Tigers'. By the time Stilwell arrived, Chennault had been fighting the Japanese in China for five years and was held in great esteem by both the Generalissimo and Meiling. From the beginning, Chennault and Stilwell were at loggerheads over strategy; inevitably the Generalissimo found himself sandwiched between the two. When President Roosevelt asked both commanders for their opinion of Chiang in a meeting in 1943, Stilwell stated: 'He's a vacillating, tricky, undependable old scoundrel who never keeps his word.' Chennault by contrast told Roosevelt: 'Sir, I think the Generalissimo is one of the two or three greatest military and political leaders in the world today. He has never broken a commitment or promise to me.'[32]

Six weeks after arriving in India, Carton de Wiart was finally on his way and with Major Dowler, his ADC 24-year-old Captain Donald Eckford,[33] a clerk, a batman and a 'a vast quantity of stores' boarded an RAF plane to take them over the 'hump' to Kunming. Ironically, his departure was overseen by Air Marshal Sir John Baldwin who had so cheerfully despatched him from the airfield in Newmarket two and a half years ago. This time there was no engine failure and the aircraft landed safely at Chongqing via Kunming on 14 December after an incident free flight over the 'hump'. Peter Fleming vividly describes landing there:

> In the winter, before the Tibetan snows had melted and swollen the Yangste, you landed on a sandbank in mid-stream, below the level of the lowest houses in this rat-coloured city. Chongqing clings to the escarpments on which it is built at an angle steeper than is to be found in any Cornish fishing village, and on the opposite side of the river its suburbs are disposed among the little jagged, tufted, willow-pattern mountains which cover so much of Szechwan. Night was generally falling when the Dakota slid past the half-seen hilltops for its run-in down the tortuous river gorge. Its headlights made an endless silver tunnel in the slanting rain, but at last, far ahead, one saw the foreshortened ribbon of illumination which marked the airstrip on the long sandbank. The city was blacked out [for this was wartime], but if you looked out of the window you could see the lights of cars moving along unseen streets above you, and not very far away. A few seconds later, as the Dakota wheeled at the end of the runway and taxied back towards a cluster of matting sheds which would vanish when the river began to rise, you were actually a shade nearer sea-level than any of the several million inhabitants on which you had descended from the air.[34]

Met at the airfield by General Chen Cheng, one of the Generalissimo's right-hand men, Carton de Wiart was taken to a house at Hua Ling Chiao which had been placed at his disposal. Situated at the bottom of a hill just outside the town, its position was far from ideal and when he spotted another house standing empty some hundred foot above it, he asked General Chen Cheng whether he could have it instead. Chen explained that they had considered it but felt that the 120 steps up to it were far from ideal; they did not know about the passing out test of 75 ascents at PG 12! Happy to accede to Carton de Wiart's request, the Chinese changed the residences and the British general's party settled in. The city was far from peaceful. General Wedemeyer recalled that on his second night there 'sirens blew, masses of people scurried into caves located along the steep cliffs on which the town is built. Sometimes a bomb would strike near the entrance to a shelter, sealing it and burying the people alive . . . the Japanese could bomb with impunity, particularly just before nightfall'.[35]

Carton de Wiart was soon made to feel at home. Lady Seymour, the wife of Sir Horace Seymour the Ambassador, gave a cocktail party for him where he met leading members of the Chinese community and the various diplomats accredited to the KMT government. 'Almost at once I felt the warmth and friendliness given out by this far country and her people; I felt they accepted me as a person, irrespective of my job or nationality.' He enjoyed going through the streets at night 'lined with vendors, whose little stalls were lit by tiny flaming torches which imbued their wares with a mysterious attraction they did not have by day'. As the house was halfway into the country, he could walk straight into the hills 'clad only in shorts and sandals and be sure of not meeting any other official'. Domestically he lived in real comfort, 'bordering on luxury, considering the times of stress. I had a most excellent staff, with a wonderful Chinese cook who cooked European food as skilfully as Chinese . . . I made it my practice to give frequent dinner parties to ten or twelve guests.'[36] On one side, his neighbours were Mr R. C. Chen, a director of the Bank of China, and his wife, 'one of the smartest and most attractive women in society' and on the other Mr T.V. Soong, the brother of Madame Chiang and a close confidant of the Generalissimo although not always in favour.

It was desirable if not essential for Carton de Wiart to strike up a friendship with the British Ambassador and fortunately the two men hit it off from the very beginning. Having served in the United States, the Netherlands, Italy and Tehran and at one stage been Principal Private Secretary to the Foreign Secretary, Seymour had been appointed Ambassador to China in 1942, just when British prestige was at an all-time low after the embarrassing defeats in Hong Kong, Singapore and Malaya. Like Carton de Wiart, his ready grasp and sympathetic understanding of Chinese problems from their point of view made him a highly effective conduit to the British government of the Generalissimo's mindset and aspirations.

From the outset, Carton de Wiart found the superior attitude of 'China hands', the foreigners who had been in China for some time, irksome as they treated him as a total ignoramus about the country and its people. To them, the Chinese were a race apart 'quite unlike any other living mortals'; this provided them with a ring-fenced area of expertise from where they could pontificate unchallenged. He saw life rather differently: 'to me there was no difference: they had the same loves, the same hates, the same tragedies, hopes and despairs, and I found it was only their customs which were different, not their characters.'[37]

After a few weeks, the enormity of the distances he had to travel flagged up the need for a personal aircraft as it was clearly impractical to rely on the

Americans to keep providing a plane for him although they were more than happy to do so. He asked Mountbatten to arrange one but the RAF said it would take several months to deliver, so he appealed to Churchill. Nevertheless, there was still a long delay and it was half way through March 1944 when Carton de Wiart received a signal from the prime minister telling him, 'I am informed that your aircraft has left for Kunming and that all arrangements for supplying it with petrol, oil and spares in China have been made. Pray report to me when the machine arrives and whether everything is satisfactory.'[38] The Wellington duly arrived at Kunming[39] but had an accident during landing when its tail geodetics were damaged by stones on the runway. After repairs, it completed 2 trips to Ceylon, 3,000 miles each way, before it crashed on landing at Chongqing and 'completely flattened out'. All its passengers emerged unscathed and its cargo of whisky bottles miraculously survived.[40] A second Wellington crashed owing to a burst tyre and had to be written off and its replacement crashed on its first flight in India. Finally, a Dakota C47 appeared and provided two years of uninterrupted flying with pilots Paddy Noble[41] and Ralph Shaw at the controls.

Top of Carton de Wiart's agenda was to keep track of the Generalissimo's intentions to support SEAC plans in Burma as outlined at the SEXTANT conference. On 17 December, he signalled Churchill that Stilwell had told him that the Generalissimo would attack 'with all his forces any time (a) full scale amphibious attack is ordered. If no attack in the spring, Chiang Kai-shek will attack in November. He then expects heavy amphibious attack mentioned in Roosevelt's telegram to take place'.[42] The next day after meeting the Generalissimo the previous evening, Carton de Wiart sent another signal that reiterated the Generalissimo would not attack with his Yunan force unless 'a big amphibious operation takes place'. The Generalissimo had told him that 'he in no way wishes to avoid fighting but he would take no risk with his Yunan force as failure would mean the invasion (by the Japanese) of that province. He was most friendly but I am convinced that nothing will change his attitude'.[43]

It appeared that Chiang Kai-shek, risk averse by necessity, was being obdurate by sticking to his demand that any Allied attack in Burma involving Chinese troops had to be made simultaneously by land and by sea. The problem was that Churchill's Indian Ocean battle fleet and Mountbatten's landing craft for his 'amphibious circus' showed no signs of appearing anytime soon; the latter had all been earmarked for the landings in France the following year.

In his last letter of 1943[44] to Ismay, Carton de Wiart wrote:

> there is not a great deal to tell you, but I have seen the Generalissimo three times this week . . .
>
> For the first time last night he said he was willing to attack without an amphibious operation having taken place, but Mandalay and Lashio must first be taken, and I don't know whether SAC can do it.
>
> Had I a plane I would have flown to Delhi today and got on with the job, but as none is available, I had to wire, which in a case like this is not the same thing; if I am to be of any use when things get moving, I feel I really ought to have one.
>
> I also want to get to the front – I feel I could give you and SAC a far better picture of events if I can go and see the form myself, without a plane it is impossible. I am in fact immobile at present.
>
> I feel, I hope correctly, that my relations with the Generalissimo improve every time I see him, and if it only goes on like that I may be of some use one of these days!
>
> I saw Stilwell the other day. He is very friendly to me at present, but a curious bird. We had a talk but he never mentioned going away and in an hour or two went off on a fortnight's trip! You can understand how difficult things are with that type of man.
>
> Whether he is straight or not, I can't say and have no proof either way at present. I only know that he has not given me a scrap of information to date.
>
> I am curious to see what his reactions will be when I want to go to the front? Anyhow, I am going to get SAC to say he wishes me to do so . . .
>
> Everyone has been charming to me here; I hope it lasts.
>
> Do you think the Prime Minister would send me a photo of himself with something nice written on it? I don't make this as a personal request, much as I would like to, but it would make an impression on these people; I would gain face – which means a hell of a lot. Don't ask if you don't think it right.

Even by his standards, 1943 had been an extraordinary year for Carton de Wiart, beginning with his escape from an Italian POW camp and ending on the other side of the world as the prime minister's personal adviser to the Head of State of the most populous country in the world. Carried by the currents of history to an unknown shore, he now had to take stock of his surroundings and make a plan to survive and thrive in the political jungles of Chongqing and SEAC.

1944

The year of the monkey

At the diplomatic level, the New Year got off to a good start. Carton de Wiart received a letter[1] and a small gift from Meiling:

> How very sweet and thoughtful of you to think of sending me a New Year present and such a nice one! Don't tell me that you found it while walking over the hills of Chungking [*sic*].
>
> I am laid up with the flu . . . one darned thing after another. I hope this will be the last of the ghosts to stalk me.
>
> With this, I am sending you an autographed copy of *Little Sister Su*. Although the story was brought out in booklet form comparatively recently, I wrote it many, many years ago when I was young and gay.
>
> I send you the best of the New Year wishes, and in the forefront of these is the hope that you will find your stay with us a happy one.

With the invasion of France now a definite fixture for the summer of 1944, the British had to adjust their plans in South East Asia as no landing craft were available for amphibious operations. Operation BUCANEER (the capture of the Andaman Islands), Operation PIGSTICK (seaborne landings on the Arakan coast) and Operation CULVERIN (a landing on the tip of Sumatra) were all cancelled. The much reduced Allied plans were now limited to continuing the Ledo Road offensive started by General Stilwell and his two US-trained Chinese divisions in October 1943 with the objectives of capturing Kamiang and Myitkyina in Northern Burma; Operation THURSDAY, Wingate's Second Chindit Expedition, in support of Stilwell; a renewed overland attack in Arakan; and an offensive across the Chindwin River in Central Burma.

After Christmas, Mountbatten sent Wingate up to Chongqing to brief the Generalissimo about his forthcoming expedition[2] and to chivvy him to send additional divisions to the Northern Front in Burma. He stayed with Carton de

Wiart who accompanied him to the meeting and he was therefore able to brief Churchill on the outcome. Confusion reigned for Chiang Kai-shek told them 'it would be better in general to postpone the attack till November as suggested to him by the President' while Stilwell's Chief of Staff, Major General Tom Hearn, told them that 'he had received a stiff note from the President to be communicated to Chiang Kai-shek urging him to attack'. Unable to reconcile these two contradictory statements, Carton de Wiart told Churchill that 'Chiang certainly did not wish to attack. If the President advises him not to, I see no hope of persuading him to do so'.[3]

Churchill responded on 21 January, asking him to personally pass a message to the Generalissimo that 'the first three battleships for the Eastern Fleet are already on their way to the Indian Ocean.[4] The destruction of the *Scharnhorst* will give still greater liberty to our naval forces'.[5] He did not mention that there would be no landing craft available for amphibious operations. The Generalissimo was delighted and asked Carton de Wiart to reply that he 'earnestly hope more naval forces will be despatched to the Far East so that the plan agreed upon between us can be put into operation at an early date'.[6]

In a 17 January letter to the recently promoted Field Marshal Sir Alan Brooke,[7] Carton de Wiart summarized his first month in China:

I have been here a month, and a good part of that time has been spent trying to induce the generalissimo to attack in the spring. I have not succeeded and in some ways am not sorry – his doing so is of no use to us, unless he does it whole heartedly, and he won't do that.

He, of course, brings up the fact that no serious amphibious operation will take place now, and that in Cairo he was promised one; but I think what is really stopping him is that he is afraid, in case of failure, the Japanese will invade Yunnan which would be very serious for him.

Stilwell wants to attack at any price, at least, so he says; his Chief of Staff told me a few days ago that he had communicated a stiff note from the President to the Generalissimo with the object of getting him to attack, but the latter told us at a conference that he thought it best to follow the President's advice and not attack until next November, so I am at a loss to know what the Americans really mean.

Stilwell is very friendly on the surface, but the fact remains he has not given me one bit of information. He left about a fortnight ago, and though I saw him a couple of hours before his departure, he never even mentioned the fact he was going, and I am supposed to be his No.2 as far as SEAC is concerned! That is only to give you an idea of how communicative he is.

Wingate was sent up by Mountbatten to give an exposé of his show to the Generalissimo in the hope he might induce him to attack. He put his case forward most excellently, and I thought at one moment he would achieve his purpose but there was no result.

The Embassy Staff are most helpful as far as I am concerned. I think I am getting on well with the Generalissimo and his other half, they are very friendly and I hope some day it will result in my being of some use.

I am immobilised by having no plane, but trust I will get one some day and be able to see the front; I have no idea what their army is like, and have not even heard a shot fired, which is all wrong.

When the photograph of Churchill, which he had asked Ismay to arrange, arrived in China, he wrote a personal thank you letter:

It was most kind of you to send me your photograph, and to send it as you did makes it a very valued possession.

The Generalissimo quite understands the position as regards the South East Asia theatre and is in full agreement with your decisions; I find him most reasonable as a rule. He knows what his troops can do and does not pretend they can drive the Japanese troops out of prepared positions.

SEAC rather take the line that he won't fight; I think this is not fair on him, he will fight when the moment comes, but I fear it will only be when we have done a lot more softening, or at any rate are in a very strong position, which we are not at present.

I have just come back from the conference in Delhi. The new strategical plan seems sound, but to my uneducated mind I should have thought the Andamans should have been tackled first; 1,200 miles from one's base is a long step even nowadays.

I cannot tell you the joy your recovery has given to everyone, but I do not include Hitler in that statement!

I must thank you again for employing me; it was very good of you and I only hope I shall justify your kindness.

Many thanks for the aeroplane, it will make all the difference to me, for it does not seem right always to ask the Americans for one. I had to this time, and though I landed twice in India before getting to Delhi, the first Englishman I saw was in Delhi!

On 5 February, Brigadier Fergusson[8] and his 16th Chindit Brigade set out from Ledo on foot and successfully penetrated into Japanese rear areas. In early March three more Chindit brigades were flown into landing zones behind Japanese lines where they remained in close contact with the enemy for the next two and a half months in support of Stilwell's advance on Myitkyina. Then, almost without warning, events in Central Burma moved centre stage as the Japanese

Fifteenth Army's bold offensive towards Dimapur in the Brahmaputra valley – Operation UGÔ – gained momentum. With still no sign of Chaing Kai-shek sending additional troops, on 24 March Churchill told Carton de Wiart that the President had telegraphed the Generalissimo urgently requesting him to utilize his Yunnan troops to assist Mountbatten in Burma, 'Should opportunity arise please inform Generalissimo that I strongly support President's request.'[9] By 6 April, the Japanese had reached Kohima. The vital Allied communications hub and supply base at Dimapur now looked vulnerable.

After flying down to Delhi for a series of meetings, Carton de Wiart wrote on 24 April to Ismay in London:[10]

I got back from India a few days ago with various messages from SAC to the Generalissimo, to get the latter to use his Yunnan force and to my surprise he has said that he will send four more divisions. . . . I must say the Generalissimo deserves full marks for from the beginning he said he would not use that force unless we staged a serious amphibious operation. His fear being that if he used it and the Japanese attacked, they might get to Kunming, and that put finis [*sic*] to this show.

I think SAC failed to see the Generalissimo's reasons but does so now; however, the latter does not think he will be attacked now and I hope he is right. I cannot say I feel positive as the Jap badly wants the Peking-Canton [*sic*] railway, and if he gets it, it will interfere with MATTERHORN and DRAKE (*ed* U.S. strategic bombing campaign from Chengtu airbase against mainland Japan) seriously.

The only real weapon we have in this country is Chennault's Air Force and he is not getting his full ration of POL (petrol, oil and lubricants) and cannot even carry on his work against Japanese shipping, which is a great pity as he is hitting them very hard.

The Generalissimo was laid up, but I had a heart to heart talk with Madame . . . (she) was very much more for the British than usual, and American shares are slumping. I am not sure that the Americans are not threatening these people, which is a fatal policy with them as they simply sit back and do nothing, when treated in that way.

Anyhow as far as I am concerned the Americans are playing up and now realise that I am only out for the war. I have told them frankly that if their businessman and ours choose to cut each other's throats after the war, it is no concern of mine, but that to finish the war is very much so. I think they like that attitude.

Mountbatten seemed keen on my going to England to put forward the Chinese point of view. I told him I thought it a bad moment to go when you had on hand all you have at present. Later on, if he thought it would help and you also thought so, it might be different. Anyhow the decision is up to you and him to make.

I am told the political situation has deteriorated in my absence. I really cannot tell for as long as the Generalissimo remains *compus menti*, I really have no worries in that line and I think as long as the war lasts we need not be anxious. Afterwards is another matter, not only in this country!

I am off to Burma and Arakan in a few days, as I think a personal report to the Generalissimo after <u>seeing</u> the front is better than all the epistolary effusions one gets on the subject.

Carton de Wiart's reference to Chennault was indicative of the senseless infighting between Stilwell, who controlled Lend-Lease supplies, and the flamboyant commander of the XIV Air Force. Vinegar Joe had long ago decided that American air bases in South-East China were indefensible against Japanese attack and that the effect of Chennault's bombers and fighters on the outcome of the war was negligible. General Takahashi, Commander-in-Chief of Japanese forces in China, disagreed. After the war, he stated that 'considering all the difficulties my armies encountered in China . . . I judge the operations of the XIV Air Force to have constituted between 60 and 75 per cent of our effective opposition in China. Without the (14th) Air Force we could have gone anywhere we wished'.[11]

In a follow-up letter dated 25 April, Carton de Wiart told Ismay that further developments had occurred which 'may seem trifling and social, at first sight, but I do know you will agree they may be very important politically'.

Madame asked me if I thought she would be welcome in England. I said I felt sure she would, but I felt it was not a moment for me to wire to ask when all the country's attention was taken up with impending events. I told her I would however write and ask the Prime Minister.

I didn't ask about dates, but I don't think much could be done before early July from this end, but your end in the one that matters.

You know her form: very intelligent, of course, but with no mean estimate of her own importance, till she knows you well, when you say anything to her . . .

In USA she had no peace – and I think one or two private visits, such as Welbeck and Blenheim would fit in well.

She is swinging pro-British so hard that it is almost embarrassing!

Taking Madame Chiang's nephew, Major Louis Kung of the Scots Guards, with him as an extra ADC, Carton de Wiart flew down to India and then hitched a ride with the Americans to a jungle airstrip where he met Major General Lentaigne[12] at Sylhet who had replaced Wingate as commander of Special Force/3rd Indian Infantry Division after the Chindit commander's death in an air crash. From there he went to the headquarters of General Slim, GOC 14th Army, and then on to Arakan where he spent time with Major General Francis Festing,[13] the commander of 36th Division. He wanted to continue on to Imphal but had to abandon the idea as the Japanese air force was too active. On his way home, he visited Archie Wavell, the Viceroy's son, who was in hospital after losing a hand when fighting with the Chindits. He reassured him that a one-handed officer had every chance of becoming a general![14] His decision to take Major Kung with him paid a handsome dividend when Meiling told Sir Berkeley Gage that 'he had the greatest affection for General Carton de Wiart and thought him the finest soldier in the world'.[15] However, much to his chagrin, all this goodwill was lost when the War Office turned down Mountbatten's request to Combined Operations to employ Tung as a staff officer.[16]

While he had been away, in North East Burma, General Wei-lihuang's (Huang Weili) 72,000 strong 'Y Force', as the American equipped and trained Chinese Divisions in Yunnan were designated, in early May had started to cross the Salween River heading for Tengchung and Lung-ling. This meant that the Japanese were now fighting on four fronts in Burma – Arakan in the south, Kohima and Imphal in the centre, Stilwell in the northwest and Wei-lihuang in the northeast. So as far as he was concerned, albeit reluctantly, the Generalissimo had delivered his pledge to his allies by taking the pressure off Stilwell and opening another front in Burma for Mountbatten.

It was around this time that Cecil Beaton, the well-known society photographer, set designer and writer, arrived in China as part of his seven-month tour of India and South East Asia. The Ministry of Information had despatched him the previous November when he had been lucky to escape with his life after his Dakota had crashed on take-off in Cornwall. After doing the rounds in India, he had flown over the hump to Kunming and then on to Chongqing where Major General Gordon Grimsdale had met him before setting out on a gruelling and at times hazardous ten-week tour of British Military Mission locations deep in the 'blue' of the Chinese countryside.

On return to Chongqing, Beaton photographed Carton de Wiart, 'Churchill's Chinese right ear' and

> although no English blood runs in his veins, his appearance and manner are those of the traditional English warrior. With one eye, one arm, the Victoria Cross, and, as he says, very few brains, he is an adventurer in the grand manner. With his Cyrano-like nose, his one remaining eye and his matchboard body, he is as dashing as the blade of a sword.[17]

Carton de Wiart's earlier misgivings about the timing of the Generalissimo sending extra divisions to Burma proved prescient when the Japanese launched Operation INCHIGÔ, a huge offensive to take out the US airbases in Central China and to open up a route between Central China and French Indo-China using the Guangzhou–Hankou railway network. The Generalissimo had warned Roosevelt of this possibility in the New Year when he told him that 'Japan will rightly deduce that practically the entire weight of the UN forces will be applied to the European Front, thus abandoning the China Theatre to the mercy of Japan's mechanised land and air forces. Before long Japan will launch an all-out offensive against China'.[18] In early March, Chennault, with whom Carton de Wiart had developed an excellent relationship, had written to him that 'my guess is that the Japanese will launch a powerful air attack on our forces in the forward area some time late in March or during April'.[19] However, the sheer scale of the offensive caught the Chinese by surprise as 500,000 men and 200 bombers headed into Central China. The Chongqing-based *Time* magazine correspondent Theodore White wrote, 'Within three weeks the Japanese had seized all their objectives; the railway to the South lay in their hands, and a Chinese army of 300,000 men had ceased to exist.'[20]

As a result of this military debacle, Roosevelt sent his Vice-President Henry Wallace to see the Generalissimo to discuss sending a US Military Mission to the Chinese Communists in Yan'an purportedly to support Operation MATTERHORN, the strategic bombing of Japan by US B-29s based in India and Chengdu in Central China. Their role would be to collect meteorological reports, dispose of wreckage of downed or crashed aircraft and rescue stranded aircrew.[21] Interested mainly in 'crops, farming and volleyball',[22] Wallace arrived in Chongqing on 20 June and surprised his hosts by insisting on pulling a rickshaw. Over the next four days, a game of diplomatic ping pong played out as he tried to persuade the Generalissimo that he should co-operate with the Chinese Communists who the Americans portrayed as 'agrarian democrats' with little in common with their Soviet namesakes.

Codenamed the DIXIE Mission, Meiling suggested that the US Army Observer Group would be a more acceptable name for the US Military Mission and, on that basis, and on the proviso that it reported to the KMT's National Military Council, the advance party under Colonel David Barratt arrived in Yan'an on 22 July. When Wallace left for Kunming, the Generalissimo suspected that this was the opening move of the American 'Left' to ingratiate themselves with Mao Tse-tung[23] and the CCP and hedge their bets. He was right for unknown to him, on his return to Washington, Wallace told the President, 'it is not believed that he (the Generalissimo) has the intelligence or political strength to run post-war China.'[24]

As Central China continued to reel under the weight of the Japanese onslaught – fourteen Japanese divisions had been redeployed from Manchuria, leaving only six in place[25] – Carton de Wiart found himself playing the role of mediator between the Generalissimo and Mountbatten for both had quite different estimates of the strength of Japanese forces engaged in the China offensive. An attitude had taken root at SEAC HQ in Kandy that the Chinese were exaggerating the numbers in order to get additional help from the Allies. In a 4 June letter to SACSEA, he pointed out that

> when people are on that tack, they generally ask for every imaginable thing they can think of. He (the Generalissimo) has asked for <u>nothing</u> but air support to deal with the attack; I feel he could not have asked for less. If the situation turns out better than it looks at present, I shall be delighted, but I think it would be a great mistake to sit back and think this will be the case unless the Chinese get substantial help, and I take it to be my job to give you the picture as it is represented here, and as I myself see it.[26]

Meanwhile the war in Burma slowly swung in favour of the British. On 30 May the Japanese withdrew from Kohima; and on 3 July they broke off their Imphal offensive and fell back to the Chindwin. General Mutaguchi's gamble to reach India had ended in disaster with his army incurring 55,000 casualties, mostly from disease and malnutrition but also 13,500 killed in action. The Allies had suffered 17,500 casualties.

Good news also arrived from North West Europe where Allied forces had secured an unassailable beach head in Normandy. Carton de Wiart sent the prime minister a telegram on 30 June, informing him that he had seen Chiang Kai-shek the previous day who told him that

> the situation here was still very serious and would get worse but that he had no fear of being forced out of the war. He wished me to tell you how wonderful he thought your achievements in France were and they would certainly help matters here. He felt that his troops would be able to continue the fight in Burma.[27]

The following week Carton de Wiart received a grumpy letter from Mountbatten, scolding him for flying down to Delhi in late June without telling him and thereby missing the chance to meet – 'I cannot fail to express my disappointed at your not having waited to see me or at least having communicated your movements to me.' It particularly irked him that the Viceroy with whom Carton de Wiart stayed had specifically asked him to remain on.[28] Colonel

Peter Fleming had incurred similar rebukes when he failed to fit in with SACSEA's somewhat arbitrary schedule. He put it down to the folly of moving SEAC Headquarters to Kandy which added a 1,800 miles round journey to Delhi.

On one of his trips down to Kandy in Ceylon, Carton de Wiart met Admiral Somerville, the C-in-C of the Eastern Fleet who offered to take him on Operation CRIMSON, a joint air-sea attack on Sabang on the northern tip of Japanese-occupied Sumatra. Tasked 'to make a mess of the air base and harbour installations and wreck any vessels found sheltering there',[29] the Fleet consisting of three capital ships, two aircraft carriers, seven cruisers and ten destroyers[30] sailed from Trincomalee in great secrecy and arrived undetected off Sabang on 25 July. Seated in a deck chair on the bridge of HMS *Queen Elizabeth*, he prepared to watch the proceedings. 'The noise was hell let loose . . . I had been expecting a great deal of noise and vibration, for everything had been removed from the walls of the ship, but it was nothing to what I heard and felt.'[31] The action was regarded as a success and it was a reinvigorated Carton de Wiart who returned to Chongqing.

In Northern Burma, after a seventy-eight-day siege, Myitkyina finally fell to Stilwell's NACC Chinese forces on 3 August; Japanese losses were put at 4,600. The advance in May of the Generalissimo's Y Force in the North East had stalled in early July and it was only in September that Tengchung finally fell. Lung-ling, which Chinese troops had entered in early June, had been wrested back by the Japanese who stubbornly held out until November.

In Hunan province, the loss on 8 August of Changsha and the strategically placed city of Hengyang after a forty-eight-day siege represented the nadir of the Generalissimo's armies. Of the 16,000 defenders all but 1,200 were killed. Yet, the Japanese had also suffered direly with casualties in excess of 20,000. For Chiang personally, it exacerbated his frustration that SEAC, for which read Stilwell, continued to hold on to the Chinese divisions in Y Force. It was entirely reasonable from his perspective to surmise if he had had them, the outcome at Hengyang may have been quite different. Yet the loss of Hengyang also marked a turning point for the Japanese who were finding it increasingly difficult to hold the ground they had taken; their lines of communication stretched nearly 700 kilometres to the nearest port.

On news of another big Japanese push in South East China in early September, Carton de Wiart flew down to Kweilin (Guilin) to get a feel of what was happening on the ground. Before he left, he wrote a personal letter to Mountbatten, expressing his sense of impending redundancy:

I have no idea as to what is to happen here but feel that I am absolutely useless . . . I wonder if it is of any use my staying on? You have a better idea from your angle, especially after being at home – and you would perhaps tell me what you think – I should be grateful if you would.[32]

For a man who rarely dropped his guard, this cry for help was indicative of his despair at the lack of British engagement with China. Matters were compounded by the prime minister's address to the House of Commons on 28 September which was construed by the Chinese as erroneous and condescending:

I was somewhat concerned to observe . . . (that) many important organs of United States' opinion seem to give the impression that the British campaign in Burma of 1944 had been a failure, or at least a stalemate, that nothing much had been done, and that the campaign was redeemed by the brilliant capture of Myitkyina . . . by General Stilwell at the head of an American Regiment of very high class commando troops and with the assistance of the Chinese. That is the picture, but I must, therefore, set matters in their true light . . .

. . . the 10 Japanese Divisions which were launched against us . . . have been repulsed and largely shattered as the result of a bloody and very costly campaign which is still being continued in spite of the monsoon conditions . . . the campaign of Admiral Mountbatten on the Burma frontier constitutes – and this is a startling fact – is the largest and most important ground fighting that has yet taken place against the armies of Japan. Far from being an insignificant or disappointing stalemate, it constitutes the greatest collision which has yet taken place on land with Japan . . .

I must here note with keen regret that in spite of the lavish American help that has been poured into China, that great country, worn by more than seven years of war, has suffered from severe military reverses involving the loss of valuable airfields upon which the American squadrons of General Chennault were counting.[33]

On his return to Chongqing in early October, he signalled the prime minister[34] with a digest of a letter which he was in the process of writing to Ismay. When Churchill later read the full letter, he arranged for it to be circulated to all members of the War Cabinet, such was the importance he placed on it:

You will have had my Amuse 23 and 24 (coded telegrams) as a result of my visit to Kweilin. To say I was shocked at what I found there is putting things very mildly.

. . . I went to the front, seventy-eight miles in a truck . . . and when I got there I was appalled at the ignorance of military matters displayed by the Chinese; I thought our Allies had given them some instruction on the subject but I was wrong.

There were two Chinese divisions holding a gorge, which could comfortably have been held by a battalion, no protection on the flanks and in the rear; although there must be fifty good rear-guard positions between the front and Kweilin, there was *not one* soldier.

The Chinese General was quite happy and said there was no Japanese force of any size within twenty miles. He pressed me to stay to lunch but as that is a lengthy business and I was very pressed for time, I declined. Within an hour of my leaving, the Japanese attacked! Those two divisions are now making their way back to Kweilin but I can get little information as to how they are getting on. However I have told you enough for you to judge the form.

The Chinese can really only do two things – run like Hell if strongly attacked or get into the nearest town and then fight well to defend it. They have little idea of attacking; if their attack fails, they merely dribble up more men, who at once get wiped out. They have no idea of staging an attack.

I was, however, very much impressed by the soldier, who looked well, was cheerful and up to lots of work; officers very poor in most cases but I didn't have time to really judge.

When I got back to Kweilin, I went and saw Brigadier-General Vincent,[35] CO of the Air Force and asked him if he wished for any information and he wanted all I could give him. When I had finished, he thanked me and said it was the first time he had *ever* had a picture of the situation! I cannot understand it: the Americans have quite a number of officers, masses of jeep, but never seem to go up and see what is happening . . .

The Chinese at Kweilin were very nice. The governor, GOC & co [*sic*] came to meet me and see me off and were all over one, never having seen a senior officer of any sort before. I told the American CO all this as I know him well and he took it very well and must have wired Stilwell as he turned up the next day. I met him on his way, and he was very friendly, although I repeated the whole story to him. I think he fully realises that I do not wish to meddle but only help.

The Americans have four beautiful airfields there, fully equipped. They were preparing to evacuate and demolish but will certainly not go before they need to for they are absolute tigers, I have never seen better.

The other Americans I believe have now left. Chennault very kindly arranged for his Chief of Staff to pick me up as I have no plane and he took me to Liuchow (Liuzhou) and Nanning. The former has a huge airfield, fully equipped but I fear it will go if the Japanese keep up their advance: Nanning is only a field for fighters and of no use for big stuff.

Kweilin may hold out for weeks, so may Liuchow, but once the Japanese are near, the airfields must be given up and we have nothing left. The Japanese can then occupy South East China in peace. Should a force of ours wish to land on the coast, they can have no land-based air support.

The whole thing is appalling. It has been obvious for months that this might happen and *nothing* has been done. I know you could do nothing about it, you told me so when I wrote to you in April. Had the Americans acted then, all this would never have happened.

I saw the Generalissimo on my return and wired you his attitude. He does not really realise what the loss of these airfields means. But nor does he know anything of our plans as you will have gathered from my wires. He must know if we want him to co-operate. I am certain one can tell him and that it will go no further. I have tested him out on small matters, and even his Staff knew nothing about the matters a fortnight later.

But to tell him the ridiculous stories that SEAC suggest: No, I can't and I won't. I am quite prepared to say I know nothing and it is generally true. I am of no value here unless I have the Generalissimo's confidence and I think I can say I have it pretty fully, but if I tell him childish stories, I shall lose it.

He should be told on broad lines what we propose to do – he will not ask for secret details.

He is very anxious we should take Rangoon and Moulmein and refers to it every time I see him, I can tell him nothing because I don't know. When I told Mountbatten before he went to England that this was the Generalissimo's wish, he was delighted as he thought it might turn the balance in favour of Rangoon when the Americans were so keen on a push from the North. Since then I have heard *nothing*.

I wired you his hopes about British troops being in the Allied Force out here and there is no need for me to add more. I think his fear is to be left entirely in the hands of the Americans.

I have seen Hurley and Nelson;[36] they tell me they had been told to contact me. I don't quite know why except Hurley spoke pretty freely about the Command out here, but you know as much and a good deal more about that than I do.

Carton de Wiart reiterated his annoyance with the Americans when in a letter to Ismay he reminded him, 'as I have told you before, I blame the Americans for the situation here, they should have made sure that the troops guarding their airfields were fit to hold up the Japanese but they never did. I know this cannot be said publicly but it should be taken into consideration when judging the situation.'[37]

Stilwell's relationship as Chief of Staff to Chiang Kai-shek had never been good since he regarded himself as the only person who understood military affairs and hence was the only person who knew what to do. Irrespective that as Commander-in-Chief of the Chinese Armed Forces Chiang Kai-shek was his superior officer, he was contemptuous of the Generalissimo's abilities and those of most of his generals, let alone his American and British peer group – he had fallen out with Wavell, Mountbatten, Wingate and Slim – although Mountbatten had little choice other than to go along with him as he was his second-in-command at SEAC. He finally exasperated Mountbatten during the protracted siege of Myitkyina in the summer of 1944. Nothing could persuade Mountbatten that Stilwell's flagrant disregard for the lives of the British Chindits justified the end; he demanded a medical assessment and of the 2,200 examined only 119 were passed fit for service. Stilwell's own version of the Chindits, Colonel Frank Merrill's 2,750 'Marauders' had also been decimated with 272 killed, 955 wounded and 980 ill with disease. However, it was not in the gift of the British to remove him but that of Roosevelt and General Marshall who continued to support him. Ironically it was to be Stilwell himself who pulled the trigger.

Having persuaded the President and General Marshal that the delay to take Myitkyina had been entirely due to the Generalissimo's procrastination in sending him additional troops and furthermore his refusal to treat with Mao Tse-tung's CCP was obstructing the war against the Japanese in China, Stilwell's game plan was to extract from Washington new terms of employment, namely he was to be given operational command of all Chinese troops, including the Communists if they came onside. He had plans to give them five divisions worth of equipment and supplies and a licence to operate to the north of the Yellow River.[38]

The Generalissimo had asked Stilwell to send the five divisions of X Force which was by now out of the line at Myitkyina to move east and help his Y Force take Long-ling which the Japanese were doggedly holding on to. Stilwell refused so Chiang responded by telling him that he would have to withdraw Y Force to Central China and use it to defend Kunming. When Roosevelt who was meeting with Churchill in Quebec (the QUADRANT conference) heard this from Stilwell who had of course placed an entirely different construction on it – namely that the Generalissimo was refusing to provide relief for troops in Burma – he asked Marshall to draft a note to send to the Generalissimo, inviting him to place 'General Stilwell in unrestricted command of all your forces'.[39] Stilwell insisted on personally delivering the note to the Generalissimo, despite the attempts of General Hurley to prevent him. It was to prove a pivotal moment in the rapidly deteriorating US–Chinese relationship mainly engineered by Stilwell. Many Americans now distrusted the Generalissimo and viewed his government as corrupt and incompetent; many Chinese were staggered by the American insouciance to the clear and present Japanese threat to Central China.

Messages went back and forth between Chongqing and Washington until Hurley grasped the nettle and told Roosevelt that 'Chiang Kai-shek and Stilwell are fundamentally incompatible. Today you are confronted with a choice between Chiang Kai-shek and Stilwell'.[40] After a final meeting with the Generalissimo on 20 October, Stilwell was on his way back to the United States, never to return to China. Major General Gordon Grimsdale, the British Military Attaché, was relieved to see the back of him and later wrote that the campaign in China 'provides examples of the old lesson that in war we cannot afford to fight with personalities clashing at the top. Divided loyalties lead to divided counsels, which in turn ensures that we will get the worst of both worlds, and only the enemy profits'.[41] He remained bewildered how Stilwell, the man who was on record as saying 'the cure for China's problems is the elimination of Chiang Kai-shek', had been allowed to continue in post for so long.

On 27 October General Al Wedemeyer received a telegram from General Marshall directing him to proceed to China to assume command of US forces in China, which at the time numbered around 28,000 men, predominantly Chennault's Army Air Force troops whom Stilwell had contemptuously called 'just a bunch of aerial chauffeurs'.[42] Wedemeyer was also named Chief of Staff to the Generalissimo Chiang Kai-shek.

Labelled by Stilwell as 'the world's most pompous prick', Wedemeyer had completed tours in the Philippines in the 1920s and in China in the early 1930s. In 1934, when he returned from a second tour in the Far East, he attended the army's Command and General Staff School at Fort Leavenworth; two years later he was sent on a two-year tour as an exchange student at the Kriegsakademie in Berlin. On his return he submitted a 147-page document that described in great detail the organization, equipment, tactical doctrines and morale of the developing German forces. In a note to President Roosevelt written soon after the attack on Pearl Harbour, Secretary of War Henry L. Stimson declared that, without the timely analysis of blitzkrieg provided by Wedemeyer, 'we should be badly off indeed'.[43]

Spotted by General Marshall as a staff officer of outstanding ability, he was assigned to the War Plans Division of the General Staff. It was in this assignment that Wedemeyer first made a name for himself as a strategist and planner, producing the far-seeing Victory Plan, a broad blueprint for US participation in a possible war against the Rome–Berlin–Tokyo Axis. In the space of nine months, he rose from major to brigadier and became head of the Strategy and Policy Group in the War Department's Operations Division, regularly on hand to assist General Marshall in presenting and defending American proposals.

At the first Quebec Conference in the late summer of 1943, when Roosevelt and Churchill decided to establish a new command in Southeast Asia to better coordinate Allied efforts, Wedemeyer was assigned, on British suggestion, as Chief of Staff to Mountbatten. At the farewell luncheon he gave for Wedemeyer in Kandy, Mountbatten gave a short speech in which he said he could not believe that Eisenhower or MacArthur had an Englishman who meant so much, or had been of such loyal help as Al Wedemeyer had been to him.[44]

When Wedemeyer arrived at Stilwell's headquarters after his dismissal, he was appalled to discover that Stilwell had intentionally departed without seeing him, thereby scuppering any sort of handover of command. Searching the offices, Wedemeyer could not find a single briefing paper or documentary record of Stilwell's plans or even records of his past operations. When he spoke with Stilwell's staff, they told him that Stilwell kept everything in his 'hip pocket'. As Carton de Wiart noted, he 'could hardly have chosen a more awkward and unenviable time to succeed to the job'.[45]

Wedemeyer had been to China the previous spring when he toured the US air fields and met the Allied team in Chongqing. Carton de Wiart was 'very struck with (him); he was a charming man, tall, well-built, with a young face and white hair; and he was a perfect staff officer with quick wits and sound judgment'.[46] In a letter to Churchill, Wedemeyer endorsed Carton de Wiart, recalling

> when I reported to SEAC several months ago, I was informed that the relations between the British and the Chinese were far from friendly. It will please you to know that quite the reverse is true now, and I attribute the change to the splendid work General de Wiart is doing. He was a most fortunate selection. His straightforward and friendly manner have won the confidence and admiration of the Chinese. I might add that the Americans I contacted in China also respect him.[47]

Shortly after Stilwell had left, the immensely experienced US Ambassador Clarence Gauss, who had spent much of his career in China, resigned on 1 November having been in post since 1941. He had finally come to the end of his tether and was deeply pessimistic about the situation in China. It did not help his cause that it was he who had recommended that the Chinese Communist forces be placed under the direct command of Stilwell, allowing them to receive directly US lend-lease aid. He was replaced on 17 November by a reluctant 'General' Patrick Hurley, who had been in China since August as Roosevelt's personal representative to Chiang Kai-shek. The President had introduced him[48] as my personal representative on military matters and you can talk to him with the utmost freedom. His principal mission is to coordinate the whole military picture under you as Military Commander-in-Chief – your being, of course, the Commander-in-Chief of the whole area – to help to iron out any problems between you and General Stilwell who, of course, has problems of his own regarding the Burma campaign and is necessarily in close touch with Admiral Mountbatten.

Born in a log cabin in Oklahoma, Pat Hurley had worked as a coalminer and cowboy to pay his way through college and, after completing his law studies, he set up a successful legal practice in Tulsa. In the First World War he went to France with the US 6th Army Corps and fought at Louppy-le-Chateau in November 1918 when he was awarded a Silver Star. Joining the Republican Party, he quickly rose up through the ranks and became the Secretary of State for War in the Hoover administration in the early 1930s and, when the Second World War broke out, General Marshal sent him as a Brigadier-General in the Reserves to the Philippines to report on the situation there. An assignment to Australia followed to arrange supplies for US troops in the Philippines. General Eisenhower, who was in charge of the Operations Division in Washington at the time, recalled 'we needed someone to organize blockade running for MacArthur and Hurley, an old-fashioned buccaneer in politics, with energy and decisiveness, was perfect for the job'.[49]

Roosevelt then sent him as his personal representative to the Soviet Union in November 1942 and from there to Iran where he organized the American side of the Tehran Conference in November 1943. Appointed Special Envoy to China in August 1944, his task was 'to promote efficient and harmonious relations between the Generalissimo and General Stilwell to facilitate General Stilwell's exercise of command over the Chinese armies placed under his direction'. En route to Chongqing, Hurley passed through Moscow when he was assured by the Russians that they had nothing in common with the Chinese Communists who were not really Communists in the first place. He believed them and after that it was a question of time before he became a political football between the Generalissimo and Mao. The historian Michael Burleigh is scathing of him:

US policy was not well served by its Ambassador to China from late 1944 onwards, a former Republican secretary of war called Patrick Hurley, a drunken idiot given to Choctaw war cries. Oblivious of China's delicate protocols, he referred to Chiang as 'Mr. Shek' and Mao Tse-tung as 'Moose Dung' in the course of shuttle trips designed to bring the two together to convert China into a springboard for the final showdown with the Japanese. Mao's cronies called Hurley 'the Clown'; his US diplomatic colleagues dubbed him 'the Albatross'.[50]

As the dust settled, Carton de Wiart wrote to Ismay on 6 November:

You can imagine how glad I was to see Wedemeyer turn up here, and if he does not make a success of the job, no one will. As far as I am concerned he will co-operate 100 per cent, so much so in fact that I wonder if I shall be of any more use.

. . . I am not happy about the Communist situation, for if the Americans go on boosting the Communists, I feel they may lose some of the ground they have gained. The Communists put as many difficulties in the way of a union with the Kuomintang as the latter do and I always think of a remark made by some well-known man to the effect that, when people went into each other's countries, they always become extremely 'left' and this is a very good example of it. I have always treated the Communist question as an internal one, and it has never even been mentioned up to date between the Generalissimo and myself. Hurley has done his best in the matter and deserves great credit for it, but I think he is realizing it is much more difficult than he thought; however, all the more credit to him if he can succeed.

The military situation here is of course bad and the Liuchow airfields will have to go and so will Kweilin but Wedemeyer hopes he will be able to hold up the Japanese West of that line and of course there will now be close co-operation between him and Chennault, a thing that was non-existent before.

The Generalissimo is very anxious for Mountbatten to stage a counter-offensive to relieve the situation here. I told him he was doing all he could with the means at his disposal. There is a good deal of feeling here against SEAC. It was started by Stilwell of course and it will take a lot to eradicate it, unless SEAC can have a definite success.

Carton de Wiart's disenchantment with his position reared up again in early November. After receiving a signal SAC 9645, he wrote to Mountbatten that:

with Al here, who is really much closer to you than I am, I do not fill any useful purpose here and that I have really shot my bolt.

I've achieved a certain amount but do not see how I am going to do anything further.

This may sound to you if I was disgruntled – I am not at all – but do not care to have a job in which I have nothing to do and one in which I am undervalued.

I am not writing to the PM on the subject as he would not know what has been taking place and I feel it is easier for you to let him know that I am of no use here . . .

I would like to thank you for all your kindness to me since I have been here and for the appreciation you expressed for the very little I have done.

Mountbatten signalled on 18 November that 'your personal letter has distressed me very much since nothing was further from my mind than the implication you refer to' and invited him to come to Kandy at his convenience. At the heart of his frustration was Mountbatten's determination to keep hold of the five Chinese divisions in X Force which were desperately needed in China. Carton de Wiart wrote to Ismay on 21 November:[51]

> The situation here is far worse than I have ever known it, and if the Japanese get Kweiyang, they can go for Kunming and Chongqing and I really would not be surprised at anything happening then.
>
> The Generalissimo wants to take some of his divisions out of Burma and one cannot blame him for they are his only good troops. I have wired Mountbatten telling him about this but am seeing the Generalissimo tomorrow, too late to write to you about what he says, but I will of course wire you.
>
> Wedemeyer and I are agreed on all points; though his Staff view on one point I don't quite share. He considers our tactical situation very bad but our strategical one good, owing to Burma and the Philippines. I agree on paper, but the tactical one dominates the strategical one to such a degree, that I don't consider the latter matters for the moment.
>
> If the Jap takes Kweiyang or Kunming as a dying effort, we may pull through but I'm afraid it hasn't got to that stage in this country.
>
> I don't know if we could send an Indian division here in preference to the Generalissimo taking his Chinese ones, it might save time if we could. It would have to be a good one or we will have Singapore or Hong Kong thrown on our heads again, and our prestige in this part of the world would be gone.
>
> I know the Chinese thought of asking for one, but they have not mentioned it to me yet.
>
> It is quite probable that we will be faced with making a decision as to whether to let China go, or else halt in Burma and give the Chinese sufficient troops from there or India to enable them to clear up this situation.
>
> Kweiyang is on the direct line of communication between here and Kunming by land; Kunming the main air base for India. If they go, we are not only in a bad way materially but the psychological effect would be more than we can compete with, I fear.

A week later, he wrote again to Ismay,[52] dismayed by a wire he had received from Mountbatten:

> I have had a wire from SAC beginning:

'Your W.786 dated 24 November is a great shock as it never occurred to me that the Generalissimo would make such an unsoldierly proposal as to withdraw any of the Chinese Army in India'.[53]

I cannot agree with his views, surely the Generalissimo's first consideration must be to save his own country, which at the present moment is in a very precarious position.

One should also remember that when things were going badly, he produced the Salween force to help us.

SAC goes on to say I am to point out to the Generalissimo that if some of the Chinese Division are withdrawn 'it will restrict our operations in Burma to his own great disadvantage'.

The point is that to derive any benefit from operations in other theatres, one must survive to reap these benefits, and if the Generalissimo cannot deal with the present situation, it is a moot point if the country will survive.

. . . Wedemeyer is going carefully into the Military Situation and hopes by tomorrow to be able to give me his views and he will do all in his power to avoid taking divisions from Burma; there is not the slightest doubt about that. But my fear is that whatever conclusions one may come to by studying the situation, one must take into consideration the fact that the troops opposing the Japs in their present advance will not stand up to them, and the only hope of checking the Japanese is by producing new troops. Whether the troops from the North will achieve this I cannot say. The troops from Burma are tried troops and might stop him.

The penny had finally dropped in London and Kandy that the crisis in China had to take priority over operations in Burma and Churchill told Carton de Wiart[54] 'to tell Generalissimo that notwithstanding cost to Operation CAPITAL (*ed* the British recapture of Burma) we are not opposing the withdrawal of these divisions from Burma. . . . Please assure Generalissimo and Wedemeyer of my full support in this matter'. Such was the concern in London that Churchill wanted Carton de Wiart to return to brief him and the Chiefs of Staff, but he signalled Ismay on 27 November that 'unless the Prime Minister wishes to see me urgently I do not feel I should leave here at present. Situation is bad and may get worse in my opinion'.[55]

On 1 December, with Wedemeyer's approval, the Generalissimo was allowed to withdraw two divisions from Burma rather than the five he had asked[56] for and send them up to Central China. In a clever compromise, Wedemeyer told the Generalissimo that the Americans would sell the Japanese false information that they were sending all five. Carton de Wiart was relieved that the impasse had been resolved though he wondered if it had been left too late. If Kunming was taken, supplies into China would be cut off and 'I think we should then have a collapse in a very short time'.[57] Wedemeyer later wrote that Mountbatten's staff had underestimated the enemy's capabilities in China while his own intelligence officers had overestimated them. 'Carton de Wiart . . . agreed with my own analysis of the situation and thought I was fully justified in requesting that two of the American-trained and equipped divisions[58] be returned from Burma to save the situation in China'.[59] By the end of December, Operation GRUBWORM had airlifted over 25,000 Chinese soldiers and over 1,500 pack animals to Kunming.

By the end of 1944, the Allied net was slowly closing in on the Japanese Empire. The relentless island by island advance of the US Navy and Marine Corps allowed the USAAF and Army Air Forces to secure forward airfields from which to bomb the Japanese mainland with the new long-range B29 bomber. In Burma, the Allied gains of 1944 had been consolidated and the US landings in the Philippines taken hold.

Although the Japanese had taken Kweilin on 24 November, a sudden halt to the Japanese advance had diminished the threat to Chongqing and Kunming. While they now held more territory than they did in 1938, the Japanese had failed in fulfilling most of their objectives. The Americans had simply moved their airfields deeper into China. Nevertheless, the attack had severely weakened Chiang's National Government, costing it somewhere in the region of 750,000 casualties and denying it both new recruits and grain from the newly enemy-occupied provinces of Henan and Hunan.

Carton de Wiart was ordered home in December[60] and on 11 January 1945, at the invitation of the prime minister, he addressed the War Cabinet[61] with a talk on his impression of the military, political and economic position in China. The only record of this talk is a note in the minutes as follows:

> A month earlier, when the Japanese had nearly reached Kweiyang in their advance from the South East, it had looked as though the situation was hopeless for there was no organised Chinese resistance. Then the Japanese had gone back due presumably to difficulties of maintenance and had devoted their efforts to opening a road along the coast to Indo-China whence they drew considerable supplies for their war effort. In his (Lt Gen Carton de Wiart) opinion, the Japanese were not likely to try again to capture Kunming in the near future. If, however, they did decide to do so, and succeeded, it should be realised that the collapse of China would follow shortly thereafter. Kunming was far more important than Chongqing for the survival of Chinese resistance.

The question therefore would be – were we prepared to provide help for China if the Japanese renewed their advance on Kunming? Admiral Mountbatten had, rather reluctantly, allowed two Chinese divisions to be withdrawn from the North Burma front and had transferred some aircraft to General Wedemeyer's control, but if the Japanese made a serious thrust towards Kunming, further help would be required from South East Asia.

The only Chinese forces capable of organised resistance were the ones which had been trained at Ramgarh: of the two which had been returned to China, only one of them was a battle-proved division with a good fighting record. The fresh troops which General Wedemeyer brought down from Sian [*sic*] could not be counted upon, although it was quite possible that the morale and effectiveness of Chinese troops everywhere could be stimulated if only the Japanese were soundly defeated in battle. The only troops capable of doing this were the American-trained forces in Burma . . . .

General Wedemeyer had done a great deal to improve things in China and the results of his efforts might raise the fighting value of the Chinese. If the Japanese decided to move towards Kunming, General Wedemeyer believed he could probably handle the situation, with the support of General Chennault's air forces, without having to necessarily call for more assistance from Burma. The Japanese would be advancing for 500 miles over a single road which passed for part of the distance through narrow ravines and gorges, presenting the air forces with perfect opportunities for attacking the lines of communication. However, if the threat re-appeared, it would probably be slow to develop, and General Wedemeyer should have time to dispose his forces to meet it. He was probably prepared to leave the remaining Chinese forces in Burma, providing he could retain the right to call them forward in an emergency.

The year 1944 had proved a momentous year in the Far East. The Japanese surprise advance to Imphal and Kohima had caught the British off-balance and Tokyo's ICHIGO offensive in Central China had put the Generalissimo temporarily on the ropes. However, despite their initial successes, neither had succeeded in fulfilling their objectives; the British were back on the Chindwin poised to retake Rangoon and US air forces in China were attacking the Japanese mainland uninterrupted. Carton de Wiart had played his hand with patience and skill, maintaining excellent relations with the Generalissimo and Meiling thereby keeping London and SACSEA informed of Chinese military policy at the highest level. Through his frankness, perspicacity and sound judgement, de Wiart had retained the trust of Churchill and Ismay and the respect and friendship of Mountbatten whom he had clashed with over the retention of Y

Force. There had been times when his morale had waned but he had overcome them with his customary resilience and cheerfulness.

The departure of Stilwell and the arrival of Wedemeyer had undoubtedly improved the atmosphere in Chongqing but, for the Allies and in particular the Americans, the contentious issue of future KMT-cooperation with the CCP had yet to be resolved. The year ahead would be make or break for Japan and, by default, the Generalissimo as well.

Special operations and 'secret society men'

When he wrote to the newly promoted Field Marshal Sir Alan Brooke on 17 January 1944, Carton de Wiart drew attention to 'our own show here':

> I do not know whether I ought to mention my opinion but if you feel you don't want it, you can simply ignore it and tell me to mind my own business.
>
> I think it is a poor show. I find the Military Mission has forty-six officers and twenty-seven BORs;[1] the Military Attaché's department has twenty-one officers and eight BORs and there are thirty odd officers besides these.
>
> The numbers are absurd and what they find to do except to get in each other's way I cannot think.
>
> I have not gone into details about their work and will not do so unless I am told to but when one thinks how badly officers are needed in many places, it seems to me a sad waste.
>
> To have a British Military Mission and an MA is already superfluous. I had a Military Mission in Poland and we did the MA's work as well and if I remember right, I had about a dozen officers and was told our work was satisfactory. Incidentally the Poles had five wars on!
>
> Their 'turn out' etc is very poor – a bad thing anywhere and particularly here; the Americans are far better. Our people also cut no ice with the Chinese and to succeed here you must do so.
>
> Anyhow I hope you won't mind me mentioning these details to you, and if we mean to take a serious part out here, I think something should be done. Whatever we mean to do, we should be well represented.[2]

The Military Mission he was referring to was the Special Operations Executive (SOE)-sponsored 204 Military Mission, set up in 1940 as 'a Corps d'Élite of Chinese guerrillas with cadres of British and Indian officers and other ranks'.[3] After endless toing and froing, it ended up spending a miserable and unproductive four months in Central China during October and November 1943 in support of Chinese forces before being evacuated to India. Its members had never once been allowed to attack the Japanese. A small contingent had remained behind, consisting of Demolition Instructors and Medical Officers attached to the Chinese 'Surprise' Battalions training school at Bihu in southern Zhejiang.

The head of the Mission, Major General Gordon Grimsdale who had also been the Military Attaché in Chongqing since 1941, had taken control of it in 1943 after the death of its commander Major General Dennys in an aircraft accident. A Military Intelligence officer of some eighteen years standing, Grimsdale had been involved in the Far Eastern Combined Bureau (FEBC) since its inception in Hong Kong in 1935 and had moved to Chongqing from FECB Singapore. The problem for de Wiart was that Grimsdale reported to the C-in-C India and the DMI India; there were no British operational commitments allocated to China Command.

In its own right SOE had also been active in China, first with John Keswick's China Commando Group which was closed down in 1942 and then with Colonel Paul Munro-Faure's SPIERS Mission,[4] tasked with inserting SOE-trained Chinese guerrilla parties from China into Burma, Thailand and French Indo-China. Its first incursion was into Kokang, a Burmese border province of Mandarin-speaking Han Chinese, where Munro-Faure dropped in February 1944. He rapidly concluded that the Chinese were hell bent on annexing the territory and signalled SOE that 'the Chinese were acting as virtual rulers of the territory (which had been British since 1897). They have attempted to suborn our interpreters; they spy on our movements and prevent our officers crossing the Salween without their permits'. Although he managed to arrange for the RAF to drop both supplies[5] and agents from India, Kokang was within the Chinese area of tactical responsibility and as he put it in a letter to the British Consular Service in Calcutta,[6] 'You will probably have heard of the unfortunate fate of the little operation I was mixed up with. Everything went wrong . . . the people in my office in India who were administering the operation, quite rightly, had no adequate comprehension of the politics involved.'

The CIGS forwarded copies of Carton de Wiart's letter to General Sir Claude Auchinleck, C-in-C India, and Lieutenant General Pownall, Chief of Staff at SEAC, asking for their views.[7] On 19 February 1944, control of 204 Mission passed to SEAC and Carton de Wiart took disciplinary control of all British personnel in Chongqing. By June, he and Pownall had agreed to expand the activities of the Mission by forming an artillery and Small arms[8] training wing in addition to its SOE sabotage and demolitions brief although this required an expansion rather than a contraction of personnel with thirty-nine new officers and nineteen BORs.[9] However, he was unhappy with Grimsdale and wrote to the CIGS in August saying that he believed Grimsdale needed a change and that 'someone with more energy was required'. He was particularly concerned that Grimsdale's relationship with Cheng Kai Ming, the new Chinese Director of Military Intelligence, was unlikely 'to produce good results'. Auchinleck agreed and a search for his replacement was put in hand.

By late 1944, SOE, represented by Lieutenant Colonel Gill-Davies at the BMM, had four units working in China.[10] In Chongqing, the Resources Investigation Institute embedded in General Wang Peng-sheng's Institute of International Relations provided SOE with access to a wealth of intelligence[11] and a Liaison Mission operated W/T links to French Indo-China, Kunming and Kweiyang. Attached to the Assistant Military Attaché's office in Kunming, SOE maintained an advanced operational base to insert Missions into enemy-occupied territory. Since 1942 SOE had loaned a number of officers to the British Army Aid Group (BAAG), and in September 1944[12] had deployed them to assist the Chinese army in delaying the Japanese advance to Kweilin.[13] In Kweilin itself, operating under the auspices of BAAG, SOE's China Coast Section produced the 'indispensable'[14] Kweilin Weekly Intelligence Summary which was widely circulated to senior Allied military commanders.

The jewel in SOE's Chinese portfolio was Walter Fletcher's Operation REMORSE.[15] Born Walter Fleischl von Marxon, before the war Fletcher had been the managing director of Hecht, Levis and Kahn, a major rubber and commodities company in the City of London. On the outbreak of war, medically unfit to serve, he haunted the corridors of Whitehall in search of employment for his particular 'trading' talents. Spotted by SOE, after a shaky start when his rubber smuggling Operation MICKLEHAM failed, he branched out to include other commodities such as agar-agar, cutch dye, benzoin oil, silk, mercury and quinine. With no time to lose, Fletcher along with an old Dunlop China hand, Colonel Lionel Davis, flew to Chongqing to put their proposal to Chiang Kai-shek to smuggle commodities out of Japanese-occupied territories into China.

Not only did the Chinese agree to it but they allowed Fletcher to set up a small company to handle the transactions, naturally with some participation by the Chinese themselves. Their first success was quinine which was desperately needed by the Australians for their troops in New Guinea. Fletcher discovered that the International Red Cross had been sending it for years to the Chinese where instead of distributing and using it, they had hoarded it. Soon a shipment arrived in Calcutta by air over The Hump but on inspection it was found to have been adulterated by the Chinese. A testing laboratory was quickly constructed, and Fletcher instigated a strict payment system relating to proven quality. By

June 1944, 25 million grains had been purchased by Fletcher and shipped to Australia.

Fletcher returned to London to table an altogether more ambitious and potentially rewarding plan. MICKLEHAM should be used to exploit the currency black market and thus enable the British to sidestep China's galloping inflation. If he did not intervene, he argued that British government costs in China would soar as it was forced to source the Chinese National dollars (CNDs) they needed to pay for their Military Missions and businesses through the Central Bank of China. To prove his point, Fletcher executed his first black market sale of Indian rupees in exchange for CNDs at a rate which showed a profit of 130 per cent. HM Treasury were suitably impressed and MICKLEHAM morphed into an entirely different operation codenamed REMORSE.

Now authorized to acquire CNDs 'through discrete banking and exchange transactions', in January 1944 Fletcher found himself at the centre of the biggest currency black market in history. Furthermore, as a result of a Chinese warlord admiring a large diamond ring on his hand, he branched out into smuggling South African sourced diamonds and other high value 'portable' goods such as watches, pearls and cigarette papers to sell on the black market in China. With its headquarters run by Colonel Davis at 9 Hsin Chin Kai in Kunming, the terminus for the Hump flights from India and hence perfectly suited for smuggling activities, the nascent organization soon sprouted branches in Kweilin, Meng-tze and Chongqing and CND bank accounts with the Chartered Bank and HSBC in London.

Soon the sheer volume of transactions outgrew the capacity of Fletcher's original company, so a new enterprise known as Syndicate B was formed in conjunction with key Chinese political and commercial interests with a fifteenth of the profits going to General Tai Li's Chinese Secret Service to provide 'a necessary insurance against guerrillas and obstruction by Customs'. Business boomed, including the diamonds for CNDs market where the exchange rate was twenty times higher than the official rate. In July 1944, REMORSE smuggled in 200 gold Swiss watches[16] sourced by SOE in Berne. Although the value of goods sold on the black market exceeded 200 million CNDs, it was dwarfed by currency exchange transactions which brought in 14,000 million CNDs. It has been estimated that during its lifetime, REMORSE gave the Allies additional spending power of over £77 million which today equates to approximately £2.5 billion. Carton de Wiart had once been heard to say, somewhat dismissively, that if one gave ten shillings to people like Fletcher, one got two and sixpence change. He could not have been more wrong.

Apart from 204 Military Mission and SOE, there were three other British intelligence organizations or 'secret society men' as Carton de Wiart was prone to call them operating in China:[17] the BAAG, the Hong Kong intelligence and escape organization started by Lindsay Ride;[18] the Secret Intelligence Service (SIS); and GBT (Gordon, Bernard and Tan). Ride, an Army doctor in Hong Kong, had been taken prisoner by the Japanese in December 1941. It was immediately apparent to him that the survival prospects for 600 British and Commonwealth officers and their 9,000 men who had been taken prisoner by the Japanese were far from rosy without adequate medical supplies. To that end he determined to escape; and on 9 January 1942 he escaped from Sham Shui-po POW camp and made his way in a *sampan* to unoccupied China, a feat for which he was congratulated by Field Marshal Wavell and appointed OBE in 1942.

Once in China he founded, formed and commanded (as a colonel in the Indian Army)[19] BAAG which helped escapees from Hong Kong, provided medical and other assistance to POWs and gathered intelligence.[20] Operating in Kwangtung and Kwangsi provinces and reporting to Grimsdale wearing his MI9 'escape and evasion' hat, BAAG gradually took on responsibility for medical services to the thousands of Chinese soldiers and their dependants, treating up to 30,000 patients a year and during the famine of 1943 feeding 6,000 people a day. 'Operating with great gallantry, skill and flair, [and] on a shoestring',[21] Ride was held in the highest esteem by SOE who co-operated with him throughout the war.

SIS in the Far East had a chequered history. Initially headed by Colonel Leo Steveni, a Russian-born British Army officer based in Delhi, it concentrated on procuring tactical intelligence on the front line. This narrow parochial focus failed to impress Mountbatten as SACSEA to the extent that Steveni became 'a complete laughing stock at the Supreme Commander's meetings'. Stewart Menzies, the Chief of SIS, tasked Brigadier Edward Beddington, his deputy director responsible for Asian activities, to find a replacement. When he visited Chongqing, Carton de Wiart found him 'utterly lacking in tact' and bemoaned the fact that he left 'a bad smell wherever he has been'.[22] The appointment of Brigadier 'Bogey' Bowden-Smith as Steveni's successor in 1944 created a new problem of credibility for he was patently a candidate of the old boy network, a former commanding officer of the 16th/5th Lancers – Beddington's old regiment – and an Old Rugbeian like Steveni. He had no track record in the Far East or as an intelligence officer.

The incumbent head of SIS in China, Lieutenant Colonel Gordon Harmon, broke the mould of SIS mediocrity. Based in the 'General Liaison Office' in

Chongqing, he oversaw a 'motley crew of old China hands' running half a dozen offices across China.[23] By the end of 1943, SIS were operating five radio stations across Nationalist China, none of which were 'molested' by General Tai Li. In all, about 25 officers handled over 400 agents throughout China. Harmon's most important human asset was Michael Lindsay, who had managed to become the principal radio adviser to Mao Tse-tung's Communists in Ya'nan. To Harmon's credit, his perspicacious attention to the CCP was a glowing example of SIS's strategic long-term intelligence mandate. Carton de Wiart rated him highly but observed that 'his people in Kandy are continually by-passing him by sending up people who take charge at Conferences etc and one doesn't quite know where one is in consequence'.[24]

Another British-sponsored intelligence network was that of Laurence Gordon, a Canadian with British citizenship who had spent some of the interwar years in Indo-China working for Texaco. Made a captain in the Intelligence Corps reporting to Major General Cawthorne, DMI India, who funded and equipped him with W/T sets, Gordon first set up shop in Chongqing and then in Kwangsi Province. In effect, he created his own private intelligence organization in Indo-China while at the same time keeping an eye on Texaco's assets and personnel. Acting as a freelance oil agent, he travelled freely through Tonkin, Annam and Cochin-China, purchasing oil and other commodities for the Chinese black market. Joined by two former colleagues, Harry Bernard and Frankie Tan, both US citizens, Gordon's network – GBT – provided first-class intelligence to General Chennault's 14th Air Force.

Since 1941, American intelligence and Special Forces activities in China had been characterized by competition between commanders and their respective services, exacerbated by the entry of General Donovan and his newly created OSS. After the departure of Stilwell who had been at daggers drawn with Chennault, Wedemeyer determined that the time had come to reign in the plethora of private armies and autonomous intelligence organizations and summoned them to a meeting on 24 January 1945. Wearing his theatre commander's hat, he laid down that all clandestine activities were to be coordinated and approved by both him and the Chinese. A week later, on the advice of SOE's Brigadier George Taylor, SEAC advocated that all British clandestine activities in China should integrate into a new single grouping headed by Carton de Wiart.[25] Ever the realist and never a dreamer, Carton de Wiart wisely restricted his participation to coordination with Wedemeyer's staff through the office of his new assistant Lieutenant Colonel Cartwright, diplomatic overwatch of the Chinese and being kept in the myriad of intelligence loops. The long-awaited replacement for

Grimsdale, Major General Eric Hayes, arrived in early 1945 and took up the new position of GOC British Troops China, reporting on policy to Carton de Wiart.[26] He was finally master of his own house

While relations with the Chinese remained good, the same could not be said of those with the Americans. When Field Marshal Wilson met Wedemeyer in Washington DC on 9 March 1945 to discuss special operations among other matters, Wedemeyer made it clear that his authority extended to full control of all clandestine organizations in China, British and American alike. Furthermore, having been recently reminded by the President 'that colonialism must be abandoned by our allies' and admonished by him not to give any supplies to clandestine French forces, he insisted that Indo-China came within the China Theatre and hence he had full control over clandestine activities there, a claim that directly contradicted the verbal agreement between Mountbatten and the Generalissimo for SEAC to conduct pre-occupational activities in the country.

The problem for the British was that the Americans held all the cards; the OSS in one guise or another had been effectively operating against the Japanese in China since mid-1944 and had nearly completed the training of 5,000 KMT commandos for long-range raids against Japanese lines of communication.[27] Five-man Special Operation groups were active throughout the war zone, some with as many as 1,500 guerrillas under command. If the British wanted to have any role in China in the next stage of the war against Japan, they would have to fall in behind Wedemeyer. Carton de Wiart knew this and soon had his work cut out. When, in the face of the Japanese advance, 204 Mission was evacuated from the OSS forward area in Chekiang by the USAAF in February, Carton de Wiart and Hayes quickly reorganized it into a fifty-strong British Training Team which eventually deployed under US Command Training HQ to Xi'an in Shensi Province. He would also need US approval for the deployment of Colonel David Stirling's new Special Air Service Regiment[28] which had been given the go-ahead by Churchill in June 1945 to support the Generalissimo. As events turned out, the war finished before it left England, in retrospect a political blessing given that its terms of reference in a telegram Arthur Sutherland sent to Carton de Wiart were 'to clobber the dreaded Chinese Communists!'[29] in direct contradiction to US policy.

17

The Generalissimo wins the war
but loses the peace

The New Year began on a high note when HM The King appointed Carton de Wiart as a Knight Commander of the Order of the British Empire.[1] It was a long overdue recognition of his outstanding record of service to his adopted country which many believed should have been bestowed on him after his return from Poland in 1923. Sadly, some tragic news followed. His friend Lieutenant General Herbert Lumsden, who had travelled out with him to India on his appointment as the prime minister's personal representative to General MacArthur, had been killed on 6 January. He had been standing on the port side of the bridge of the battleship USS *New Mexico*, watching the bombardment at Lingayen Gulf, when a Japanese suicide bomber struck the bridge and killed him instantly. He was buried at sea that night.

The prime minister had given Carton de Wiart a letter to hand to the Generalissimo on his return. 'General Carton de Wiart has told me of your kindness to him and of the trust you repose in him. I have no doubt that his services in linking us more closely are of great assistance to our common cause.' It got the year off to a good start.

On the morning of 28 January, the official Ledo Road inaugural 113 vehicle convoy set off from Ledo; a week later the column of trucks and jeeps, some towing 105-mm. and 75-mm. howitzers, entered Kunming, marking the triumphant completion of General Stilwell's grand plan to open a land route to China. Shortly after its opening, the Generalissimo suggested that it be renamed the Stilwell Road. Given the poisonous relationship between the two men, maybe he had found a subtle way to associate his bête noir with failure for, far from the wildly optimistic projections of the road handling 100,000 tons a month, in July 1945 only 6,000 tons were moved along it compared to 71,000 tons flown over the Hump. Stilwell's obsession had turned out to be a $2 billion White Elephant.

Major General Gordon Grimsdale, a seasoned China-watcher, had consistently questioned the rationale of the road, pointing out that even at the height of its usefulness before the fall of Burma, it had carried less than 20,000 tons per month, the equivalent of two medium-size cargo ships. Furthermore, since all the Chinese ports remained in the hands of the Japanese, until Rangoon was recaptured there would be no Burmese harbour to unload the cargo ships carrying the Lend-Lease supplies for China.

On 29 January, Mountbatten as SACSEA issued two new directives.[2] The first redefined Carton de Wiart's role. In addition to being the prime minister's representative in China, he was appointed head of all British Armed Services in China and the co-ordinator of all British activities there, including those of BAAG and E Group. Furthermore, the GOC 204 Military Mission would be responsible to him for all matters of policy and any approach to the Generalissimo or Wedemeyer had to be made through him. Colonel Cartwright, Mountbatten's representative, was tasked to coordinate all SIS, SOE and specific BAAG activities. Carton de Wiart's earlier missives to Mountbatten about being of 'no use' had been heeded. Even better, they were now on first name terms after Mountbatten had written to him, beginning 'My dear Adrian (if I may call you after fifteen months of friendship)' to which he replied 'My dear Dickie'.[3]

The second directive was addressed to Major General E. C. Hayes, the new GOC 204 Military Mission. Instructed to 'do everything in your power to improve the fighting efficiency of the Chinese army', Hayes's troops were limited to training and had no operational role as such although they were 'at liberty to keep in touch with the Chinese General Staff . . . on such matters as the strategical and tactical dispositions, plans for raids on enemy communications and installations and all other matters including the health of the Chinese troops'. While the bulk of 204 Military Mission had been moved from Eastern China, Mountbatten reminded him of the importance of British prestige and asked him not to move the remainder so long as they were performing a useful operational and intelligence role. If the rhetoric sounded hollow, it was because by the summer of 1945, there were 34,726 US air force personnel and 22,151 ground troops in the China Theatre.[4] As Major General Gordon Grimsdale concluded, 'by comparison with the immense efforts of the US in China, especially the USAAF, the British effort was almost negligible'.[5]

In early March, Mountbatten and his wife Edwina paid an official visit to Chongqing,[6] an event eagerly awaited by the Generalissimo although Meiling was in America recuperating from an illness. After dining with Carton de Wiart the first night, the next day Mountbatten met with the Generalissimo with T. V.

Soong acting as interpreter and then with General Chen Cheng before an official dinner with the Generalissimo. Edwina's programme focused on the Red Cross with visits to hospitals and children's orphanages. It was an unqualified success; and Mountbatten wrote to Carton de Wiart a few days later:

> I am astounded at the difference in the atmosphere of Chongqing between October 1943 and March 1945 and I realise this change has been brought about largely by your personal influence and prestige and actions. I knew this before and it was on this basis that I recommended you for a knighthood to the Prime Minister but I was not prepared for the degree to which you had succeeded. This is indeed a very wonderful feather in your cap and must surely be measured as your greatest service to the Empire, great as your other services as a soldier'.[7]

French Indo-China (FIC) continued to dominate the relationship with Wedemeyer. At one point Carton de Wiart tripped up by writing a poorly worded letter in which he appeared to suggest to Wedemeyer that the United States and China 'in conjunction' should attack FIC. What he had intended to say was that once the political oversight of the FIC had been resolved, the French, with some outside help, could retake FIC and at that point, the United States and China could launch an attack on Japanese-occupied South China with the object of capturing a port.[8] It was indicative of just how prickly the situation had become and at every opportunity Wedemeyer would tell Carton de Wiart how he resented any operation being implemented in FIC without his consent being obtained.[9] Mountbatten put it down to Wedemeyer's problem in coming to terms with the fact that although he was now the Commanding General of a US Theatre, he was still subordinate in the SEAC area to SACSEA who had been appointed by the Combined Chiefs of Staff with the approval of the President and the Prime Minister. None of this would have mattered but the advance of the Americans from their SWPA bases had focused the minds of the Japanese High Command on the possibility of a US invasion of Indo-China. Consequently, troop levels were increased to around 60,000 and the coastal areas of Annam and Tonkin were reinforced. The key question was whether the French Vichy army would remain loyal to Tokyo.

Without waiting for an answer, on 9 March 1945 the Japanese puppet government seized key points all over the country and mercilessly dealt with all opposition, known and potential.[10] The French Army was disarmed and interned; Admiral Decoux and General Mordant were imprisoned. In some garrisons, the French were subjected to dreadful atrocities: in Dong Dang and Lng Son 80 per cent of French military personnel were beheaded. Two French Jedburgh officers, Captain Maurice Stasse and Second Lieutenant Roger Villebois, were killed in action on 9 March; another, Lieutenant Pierre Roussett, was captured after dropping on 18 April and later beheaded. The timing could not have been worse for the French as the renewed offensive in Burma was using up all the resources of Force 136, especially aircraft and supplies.

Then, as news of the disaster began to filter into Kandy, it was apparent that some 10,000 French troops were still fighting. SOE therefore decided to reinforce General Alessandri who was holding out with 4,000 men (including the formidable 5th Infantry Regiment of the French Foreign Legion) in the Black River sector of West Tonkin. They provided him with thirteen W/T stations and dropped three actions groups – DAMPIERRE, GASSET and CORTADELLAS – together with arms and ammunition.[11]

It was a race against time. Lord Selborne, the minister in charge of SOE, wrote to the prime minister on 15 March, advising him of the need to give 'our French Allies' the earliest possible support 'before it is too late'. To that end, he implored him to approach President Roosevelt as soon as possible to clarify the question of responsibility between SEAC and China Command for operations in Indo-China. After fifty-two days of bitter fighting and incessant marching, General Alessandri's troops reached China on 2 May where they received a cool welcome from both the Chinese and the Americans. The latter had initially refused to help, prompting Colin Mackenzie, the head of SOE in the Far East, to signal 'American name is mud, repeat mud, with French and British alike in this whole episode'. It had been, as he put it, 'a very poor show indeed'. Churchill had felt equally strongly, writing to Field Marshal Wilson that 'it will look very bad in history if we were to let the French force in Indo-China be cut to pieces by the Japanese through shortage of ammunition,[12] if there is anything we can do to save them'. It was only on 18 March that Roosevelt ordered US Air Forces in China to come to the aid of the French.

However, the war in the Pacific was above all an American war and in early 1945 the end game was slowly coming into sight. The combination of American industrial might and huge manpower resources meant the US military–industrial machine was inexorably closing in on Japan, its air forces pulverizing cities with incendiaries and HE bombs and decimating seaborne lines of communication. The resultant pockets of Japanese resistance in the Pacific were formidable but containable in the knowledge that it was only a matter of time before they capitulated. Although the Allies still believed that the war would not end until 1947, for the KMT the key question was no longer the defeat of Japan but what was going to happen next in their huge country as it teetered towards the brink of civil war. Never before had the Generalissimo been in such need of true friends.

Despite its 900,000 strong army and a militia of 2.2 million living in areas it controlled,[13] Mao's Tse-tung's CCP had done little to take the fight to the Japanese during the INCHIGÔ offensive. A summary in an earlier intelligence assessment of the Japanese North China Area Army dated 1 October 1940 provides an explanation:[14]

> The CCP's ultimate goal is simply to overthrow the Chongqing Government and seize control of the whole of China itself. However, the CCP is still weak at present and is not strong enough to replace the KMT and take power. And so the mission of the CPC forces for the time being is to make Japan and the Chongqing Government fight each other as long as possible and build up their own strength in the meantime. This is why, outwardly, they look like they are obeying the Chongqing Government, believing that intensifying the opposition between the KMT and CCP forces is detrimental to the expansion of their own troops, when in actual fact they are moving to prevent Japan engaging in peace talks with the Chongqing Government. Because unless the Japanese Army and the Chongqing Government keep on fighting as long as possible, the CCP forces will not have the time they need to grow stronger.[15]

Not surprisingly, the Generalissimo was piqued about the US Dixie Mission to Ya'nan and Ambassador Hurley's November visit to Mao and his resultant five-point plan to bring the CCP into a coalition government. The OSS, adopting the same attitude as the British had done with Tito in Yugoslavia, backed the idea of supporting Mao for, in their opinion, his troops were more likely to inflict serious damage on the Japanese than the KMT. Unlike Tito's proven record, there was little evidence to support this.

When at the beginning of February, Roosevelt, Churchill and Stalin had met in Yalta to discuss the fate of post-war Europe and the next stage of the war against Japan, including Russian participation, pointedly the Generalissimo had not been invited and was naturally suspicious that Chinese interests had been side-lined. He was right for the terms of Russian participation were hidden in a series of secret codicils. It was Hurley who came to his rescue by announcing at a press conference in Washington on 2 April[16] that the United States would recognize only the national KMT government. Events then moved quickly. On 12 April Roosevelt died and a new president Harry S. Truman took over. A month later, on 5 May, Germany surrendered, and Stalin stood by the promise he had made at Yalta to declare war against the Japanese within ninety days of

VE day. The Generalissimo sent T. V. Soong to Moscow to negotiate terms since the Americans and British were too busy preparing for the Potsdam Conference and could not intermediate. The Soviet demands which had tentatively been agreed at Yalta behind the Generalissimo's back were onerous including the independence of Outer Mongolia and a privileged status in Manchuria.

British military intelligence (M 12) reported in May that 'in actual fact, very little indeed is going on in China in spite of the large amount of paper that comes in. Most of the ops are of very small importance to the main strategical picture . . . many of which have obviously only taken place in the imagination of the Chinese'.[17] For Carton de Wiart and the British troops in Chongqing, the picture was rather different for a cholera epidemic had just started, one that would reach its peak at the end of June.[18] One US officer wrote home:[19]

> We began noticing it about three weeks ago. These sedan chairs were carrying an increasing number of people with their faces covered up or, if exposed, their arms, legs and faces were an ashen white. Then the long blanket wrapped bundles suspended on bamboo poles with chickens on top began to become more noticeable. . . . There is no census – the sick are not treated (except a very, very few richer folk) and the dead cannot be counted because there is no registration. The only means to check is by the number of coffins bought, but these blanket covered bundles don't go in coffins.

Then on 25 July, there was an unexpected political upheaval in Britain. Labour won a landslide general election and technically Carton de Wiart was no longer Churchill's personal representative. The Chinese were quickly on to it and sent Lieutenant General Ho Hao Jo, the head of Foreign Affairs Bureau, to find out whether he was staying on. Mountbatten signalled Ismay to this end.[20] From his home in London, Churchill sent a telegram to Carton de Wiart, 'I am deeply grateful to you for the splendid work you have done. I was always proud to be represented by a man like you. Thank you for your kind expressions.'[21] Fortunately Clement Attlee, the new prime minister, was equally quick off the mark and telegrammed the Generalissimo that he wished to keep de Wiart in place. He forwarded copies to Carton de Wiart with a note saying,

> I would like you to know that I am well aware of the success with which you have in the past discharged the tasks falling to you. I have the fullest confidence in your continued ability to meet these responsibilities which at present and probably for some time to come will, I am convinced, exercise your powers to the full.[22]

This was reassuring since Carton de Wiart had told Mountbatten that 'our allies are getting more and more difficult – they want a complete monopoly on this country – and though they are very nice to me – I'm getting heartily sick of them'. He was particularly upset by Chennault's resignation which was 'a very bad mark . . . in Chinese eyes'.[23]

By now the Japanese economy stood close to collapse. Devastating B-29 raids on Tokyo had destroyed fifteen square miles of the city in early March and other cities such as Nagoya and Osaka had been pounded. Then on 6 August, the Americans dropped the first atomic bomb on the city of Hiroshima, instantly killed 66,000 people and irradiating thousands more. Three days later, on 9 August the Soviet Union declared war on Japan and launched an all-out offensive in Manchuria. The same day the Americans dropped another atomic bomb, this time on Nagasaki, killing a further 44,000 people. Japan surrendered unconditionally on 14 August.

The immediate concern of the British in China after the Japanese surrender was the reestablishment of British administration in Hong Kong, the centre of their financial and trading activities in the Far East. Various plans had been made in 1944 to use BAAG and 204 Mission to train a Chinese guerrilla army in the nearby area which could then conveniently assist in the liberation of Hong Kong. These were refined in 1945 despite the intense suspicions of the Chinese about British intentions and the need to clear them with the Americans. In his new role as head of all British military activities in China, Carton de Wiart played a central part in securing approval from Wedemeyer and the OSS for the British to operate in the Poseh area to the southeast of Kunming and in preventing friction between SOE and the OSS.

In the event, SOE through BAAG was able to deter the KMT and Communists from fighting one another for control of the Territory and to support Franklin Gimson, the former Colonial Secretary, who had declared himself Acting Governor as soon as he heard of the Japanese surrender. Setting up an office in the former French Mission Building in Victoria on 1 September, Gimson and his skeleton administration dealt with the pressing problems of freeing and feeding former Allied POWs and civilian detainees and in containing 10,000 surrendered Japanese troops until, on 30 August, Rear Admiral Cecil Harcourt[24] sailed his Task Force[25] into Victoria Harbour (Operation ARMOUR) to establish British Military Administration in the colony. On 16 September, on behalf of Britain and the Generalissimo, he formally accepted the Japanese surrender from Major General Umekichi Okada and Vice Admiral Ruitaro Fujita at Government House.

For the Chinese government, the actions of the British appeared perfidious and high-handed for they had not been party to these plans. Hong Kong clearly lay in the Generalissimo's theatre of operations; indeed, in good faith, he had delegated the powers for surrender to the British on that understanding.[26] Carton de Wiart found 'British diplomacy may have been questionable at this time' and gave great credit to Rear Admiral Harcourt and Major General Frankie Festing, Commander British Forces Hong Kong, who between them devised a modus operandi with the Chinese and oversaw the return of civilian rule over the following nine months.

China's eight-year war with Japan was suddenly over. Some 14 to 20 million people are estimated to have perished in the conflict, a number so large as to be incomprehensible in terms of individual lives. The Generalissimo, who had been taken unawares by the A-bomb like everyone else, now realized he needed to act quickly to gain control in the sudden vacuum. After signing a Sino-Soviet Treaty of Friendship neatly wrong-footing Mao who saw Moscow as his natural ally, he invited the CCP leader to come to Chongqing for talks about plans for the future. For six weeks the two men sat down in an attempt to come to some sort of binding and sustainable agreement, but it remained elusive as both sides prepared for civil war.

Ismay sent Carton de Wiart down to Kandy to see Mountbatten and when he returned to Chongqing on 22 August, he reported:

> I do not see how civil war can be avoided here, and what distresses me is that after speaking to Mountbatten I gather the feeling at home is that the Generalissimo wants civil war. That is absolutely false, but when Mountbatten said the Generalissimo should retire before the Communists, if the latter attack, to put them in the wrong, it is really going too far. I doubt any Government doing so in similar circumstances, and in this country he could not show his face again if he did.
>
> He will do all he can to avoid civil war, but the Americans have made too much of the Communists and the latter have raised their price in consequence and that makes the situation very complicated.
>
> . . . I have been to see Wedemeyer since writing the above. He tells me the Chinese are very sore at the wording of our announcement that we were going to Hongkong. He says we told them we were going whether they wished it or not, which I suppose is true, but I feel he is really more sore about it than the Chinese themselves.[27]

Mountbatten invited Carton de Wiart to attend the surrender ceremony in Singapore on 12 September 'where the Japs looked such insignificant little objects that I could not help wondering how they had kept us occupied for so long'.[28] From there he flew to London where his first engagement was a lunch with the Belgian Ambassador with the diplomat Lord Killearn and Lady Cunard among others.[29] On 28 September, he addressed the Chiefs of Staff Committee[30] on China. MI2 had reported earlier in the month[31] that:

> We are in agreement with General Carton de Wiart that the danger of a civil war in China with the next two years is real unless the US Government continues to give strong political, military and economic support to the Generalissimo.
>
> Civil War has virtually been endemic in China from time immemorial; even during the war against Japan the country was weakened because it had been divided among the followers of Chiang Kai-shek, the followers of Wang Ching-wei[32] (later succeeded by Cheng Kung-po)[33] who came to terms with the Japanese, the Chinese Communists centred on Yan'an, and certain Provincial War Lords in Southwest China e.g. in Yunan, who have remained largely independent of Chongqing.
>
> On the other hand, we are not altogether convinced that the Provincial War Lords will come to terms with the Communists to overthrow the Central Government . . .
>
> Much of course depends on the future attitude of the Soviet Government to the Communists. It is possible that despite this treaty with Chiang Kai-shek, the Russians might consider it worth their while to maintain clandestine relations with the Communists as a means of blackmailing the Central Government into acceptance of Russia domination, or at any rate predominant influence, in such areas as Manchuria, Singkiang and Outer Mongolia.
>
> If, however, Russia and the US more or less disinterested themselves in the internal political affairs of China, the fact that the Kuomintang have some well-trained troops, American arms and the bulk of the armaments of the surrendered Japanese, might impel the Chinese communists to do a deal with Chiang Kai-shek and accept some sort of federal government.
>
> But we agree that in view of the poor communications in China and the immense size of the population and the country and the character of the Chinese War Lords, a stable regime is unlikely for many years.

He told the Committee that he thought the likelihood of civil war had diminished but if the movement of the Communists into Manchuria continued, then it could exponentially increase the threat. Asked whether there was any substance as to whether the Americans would increase their troop levels there, he understood to the contrary that they were planning to half their 300,000 men by December. He was delighted to report that relations with the Generalissimo continued to be good and their talks always very friendly and frank. On the question of the French General Le Clerc using British airfields to fly troops into Indo-China, he referred it to the Chiefs of Staff themselves.

Now that the war with Japan was over, he wondered what the British military organization in China should look like and suggested a Military Attaché with three or four assistants to cover the ground, an Air Attaché and assistant and a Naval Attaché. The Air Mission to the Chinese Staff College should ideally remain in place[34] depending on the wishes of the Chinese. Similarly, an air route Rangoon-Hanoi-Hong Kong-Shanghai-Japan would need to be cleared with the Chinese. The last item on the agenda was his continued tenure in post. In view of the unsettled circumstances, he was prepared to return if required. With the approval of Prime Minister Attlee and Ernest Bevin, the new Foreign Secretary, Field Marshal Lord Alanbrooke warmly welcomed his offer and he was on his way back on 10 October.

His return to China turned out to be an astute move on Alanbrooke's part for, on his return, he met with Meiling who relayed him some of the Generalissimo's concerns about the United States:

> He thought their policy was always liable to change owing to their political administration, but once Britain offered its friendship it was of a much more permanent nature. He of course owed the US a great debt of gratitude and he felt it deeply but he could not overlook a change of attitude. . . . She told me that the Generalissimo had applied to our embassy for 100,000 tons of shipping and she asked if I could do anything to get 50,000 tons in the course of next month . . . she spoke of the Communist situation but she did not seem to me to be unduly worried about this except insofar as Russia was concerned . . . hinting that Russia might use force. She said that the Generalissimo had asked her to tell me all this as a friend, as they were points he did not want to talk about officially.[35]

Around this time, de Wiart met Mao Tse-tung and he described the meeting to Ismay:

> I met Mao Tse-tung, the Communist leader, at a small party given by Colonel Harmon, our SIS representative here. Mao Tse-tung, his chief of staff[36] and a female secretary, who spoke good English, were the only ones present.
>
> If the Generalissimo can effect a compromise with him, I will be more than surprised. Harmon started off by asking Mao if he was pleased with the appointment the Generalissimo had made in putting General Li Tsung-jen in command of the forces in Peking and the North. Mao's reply was that the Generalissimo ought to have put in a Communist there, which I thought very uncompromising. Before starting our conversation, I pointed out to Mao that I was merely speaking as a private individual and a looker on who wished China well. If he was prepared to talk on this condition, I would tell him what I thought, and he agreed.

Mao then told me that he had tried to co-operate with the Generalissimo, and I said that was all very well but what he had done was not my idea of co-operation. It was quite true that both Mao's and the Generalissimo's forces had fought the Japs but the whole time they were looking over their shoulder at each other and hoping they might have a chance to deal each other a crippling blow. I pointed in my opinion co-operation could only be really effective if both parties trusted each other. He agreed with me though he did not much like my remarks.

He added that he thought beating the Japanese was the first objective and that they could try and come to terms with the Generalissimo. I said I felt that no harm could have been done if he at the same time tried to come to terms before the fighting had finished. It would have helped matters then and simplified them now.

Mao is quite a good type of man, but a fanatic, and I cannot believe he really means (to do) business, though I hope I may be wrong. His Chief of Staff was much easier to deal with, but I didn't feel he had great influence over Mao.

The latter asked me why I had never come up to see them and I said I had avoided doing so as I considered the KMT-Communist controversy as concerning China and no one else and I had no instructions, right or desire to meddle in it.

I am afraid the result of my meeting with Mao does not give me any more confidence in a settlement than I had before.

Mao himself never concealed his political views. 'Definitely and beyond all doubt, our future or maximum programme is to carry China forward to socialism and communism. Both the name of our Party and our Marxist world outlook unequivocally point to this supreme ideal of the future, a future of incomparable brightness and splendour.'[37]

He had also met with T. V. Soong; and in a signal to Ismay on 21 November, he reported that Soong was

undoubtedly considerably perturbed by the Communist situation in the North as I think he has every cause to be for in my opinion there is absolutely no doubt that Chiang Kai-shek's only chance of dealing with the present situation is by a quick show of force, which although it may become involved in open hostilities, might achieve the desired object by merely being on the ground, hence Soong's desire to transport troops to focal points as soon as possible.

Carton de Wiart's Chief of Staff, Major Dowler, had had to return to England after a serious operation; his replacement was Colonel John Chapman-Walker.[38] A Conservative politician and Bond Street solicitor in peacetime, Chapman-Walker had taken on the role of Director Special Operations Australia in March

1943, dealing with a myriad of interests: British, American, Australian, Dutch, Portuguese and French. He scarcely put a foot wrong and presided over a highly effective office that soothed ruffled feathers on countless occasions and delivered a number of remarkable successes in the field despite, on occasions, in the teeth of American opposition.[39]

At the beginning of December, Carton de Wiart gave a dinner party in Chongqing for Lester Little, the first American to be appointed Inspector General of Chinese Customs,[40] who had been in post since 1943. Few people in China were better informed about trade, finance and politics than Little, so it was not surprising that the other guests included the banker Reignson Chen and his wife, the intelligence chief General Ho Hao Jo, Geoffrey Wallinger of the British Legation, Colonel Harman of SIS and Colonel Eckford of SOE. Beginning with a cocktail of one measure of rum, half a measure of brandy, and the juice of one lime and one orange, the evening got off to a good start until Little declined on health grounds to eat the fresh crabs the General had brought back from Nanking that day and made do with ham and eggs.[41] Naturally no offence was taken, and conversation went on late into the night.

Shortly afterwards, an opportunity to visit Peking arose and Carton de Wiart flew up to find it covered in snow. 'Feasted and feted for several wonderful days,'[42] he found the city beguiling, fascinating and lovable as he toured the Forbidden City, the Temple of Heaven and the Summer Palace. When he was back in Chongqing, a letter dated 20 December arrived from the Mayor of Peking:

> For favour of perusal by General Carton de Wiart
>
> The recent gracious visit of the Mighty Chariot added lustre to the appearance of the City. How sad, how regrettable that it was not possible to stay long and that feelings of the host could not be adequately expressed.
>
> It was heard with deep relief that the Mighty Chariot had returned in safety to Chongqing. Many exposures were taken by attendants of the places visited while in Peking; herein, presented with both hands, to form 'the imprint of the wild swan on the snow and mud' and a souvenir of former travels.
>
> It is respectfully suggested that they may be accepted with a smile (of benevolent condescension); this is my earnest prayer.
>
> Respectful wishes for the Sage's birthday.
>
> Respectfully written by Hsuing Pin

As to the continued presence of British troops and clandestine services in China, after talking to the Ambassador and Major General Hayes, Carton de Wiart recommended that British troops in China should be disbanded as practicably as possible and all paramilitary forces such as SOE should be wound up and

BAAG dissolved. The future of the SIS station was particularly tricky since they had worn uniforms throughout the war and were all well known to the Chinese. He thought it would be necessary to change the entire personnel.

On 31 December 1945, SOE ceased operating and formally closed down on 15 January 1946. The exception was in the Far East and in February 1946 the Chiefs of Staff agreed with SACSEA that the retention of 569 SOE personnel would become a War Office/ALFSEA responsibility. Tasked with resettling ex-guerrilla forces in Burma, Siam and Malaya, General Browning, Chief of Staff ALFSEA, was committed to liquidating them as soon as possible.

On 28 December Carton de Wiart confronted the Generalissimo about a letter the embassy had received from the Ministry of Foreign Affairs which suggested that 'we were not wanted here and the sooner we get out, the better'.[43] The Generalissimo was

> very apologetic. . . . He would always welcome our ships and he felt that all that had happened arose out of inexperience and stupidity on the part of his people who were handling these matters. . . . He assured me there was no discrimination between the US and British navies and that no discourtesy was ever meant. I also tackled him on the question of a staging post for our planes in Shanghai, another request to which we have had no answer . . . he told me we could have one . . . I hope things will go better now and the Generalissimo could certainly not have been nicer than he was, but there is no question of getting anything done here except through him.[44]

In November 1945 President Truman made it clear that US forces would not fight for the Nationalists which precipitated the resignation of Ambassador Hurley, opening up a rift in US foreign policy that had long been in gestation. In his letter of resignation, Hurley fumed that 'the chief opposition to the accomplishment of our mission came from the American career diplomats in the Embassy at Chongqing and in the Chinese and Far Eastern Divisions of the State Department'.[45] Truman's response was to send the former Chief of Staff of the Army, General of the Army George C. Marshall, to China to broker a deal between the CCP and KMT factions who were now increasingly warring rather than sparring.

With the arrival of General Marshall in Chongqing on 22 December, the Americans took centre stage; and on 10 January 1946, the newly formed Committee of Three – Marshal, Zhou Enlai and the Generalissimo – announced a truce between the KMT and CCP and the deployment of tripartite 'truce teams' into the contested areas in the north. By February, Mao Tse-tung was briefing journalists that 'China has stepped into a stage of democracy' and it began to look as if Marshall had pulled off the Chinese Goldfish Bowl Trick when an agreement between the KMT and CCP for 'the reorganization and integration' of their two armies was announced on 25 February. The prospect of peace appeared to be imminent.

By now a seasoned observer, Carton de Wiart was unusually alarmist and pessimistic after a trip to Shanghai in February. He wrote to Ismay that

> The Communist situation has also deteriorated, and it is hard to predict what may or may not happen. I feel the Generalissimo has gone as far as he can and now all depends on Marshall's report. If the Americans withdraw their troops, there is almost bound to be a civil war and in that case the Generalissimo might very easily decide to raise a Japanese army. Should this happen the yellow peril will become a fact. I am afraid I had always looked upon it as a myth: I don't know. One must remember that the Chinese have no real hatred for the Japanese and it will take very little to bring them together.[46]

Marshall had returned to Washington half way through March to report to President Truman. His absence triggered a breakdown of the truce and the deliberations of the Committee of Three seemed little more than hollow rhetoric. Far from implementing the agreement, Zhou had stalled on the CCP's undertaking to give the truce teams access to Manchuria. Marshall had no choice other than to return, this time with his wife Katherine.

Carton de Wiart had returned to London in late March and was asked to brief the Chiefs of Staff Committee on 3 April.[47] After a general discussion about China and Indo-China, mundane matters like the repatriation of Japanese troops through Hong Kong and the niceties of British ships 'visiting' Shanghai rather than 'relieving' other ships on station there were summarily dealt with by Carton de Wiart, who by now was an arch practitioner of Chinese diplomacy.

Asked to stay on in China until 31 October, he relocated his office which by now consisted of himself and his ADC, Captain Bob McMullan,[48] to Nanking where the Generalissimo had moved his government. Although he was given a pleasant house in the compound of the university, ironically the former home of the best-selling US writer Pearl Buck who detested and chastised the British Empire at every opportunity, he missed the 'hurly-burly of that overcrowded city (Chongqing) and its cheerful informality bred by war; the little shopkeeper and the ordinary citizens were of infinitely more interest than the State officials'.[49] The one consolation was a daily hour and a half walk up the 2,000-foot Purple Mountain. Naturally, he took the steepest path.

The tempo had markedly slackened as Attlee preferred to deal with him either through the Foreign Office or War Office. This in turn impacted on the frequency of his access to the Generalissimo although they continued to meet as friends. At the beginning of May, the Russians pulled out of Manchuria taking with them an estimated 70 per cent of Manchurian industrial assets which prompted the opportunistic CCP to occupy Siping which in turn provoked the KMT to attack them. Carton de Wiart sent Ismay a note on 15 May:

> Things here are far from bright; I never saw a solution to the Communist question except by giving them a good beating and, as they keep on attacking towns, I hope the Generalissimo will go for them one of these days.
>
> I do not believe Russia would react to this except by supplying more arms etc to the Communists but, as they are already doing this, it would change nothing in that respect.
>
> Marshall is doing all that is humanly possible to do to bring about a peaceful solution, but I simply do not believe that it can be done unless the economic situation could be restored to such an extent as to eliminate the various evils resulting from it. Famines, strikes, soaring prices are all playing into the Communists hands.

Marshall was indeed struggling to bring peace to China but managed to persuade the Generalissimo to declare a fifteen-day ceasefire on 6 June after three months of non-stop fighting, followed by an extension to 30 June.

That summer, the Generalissimo provided Carton de Wiart with a summer house at Guling, a small village perched on top of a 3,500-foot mountain above Kukiang, where treaty-port residents would move to escape the malaria-infested plains in the hot summer months. The Chiang Kai-sheks had bought a house there in 1933 in the days when it was still a British-built village[50] with the Fairy Glen Hotel and the Journey's End Inn still run by British nationals. The only way up was by foot and declining the offer of being carried for five miles in a chair borne by two coolies, he set off up the 1,000 stone steps, arriving at the top 'virtually in a state of collapse'![51] He was deeply touched by Chiang's thoughtfulness and relished the long walks in the wood-covered hills. General Marshall and his wife were also provided with a summer house in the village.

After making a short trip back to England to report, he was thrilled to be given an Avro 691 Lancastrian passenger plane (a derivative of the Lancaster bomber) for his return journey which to his amazement involved only four stops. Soon after arriving back in Nanking, he flew to Tokyo where he had lunch with General MacArthur, 'a tremendous personality and a charming man'.[52] In July, Sir Horace and Lady Seymour left for England, a sad moment for Carton de Wiart who had been welcomed by them on the day he first arrived in Chongqing. The new Ambassador, Sir Ralph Stevenson,[53] had been Ambassador Extraordinary and Minister Plenipotentiary to His Majesty the King of Yugoslavia, and if de Wiart's plane had not crashed in 1941, the two men would have most likely worked together.

The picture in China looked bleak as the American elements of the truce teams made their way back to their Executive Headquarters in Beijing. Marshall left Kuling on 17 September and relocated to Nanking where he attended a remembrance service for General Stilwell in mid-October when some 1,500 Americans and Chinese gathered in a large ceremonial hall. Flowers covered the altar, incense smouldered and panels of Chinese calligraphy covered the wall with tributes from leading dignitaries.[54] The eternally changing choreography of the battle between the KMT and CCP continued to frustrate Marshall as he gamely stayed the course to try to settle their differences in the interests of a united China.

By now it was clear that the Soviet Union and the CCP were both playing the same game to discredit the United States and remove the Generalissimo, who was holding on by vigorously prosecuting the war – with an unexpected degree of success – on the expectation that the Americans would have to come off the fence and support him. The stark reality that Marshall faced was there was no appetite for such a commitment for, as far as the American people were concerned, the war had ended. So, although by now it was obvious that Chiang Kai-shek was the lesser of two evils, he had to be persuaded that social and economic collapse driven by hyperinflation and food shortages were more of a threat to his government than the CCP and if these were not averted by wide-ranging and meaningful reforms, the fallout would play straight into Mao's hands.

As to the United States supporting the KMT, Marshall warned that Washington would 'have to be prepared to take over the Chinese Government, practically, and administer its economic, military, and government affairs'. That would 'involve [the US] Government in a continuing commitment from which it would be practically impossible to withdraw', as well as a 'dissipation of resources' that would 'inevitably play into the hands of the Russians'. Yet to Marshall, the challenge was not just about resources. A full-scale military commitment would involve 'obligations and responsibilities . . . which, I am convinced, the American people would never knowingly accept. We cannot escape the fact that the deliberate entry of this country into the armed effort in China involved possible consequences in which the financial costs, though tremendous, would be insignificant when compared to the other liabilities involved.'[55]

By October 1946, Carton de Wiart was on his way home. On 12 October, the prime minister sent him a fulsome telegram,

> on relinquishing the appointment which you have filled with such conspicuous success for the past three years, I ask you to accept my warmest thanks for the services that you have rendered. You have built up a very special position in China and the part that you have played in winning the confidence of Generalissimo Chiang Kai-shek and in fostering the good relations between ourselves and the Chinese is deserving of the highest praise.[56]

Two days later, General Ismay received a note from 10 Downing Street informing him that his suggestion that Carton de Wiart was deserving of a higher honour that the KBE for example a KCB or KCMG, which Mountbatten had recommended him for in 1945, had been forwarded to the Foreign Office who felt they had many other candidates to consider and thus they were unable to include him on their forthcoming list.[57] It begged the question as to how 'the highest praise' by the prime minister could be converted into an honour or award. Carton de Wiart was not the only one whose citation was rejected. Colin Mackenzie, who had run SOE in the Far East for four years, had been put forward by Mountbatten for a knighthood; he received a CMG, much to the chagrin of Mountbatten who told him, 'he was shocked and grieved not to see your name among the Knighthoods in the New Year's Honours list of 1946'.

It must have been of some consolation when 10 Downing Street put out a statement on 15 October to the effect that, following the termination of his appointment as the prime minister's special military representative,

> His Majesty's Government in the United Kingdom are glad to take this opportunity of paying tribute to the valuable services rendered by General Carton de Wiart during the three years of his appointment, and to the excellent personal relations which he established with the Chinese authorities. His work was in the best traditions of Anglo-Chinese friendship, and His Majesty's Government look forward confidently to maintaining equally close liaison as before with the Generalissimo through the ordinary diplomatic channels.

The Times chose to give the announcement due prominence.[58]

Flying via Saigon where he had dinner with Admiral Georges Thierry d'Argenlieu, the Free French High Commissioner for Indo-China, he stopped over in Rangoon to stay with Brigadier Duke who had worked for him as a

Major in 61st Division in Oxfordshire and Ballymena in 1940. After a modest lunch, he went up to his room for a siesta, and on coming down slipped on the coconut matting and crashed to the bottom of the stairs. 'I hit my head on the wall knocking myself almost unconscious, broke my back, crushing a vertebra, and was very lucky not to break my neck.'[59] Fortuitously, he was put in the care of the Australian orthopaedic surgeon Colonel J. G. Bonnin, who put him in plaster of Paris which enabled him to fly home. Looking akin to an Egyptian mummy, he stayed with the Wavells in Delhi, Lieutenant General Charles Allfrey[60] in Cairo, Sir Clifford and Lady Norton[61] in the embassy in Athens until; on arrival in Great Britain, he was hospitalized at The Royal Masonic Hospital in London.

> For seven months they operated on me, nursed me, housed me and fed me, and all with unremitting kindness and skill; and no man has more reason to be grateful to them. Not only did they mend my back, but they tidied me up inside and outside, excavated all sorts of old bits of scrap-iron, and sent me away a fitter if not wiser man.[62]

Even the prime minister sent him a Telegram: 'I am very sorry to hear of your unfortunate accident. I hope you are making good progress towards an early recovery.'[63] On 17 December, Carton de Wiart replied to him from The Royal Masonic Hospital in London:[64]

> When I went to say goodbye to the Generalissimo, he asked me if I would come back to him as his Adviser. I thanked him for the honour done to me by this offer but said I would like to think it over.
>
> He told me that if I felt inclined to accept, he would apply for me officially to the British government.
>
> Frankly, I would prefer not to accept, but should you consider my acceptance would prove of any help to Sino-British relations then I would do so.
>
> I think it is very significant that this offer has been made to an Englishman in preference to an American, as it clearly shows the Generalissimo's desire for good relations with the British.
>
> Unfortunately, I have just had an operation, but I hope soon to be fit enough to see you and make my report on leaving your service. Perhaps then you would allow me to discuss this question with you.

As it happened, he was laid up too long to be able to accept the Generalissimo's invitation although Chiang Kai-shek offered to keep the job open for him indefinitely.

Back in China, after a final meeting with the Generalissimo on 1 December, having embargoed all arms and ammunition supplies to China[65] in a final attempt

to convince him to buy into the American peace plan, Marshall threw the towel
in and left the Nationalists and Communists to fight it out between themselves.
For the next two years, beset with problems of rampant inflation, strikes, student
protests and extended lines of communication, the Nationalists were on the back
foot, outgeneralled and outsmarted as the Communists switched from guerrilla
to conventional warfare.[66] The Generalissimo's strategy of dispersing his forces to
hold the main cities in areas captured from the Communists proved to be flawed
for it exposed his troops to battles of encirclement and attrition. On 21 January
1949, the Generalissimo left Nanking for the last time; two day later the People's
Liberation Army marched into Beijing. His wartime capital Chongqing fell to
Communist forces on 1 December and on the 10th he left the Chinese mainland
for his new base, the offshore island of Taiwan. Earlier, on 21 September, Mao
Tse-tung had proclaimed the establishment of the People's Republic of China
and began his twenty-seven years of uninterrupted power as the leader of a
totalitarian Communist state.

In his summary of *China's War with Japan*, Rana Mitter writes that:

> Without Chinese resistance, China would have become a Japanese colony as
> early as 1938. This would have allowed Japanese dominance over the mainland
> and would have allowed Tokyo to turn its attention to expansion in Southeast
> Asia even more swiftly, and with less distraction. A pacified China would also
> have made the invasion of British India more plausible. Without the China
> Quagmire – a quagmire caused by the refusal of the Chinese to stop fighting –
> Japan's imperial ambitions would have been much easier to fulfil.[67]

With the benefit of hindsight, it is easy to criticize Seymour and Carton de
Wiart as the senior representatives of the British government in China for their
passive acceptance of the endemic corruption over which the Generalissimo
and his ministers shamelessly officiated. This belies the facts that, first, China
was still transitioning from an autocratic Imperial state, which had disintegrated
into regional fiefdoms, into a centralized modern state with all the necessary
institutions – a transition that had been abruptly arrested by the Japanese invasion
of 1937. Secondly, more important, its embattled government, 'struggling to
continue a long war against a modern industrial power',[68] was a pivotal ally in
the war against Japan and Germany, leaving the Allies little room to demand
changes of economic and social policy or indeed terms of engagement as long
as the KMT continued to tie down one and a half million Japanese soldiers. It
is fanciful to suggest that either man could have better discharged his duty by
scolding the Generalissimo for his shortcomings.

Part X

Retirement

A contented old age

Several months after being admitted to the Royal Masonic Hospital with a broken back, in June 1947 Carton de Wiart was finally discharged and thanks to the generosity of a friend he moved into 3 Headford Place, a small house off Halkin Street near Hyde Park Corner. His old soldier servant Pritchard took charge of the household and despite stringent rationing managed to produce memorable meals when Carton de Wiart entertained his many friends. Visitors to the house included fellow 4th Dragoon Guards officers Bob Ogilby, Arthur Fitzgerald and Tony de Rothschild; General Pug Ismay from his Somaliland escapade; Peter Fleming, who had worked closely with him in Norway and China; and General Dick O'Connor and Dan Ranfurly from PG 12, all of whom had become good friends after a lifetime of shared adventures. He was much in demand as a godfather, first to Sir Geoffrey and Lady Davson's daughter Caroline in 1947 and then to the Ranfurlys' daughter, also a Caroline, in 1949.

The famous Carton de Wiart exercise regime focused on walks around Richmond Park, supplemented by long hikes across the South Downs near his old stomping ground at Brighton. Within a remarkably short time, he had regained his legendary fitness and after a few sessions at James Purdey's shooting school was back on the lists of invitations for pheasant shooting that autumn. In October, according to the *Dundee Evening Telegraph*,[1] he had 'gone into business and become chairman of Yangtye (London) Ltd, an import and export firm which has roots in a large Chinese trading corporation'.

White's Club in St James's celebrated the return to health of one of its most popular and long-standing members – he had been first elected in 1908 – by making him a life member and commissioning fellow member Simon Elwes to paint his portrait.[2] An Old Oratorian like de Wiart, in 1945 Elwes had lost the use of his right 'painting' arm as the result of a stroke. Through hard practice and determination, he taught himself to paint with his left arm and his portrait of Carton de Wiart hangs in the club today opposite Oswald Birley's portrait of Field Marshal Earl Alexander of Tunis.

By now held in fond esteem by the British public, Peter Fleming affectionately described him in his *Stryx* column[3] in *The Spectator*:

> The General has a fierce eye, a soft voice and the best manners in the world. He is a good judge of risks and has never refused one that he liked the look of. His standards of conduct are high and rigid. He is a very fastidious man – fastidious in his likes and dislikes, in his quite extraordinary consideration for others, in his dress, in the fairness which he assesses people and situations and things . . . his manners are impeccable, his canons are unashamedly those of the day before yesterday, he never appears to be trying very hard, he has tremendous style. He is also very witty, and quite impossible to replace. It is a good thing that the standard of marksmanship among foreigners is not just a shade higher.

The full article also appeared in the Candid Cameo column of the *Daily Sketch* in 1947. Carton de Wiart was given the opportunity to reply:

> Judging by all the things Peter Fleming has found to write about me, I feel he should be a writer of fiction. But it seems hardly fair for such a famous man of letters to expect me to bandy words with him, when he knows perfectly well that soldiers generally use words of one syllable only, and only rise to two syllables on special occasions.
>
> I share his pleasure that the standard of marksmanship of foreigners was not higher, for had it been I am sure Peter would not be here either. To lose an eye is a bore; a hand one seldom misses, and it is amusing to find out how much one can do with one only.
>
> The truth is that I was born lucky; I have taken the opportunities that came my way; and I have no politics.

Possessed of an irresistible love of driving, when passing by a car showroom in Piccadilly he made a spur of the moment decision to buy a black convertible Touring Lagonda. This may explain why he sold a Queen Anne footed salver at Christies for £440! Soon, he was on the road to the South of France, a journey that became an annual pilgrimage for the sun worshipping veteran. One year he dined with Winston Churchill, another habitué of the French Riviera, who was staying with his American literary agent, Emery Reves, at the Villa La Paula built by the Second Duke of Westminster for his mistress Coco Chanel.

The plight of disabled veterans became a particular concern for him in the years of post-war austerity. In August 1948, he wrote to *The Times* adding his support to the British Legion's campaign to draw attention to the 650,000 disabled ORs who received no supplementary benefits and relied entirely on their basic forty-five shillings pension. Pointing out that in 1919 a select committee had fixed the basic rate at forty shillings, he questioned whether 'our disabled should be asked to shoulder the burden of the decreased purchasing power of the pound'. With his customary tenacity he returned to the topic with another letter in February 1951[4] after the primacy of disability over unemployment compensation had been debated in the House of Commons. Carton de Wiart reminded readers that 'the national conscience' had decided that a disability allowance was not a substitute for the dole.

Events in the Far East remained centre stage for British foreign policy. The French and the Dutch were struggling to subdue nationalist movements in their respective pre-war colonies, the civil war between the Nationalists and Communists raged on in China; and in Malaya, the Malayan Communist Party had embarked on a guerrilla war against the British colonial administration. Carton de Wiart was delighted if somewhat surprised when he was invited to lecture at an Ashridge House seminar at Berkhamsted with three distinguished journalists – *Reuter*'s Gerald Samson, *Newsweek*'s Joseph B. Phillips and the *Observer*'s Patrick O'Donovan.[5]

On 6 July 1949, Rikki died in Vienna, a city she knew and loved above all others. Her beloved sister Sylvia had died there in April; their mother Nora had also died there in March 1945 just as the Soviet army approached.[6] Carton de Wiart was in Hyères on the French Riviera at the time and wrote to Anita,[7] 'I only hope she did not suffer a lot and that she enjoyed those last few months in Vienna. Our ways parted long ago but that does not make me feel her death any the less. I know how she loved to enjoy life and I should like to think that she enjoyed it to the end.' When her estate was wound up, he told Anita he did not want any money but would like the cigar case given to him by President Paderewski and a small gift box, 'both of which I consider are very personal things'.[8] His brother-in-law, Major General Prince Leopold Fugger von Babenhausen, had been captured by the Russian Army in 1945 and was still being held in captivity.[9]

By now Carton de Wiart had entered into a relationship with Joan Sutherland,[10] a divorcee in her early forties who had been previously married to Lieutenant Colonel Arthur Sutherland. Carton de Wiart and Arthur were old friends and had kept in touch after the Great War; David Sutherland, Arthur's elder son, refers to Carton de Wiart as his father's 'old WW1 buddy'.[11] It has not been possible to establish when they first met but after her divorce from Arthur in 1943, Joan moved to London to work for the War Office and she told her niece that she had written to Carton de Wiart when he was a POW in Italy.[12] It was Joan who as a regular visitor to the Royal Masonic Hospital had helped him recover after he returned from the Far East with a broken back.

Sutherland's first marriage had been to his nurse Ruby Miller, the vivacious and pretty eighteen-year-old step-daughter of his friend Major Guy Vivian,[13] who had been wounded serving with the Grenadiers in France. Guy was recovering at the family home at Foxborough Hall in Suffolk which had been turned into a military convalescent home; and when he heard that Arthur had lost his leg with the Black Watch at Aubers Ridge, he arranged for him to come and recuperate with him. Arthur had then returned to duty as a Staff Officer in France, retiring from the Army in 1922 to work for the family business Begg Roberts & Co in London which had extensive interests in India. Their son David, who was to become an outstanding SAS and SBS leader in the Second World War, was born in 1920 but the marriage failed and they were divorced in 1927.

A year later, Arthur married 25-year-old Joan, daughter of George McKechnie, a city businessman and a director of Findlater, Mackie, Todd & Co Ltd wine merchants. Brought up in Beaufort Gardens in Knightsbridge, Joan attended the Glendower House school where she excelled at games.[14] They had two children, Caroline born in 1928 and Fergie in 1931. That marriage failed too and in 1943 Sutherland married Mrs Elizabeth Warburton-Lee,[15] the widow of Captain Bernard Warburton-Lee, VC, who had been killed in action in the 1940 raid on St Nazaire.

In 1950, Carton de Wiart's autobiography, *Happy Odyssey*, was published by Jonathan Cape. With a foreword by none other than Winston Churchill which told of a 'vigorous, varied and useful life' and assured readers that 'his story will command the interest of all men and women whose hearts are uplifted by the deeds and thoughts of a high-minded and patriotic British officer', it became an instant success with five impressions within the first year. Sir Keith Officer, the former Australian Ambassador to Chungking, told Peter Fleming that Carton de Wiart had written it 'under duress' when he was in the Royal Masonic Hospital. There were some extraordinary omissions, one of which was the award of the Victoria Cross which the publisher turned into a positive by using the back of the book jacket to point out that 'in his book General Carton de Wiart makes no mention of the fact that he was awarded the Victoria Cross. Because, as readers will agree, his conduct was no more than characteristic, the citation is here quoted in full'. More puzzling was that not once did he mention his marriage to Rikki, his two daughters or his grandchildren. They had been airbrushed out of his account of his life like disgraced members of the Politburo erased from a group photograph taken on the reviewing stand in Red Square on a May Day parade.

The following year, Carton de Wiart and Joan were married in Tiverton where her sister-in-law lived[16] and decided to leave London in search of open spaces, fresh air and shooting, the complete antithesis of city life. Several newspapers latched on to it as a secret marriage, describing Joan mysteriously as 'a secret bride'. In their search for a place to live, preferably in a sporting paradise, however alluring the charms of Italy, Austria and France were, the major factor was that it had to be somewhere the British government could pay his pension. Ireland fitted the bill perfectly, the more so since Carton de Wiart admired and liked the Irish – 'each man who has a snipe in his swamp, a woodcock in his brushwood or a fish in his pond, invites you to share it with him'[17] – and, with the royalties that had accumulated from sales of *Happy Odyssey*, they bought an empty former priory called Aghinagh House in Killinardrish, County Cork, on the banks of the River Lee. It was as near he could get to his beloved Pripet marshes for just to the west of Aghinagh lies the Gearagh, an alluvial woodland which hosts a diversity of wildfowl such as mallard, wigeon, teal and Greylag geese. The river was famed for its salmon although shortly after they moved there, the fishing was disrupted by the building of two dams to provide electricity for the city of Cork.

After leaving Eton, his step-son Fergie went on to Sandhurst and was commissioned into the 5th Royal Inniskilling Dragoon Guards. Sent to Korea in 1951, he lost his left leg in an explosion while on reconnaissance. 'Going up a hill, one of the four troops I was with tripped the wire of a landmine and set off the blast,' Sutherland recalled. 'I was the only one badly injured. One of the troops said "You're OK, Mr Fergie, it's only the leg". I knew that because I had already checked.'[18] He was taken to the Field Hospital, where the surgeons prepared to amputate his right leg as well. The story has it that Sutherland slowly cocked his loaded revolver and indicated to them, in words of one syllable, that under no circumstances should they attempt to do so. Surely his step-father would have approved.

The doctors later told Sutherland – who had loved horses since childhood – that his riding days were over. He ignored this diagnosis, and with the help of his mother and Carton de Wiart who found him a splendid grey mount called Munster Man,[19] he continued to ride to hounds and compete in point-to-points. He had specially adapted artificial legs for specific activities – for example, one for riding, one for shooting and one for dancing. According to his son Harry: 'We grew up in houses full of legs. There were legs in every cupboard.'

Carton de Wiart and his wife spent the next twelve years at Aghinagh where, in between looking after the kitchen and flower gardens and running a little dairy, 'the General's tireless physical activity found ample outlets in the pursuit of snipe and salmon'.[20] In 1949 he had taken on the role of President of the Military Historical Society and he attended its annual dinner in London whenever possible. Much to his surprise and delight, he was made an honorary Fellow of Balliol[21] and an honorary LL.D. of Aberdeen University. Old age started to catch up with him and Joan's grandchildren remember him in a wheel chair out blackberry picking.[22] He never forsook style and enjoyed half a bottle of champagne with Joan before lunch every day.

Joan's granddaughter remembers visiting Aghinagh as a child where 'the house was very well organized and comfortable . . . filled with flowers'. Her grandmother loved 'theatre and musicals, particularly Gilbert and Sullivan. . . . She really loved and admired the general and I think her happiest days were with him . . . going together in his Lagonda to Monte Carlo and the South of France, fishing and shooting in Ireland and enjoying picnics and outings'.[23]

In June 1956, Carton de Wiart and Joan travelled to London to attend four days of events marking the centenary of the introduction of the Victoria Cross as a gallantry award. The main event was a review of 300 VC holders from all over the Commonwealth, together with the widows and families of posthumous awards. Ninety-nine years to the day after her great-great-grandmother Queen Victoria had invested 62 of the 111 Crimean War recipients, HM Queen Elizabeth took the salute as the VCs led by Lieutenant General the Lord Freyburg, marched past in Hyde Park. Carton de Wiart was in the front rank between Colonel James Carne, who had won a VC commanding the Gloucesters in Korea in 1951, and the one-legged Private Willie Chafer, who had won his in 1916 in France. Immediately behind him marched Brigadier Charles Hudson, the winner of a VC in Italy in 1918 as the 26-year-old commanding officer of the Sherwood Foresters.

In her address to the parade, HM the Queen spoke of the 1,344 men who had won the VC,

> men of all ranks and . . . from all walks of life. They were of different colours and creeds. They fought in many lands and with many different weapons. But their stories are linked by a golden thread of extraordinary courage. Each man of them all gave the best that a man can give, and all too many gave their lives. Some, careless of danger, stood firm in battle to hold or secure a position. Some with sublime self-sacrifice, gave their lives to help wounded comrades. Many exposed themselves time after time to death in conditions of battle beyond the imaginations of our forefathers. All met with honour those demands of war which urge the valiant spirit to the limits of human endeavour and endurance. They dared mightily, and 'turned their necessity to glorious gain'.

Apart from the parade, the Carton de Wiarts attended the Service of Commemoration in Westminster Abbey followed by a government reception in Westminster Hall on the Monday, a garden party at Marlborough House on the Tuesday, and a reception at Windsor Castle and an evening reception at the Guildhall on the Wednesday. And if that was not enough, the VC holders and their guests could view an exhibition of VCs in Marlborough House, join the directors of Mecca at a Tea Party and Cabaret at the Lyceum Theatre in the Strand, go to Lord Mountbatten's British Empire Service League reception in Great Smith Street, enjoy a visit to the cinema courtesy of the Rank Organization or join BBC Television at the King's Theatre in Hammersmith for a performance of Henry Hall and the BBC Dance Orchestra in *Here's to the Next Time*. Lionized wherever they went, it was a memorable week for the Carton de Wiarts.

In June 1957, Carton de Wiart took Joan to Belgium to introduce her to members of his father's family there. Met in Bruxelles by Count Edmund Carton de Wiart and his daughter Renée-Victoire, Marquise de la Boëssière-Thiennes, after an audience with King Baudouin,[24] they toured the Ypres and Passchendaele battlefields with his cousin, Baron Christian Houtart, and then stayed with Renée-Victoire at her husband's family Chateau at Lomside. From here they visited the Carton de Wiart house at Hastières par delà where he had often spent his holidays as a boy.[25] Over the next years, several of his Belgian cousins came to stay at Aghinagh, maintaining the renewed family links. Under the guidance and love of Joan, especially after his heart attack in Aix-en-Provence in 1960 when according to Joan 'the after-effects of his old wounds suddenly became very serious . . . and left him unable to walk unaided',[26] these last years of his life revolved around her extended family to which he happily played the role of devoted step-father[27] and patriarchal grandfather; his own family remained in the background, a choice he had made nearly fifty years before.

In August 1962, Hugh Molyneux, the 7th Earl of Sefton,[28] as a result of meeting several of Carton de Wiart's friends and contemporaries at a house party at Goodwood during race week, wrote to Lord Ismay suggesting that a biography of Carton de Wiart was long overdue and that he, Ismay, would be the best man to head it up.[29] Ismay whose *Memoirs* had been published by Heinemann two years previously reacted favourably and after receiving a letter of encouragement from both Joan and Carton de Wiart, he started to recruit contributors. General Sir Richard O'Connor agreed to provide a chapter on their time together as POWs in Italy; Ismay himself offered to write a chapter on Somaliland. This 'compilation' strategy needed an editor to oversee it and the first name put forward by Peter Fleming was that of Dennis Kelly,[30] the mainstay of Churchill's literary team who had been making 'Cosmos out of Chaos' for the last thirteen years. At the same time, Ismay approached Ben Glazebrook at Constable & Co[31] to see whether he would be interested in publishing a biography.

Keen to get on with his career as a barrister, Kelly gracefully declined in February 1963 which triggered a new search and Fleming put forward two further names, Alistair Horne and Brigadier James Davidson-Huston.[32] Horne, who had just completed *The Price of Glory: Verdun 1916*, had just embarked on his next book *The Fall of Paris*, which ruled him out, leaving Davidson-Huston in the running. On paper he looked an excellent choice, fluent in Chinese since his time with the Shanghai Defence Force in 1927–8 and then as Assistant Military Attaché China from 1930–3. In the Second World War, he had commanded the commando units in 204 Military Mission and had been with General Stilwell on the 'walk out' to India in May 1943. He was also a published author with *Yellow Creek, the Story of Shanghai* (1962), *The Piracy of the Nanchang* (1961), and *Russia with Your Eyes Open* (1962), all favourably reviewed. Nothing came of this approach, so Constables put forward the name of Christopher Sykes,[33] Robert Byron's companion on *The Road to Oxiana*, who had written the biography of Major General Orde Wingate three years earlier. Due to prior work commitments, he turned it down.

Seven months had now passed since Ismay had sponsored Sefton's idea and there was still no sign of an editor. Constables then came up with Reginald Pound,[34] who had just completed the biography of the press baron Lord Northcliffe. A former officer in the Royal Sussex Regiment in the First World War, Pound had gone on to become a successful journalist with the *Daily Express* and then the *Daily Mail* as well as editor of the *Strand Magazine*.

It was at this point that Carton de Wiart died in his sleep on the night of 5 June 1963 at Aghinagh House. Leaving her husband in the care of his nurses and staff, Joan had set off to London earlier that day to attend the wedding of her niece (and god-daughter) Deidre to Michael Constable-Maxwell-Scott. As soon as she arrived, news of his death came through and she headed straight back home.[35] Having nursed and cherished him since his stroke, his death caused great distress to her for she had not been at the bedside of the man she adored. He was buried just outside the Caum graveyard of Killinardrish Church in Creek field, a piece of land belonging to the house where an impressive stone memorial was later erected by Joan.

Tributes came in from all over the world and a Requiem Mass was held on 24 July at Westminster Cathedral in London. The Armed Services were represented by the Chief of the Defence Staff, Earl Mountbatten, and Sir Winston Churchill by Brigadier Sir John Smythe, VC, MP. Joan was accompanied by her son Fergie; Carton de Wiart's daughters, Anita and Ria, by their husbands and two of their children. Old friends such as Countess Wavell, Dan Ranfurley, Field Marshal Sir Frankie Festing, Lieutenant General Sir Philip Neame and Bob Ogilby were ushered to their seats by officers of the 4/7 Royal Dragoon Guards and the service concluded with the Last Post and Reveille fittingly sounded by the regimental trumpeters.

Ismay was fulsome in his tribute to his old friend:

> Carton de Wiart was a happy warrior if ever there was one. He always scorned the safe and easy way. He was literally shot to pieces, but his wounds only seemed to quicken his fighting spirit. His courage was not only superlative: it was infectious. I have seen half-trained troops follow him gaily into a tight corner as though they were veterans. No soldier of his generation was more admired or more loved.[36]

Shortly after Carton de Wiart's death, Major Bryan Lewis of the Worcestershire Regiment[37] wrote to Ismay about a proposed BBC tribute to Carton de Wiart and asking for his contribution. Lewis then put himself forward as a potential editor for the biography,[38] an offer supported by Constables but not by Joan who vigorously opposed it[39] on account of Lewis's clumsy overtures to the family. 'We don't want Adrian's spirit disturbed – do we?' she wrote to Ismay in August.[40] In the meantime, at the request of Ismay and the family, Fleming had been making some inquiries about Lewis and concluded that he was 'wholly incapable of writing and devoid as in his communications of any literary perception'; he suspected that Lewis, 'if left to himself, would never produce a completed MS and certainly not one fit for publication'.[41]

By the year end, Ismay was ready to give up, suggesting to Joan that she could compile it herself notwithstanding the difficulty in unravelling the contract between Constables and Lewis.[42] Fleming then volunteered to take on the project, but the issue of Lewis and his contract with Constables had still not been resolved. By now Ismay was far from well and he died in December 1965, two years after his Somaliland brother officer whose biography he had worked so hard to champion.

On 19 January 1964, the BBC Home Service *In Our Time* programme broadcasted a tribute to Carton de Wiart called *Genius in Courage*. Narrated by Edward Ward, contributors included his daughter Ria, Earl Alexander of Tunis, Earl Mountbatten, Lord Ismay, Peter Fleming, fellow escapers from the Italian POW camp, and officers and men who had served under him. Fergie Sutherland told one of his sons: 'There are men who talk and there are men who are talked about, but they are talked about for what they do, not what they say. If I were you, I would strive, if you can, to be one of the latter.'[43] He presumably had his step-father in mind.

In his 1951 *Sunday Times* article about life in Eire, Carton de Wiart recalled how Irishmen have the charming habit of telling you what they think you want to hear, and that for the most delightful reason: no more than a wish to make you happy. Not long ago, high up in the hills, he had lost his way on a deserted road. What a relief it was when he happened to stumble on a pretty girl and was able to ask her where the road led to. With a smile, she answered: 'Oh, anywhere you'd like it to go.' Whereupon his imagination was immediately filled with 'heavenly places': Paris — London — Heaven — Dublin perhaps. She was so right, he mused; what did it really matter?[44] He had, of course, been going down that road since he was nineteen and what an adventurous journey it had been.

Peter Fleming's obituary of Carton de Wiart perfectly captured the man:

> It was to the age of chivalry that Adrian de Wiart [*sic*] properly belonged. He saw life as a list in which honour (when nothing much was happening) and duty (when his country was in peril) engaged him automatically as a contestant. It was once said of him that in the world of action he occupied the same sort of niche that Sir Max Beerbohm occupied in the world of letters; and this was true, for he was in all things a stylist.
>
> De Wiart's appearance was distinguished and, thanks partly to a black eye-patch and one empty sleeve, faintly piratical. He could be fierce and was intolerant of fools; but his mind had an almost feminine perceptiveness, and he was unfailingly considerate to others. He accepted, with an air of quizzical insouciance, every challenge that life offered. He might not have agreed – for he disliked empty or pretentious language – that danger has bright eyes; but he found them irresistible.

Lady Carton de Wiart gave her husband's medals to the Ogilby Trust, set up by his old friend Colonel Robert Ogilby, which entrusted them to the National Army Museum in London where they are on display today.

Apart from his astonishing record of courage in the First World War service and his inspirational leadership of 1939 British Military Mission to Poland and the Norwegian Expeditionary Force to Namsos for which he is best remembered today, Carton de Wiart deserves recognition for the significant roles he played in the 1919 Inter Allied Polish Military Mission and as the prime minister's personal representative to Chiang Kai-shek. He rarely put a foot wrong and his counsel was unerringly accurate. His keen intelligence, his natural empathy with people he was working with, his determination to express his own frank opinions irrespective of the rank or status of the recipient, his charm and loyalty to his friends and staff, his openness and embrace of people from all walks of life made him much more than a battlefield hero. It made him the trusted emissary and confidant of prime ministers and national leaders, a role in which he served both his adopted country and others with great distinction. As Peter Fleming put it in a letter to Ismay, 'Adrian was called in to deal with things that were <u>important</u>, not merely adventurous.'[45]

His personal life reveals a more vulnerable and insecure figure who, by his own volition, became estranged from his wife and two daughters at an early stage in their married life. Observing his fellow officers in the Abyssinian campaign in early 1940, Bill Allen wrote[46] that

> every man has manifold personalities; there is the self which he never knows; the self which he sees himself; the self which he presents to the world; and the self which the world accepts; lastly, the ever-changing self of the future – battered, shorn, remoulded by external events, worked down, destroyed and raised again by the inner experience of the man.

Somewhere in this latter category lies the reason for de Wiart's decision to distance himself from Rikki and his daughters.

On the one hand enjoying the companionship of friends, both men and women, and the comradeship of gregarious soldiers, and on the other hand, retreating into a cocoon of self-sufficiency content with his own company – a response he had acquired as a small boy – for Carton de Wiart did not equate solitude to loneliness. This would explain how the idea of marriage to Rikki, an outgoing bubbly personality brought up by a mother who revelled in the whimsicality of Habsburg Imperial society, together with the demands of domesticity which ensued, soon collided with his alter ego that thirsted for a life of an adventurer with no ties attached. Beloved by the British, cherished by the Belgians, revered by the Poles, admired by the Americans and held in high esteem by the Nationalist Chinese, what an extraordinary life he had lived.

Notes

Chapter 1

1   Reading University Library (Hereafter RUL) 1391/B14 Peter Fleming.

2   A.-M. Pagnoul in his introduction to the inventory of the first instalment of Carton de Wiart family archives.

3   Brigadier Sir Bill Williams CB, CBE, DSO, the Editor of the Dictionary of National Biography, erroneously stated that Léon's wife was M. I. James. Anne James was his second wife.

4   D'Esquelbecque, d'Ardinais, de Thouars and de St. Vrain.

5   Bruxelles Municipal Archives.

6   RUL 1391/B14 Peter Fleming.

7   RUL 1391/B44 Peter Fleming.

8   RUL 1391/B44 Peter Fleming.

9   Muchinov, Ventsislav, *Ottoman Policies on Circassian Refugees in the Danube Vilayet in the 1860s and 1870s*, https://dergipark.org.tr/tr/download/article-file/226241 (accessed 15 June 2021).

10 RUL 1391/B14 Peter Fleming reference to conversation with Bill Cavendish-Bentinck.

11 When he was sixty-six, Leopold II took up with a sixteen-year-old French prostitute, Caroline Lacroix.

12 Document www.flickr/photos/halflants/31941441014/in/photostream (accessed 15 June 2021).

13 Hélène was married to Arthur De Ryckman De Betz, a member of a Brabant family which had been ennobled in the 1820s. In 1886 she had three children – Jeanne (5), Andre (2), Raoul (1).

14 Rahimlou, Youssef (1988), 'Aspects de l'expansion Belge en Egypte sous le Regime d'Occupation Britannique (1882–1914)', *Civilisations*, Vol. 38, No. 1, pp. 101–78. *JSTOR*, www.jstor.org/stable/41229365 (accessed 15 June 2021).

15 Tignor, R. (1980), 'The Economic Activities of Foreigners in Egypt, 1920-1950: From Millet to Haute Bourgeoisie', *Comparative Studies in Society and History*, Vol. 22, No. 3, pp. 416–49, http://www.jstor.org/stable/178757 (accessed 24 August 2020).

16 Carton de Wiart, A. (1951), *Happy Odyssey*, London: Jonathan Cape (Hereafter *Happy Odyssey*).

17 *Happy Odyssey*, p. 11.

18 RUL 1391/B14 Peter Fleming.

19 Certificate dated 15 June 1903 signed Hugh Shield.
20 Convened in 1876, the Mixed Courts of Egypt dealt with disputes between Egyptians and foreigners and arbitrated between foreign nationals in Egypt. A blend of the French Civil Code, British Common Law and Islamic legal principles proceedings were held in French.
21 *Happy Odyssey*, p. 13.
22 RUL 1391/B15 Peter Fleming, loose paper signed E.T.W.
23 Francis Fortescue Urquhart, Fellow and Dean of Balliol College.
24 Jones, J. (1997), *Balliol College, A History* (Second edition), Oxford: Oxford University Press.
25 There were exceptions – the *Daily Chronicle*'s editor Henry Massingham retired after falling foul of Prime Minister Asquith when he advocated a policy of reconciliation in South Africa. Likewise, the *Manchester Guardian* called for restraint and negotiation.
26 *The Times*, 5 October 1899.
27 Carton de Wiart, A., *Happy Odyssey*, p. 16.
28 RUL 1391/B14 Peter Fleming.
29 http://www.militarysunhelmets.com/2012/pagets-horse-in-the-boer-war (accessed 15 June 2021).
30 Rose-Innes, C. (1901), *With Paget's Horse to the Front*, London: John MacQueen.
31 Carton de Wiart, A., *Happy Odyssey*, p. 18.
32 Carton de Wiart, A., *Happy Odyssey*, p. 18.
33 *London Gazette*, 26 January 1900.
34 Carton de Wiart, A., *Happy Odyssey*, p. 18.
35 TNA: HO 144/5444. Léon is shown on a UK naturalization page as living in St Anne's, Hampton Wick, with Adrian and Maurice shown as his dependents.
36 Later killed at the Somme in 1916 when serving with the Grenadier Guards.

Chapter 2

1 *London Gazette*, 14 December 1900.
2 Carton de Wiart, A., *Happy Odyssey*, p. 23.
3 Carton de Wiart, A., *Happy Odyssey*, p. 23.
4 Seventy-eight VCs were awarded during the Second Boer War.
5 *London Gazette*, 27 April 1905.
6 Carton de Wiart, A., *Happy Odyssey*, p. 24.
7 Carton de Wiart, A., *Happy Odyssey*, pp. 24–5.
8 TNA WO 76/2.
9 Lieutenant General Sir Charles Briggs, KCB, KCMG (1865 –1941). Briggs was later to become Head of the 1919 British Military Commission to General Denikin in Russia when Carton de Wiart was in Poland.

10 TNA: WO 76/1 and WO 76/2.

11 In 1922 it was amalgamated with 7th Dragoon Guards (Princess Royal's) to form the 4th/7th Dragoon Guards.

12 A misnomer used by the British Army as muzzle-loading muskets had long been withdrawn from service.

13 Wardrop, Major A. E. (1914), *Modern Pig-Sticking*, London: Macmillan & Co.

14 Woodruff, Philip (1954), The *Men Who Ruled India – The Guardians,* London: Jonathan Cape.

15 Carton de Wiart, A., *Happy Odyssey*, p. 33.

16 Fugger, Nora (1932), *The Glory of the Habsburgs, the Memoirs of Princess Fugger,* London: George G. Harrap & Co Ltd, p. 7.

17 Nora was the youngest; her elder sister Marie married Albert Lonyay de Nagy-Lónya et Vásáros-Namény; and her brother Johannes married Archduchess Anna of Austria, Princess of Tuscany.

18 King, Greg and Wilson, Penny (2017), *Twilight of Empire*, New York: St. Martin's Press, p. 68; Fugger, Nora, *The Glory of the Habsburgs, the Memoirs of Princess Fugger*, p. 200.

19 His squadron was based in Boldogasszony (Frauenkirchen) where they managed to find rooms for the family.

20 Fugger, Nora, *The Glory of the Habsburgs, The Memoirs of Princess Fugger*, p. 313.

21 Keegan, John and Wheatcroft, Andrew (2001), *Who's Who in Military History from 1453 to the Present Day*, London: Routledge, p. 12.

22 RUL 1391/B44 Peter Fleming. Princess Hanau to Fleming.

23 Fugger, Nora, *The Glory of the Habsburgs, the Memoirs of Princess Fugger*, pp. 294–6.

24 Later eneral Sir Reginald Hildyard, KCB, CMG, DSO (1876–1965).

25 Lieutenant Colonel Dudley Churchill Marjoribanks, 3rd Baron Tweedmouth, CMG, MVO, DSO (1874–1935).

26 Dudley Marjoribanks inherited the family title in 1909, becoming 3rd Baron Tweedmouth. Muriel is often referred to as Lady T.

27 Hastings, Max (1985), *The Oxford Book of Military Anecdotes*, Oxford: Oxford University Press, p. 314.

28 Carton de Wiart, A., *Happy Odyssey*, p. 40.

29 Fugger, Nora, *The Glory of the Habsburgs, the Memoirs of Princess Fugger,* p. 168–71.

30 TNA: HO 334/67/61.

31 RUL 1391/B44 Peter Fleming.

32 RUL 1391/B44 Peter Fleming.

33 RUL 1391/B44 Peter Fleming.

34 RUL 1391/B44 Peter Fleming.

35 Fugger-Babenhausen archive: FA 7a.1.1 ¼, letter dated 20 October 1908 from the Fürstlich Fugger'sche Domanial-Kanzlei to the Fürstliches Rentamt und Forstrevier Babenhausen.

36 *The Times*, 29 October 1908.

37 Baron Christian Carton de Wiart to author.

38 RUL 1391/B44 Peter Fleming.

39 Carton de Wiart, A., *Happy Odyssey*, p. 43.

40 Carton de Wiart, A., *Happy Odyssey*, p. 43.

Chapter 3

1 Fugger, Nora, *The Glory of the Habsburgs, The Memoirs of Princess Fugger*, pp. 300–1.

2 Carton de Wiart, A., *Happy Odyssey*, p. 44.

3 Bradley, Cuthbert (1910), *Good Sport Seen with Some Famous Packs*, London: George Routledge.

4 Fox, Frank (1923), *The History of the Royal Gloucestershire Hussars Yeomanry 1898–1922*, London: Philip Allan & Co.

5 Carton de Wiart, A., *Happy Odyssey*, p. 45.

6 Rahimlou, Youssef: Aspects de l'expansion Belge en Egypte sous le regime d'occupation Britannique (1882–1914), Civilisations 38, no. 1 (1988): pp. 101-78, http://www.jstor.org/stable/41229365 (accessed 15 June 2021).

7 1900 La Compagnie Immobilière d' Egypte; 1902 La Sociétè Fayoum Light Railway; 1903 La Caisse Hypothécaire d'Egypt – Cousin Edmond was on the board; 1905 Sociétè des Travaux Publics du Caire; 1906 Cairo Electric Railway Company and Heliopolis Oases Company; 1906 Anglo-Belgian Company of Egypt – investor in Fayoum; 1906 La Sociétè Egyptienne des Terrains du Caire et sa banlieue.

8 *Egyptian Gazette*, 27 January 1915.

9 Fox, Frank, *The History of the Royal Gloucestershire Hussars Yeomanry 1898–1922*, pp. 56–7.

10 Lieutenant Colonel Alexander Cobbe (6 October 1902), Captain William Walker (22 April 1903), Major George Roland (22 April 1903), Major Johnnie Gough (22 April 1903), Captain Herbert Carter (19 December 1903), Lieutenant Clement Smith (10 January 1904).

11 Carton de Wiart, A., *Happy Odyssey*, p. 46.

12 RUL 1391/B15 Peter Fleming.

13 His parent regiment, the 4th Royal Irish Dragoon Guards, was likewise mobilized and despatched to France.

14 Mgr de Wiart was later an officer of the Order of Leopold, Knight of the Order of the Crown (Belgium), and an Officer of the British Empire. He received the gold medal of the Reconnaissance Française and the Belgian Medal, First-Class for Civilians.

15 From Dollis Hill, the Hospital of St John and St Elizabeth and Miss Fullerton's Homes.

16 Fr Nicholas Schofield, Oremus, the Westminster Cathedral Magazine.

17 One million Belgians fled to the Netherlands, 250,000 to France and another 250,000 to England. This is still being the largest refugee movement in British history.

18 Obituary in *Pourquoi Pas?* Gazette Hebdomadaire, 24 April 1936.

19 RUL 1391/B44 Peter Fleming. Lady Monk Bretton recalled Rikki being in Austria with her daughters when war was declared.

20 Fugger, Nora, *The Glory of the Habsburgs, The Memoirs of Princess Fugger,* p. 310.

21 Gudule and Marie-Gislaine, two of Henri Carton de Wiart's children, both married into the Houtart family. Gudule's husband was Baron Paul Houtart.

22 RUL 1391/B44 Peter Fleming.

Chapter 4

1 Jardine, Douglas (1923), *The Mad Mullah of Somaliland,* London: Herbert Jenkins.

2 RUL MS 1391 B/13 Peter Fleming.

3 Jardine, Douglas, *The Mad Mullah of Somaliland,* p. 39.

4 Jardine, Douglas, *The Mad Mullah of Somaliland,* pp. 53–4.

5 Brigadier Sir Eric Swayne, KCMG, CB (1863–1929).

6 Jardine, Douglas, *The Mad Mullah of Somaliland,* p. 94.

7 HC Deb 3 March 1910 Vol. 14 cc1019-53.

8 Churchill, Winston (1930), *My Early Life, A Roving Commission,* London: Thornton and Butterworth.

9 Carton de Wiart, A., *Happy Odyssey,* p. 49.

10 Cubitt had served in five West African campaigns between 1898 and 1902.

11 Later General Hastings Ismay, 1st Baron Ismay, KG, GCB, CH, DSO, PC, DL.

12 TNA: WO 106/272.

13 Carton de Wiart, A., *Happy Odyssey,* p. 51.

14 Ismay, Lord (1960), *The Memoirs of General the Lord Ismay,* London: Heinemann, p. 14.

15 Later Sir Arthur Lawrence, Governor of Somaliland.

16 Carton de Wiart, A., *Happy Odyssey,* p. 52.

17 Supplement to the *London Gazette* 2 August 1916: The Despatches of the Commander-in-Chief and the Commander of the Troops in Somaliland. Para 5.

18 Ismay, Lord, *The Memoirs of General the Lord Ismay,* p. 10.

19 RUL MS 1391 B/13 Peter Fleming.

20 TNA: WO 106/23.

21 RUL 1391/B13 Peter Fleming.

22 Carton de Wiart, A., *Happy Odyssey,* p. 53.

23 Based at Clarke's house Artillery at Rupertswood, Sunbury.

24 The Fink family had emigrated from Guernsey to Melbourne in 1861. Benjamin became a successful businessman but was declared a bankrupt after the property crash in the early 1890s. Leaving debts of £1.5 million behind (about £124m in 2017), the family fled to London where he transferred his remaining considerable wealth to his wife Catherine. He died in 1909. (Cannon, Michael (1972), *Fink, Benjamin, Australian Dictionary of National Biography Vol 4*, Melbourne University Press).

25 Among his distinguished patients were the Grand Duke Alexander of Russia, Ramsay MacDonald MP, John Galsworthy, Sir James Barrie, Dame Nellie Melba and (Sir) Donald Bradman.

26 Carton de Wiart, A., *Happy Odyssey*, p. 55.

Chapter 5

1 Gibb, the Rev Harold (1923), *Record of the 4th Royal Irish Dragoon Guards in the Great War 1914–1918*, London: Saward, Baker & Co.

2 TNA: WO95/1112 War Diary of 4th Dragoon Guards.

3 Carton de Wiart, A., *Happy Odyssey*, p. 63.

4 Extract from *The Ypres Book of Valour* – An account of the 4th Royal Irish Dragoon Guards in the Ypres Salient by Major General A. Solly-Flood, CMG, DSO.

5 *London Gazette*, Supplement Friday 14 May 1915.

6 *The Times* 9 June 1915.

7 *The Globe* 11 June 1915.

8 Rahimlou, Youssef: Aspects de l'expansion Belge en Egypte sous le regime d'occupation Britannique (1882–1914), Civilisations 38, no. 1 (1988): pp. 101-78, http://www.jstor.org/stable/41229365 (accessed 15 June 2021).

9 Carton de Wiart, A., *Happy Odyssey*, p. 65.

10 About £15,000 in 2017. TNA purchasing power calculator.

11 Wyrall, Everard (1932), *The History of 19th Division*, London: Edward Arnold.

12 Gough, Hubert (1931), *The Fifth Army*, London: Hodder & Stoughton pp. 127–8.

13 He was one of nearly 240 Cavalrymen to command infantry battalions in the First World War.

14 Bridges, Thomas (1938), *Alarms and Excursions,* London: Longman Green & Co, p. 140.

15 Carton de Wiart, A., *Happy Odyssey*, p. 67.

16 TNA: WO 95/2085, WO 95/2085/1, WO 98/8/262.

17 RUL 1391/3/1 Peter Fleming, Capt Walter Parkes, Draft for BBC broadcast Jan 1964.

18 RUL 1391/3/1 Peter Fleming, Capt Walter Parkes, Draft for BBC broadcast Jan 1964.

19 Wyrall, Everard, *The History of 19th Division*, pp. 34–5.

20 Keegan, John (1999), *The First World War*, London: Hutchinson, p. 200.

21 Wyrall, Everard, *The History of 19th Division*, pp. 34–5.

22 TNA: WO 95/2083 July 1916.

23 Keegan, John, *The First World War*, p. 200.

24 Carton de Wiart, A., *Happy Odyssey*, p. 72.

25 Bridges, Thomas, *Alarms & Excursions*, p. 159.

26 Carton de Wiart, A., *Happy Odyssey*, p. 73.

27 RUL 1391/3/1 Peter Fleming: Capt Walter Parkes, Draft for BBC broadcast Jan 1964.

28 TNA: WO 95/2085/.1.

29 Carton de Wiart, A., *Happy Odyssey*, p. 76.

30 Thynne was twice wounded in the Battle of the Somme in 1916 and awarded the DSO and the Croix de Guerre. He was killed in action in France on 14 September 1918, aged forty-five, while commanding 6th (Royal Wiltshire Yeomanry) Bn. Wiltshire Regiment and was buried at Béthune Town Cemetery.

31 Captain Eric Bell, the Royal Inniskilling Fusiliers; Captain Anketell Read, the Northamptonshire Regiment; Private Jacob River, the Sherwood Foresters; Private Abe Acton, the King's Own Border Regiment; Private George Peachment, KRRC; Sapper William Hackett, RE; Lieutenant Geoffrey Cather, Royal Irish Fusiliers.

32 Asquith, Lady Cynthia (1968), *Diaries 1915–18*, Hutchinson, London, p. 244.

33 Gough, Hubert (1954), *Soldiering On*, London: A. Barker, p. 149.

Chapter 6

1 Or equivalent subunits in other Arms.

2 Third Army was comprised of four corps – Cavalry Corps under Kavanagh, VI Corps under Haldane, VII Corps under Snow and XVII Corps under Fergusson.

3 General Sir Charles Fergusson, 7th Baronet, GCB, GCMG, DSO, MVO (1865–1951).

4 Fergusson had three other divisions under command – 9th (Scottish) Division under Major General Henry Lukin, 34th Division under Major General Nicholson and and 51st (Highland) Division under Major General Harper.

5 Major-General the Honourable Sir William Lambton, KCB, CMG, CVO, DSO (1863–1936).

6 Mullock was killed in action, and from 12 April 1917 Lieutenant Colonel N. M. S. Irwin assumed command.

7 James was the eldest son of James Fison, a manufacturer of chemical fertilizer, and his wife, Lucy Maud, of Stutton Hall, Suffolk, a fine Tudor House overlooking the

Stour estuary. Educated at Charterhouse, he went up to Christ Church as a Scholar in 1909. He joined the 4th Battalion the Suffolk Regiment at the outbreak of war and was awarded the Military Cross on 14 June 1916 and twice mentioned in Despatches in France in 1916 and 1917. He married Charlotte Elliot aged twenty-two at Holy Trinity Church, Brompton on 8 March 1917. Died aged twenty-seven while on sick leave at Wherstead, Suffolk.

8   TNA: WO 95/1502/4.

9   Sharp, Everett, *The Battle of Arras: An Overview,* (http://ww1centenary.oucs.ox.ac .uk/?p=507) (accessed 15 June 2021).

10 Keegan, John, *The First World War.*

11 TNA: WO 95/1502/5.

12 LHCMA: Ismay 4/5/70/2.

13 TNA: WO 95/1502 12 Bde War Diary.

14 Sixteen per cent of Commanding Officers of Service battalions were killed in the First World War.

15 Major General Sir Colin Gubbins, KCMG, DSO, MC (1896–1976).

16 Wilkinson, Peter and Bright Astley, Joan (1993), *Gubbins and SOE,* London: Leo Cooper, p. 19.

17 TNA: WO 95/150212th Infantry Brigade No. O.R.1022/1 dated 22 April 1917.

18 TNA: WO 95/1502 No. OR 1022 Report on 12th Infantry Brigade Attack.

19 Later Lieutenant General Sir Oswald Cuthbert Borrett, KCB, CMG, CBE, DSO & Bar.

20 TNA: WO 95/1503/1 12th Infantry Brigade G.R. 1153 Account of Operations on 3 May 1917.

21 12th Infantry Brigade No. G.R.1132.

22 On 12 July, Borrett was promoted to Brigadier of 197th Infantry Brigade and was replaced by Lt Col A. G. Horsfall, DSO.

23 2/Essex: 7 officers and 180 ORs; 2 W.Rid.R: 2 officers and 30 ORs; 4 detachments, each of 3 sappers.

24 TNA: WO 95/1503/1.

25 Keegan, John, *The First World War,* pp. 139–40.

26 TNA: WO 95/1503/3.

27 The Household Battalion was formed in September 1916 from the reserves of the Household Cavalry regiments to help fill the ever-increasing demands for infantry on the Western Front.

28 TNA: WO 95/1503/4.

29 TNA: WO 95/1503/4.

30 Carton de Wiart, A., *Happy Odyssey,* p. 84.

31 TNA: WO 95/1503/3.

32 TNA: WO 95/1503/5.

33 TNA: WO 95/1503/5.

34 Carton de Wiart, A., *Happy Odyssey*, p. 86.

35 TNA: WO 95/2486/2.

36 TNA: WO 95/2486/3.

37 TNA: WO 95/2554/5 113 Inf Bde War Diary.

38 Carton de Wiart, A., *Happy Odyssey*, pp. 89–91.

Chapter 7

1 Carton de Wiart, A., *Happy Odyssey*, p. 92.

2 Dillon, E. J. (1920), *The Inside Story of the Peace Conference*, New York and London: Harper & brothers (Project Gutenberg EBook December 2004).

3 Davies, Norman (1972), *White Eagle, Red Star, the Polish-Soviet War 1919–20 and 'the miracle of the Vistula'*, London: Macdonald & Co, p. 19.

4 Later 1st Baron Howard of Penrith, GCB, GCMG, CVO, PC.

5 Lord Hardinge diary entry (Cambridge University) quoted by Howard.

6 Later Commercial Secretary at the Embassy in Warsaw.

7 TNA: FO 608/57.

8 TNA: FO 608/57.

9 Howard, Esme (1935), *Theatre of Life,* London: Hodder and Stoughton.

10 Noulens was President of the Commission as Poland was in the French zone.

11 Sir William Tyrrell, KCMG., CB, Minister Plenipotentiary, Assistant to the Administrative Director, Assistant Under Secretary of State for Foreign Affairs.

12 Howard, Esme, *The Theatre of Life.*

13 Howard, Esme, *The Theatre of Life.*

14 TNA: FO 608/59.

15 3 February 1919.

16 TNA: FO 608/59.

17 Howard, Esme, *The Theatre of Life.*

18 Howard, Esme, *The Theatre of Life.*

19 TNA: FO 608/59.

20 A Foreign Office memo of October 1919 refers to a house Baron Taube had put at the disposal of the Commission.

21 Later Ambassador to Washington 1941–45.

22 Later Ambassador to Washington 1936–40.

23 Born in 1876, he was educated at Winchester and then joined the Royal Sussex Regiment in 1900 and served with them in South Africa (five clasps). Resigned due to ill health, he was appointed Comptroller of the household of the Governor General of Canada (Earl Grey at the time). In the Great War served as a railway

transport officer and then as an interpreter in Corfu assisting displaced Serbians. On 20 November 1918 he was appointed Assistant Military Attaché to Lord Derby, the British Ambassador in Paris with special responsibility for Czecho-Slovak matters.

24 Howard, Esme, *Theatre of Life*.

25 TNA: FO 608/59 Cypher telegram 12 January 1919.

26 Carton de Wiart, A., *Happy Odyssey*, p. 94.

27 Howard, Esme, *Theatre of Life*.

28 Wasilewski edited and published Przedświt, the PPS Review in London.

29 *Pamiatka Majowa*, published by A. Dębski in London in 1896.

30 Piłsudska, Alexandra (1940), *Memoirs of Madame Pilsudski*, London: Hurst & Blackett, pp. 164–6.

31 Correspondence Piłsudski Institute 19 November 2020.

32 The Combat Organization of the Polish Socialist Party, or *bojówki*.

33 The Habsburg stratagem to install the pro-Polish Archduke Karl Stephan von Habsburg-Lothringen as regent and then king came to nought.

34 Zamoyski, Adam (2008), *Warsaw 1920 – Lenin's Failed Conquest of Europe*, London: William Collins 2014, p. 4.

35 Oberkommando-Ostfront stretched from the Baltic to the Sea of Azov.

36 Howard, Esme, *Theatre of Life*, p. 318.

37 Charaszkiewicz, Edmund (1955), *Przebudowa wschodu Europy* (The Restructuring of Eastern Europe), London: Niepodległość (Independence), pp. 125–67.

Chapter 8

1 Major General Sir Frederick Poole, KBE, CB, CMG, DSO, DL.

2 Later commanded by Field Marshal William Ironside, 1st Baron Ironside, GCB, CMG, DSO.

3 Major General Sir Charles Maynard, KCB, CMG, DSO.

4 Major General Sir Alfred Knox, MP.

5 Lieutenant General Sir Herbert Holman, KCB, CMG, DSO.

6 General Sir Hubert Gough, GCB, GCMG, KCVO.

7 Brigadier Alfred Burt, CB, CMG, DSO.

8 Telegram Lord Curzon to Mr Balfour 8 February 1919.

9 Captain W. H. F. Maule, DSO. Educated Winchester and Magdalene College, Cambridge; 2nd Lt., N. Lancs. R.; wounded once in the Anere Valley and twice in the Ypres Salient; mentioned in despatches twice.

10 Later Admiral Sir Henry Rawlings, GBE, KCB.

11 TNA Currency converter.

12 Vernon Kellogg, '*Review of The Children of Warsaw,*' 14 August 1919, Vernon Kellogg Papers, Box 1, Folder 11, Hoover Institution Archives, Stanford, California.

13 TNA: FO 608/59.

14 TNA: FO 608/59.

15 TNA: FO 608/268.

16 It was not until 26 February that an Army Law was passed. At that point its strength was estimated as 110,000, a mixture of the Polnische Wehrmacht, former members of Piłsudski's legions and other volunteers.

17 Puslowski represented the Government of Grodno, a city on the eastern border that had remained under German military control until 27 April 1919.

18 Later Brigadier Frederick Hermann Kisch, CBE, CB, DSO (1888–1943).

19 Major Harry Wade (1873–1959), fourth son of Sir Thomas Francis Wade (1818–95), the diplomat and Sinologist and his wife Amelia Herschel (1841–1926), daughter of the astronomer John Herschel. Born in Peking, after attending Harrow (along with classmate Winston Churchill), he joined the army in 1893. In the Great War, he served on the staff of the 1st Army Corps in France and then as military attaché in Denmark.

20 TNA: FO 608/268.

21 TNA: FO 608/268.

22 Davies, Norman, *White Eagle, Red Star*, p. 23.

23 Carton de Wiart, A., *Happy Odyssey*, p. 99.

24 Ludwik Bernsztejn vel Niemirowski, who had been born in Russian-administered former Polish territory, became a British national in 1913.

25 TNA FO 800/215 Drummond to Kerr 18 January 1919.

26 It is not disputed that Archduke Wilhelm von Habsburg-Loringen, the young pretender to the putative crownland of Eastern Galicia, had sent soldiers from his Battle Group to fight for the Ukrainian cause in Lwów.

27 Between 1349 and 1772 it has been in the Rus' Palatinate of the Polish Kingdom.

28 *The Times*, 17 February 1919 – Professor Robert Howard Lord (USA), De Wairt, Gen Longhena (Italy) and Gen Barthélemy (France) travelled to Lemberg/Lvov to secure an armistice with Pavlenko, leader of the Ruthenian forces.

29 Carton de Wiart, A., *Happy Odyssey*, p. 98.

30 Carton de Wiart, A., *Happy Odyssey*, p. 100; TNA: FO 608/59.

31 TNA: FO 608/57 CDW to Balfour 4 March 1919.

32 Orpen, William (1921), *An Onlooker in France 1917–1919*, London: Williams and Norgate, Chap. XIV.

33 Lawrence was in Paris advising the Emir Faisal.

34 During his stay in Paris, Orpen also painted Major General Sir Charles Sackville-West, Major General Sir Henry Burstall, General Sir Herbert Plumer, General Sir Henry Seymour Rawlinson and many others.

35 TNA: FO 608/59 Kimens to British Minister Berne 8 April 1919.

36 Intelligence Report 8 April 1920 to Lt Col Kirsch.

37 TNA: FO 608/59.

38 TNA: FO 208/59 CDW to Kisch 13 April 1919.

39 TNA: FO 608/58 Letter Thwaites – Hankey 13 June 1919.

40 400 were instructors.

41 Białystok.

42 General Count Stanisław Maria Jan Szeptycki (1867–1950).

43 General Antoni Listowski (1865–1927).

44 Davies, Norman, *White Eagle, Red Star*, p. 57.

45 TNA: CAB 208/58 Telegram 9 May 1919.

46 TNA: CAB 208/58 BMM to DMI 11 May 1919.

47 Lwów.

48 Berezina River, also spelled Byarezina.

49 TNA: CAB 208/58.

50 TNA: CAB 208/58 Telegram 553.

51 Howard papers, Cumbria County Record Office quoted McKercher.

52 Dillon, E. J., *The Inside Story of the Paris Peace Conference*.

53 About 7,000 Euros re gold price comparison.

54 Later he joined the South Australian Police, then became a tea planter in Indonesia. He died in Perth, W. Australia, in 1942.

55 Carton de Wiart, A., *Happy Odyssey*, p. 118.

56 TNA: FO 608/58 Telegram 1405 From Curzon to Astoria.

57 TNA: FO 608/58 Telegram 249 Rumbold to FO 19 November 1919; also quoted by Norman Davies as WO 106/967 G 1285.

58 TNA: FO 608/58 Letter War Office 5 November 1919.

59 Churchill to Wilson 31 December 1919, Wilson papers IWM; Churchill to Holman 11 January 1920, CHAR 16/55, CAC.

60 Today Brickenhof Manor is in Tartu county in Estonia.

61 RUL MS 1391 B/44 Peter Fleming, see M. A. Henry entry.

62 Later 9th Duke of Portland.

63 Howarth, Patrick (1986), *Intelligence Chief Extraordinary, the Life of the 9th Duke of Portland*, The Bodley Head, London, p. 30.

64 The Radziwiłł family owned a Palazzo on the Via Gregoriana in Rome.

65 RUL MS 1391 B/44 Peter Fleming.

66 Carton de Wiart, A., *Happy Odyssey*, pp. 112–14.

67 MacMillan, Margaret (2001), *Paris 1919 – Six Months that Changed the World*, John Murray, London, p. 226.

Chapter 9

1 FO 371/5448 (Major General Sir H. C. Holman's Final Report of the British Military Mission, South Russia, April 1920).

2 Information can be found in three White Papers, *Statement of Expenditure on Naval and Military Operations in Russia*, Cmd 307, 11.11.1918-31.7.1919; Cmd 395, to 31.10.19, Expenditure on; Cmd 772 revised.

3 Zamoyski, Adam, *Warsaw 1920 – Lenin's Failed Conquest of Europe*, p. 43 Endnote 16.

4 Ullman, James (2019), *Anglo-Soviet Relations, 1917–1921, Volume 3: The Anglo-Soviet Accord*, Princeton University Press.

5 Carton de Wiart, A., *Happy Odyssey*, pp. 104–5.

6 *The Times*, 7 July 1920.

7 HC Deb 7 July 1920 Vol. 131 c1424.

8 Hansard House of Commons Vol. 132, col.484, quoted Gilbert and Ullman.

9 Edgar Vincent, 1st Viscount D'Abernon, GCB, GCMG, PC, FRS (1857–1941).

10 General Sir Percy Pollexfen de Blaquiere Radcliffe, KCB, KCMG, DSO (1874–1934).

11 Carton de Wiart, A., *Happy Odyssey*, pp. 106–7.

12 D'Abernon, Lord (1931), *The Eighteenth Decisive Battle of the World – Warsaw 1920*, London: Hodder & Stoughton, p. 40.

13 Davies, Norman, *White Eagle, Red Star*, p. 177.

14 HC Deb 10 August 1920 Vol. 133 cc 253–351.

15 Nicolson, Harold (1934), *Curzon, The Last Phase 1919–1925*, London: Constable & Co Ltd, p. 206.

16 Malaparte, Curzio (1931), *Technique du Coup d'Etat*, Paris: Bernard Grasset 'Les Ecrits'.

17 Wojciech Trompczinski, Marshal of The Polish Sejm 1919–22.

18 Jan Henryk Dąbrowski (1755–1818).

19 The total headcount was about 500,000 of which 20 per cent were 'bayonets'.

20 Davies, Norman, *White Eagle, Red Star*, pp. 224–5.

21 D'Abernon, Lord, *The Eighteenth Decisive Battle of the World – Warsaw 1920*, pp. 121–3.

22 TNA: WO 32/5422.

23 TNA: WO 32/5422.

24 TNA: WO 32/5422.

25 General Sir Richard Haking, GBE, KCB, KCMG, (1862–1945).

26 RUL 1391 B/44 Peter Fleming, quoted from Lady Carton de Wiart family letters.

27 Field Marshal Philip Chetwode, 1st Baron Chetwode, 7th Baronet of Oakley, GCB, OM, GCSI, KCMG, DSO. (1869–1950).

28 Nicolson, Harold, *Curzon, The Last Phase 1919–1925*, p. 206.

29 TNA FO 371/8143.

30 BNA Tatler 16 March 1921.

31 HC Deb 3 April 1922 Vol. 152 cc 1885–996.

32 Morgan, Kenneth (1986), *Consensus and Disunity; The Lloyd George Coalition Government 1918–1922*, Oxford: Clarendon Press, p. 315.

33 The economic package was signed a year later.

34 *The Times*, 4 April 1923.

35 Carton de Wiart, A., *Happy Odyssey*, p. 117.

36 Davies, Norman, *White Eagle, Red Star*, pp. 93–4.

37 TNA: FO 688/14/4.

38 TNA: FO 688/14/4.

39 Manfred, Alexander (1973), 'Marshal Foch's Trip to Warsaw and Prague in the Spring of 1923', *A Journal of History and Civilization in East Central Europe*, Vol. 14 No. 1, p. 507.

40 Tommasini, Francesco (1928), *Odrodzenie Polski*, Warsaw, pp. 300–1.

41 Later Major General Frederick Beaumont-Nesbitt, CVO, CBE, MC (1893–1971).

42 TNA: FO 688/14/1.

43 TNA: FO 688/14/1.

44 Carton de Wiart, A., *Happy Odyssey*, pp. 120–1.

Chapter 10

1 19 December 1923.

2 General Sir William Peyton, KCB, KCVO, DSO (1866–1931).

3 Harrison, E. D. R., *An Absolute Non-Ducker*, pp. 113–16.

4 Now in South Belarus -Mankovichi near Stolin on the Horyń River. The house has been destroyed but the park survives.

5 McCormick, M. (1995), 'Byzantium and the West, 700–900', in R. McKitterick (ed.), *The New Cambridge Medieval History* (The New Cambridge Medieval History, pp. 349–80). Cambridge: Cambridge University Press. doi:10.1017/CHOL9780521362924.017.

6 A term used for the Polish nobility from the fifteenth century onwards.

7 The Radziwiłłs received confirmation of their right to the title of Prince of the Holy Roman Empire in 1547; in Poland in 1564/1569; in Austria in 1784 and 1882; in the Kingdom of Poland in 1824 and in Russia in 1845, 1867 and 1899. The qualification of Serene Highness was accorded in Prussia in 1859 and 1861 and in Austria in 1905.

8 Later, the palace later became the seat of the German Chancellor. Hitler's Führerbunker was built in its courtyard.

9 Lednicki, Wacław (1971), *Reminiscences: the Adventures of A Modern Gil Blas during the Last War*, De Gruyter Mouton, Berlin and Boston, Reprint 2019 Edition.

10 Carton de Wiart, A., *Happy Odyssey*, p. 122.

11 Prior to the Treaty of Riga it amounted to 250,000 hectares.

12 Carton de Wiart, A., *Happy Odyssey*, p. 123.

13 De Wiart says forty miles. It is fifteen miles as the crow flies.

14 Prostyń nad Lwą (on River Lva [Lion]/Mostva) is a forester's lodge in Błoty Olmańskich, a day away from Mankiewicz.

15 Carton de Wiart, A., *Happy Odyssey*, p. 122.

16 RUL 1391/B44 Peter Fleming.

17 Carton de Wiart, A., *Happy Odyssey*, p. 128.

18 Howarth, Patrick, *Intelligence Chief Extraordinary*, p. 30.

19 Lednicki, Wacław, *Reminiscences: The Adventures of A Modern Gil Blas during the Last War,* p. 96.

20 General Sir Richard Haking GBE, KCB, KCMG (1862–1945).

21 Mary died in 1932 and left de Wiart her estate worth £29. Her address (see Maurice) was Stone Gap bungalow, Stone Road, Broadstairs.

22 Carton de Wiart, A., *Happy Odyssey*, p. 132.

23 Carton de Wiart, A., *Happy Odyssey*, p. 133.

24 Radziwill, Michael (1971), *One of the Radziwills*, London: John Murray, p. 77.

25 Very different to the English snipe. De Wiart describes them as 'pig fat and fly very slowly and straight'.

26 Carton de Wiart, A., *Happy Odyssey*, p. 146.

27 Arthur Sutherland's Game Book 1924-32 (privately owned).

28 Carton de Wiart, A., *Happy Odyssey*, p. 152.

29 Dzikowski, Stanisław (1931), *Egzotyczna Polska*, Warswaw: Gebethner i Wolff.

30 *The Boston Globe*, 4 May 1920.

31 Pilsudski, Alexandra, *Memoirs of Madame Pilsudski*, p. 297.

32 Wiatr, Jerzy (2019), *The Soldier and the Nation, the Role of the Military in Polish Politics 1815–1985*, London: Routledge.

33 *The Times,* 13 May 1935.

34 Chervov, Victor, *Joseph Pilsudski –From Socialist to Autocrat*, Foreign Affairs, October 1935, Vol. 14 No. 1, https://www.jstor.org/stable/20030709 (accessed 18 October 2020).

35 https://ninateka.pl/film/mankiewicze-zofia-chometowska (accessed 15 June 2021).

36 Henryk Uziembło (1879–1949), artist and writer.

37 Julian Fałat (1853–1929) was one of the most prolific Polish watercolour painters and one of the country's foremost landscape painters.

38 Wojciech Kossak (1856- 942) was a celebrated Polish painter noted for his equestrian pictures.

39 Szejnert, Małgorzata (2015), *Building Mountains – Stories from the Polesie Region*, Warsaw: Znak.

40 RUL 1391/B14 Peter Fleming.

41 Lieutenant Colonel Anthony Muirhead, MC and bar, MP for Wells 1929-1939 (1890–1939).

42 Lieutenant Colonel Sir Rex Benson, DSO, MVO, MC (1889–1968).

43 Wake, Jehanne, *Oxford Dictionary of National Biography*, https://doi.org/10.1093/ref :odnb/30716 (accessed 15 June 2021).

44 Brian Beaumont-Nesbitt to author June 2020.

45 Letter addressed to her c/o Mankiewicze postmarked 7 October 1931. Returned to 5 St James's Square, the Stafford home in London.

46 Lady (Florence) Elizabeth Alice Byng (1897–1987).

47 Julian Michael Edmund Byng.

48 Shohet, Azriel (2013) *The Jews of Pinsk 1881 to 1941*, Stanford University Press, Preface.

49 He has the wrong woman – in 1936 Balala aged twenty-one had married Prince Edmund Radziwiłł.

50 *The Times*; the Bannacker polo venture is described by Richard Weininger in his memoir *Exciting Years* (Ed. Rodney Campbell, New York: Exposition Press, 1978).

51 RUL 1391/B44 Peter Fleming. Lady Ruth Monk Bretton, née Brand, first knew CdW and made a great effort to befriend Rikki.

52 Bought by the industrialist Richard Freiherr Drasche von Wartinberg, on his death in 1922 it was sold to the Belgian government.

53 His first wife had been killed in a car accident in June 1935.

54 From 1919 to 1920, he was the Polish envoy to London and served as the Polish Foreign Minister from 1920 to 1921.

55 Now in the Ukraine between Lutsk and Rivne.

56 Walker was in the Army at the time and stationed there; his family came from Lancashire.

57 RUL 1391/B44 Peter Fleming. Letters CdW to Ria 26 June 1937 and 10 October 1937. The drought persisted well into October when CdW wrote that he 'still could not get to my place . . . shooting nil'.

58 De Wiart was still in England in December for on 17th he attended Queen Mary's 'Not Forgotten' Christmas Party at the Riding School, Buckingham Palace (*The Times*, 18 December 1937).

59 https://ifthosewallscouldtalk.wordpress.com/2018/12/24/hidden-histories-the-stre et-heath-charnock-rivington/ (accessed 15 June 2021) the 1939 Register.

60 In February 1938 he presided over the twentieth anniversary reunion dinner of the 8th Gloucestershires with more than 300 attendees.

61 Carton de Wiart, A., *Happy Odyssey*, p. 153.

62 Chamberlain's *Peace through Strength* speech delivered to Women Conservatives at the Albert Hall, 11 May 1939.

63 HolocaustResearchProject.org/euthan/Koscian.html.

64 Radziwill, Michael, *One of the Radziwills*, p. 58 'taking up residence . . . not without the connivance of MI5'.

65 Carton de Wiart, A., *Happy Odyssey*, p. 161.

Chapter 11

1 HC Deb 28 September 1938 Vol. 339 cc5-28.

2 HC Deb 31 March 1939 Vol. 345 cc2415-20.

3 HC Deb 3 April 1939 Vol. 345 cc2475-588.

4 At that time Inspector General of Overseas Forces.

5 General the Lord Ironside (1962), *The Ironside Diaries 1937–40*, London: Constable, p. 81.

6 Carton de Wiart, A., *Happy Odyssey*, p. 153.

7 Carton de Wiart, A., *Happy Odyssey*, pp. 153–4.

8 Carton de Wiart, A., *Happy Odyssey*, p. 154.

9 On 30 August 1939, three destroyers (ORP *Błyskawica*, ORP *Grom*, and ORP *Burza*) sailed to the British naval base at Leith in Scotland. Also, two Polish submarines managed to flee from the Baltic through the Skagerrak, reaching Great Britain soon after. Source: https://www.naval-encyclopedia.com/ww2/polish-navy (accessed 15 June 2021).

10 Carton de Wiart, A., *Happy Odyssey*, p. 154.

11 MIR stood for Military Intelligence Research.

12 Linderman, Aaron(2016), *Rediscovering Irregular Warfare,* University of Oklahoma Press, p. 46.

13 TNA: HS 8/256.

14 Harrison, E. D. R. (2000), 'The British SOE and Poland', *The Historical Review*, Vol. 43, No. 4, pp. 1071–91.

15 Polskie Linie Lotnicze LOT, the state-owned airline.

16 TNA: HS 4/223.

17 Wilkinson, Peter (1997), *Foreign Fields*, London: I.B. Tauris, p. 71.

18 Formerly Grenadier Guards.

19 IWM 13289 Sir Peter Wilkinson Reel 2.

20 TNA: WO 216/47 Report by Capt T. F. Davies p. 3.

21 TNA: WO 216/47 Report by Capt T. F. Davies p. 3.

22 On 4 September, the RAF launched a bombing raid on Wilhelmshaven and Brunsbüttel with a loss of seven aircraft. Minimal damage was inflicted. The next raid against German naval targets was on 29 September.

23 Carton de Wiart, A., *Happy Odyssey*, 156.

24 Carton de Wiart, A., *Happy Odyssey*, 157.

25 IWM 13289 Sir Peter Wilkinson Reel 3.

26 TNA: HS4/223 Despatch by Major Gen A. Carton de Wiart, Appendix C – BMM to Poland Diary of Events.

27 TNA: HS4/223 Despatch by Major Gen A. Carton de Wiart, Part 1 Para 11.

28 Polityka – nr 37 (2469) z dnia 2004-09-11; s. 66–67 Historia / Wrzesień '39 Krzysztof Żwikliński Tajemnica zamku Vincennes; Mazur, Wojciech (March 2009). 'Pomocnik Historyczny'.

29 Higham, Robin D. S. and John, Stephen (2006), *Why Air Forces Fail: The Anatomy of Defeat*. Harris University Press of Kentucky. See also Michael Peszke – Polish Military Aviation 1939.

30 Wilkinson, Peter, *Foreign Fields*, p. 77.

31 TNA: WO 216/47.

32 Fairey Battles were single engine light bombers designed in the 1930s. The RAF had seventeen squadrons by May 1939.

33 TNA HS4/223 BMM Despatch, Part 1, para 18.

34 TNA: WO 216/47.

35 IWM 13289 Reel 3.

36 TNA: HS 4/223.

37 TNA: HS 4/223.

38 TNA: WO 216/47.

39 TNA: HS 4/233 Para 23.

40 TNA: HS 4/223 Para 30.

41 Carton de Wiart, A., *Happy Odyssey*, 159.

42 Sapieha, Virgilia (1940), *Polish Profile*, London: William Heinemann Ltd.

43 Wilkinson, Peter, *Foreign Fields*, p. 83.

44 Tarnowski, Andrew (2006), *The Last Mazurka*, New York: St Martin's Press, p. 116.

45 Later Sir Denis Wright GCMG (1911–2005), Ambassador to Ethiopia and then Iran.

46 IWM Sir Peter Wilkinson Reel 3.

47 English version of the introduction written by Dennis Deletant to *The Great Fortune*, translated as Marea Sansa (Editura Univers, 1996), pp. 5–15.

48 Carton de Wiart, A., *Happy Odyssey*, p. 160.

49 1939 Register (29 September).

50 *Daily Telegraph* (London Day by Day column), 29 September 1939.

51 TNA: WO 216/47 The German attack on Poland: report from Major General Carton de Wiart.

52 Astley, Joan Bright, *Gubbins and SOE*.

53 TNA: HS 4/223 Conclusion.

54 *London Gazette*, 11 April 1941.

55 *The Times*, 11 October and 16 November 1939.

56 Dr Ihar Melnikau, the Belorussian historian, told the author that a 2015 expedition had reached the exact location but found no sign of the Prostyn estate lodge. Satellite images confirm this.

57 HC Deb 3 September 1939 Vol. 351 cc291-302.

58 24 September 1939.

Chapter 12

1 Carton de Wiart, A., *Happy Odyssey*, p. 163.
2 Major General Robert John Collins, C.B., C.M.G., D.S.O., p.s.c, a retired officer recalled to Active Service, had assumed command of the new division on its formation with effect from 1 September 1939, but was then posted to become the commandant of the Staff College in place of Major General Paget.
3 Carton de Wiart, A., *Happy Odyssey*, p. 164.
4 General the Lord Ironside, *The Ironside Diaries 1937–40*, p. 257.
5 TNA: CAB 83/3.
6 Carton de Wiart, A., *Happy Odyssey*, p. 165.
7 *London Gazette*, Supplement 29 May 1946.
8 TNA: WO 106/2013.
9 166 Light AA Battery RA and 193 AA Battery AA.
10 TNA: HS 8/261.
11 Later killed in Normandy in 1944 when serving with the Parachute Regiment.
12 TNA: HS 8/263.
13 RUL 1391 B/2 Peter Fleming.
14 The War Office did receive a message from MIR timed 7.45 pm on 14 April that 'no enemy in or near Namsos.' Am stopping all outward telegraph, telephone and road communications. Trying to get pilots. Fleming.
15 TNA: WO106/1916.
16 Carton de Wiart, A., *Happy Odyssey*, pp. 166–7. He uses Fleming's 1945 rank of Colonel.
17 TNA: WO 106/1916.
18 TNA: WO 106/2013.
19 General the Lord Ironside, *The Ironside Diaries 1937–40*, p. 243.
20 General the Lord Ironside, *The Ironside Diaries 1937–40*, p. 243.
21 MIR War Diary 24 April.
22 Haarr, Geirr (2010), *The Battle for Norway April-June 1940*, Barnsley: Seaforth Publishing, p. 118.
23 Hart-Davis, Duff (1974), *Peter Fleming – A Biography*, London: Jonathan Cape, p. 226.
24 Report of Sgts Berriff and Bryant.
25 Carton de Wiart, A., *Happy Odyssey*, p. 169.
26 TNA: ADM 199/475.
27 TNA: ADM 186/798.
28 Hart-Davis, Duff, *Peter Fleming –A Biography*, pp. 226–7.
29 TNA: CAB 44/73.

30 Derry, T. H. (1950), *Official History of Norwegian Campaign*, London: HMSO, p. 87.

31 Haarr, Geirr, *The Battle for Norway April- June 1940*, p. 118 and p. 126.

32 Derry, T. K., *Official History of Norwegian Campaign*.

33 Other calculations make it eighty-two miles in sixty-seven hours depending on their final destination.

34 Derry, T. K., *Official History of Norwegian Campaign*.

35 Plevy, Harry (2007), *Norway 1940 Chronicle of a Chaotic Campaign*, Brimscombe: Fonthill Media.

36 Plevy, Harry, *Norway 1940 Chronicle of a Chaotic Campaign*.

37 TNA: WO 106/2013.

38 General the Lord Ironside, *The Ironside Diaries 1937–40*, p. 270.

39 Major General Frederick Hotblack, DSO and bar, MC (1887–1979).

40 Major General Horatio Berney-Ficklin, CB, MC (1892–1961).

41 General Sir Bernard Paget, GCB, DSO, MC (1887–1961).

42 Major General Harold de Riemer Morgan, DSO (1888–1964).

43 Derry, T. H., *Official History of Norwegian Campaign*, p. 128.

44 Leland Stowe, Stockholm correspondent of the *Chicago Times*, had filed a report that Stockholm radio had announced that Captain Fleming had been killed, and so on.

45 Hart-Davis, Duff, *Peter Fleming, A Biography*, p. 229.

46 Carton de Wiart, A., *Happy Odyssey*, p. 171.

47 Carton de Wiart, A., *Happy Odyssey*, p. 171.

48 Later Major General Sir Rohan Delacombe, KCMG, KCVO, KBE, CB, DSO, KStJ.

49 Supplement to the *London Gazette*, 19 May 1946.

50 Lieutenant General Hugh Massy, CB, DSO, MC (1884–1965).

51 TNA: WO 106/2013.

52 In the *Times* obituary of Fleming, the writer states that Fleming remained behind in Norway to organize Stay Behind Parties and came out via Sweden. There is no documentary evidence to support this and he may have confused him with Malcolm Munthe or Andrew Croft.

53 BNA *Daily Mirror*, 6 May 1940.

54 Fleming, Peter (1957), *With the Guards to Mexico*, London: Rupert Hart-Davis.

55 Fleming Family archives: Letter Peter Fleming to Celia Johnson, 6 October 1944.

56 General the Lord Ironside, *The Ironside Diaries 1937–40*, p. 296.

57 HC Deb 07 May 1940 vol 360 cc1073-196.

58 *London Gazette*, Supplement 29 May 1946.

59 TNA: WO 106/2013.

60 Ed. – Clemmensen, Michael and Faulkner, Marcus (2013), *Northern European Overture to War, 1939–1941: From Memel to Barbarossa*, Leiden/Boston: Brill.

61 Corrigan, Gordon (2006), *Blood, Sweat and Arrogance, The Myths of Churchill's War*, London: Weidenfeld & Nicolson.

62 Fraser, Sir David (1988), *And We Shall Shock Them – The British Army in the Second World War*, London: Sceptre.

63 Sykes (1977), *Evelyn Waugh*, London: Penguin, pp. 555–6.

64 Cathleen Mann RA was an official Ministry of Information war artist.

65 BNA *Illustrated London News*, 4 May 1940.

66 BNA *Yorkshire Post*, 4 May 1940.

Chapter 13

1 Lieutenant General Sir Edmund Schreiber, KCB, DSO, KStJ, DL (1890–1972).

2 Stephan, Enno (1963), *Spies in Ireland*; translated from German by Arthur Davidson, London: MacDonald.

3 Carton de Wiart, A., *Happy Odyssey*, p. 176.

4 Later Sir John Figges KBE, CMG, Military Attaché Japan and Information Counsellor British Embassy Tokyo.

5 IWM 11316 Sir John Figges Reel 2.

6 Major General Sir Hubert Jervoise Huddleston, GCMG, GBE, CB, DSO & Bar, MC (1880–1950).

7 Lieutenant General Sir Henry Royds Pownall, KCB, KBE, DSO & Bar, MC (1887–1961).

8 Carton de Wiart, A., *Happy Odyssey*, p. 179.

9 TNA: CAB 121/674 Extracts from 128th meeting.

10 TNA: CAB 121/674.

11 The Internal Macedonian Revolutionary Organization, a terrorist network, seeking to change state frontiers in the Macedonian regions of Greece and Yugoslavia.

12 An area ruled by a *Ban* in medieval Slavonia and later a title conferred on viceroys of military regions by the Hungarian kings.

13 TNA: CAB 121/674 JIC (41) 123 28 March 1941.

14 TNA: CAB 121/674 Dill signal to WO 31 March 1941.

15 TNA: CAB 121/674.

16 General Sir Robert Hadden Haining, KCB, DSO, JP (1882–1959).

17 Brigadier George Davy, CB, CBE, DSO, formerly Queen's Own Hussars (1898–1983).

18 Carton de Wiart, A., *Happy Odyssey*, p. 179.

19 Later 4th Baronet and 22nd Knight of Kerry.

20 Air Marshal Sir John Baldwin, KBE, CB, DSO, DL (1892–1975).

21 Major General Sir Sanford Scobell, KBE, CB, CMG, DSO (1879–1955).

22 Lieutenant General Sir William Dobbie, GCMG, KCB, DSO (1879–1964).

23 Carton de Wiart, A., *Happy Odyssey*, p. 183.

24 Leeming, John (1950), *Always Tomorrow*, London: George Harrap.

25 RUL 1391 B/17 Peter Fleming, O'Connor note 16 December 1962.

26 Neame, Sir Philip (1947), *Playing with Strife*, London: George Harrap, p. 285.

27 RUL 1391/B44 Peter Fleming.

28 RUL 1391 B/17 Peter Fleming, O'Connor note 16 December 1962.

29 Address at Memorial Service St Columba's Church London SW1 on 15 July 1981.

30 Campo concentramento di prigionieri di Guerra.

31 Carton de Wiart, A., *Happy Odyssey*, p. 192.

32 WO 32/10706 The Red Cross report on Camp for British General at Vincigliata.

33 Carton de Wiart, A., *Happy Odyssey*, p. 196.

34 Carton de Wiart, A., *Happy Odyssey*, p. 198.

35 Carton de Wiart, A., *Happy Odyssey*, p. 206.

36 RUL 1391 B/17 Peter Fleming, O'Connor note 16 December 1962.

37 RUL 1391/B44 Peter Fleming; on 30 May 1942, CdW had written to Anita that 'my first hopes of repatriation have gone. I must be too young or not sufficiently knocked about!'

38 Leeming, John, *Always Tomorrow*, pp. 137–8.

39 Carton de Wiart, A., *Happy Odyssey*, p. 214.

40 Felton, Mark (2017), *Castle of the Eagles*, London: Icon Books, p. 203.

41 RUL 1391 B/17 Peter Fleming, O'Connor note 16 December 1962.

42 Neame, Sir Philip, *Playing with Strife*, p. 509.

43 RUL 1391 B/17 Peter Fleming, O'Connor note 16 December 1962, p. 25.

44 RUL 1391 B/17 Peter Fleming, O'Connor note 16 December 1962, p. 30.

45 He was accompanied by Italian diplomat Franco Montanari.

46 Campbell was in a muddle here – Roatta was Chief of the Army General Staff and Vittorio Ambrosio Chief of the General Staff (Commando Supremo).

47 https://history.state.gov/historicaldocuments/frus1943/d540 (accessed 6 January 2021).

48 https://history.state.gov/historicaldocuments/frus1943/d542 (accessed 6 January 2021).

49 Brigadier N. R. Crockatt, CBE, DSO (1894–1956).

50 Major General F.N.H. Davidson CB, DSO, MC (1892–1973).

51 Carton de Wiart, A., *Happy Odyssey*, p. 234.

52 HC Deb 21 September 1943 Vol. 392 cc69-170.

53 *London Gazette*, 9 December 1943.

Chapter 14

1 Carton de Wiart, A., *Happy Odyssey*, p. 235.

2 Lieutenant General Herbert William Lumsden, CB, DSO & Bar, MC (1897-1945).

3 TNA: CAB120/816: Prime Minister personal minute No.M.622/3 2 October 1943.

4 Theseira, Julian (2015), "'When we spoke at Versailles": Lou Tseng-Tsiang and the Chinese Delegation at the 1919 Paris Peace Conference, A Frustrated Quest for Justice', *Global Histories*, Vol. 1, No. 1 pp. 39–60.

5 Elleman, Bruce (2002), *Wilson and China – A Revised History of the Shandong Question*, London: Routledge, p. 42.

6 Elleman, Bruce, *Wilson and China – A Revised History of the Shandong Question*, p. 44.

7 Portwood, Matthew and Dunn, John (Winter 2024), *A Tale of Two Warlords*, Education about Asia, Vol. 19, No. 3.

8 This is the figure which modern researchers accept as the base line. The 1946 International Military Tribunal for the Far East (Tokyo) estimated 200,000.

9 Kirby, Maj-Gen Woodburn (1965), *The War against Japan*, London: HMSO, pp. 106–8.

10 In 1935, the trading organization HARPO (Handelsgesellschaft zur Verwertung industrieller Produkte) was established. Its goal was to funnel German military goods to Chiang Kai-Shek through commercial cover. Trade to China not only contained items such as uniforms, guns, munitions, and tanks but it also included manufacturing know-how, railroad technologies, munitions plants, and communications technologies.

11 Pratt, Sir John (1943), *War and Politics in China*, London: Jonathan Cape.

12 The United States also continued its silver purchases, which gave China US $252 million in cash.

13 BNA Belfast News Letter 5 May 1944 quoting Maclean's Magazine; the photograph was published in October 1946 in Arthur Bryant's Our Notebook in the *Illustrated London News*.

14 Carton de Wiart, A., *Happy Odyssey*, p. 236.

15 Carton de Wiart, A., *Happy Odyssey*, p. 236.

16 Together with Admiral Mountbatten, the newly appointed SACSEA.

17 Carton de Wiart, A., *Happy Odyssey*, p. 239.

18 Fleming, Peter (1934), *One's Company*, London: Jonathan Cape.

19 Isherwood, Christopher and Auden, W. H. (1939), *Journey to War*, London: Faber & Faber, p. 65.

20 Carton de Wiart, A., *Happy Odyssey*, p. 239.

21 https://history.state.gov/historicaldocuments/frus1943CairoTehran/d255 (accessed 21 September 2020).

22 https://history.state.gov/historicaldocuments/frus1943CairoTehran/d255 (accessed 21 September 2020).

23 Text National Diet Library, Japan.

24 Combined Chiefs of Staff C.C.S. 284/5/D: General Directive of Deceptions Measures against japan in 1943–4.

25 He actually took over on 8 November after the defence of India against the Japanese had legally been transferred to his command.

26 Field Marshal Sir Claude Auchinleck, GCB, GCIE, CSI, DSO, OBE (1884–1981).

27 Louis, Allen (2000), *Burma, The Longest War*, London: J.M.Dent and Sons, p. 110.

28 Carton de Wiart, A., *Happy Odyssey*, p. 240.

29 Li, Laura Tyson (2007), *Madame Chiang Kai-shek, China's Eternal First Lady*, New York: Grove Press, quoted p. 247.

30 White, Theodore (1978), *In search of History*, London: Jonathan Cape.

31 Li, Laura Tyson, *Madame Chiang Kai-shek, China's Eternal First Lady*, quoted p. 24.

32 Fenby, Jonathan (2004), *Chiang Kai-Shek China's Generalissimo and the Nation He Lost*, New York: Carrol & Graf, p. 400.

33 Born in Tsingtao in 1919; Indian Army officer.

34 Fleming, Peter (1956), *My Aunt's Rhinoceros and Other Reflections*, London: Rupert Hart-Davis.

35 Wedemeyer, Albert (1958), *Wedemeyer Reports!* New York: Devin Adair, New York, p. 278.

36 All quotes in this para from Carton de Wiart, *Happy Odyssey*.

37 Carton de Wiart, A., *Happy Odyssey*, p. 264.

38 TNA: FO 954/6 Cypher No.6 FO to General Carton de Wiart 16 March 1944.

39 TNA: FO 954/6 Cypher No.6 General Carton de Wiart to FO 22 March 1944; CAB 120/816.

40 Carton de Wiart, A., *Happy Odyssey*, p. 247.

41 28-year-old Belfast-born William Noble had flown Spitfires in the Battle of Britain before being commissioned in 1941. Source: http://www.bbm.org.uk/airmen/NobleWJ.htm (accessed 21 September 2020).

42 TNA: FO 954/6 Cypher No.1 General Carton de Wiart to FO 17 December 1943.

43 TNA: FO 954/6 Cypher No.2 General Carton de Wiart to FO 18 December 1943.

44 TNA: CAB 120/816 Extracts from a letter dated 28 December 1943 from CdW to Ismay.

Chapter 15

1 With kind permission of Anthony Loyd.

2 Hartley Library, University of Southampton (HLUS) MB1/C42/6/2 CdW to Mountbatten 30 December 1943, p. 3.

3 TNA: FO 954/6 Cypher No.3 General Carton de Wiart to FO 2 January 1944.

4 HMS *Queen Elizabeth*, HMS *Valiant*, HMs *Renown*.

5 TNA: FO 954/6 Cypher No.2 FO to General Carton de Wiart 21 January 1944.

6 TNA: CAB 120/816 Chongqing to FO No.5 Amuse 26 January 1944.

7   TNA: WO 106/3564.

8   Brigadier Bernard Fergusson, Baron Ballantrae, KT, GCMG, GCVO, DSO, OBE (1911–1980).

9   TNA: FO 954/6 Cypher No.8 FO to General Carton de Wiart 24 March 1944.

10 TNA: FO 954/7 Copy of letter dated 24 April 1944 from General Carton de Wiart to General Ismay; CAB 120/816.

11 Grimsdale, Maj-Gen G. E. (1950), 'The War against Japan in China', *RUSI Journal*, Vol. 95, No. 578, p. 266.

12 Lieutenant General Walter Lentaigne, CB, CBE, DSO (1899–1955).

13 Field Marshal Sir Francis Festing, GCB, KBE, DSO, DL (1902–1976).

14 *The Times*, 1 January 1954 – letter to the editor from Sir Walter Fletcher.

15 HLUS MB1/C42/26/2.

16 HLUS MB1/C42/40 1 De Wiart to SACSEA 3 July 1944.

17 Beaton, Cecil (1991), *Chinese Diary & Album*, Hong Kong: Oxford University Press, pp. 73–4.

18 Van der Ven, Hans (2012), *War and Nationalism in China 1925–45*, London: Routledge.

19 HLUS MB1/C42/20/3 Chennault to De Wiart 5 March 1944.

20 White, Theodore and Jacoby, Annalee (1946), *Thunder Out of China*, New York: William Sloane.

21 The Air Ground Aid Service.

22 Newman, Robert (1992), *Owen Lattimore and the Loss of China*, Oakland: University of California Press.

23 I have used the wartime spelling of Mao's name throughout rather than the more recent Mao Zedong.

24 Fenby, Jonathan (2004), *Generalissimo Chiang Kai-Shek and the China He Lost*, New York: Carol & Graf.

25 HLUS MB1/C42/33 and 34 CdW to SACSEA dated 29 May 1944 (after being briefed by General Ho Ying-chin).

26 HLUS MB1/C42/35 1 CdW to SACSEA dated 4 June 1944.

27 TNA: CAB 120/816 Chongqing to FO No. 20 Amuse dated 30 June 1944.

28 HLUS MB1/C42/41 SACSEA to CdW 6 July 1944.

29 Murfett, Malcolm H. (2008), *Naval Warfare 1919–45: An Operational History of the Volatile War at Sea,* London: Routledge, p. 357.

30 Willmott, H. P. (1996), *Grave of a Dozen Schemes*, London: Airlift Publishing, p. 163.

31 Carton de Wiart, A., *Happy Odyssey*, pp. 261–2.

32 HLUS MB1/C42/42 CdW to SACSEA 10 September 1944.

33 HC Deb 28 September 1944 Vol. 403 cc421-604.

34 TNA: FO 954/7 Cypher No.23 General Carton de Wiart to FO 14 September 1944.

35 Brigadier General Clinton 'Casey' Vincent (1914–1955).

36   Major General Patrick Hurley and Mr Donald M. Nelson had been sent to China as personal representatives of President Roosevelt to smooth relations between the Generalissimo and Stilwell.

37   TNA: CAB 120/816 Extract from letter CdW to Ismay dated 10 October 1944.

38   Tuchman, Barbara (1971), *Stilwell and the American Experience in China 1911–1945*, New York: The MacMillan Company, p. 495.

39   The Office of the Historian in the United States Department of State, Foreign Relations of the United States series (FRUS) 1944: China 2 October 1944, p. 164.

40   FRUS, 1944: China 9 October 1944, p. 169.

41   Grimsdale, Maj-Gen G. E., 'The War against Japan in China', p. 267.

42   Crouch, Gregory (2012), *China's Wings: War, Intrigue, Romance, and Adventure in the Middle Kingdom during the Golden Age of Flight*, New York: Random House.

43   Hoover Foundation – https://www.hoover.org/research/uncommon-soldier (accessed 22 September 2020).

44   Ed. Zeigler, Philip (1988), *Personal Diary of Admiral the Lord Louis Mountbatten 1943-46*, London: Collins, p. 8.

45   Carton de Wiart, A., *Happy Odyssey*, p. 258.

46   Carton de Wiart, A., *Happy Odyssey*, p. 255.

47   Wedemeyer, Albert, *Wedemeyer Reports!*, p. 265.

48   FRUS: Diplomatic Papers, 1944, China, Vol. VI (Documents 227–251).

49   Smith, Jean Edward (2012), *Eisenhower in War and Peace*, New York: Random House, p. 183.

50   Burleigh, Michael (2013), *Small Wars, Faraway Places*, New York: Viking, p. 103.

51   FO 954/7 Memo Ismay to Foreign Secretary re extract of Carton de Wiart letter dated 21 Nov 1944; WP (44) 631, 8 November 1944.

52   FO 954/7 Memo Ismay to Foreign Secretary re copy of Carton de Wiart letter dated 28 November 1944.

53   De Wiart replied to Mountbatten that 'I do not think you are being fair to the Generalissimo and you must forgive me saying so. I cannot see his conduct is unsoldierly, if you put yourself in his position, what else could you do? And he has always done his best to help you and is very loyal to you'. (HLUS MB1/C42/53).

54   TNA: FO 954/7 Cypher No.16 FO to General Carton de Wiart 7 December 1944.

55   TNA: CAB 120/816 Cypher CdW to Ismay.

56   14th, 22nd, 38th, 50th and 30th.

57   TNA: CAB 120/816 Signal to Ismay from CdW dated 1 December 1944.

58   The vast majority of US Lend Lease military equipment went to X and Y Force in India; very little reached mainland China.

59   Wedemeyer, Albert, *Wedemeyer Reports!*, p. 291.

60   He left on 21 December and arrived on 27 December.

61   TNA: CAB 65/49 and CAB 79/28.

Chapter 16

1   British other ranks.

2   TNA: WO 106/3564.

3   TNA: WO 106/3579.

4   TNA: HS 1/4, HS 1/5.

5   357 Squadron dropped 27 containers in March 1944.

6   A. G. N. Ogden.

7   TNA: WO 106/3546.

8   3.7mm howitzers, mortars, small arms and signals equipment.

9   TNA: WO 106/3564.

10 TNA: HS 1/135.

11 RII also provided intelligence to SIS London and DMI India.

12 In June that year an informal agreement was made between SOE and GHQ India whereby if SOE was authorized to work in China they could use BAAG as cover with the proviso that Ride agreed.

13 Majors Teesdale, Cowie and Salinger all contributed to the demolition of roads and bridges, forcing the Japanese to abandon their frontal attack.

14 TNA: WO 208/517 (March 1944).

15 TNA: HS 1/135, HS 1/276, HS 1/291, HS 1/292, HS 1/293.

16 Rolexes, Omegas, Longines, Jaeger Le Coutre and other brands.

17 HLUS MB1/C42/13/2-2.

18 Ride, Edwin (1981), *BAAG [British Army Aid Group]: Hong Kong Resistance 1942–45*, Hong Kong: Oxford University Press.

19 Ride had the distinction of being commissioned a Second Lieutenant and promoted to Lieutenant Colonel on the same day.

20 TNA: WO 203/3357, WO 203/3355, WO 203/5381.

21 Foot, Michael and Langley, Jimmy (1979), *MI 9, British Escape & Evasion 1939–45 & Its US Counterpart*, London: Bodley Head.

22 HLUS MB1/C42/13/2 CdW to Mountbatten 18 January 1944.

23 Dimitrakis, Panagiotis (2017), *The Secret War for China, Espionage, Revolution and the Rise of Mao*, London: Bloomsbury.

24 HLUS MB1/C43/1_3 CdW to SACSEA 23 February 1945.

25 Aldrich, Richard (2000), *Intelligence and the War against Japan*, Cambridge: Cambridge University Press, pp. 364–7.

26 SEAC Operational Directive No. 23, 25 January 1945.

27 *The Overseas Targets, War Report of the OSS*, Volume 2, New York: Walker & CO, 1976, pp. 415–58.

28 TNA: WO 203/3774; WO 203/3426.

29 Sutherland, David (1998), *He Who Dares*, Barnsley: Leo Cooper, pp.172–3.

Chapter 17

1   *London Gazette*, 1 January 1945.
2   TNA: WO 106/5015.
3   HLUS MB1/C42/63 and 65.
4   Romanus, Charles and Sunderland, Riley: CBI Theatre – time runs out in CBI.
5   'British Effort in China' – Thunder in the East, IWM.
6   TNA WO 203/5629 Mountbatten visit to Chongqing March 1945.
7   HLUS MB1/C43/7 SACSEA to de Wiart.
8   HLUS MB1/C43/2 8 March 1945.
9   HLUS MB1/C43/12, 14 and 15.
10 Massacres of POWs and internees were reported at Long Son, Dinh Lap, Thakhek, Tan Qui, Dong Dang, Ha Giang and Tonkin.
11 The weather was appalling – between 9 March and 30 April, only twenty-seven out of seventy-two Liberator drops were successful.
12 Chennault's US 14th Air Force had accidentally bombed the French artillery depot. He later claimed that bad weather and lack of equipment prevented him from assisting the French.
13 Garver, John (1993), *Chinese-Soviet Relations 1937–45: The Diplomacy of Chinese Nationalism*, Oxford: Oxford University Press, pp. 258–9.
14 Office of War History in the National Institute for Defense Studies of the Ministry of Defense Institute (1968), *The War of Pacification in North China*, Vol. 1, Tokyo: Asagumo Shimbunsha Inc., p. 384.
15 Quoted by Endo Homare in *Mao Zedong: The Man Who Conspired with the Japanese Army*, 2015.
16 Garver, John, *Chinese-Soviet Relations 1937–45*, pp. 258–9.
17 TNA: WO 106/3589.
18 There were over 8,000 cases reported between 5 and 25 June 1945. See US Army Medical Department, Office of Medical History Chapter 21; Public Heath Engineering Abstracts Vol. 27, University of Michigan 2009.
19 Caughey, John (2018), *The Letters and Diaries of Colonel John Caughey*, London: Rowman & Littlefield.
20 TNA: CAB 120/816 Cypher SACSEA to WO dated 15 August 1945.
21 TNA: CAB 120/816 Cypher SACSEA to WO dated 18 August 1945.
22 TNA: CAB 120/816 Copy of note August 1945.
23 HLUS MB1/C43/25 CdW to SACSEA 25 July 1945.
24 Admiral Sir Cecil Harcourt, GBE, KCB (1892–1959).
25 TG 111.2 Two aircraft carriers, a battleship, three cruisers, four destroyers and an anti-aircraft ship.

26 Tsang, Steve (2003), *A Modern History of Hong Kong 1841-1997*, London: I.B. Tauris, London, p. 138.

27 TNA: CAB 120/816.

28 Carton de Wiart, A., *Happy Odyssey*, p. 272.

29 *The Times*, 15 September 1945.

30 TNA: CAB 79/39 p. 321.

31 TNA: WO 208/473 Ref COS (45) 224.

32 Wang was a close associate of Sun Yat-sen for the last twenty years of Sun's life. After Sun's death in 1925 Wang engaged in a political struggle with Chiang Kai-shek for control over the KMT but lost. Wang remained inside the KMT but continued to have disagreements with Chiang until the outbreak of the Second Sino-Japanese War in 1937, after which he accepted an invitation from Tokyo to form a Japanese-supported collaborationist government in Nanjing. Wang served as the head of state for this puppet government until he died, shortly before the end of the Second World War.

33 Cheng Gongbo.

34 Run by Air Marshal Sir Lawrence Pattinson, KBE, CB, DSO, MC, DFC at Chengtu; then by Air Vice- Marshal William Foster McNeece Foster, CB, CBE, DSO, DFC.

35 TNA: WO 208/473.

36 Zhou En-lai.

37 Tse-tung, Mao (April 1945), On Coalition Government *Selected Works*, Vol. III, China: Foreign Languages Press, Peking, p. 282.

38 Chapman-Walker had previously run SOE's USA and South American desks.

39 He later became Chief Publicity Officer for Central Office from 1949–55 and then a Managing Director of *The News of the World*.

40 Founded in 1854 and largely staffed at senior levels by foreigners, the Chinese Maritime Customs Service was a Chinese governmental tax collection agency and information service.

41 Edited Chang, Chihyun (2018), *The Chinese Journals of L.K. Little 1943–54: My Eyewitness Account of War and Revolution,* Vol. 1, London: Routledge, Taylor & Francis.

42 Carton de Wiart, A., *Happy Odyssey*, p. 274.

43 TNA: WO 208/473.

44 TNA: WO 208/473.

45 FRUS: Diplomatic Papers, 1945, The Far East, China, Vol. VII 123 Hurley, Patrick J.

46 TNA: CAB 120/816 Extracts from letter CdW to Ismay dated 27 February 1946.

47 TNA: CAB 79/46.

48 McMullan was born in China to a family of missionaries turned traders. Fluent in Mandarin, he was recruited by SOE and sent to Kunming in 1944 as leader of

a four-man Jedburgh Mission. Source: The Cheltonian Association and Society Floreat 16, Obituary Supplement.

49   Carton de Wiart, A., *Happy Odyssey*, p. 276.

50   Founded by an English missionary, Edmund Selby Little, who leased the land from the Chinese from 1895 to 1936.

51   Carton de Wiart, A., *Happy Odyssey*, p. 277.

52   Carton de Wiart, A., *Happy Odyssey*, p. 279.

53   Sir Ralph Clarmont Skrine Stevenson, GCMG, MLC, CP (1895–1977).

54   Taylor, Jay (2009), *The Generalissimo, Chiang Kai-Shek and the Struggle for Modern China*, Harvard: Belknap Press, Harvard University.

55   Kurtz-Phelan, Daniel (2018), *The Marshall Plan that Failed*, The Atlantic, 30 July.

56   CAB 120/816 Cypher telegram Prime Minister to CdW dated 12 October 1946.

57   CAB 120/816 Downing Street to Ismay 14 October 1946.

58   *The Times*, 15 October 1946.

59   Carton de Wiart, A., *Happy Odyssey*, p. 281.

60   Lieutenant General Sir Charles Walter Allfrey, KBE, CB, DSO, MC & Bar, DL (1895–1964).

61   Sir Clifford Norton, K.C.M.G., C.V.O. (1891–1990).

62   Carton de Wiart, A., *Happy Odyssey*, p. 282.

63   CAB 120/816 Prime Minister Personal; telegram 20 October 1946.

64   CAB 120/816 letter CdW to Minister dated 17 December 1946.

65   Truman's administration also delayed the implementation of the China Aid Act in 1948.

66   Dreyer, Edward (1995), *China at War, 1901–49*, London and New York: Longman.

67   Mitter, Rana (2013), *China's War with Japan 1937–45 – the Struggle for Survival*, London: Allen Lane.

68   Barker, Mark (June 2016), 'Spaces of Starvation: State and Province in the Henan Famine, 1942–43', *Macmillan Yale Agrarian Studies*.

Chapter 18

1   *Dundee Evening Telegraph*, 7 October 1947.

2   Joan Carton de Wiart's Epilogue to French edition of *Happy Odyssey* – Mémoires de la Reine Victoria à Mao Tse-toung, Document Duculot, p. 236.

3   Fleming, Peter, *With the Guards to Mexico*, pp. 146–7.

4   *The Times*, 7 August 1948, 26 February 1951.

5   *The Times*, 14 September 1949.

6   Her remains were later relocated to the Holy Trinity Chapel at the Von Hanau's Schloss Meiselberg to the north of Klagenfurt.

7   RUL 1391/B14 Peter Fleming.

8   RUL 1391/B14 Peter Fleming.

9   He was one of the last to return in 1955. He died in Hamburg in 1966.

10 Née McKechnie.

11 Sutherland, David (1998), *He Who Dares, Recollections of Service in the SAS, SBS and MI5*, London: Leo Cooper, p. 174.

12 Deidre, Lady Maxwell Scott, to author 7 May 2020.

13 Sutherland and Vivian had both served as ADCs to the governor of Bengal.

14 Conversation author and Rosie Sutherland April 2020.

15 Née Campbell Swinton.

16 Her brother Alec had died in 1950 and her sister-in-law Pamela had remarried to Walter Lord.

17 CdW writing in the *Sunday Times*, 18 November 1951.

18 *Irish Sunday Independent*, 18 November 2012.

19 Conversation author and Rosie Sutherland April 2020.

20 *The Times* obituary written by Peter Fleming.

21 He had received an honorary degree from Oxford on 14 December 1947.

22 Conversation author and Rosie Sutherland April 2020.

23 Correspondence author and Rosie Sutherland.

24 Archiviste du Palais royal de Bruxelles – Le registre des audiences du Roi Baudouin 26 June 1957.

25 Baron Christian Houtart to author April 2020.

26 Afterword to French edition of *Happy Odyssey*, p. 239.

27 In 1959, de Wiart became a godfather to Fergie's son Adrian.

28 1898–1972; served Royal Horse Guards (3rd Bn Guards Machine Gun Regiment 1918); Lord Mayor of Liverpool; chairman Jockey Club.

29 Liddell Hart Centre for Military Archives (LHCMA) Ismay 4/5/6.

30 LHCMA Ismay 4/5/12.

31 LHCMA Ismay 4/5/15.

32 LHCMA Ismay 4/5/50.

33 LHCMA Ismay 4/5/53.

34 LHCMA Ismay 4/5/58.

35 Lady Maxwell-Scott to author 1 July 2020.

36 *Journal of the Royal Central Asia Society,* Vol. 50, 1963 – No. 3–4, p. 352.

37 Commissioned October 1938. Served with 10th Battalion in UK and Northern Ireland on home defence duties.

38 LHCMA Ismay 4/5/72.

39 LHCMA Ismay 4/5/78 and 4/5/83.

40 LHCMA Ismay 4/5/78/7.

41 LHCMA Ismay 4/5/87.

42 LHCMA Ismay 4/5/108.

43 *Irish Sunday Independent*, 18 November 2012.

44 *Sunday Times*, 18 November 1951.

45 KCLMA; Ismay 4/5 8 August 1962.

46 Allen, Bill (1943), *Guerrilla War in Abyssinia*, Harmondsworth: Penguin Books.

Bibliography and Other Sources

Books

D'Abernon, Lord: *The Eighteenth Decisive Battle of the World – Warsaw 1920*, Hodder & Stoughton, London, 1931.

Adams, Jack: *The Doomed Expedition, the Campaign in Norway 1940*, Leo Cooper, London, 1989.

Aldrich, Richard: *Intelligence and the War against Japan*, Cambridge University Press, Cambridge, 2000.

Allen, Louis: *Burma: The Longest War*, J.M. Dent and Sons, London, 1984.

Amery, Julian: *Approach March: A Venture in Autobiography*, Hutchinson, London, 1973.

Asquith, Lady Cynthia: *Diaries 1915–18*, Hutchinson, London, 1968.

Bayley, Chris and Harper, Tim: *Forgotten Armies – Britain's Asian Empire and the War with Asia*, Penguin Allen Lane, London, 2004.

Beamish, John: *Burma Drop*, Elek Books, London, 1958.

Beaton, Cecil: *Chinese Diary & Album*, Oxford University Press, Hong Kong, 1991.

Bonsal, Stephen: *Suitors and Suppliants*, Prentice Hall, New York, 1946.

Bridges, Thomas: *Alarms and Excursions*, Longman Green & Co, London 1938.

Buhite, Russell: *Patrick J. Hurley and American Foreign Policy*, Cornell University Press, 1973.

Burleigh, Michael: *Small Wars, Faraway Places*, Viking, New York, 2013.

Chang, Chihyun (ed.): *The Chinese Journals of L.K. Little 1943–54: My Eyewitness Account of War and Revolution*, Vol. 1, Routledge, Taylor and Francis, London, 2018.

Charaszkiewicz, Edmund: *Przebudowa wschodu Europy* (The Restructuring of Eastern Europe), Niepodległość (Independence), London, 1955.

Chennault, Claire Lee: *Way of a Fighter*, G. P. Putnam's Sons, New York, 1949.

Cherry, Niall: *Doomed Before the Start: The Allied Intervention in Norway 1940 Volume 1 – The Road to Invasion and Early Moves*, Helion, Warwick, 2016.

Cherry, Niall: *Doomed Before the Start The Allied Intervention in Norway 1940 Volume 2 – Evacuation and Further Naval Operations*, Helion, Warwick, 2017.

Churchill, Winston: *My Early Life, a Roving Commission*, Thornton Butterworth, London, 1930.

Churchill, Winston: *The World Crisis*, Volume 4, Thornton Butterworth, London, 1923.

Clemmensen, Michael and Faulkner, Marcus (eds): *Northern European Overture to War, 1939–1941: From Memel to Barbarossa*, Brill, Leiden/Boston, 2013.

Clifford, Rollo: *The Royal Gloucestershire Hussars*, Alan Sutton, Stroud, 1991.

Corrigan, Gordon: *Blood, Sweat and Arrogance, the Myths of Churchill's War*, Weidenfeld & Nicolson, London, 2006.

Crouch, Gregory: *China's Wings: War, Intrigue, Romance, and Adventure in the Middle Kingdom During the Golden Age of Flight*, Random House Inc, New York, 2012.

Crouchley, A. E.: *The Economic Development of Modern Egypt*, Longmans, Green & Co, London, 1938.

Cruikshank, Charles: *SOE in the Far East*, Oxford University Press, Oxford, 1983.

Cuthbert, Bradley: *Good Sport Seen with Some Famous Packs*, George Routledge, London, 1910.

Davies, Norman: *God's Playground. A History of Poland in Two Volumes. 1795 to the Present*, Volume 2, Clarendon Press, Oxford, 1982.

Davies, Norman: *White Eagle, Red Star*, Pimlico, London, 2003.

Dear, Ian: *Sabotage and Subversion – SOE and OSS at War*, Phoenix, London, 1999.

Derry, T.K.: *The Campaign in Norway*, HMSO, London, 1950.

Dillon, Dr E.J.: *The Inside Story of the Peace Conference*, Harper & Brothers, New York and London, 1920.

Dimitrakis, Panagiotis: *The Secret War for China, Espionage, Revolution and the Rise of Mao*, Bloomsbury, London, 2017.

Dreyer, Edward: *China at War, 1901–49*, Longman, London and New York, 1995.

Dzikowski, *Stanisław: Egzotyczna Polska*, Gebethner i Wolff, Warsaw, 1931.

Elleman, Bruce: *Wilson and China – A Revised History of the Shandong Question*, Routledge, London, 2002.

Elsie, R.: *Traveller, Scholar, Political Adventurer, The Memoirs of Franz Kopsca*, Central European University Press, Budapest, 2014.

Felton, Mark: *Castle of the Eagles, Escape from Mussolini's Colditz*, Icon Books, London, 2017.

Fenby, Jonathan: *Chiang Kai-shek China's Generalissimo and the Nation He Lost*, Carrol & Graf, New York, 2004.

Fenn, Charles: *At the Dragon's Gate, with the OSS in the Far East*, Naval Institute Press, Annapolis, 2004.

Fleming, Peter: *My Aunt's Rhinoceros and other Reflections*, Rupert Hart-Davis, London, 1956.

Fleming, Peter: *News from Tartary*, Jonathan Cape, London, 1936.

Fleming, Peter: *With the Guards to Mexico*, Rupert Hart-Davis, London, 1957.

Foot, Michael and Langley, Jimmy: *MI 9, British Escape & Evasion 1939-45 & Its US Counterpart*, Bodley Head, London,1979.

Ford, Douglas: *Britain's Secret War against Japan 1937–48*, Routledge, London, 2006.

Forczyk, Robert: *Case White – The Invasion of Poland 1939*, Osprey, Oxford and New York, 2019.

Fox, Frank: *The History of the Royal Gloucestershire Hussars Yeomanry, 1898–1922: The Great Cavalry Campaign in Palestine*, Philip Allan & Co, London, 1920.

Fraser, Sir David: *And We Shall Shock Them – the British Army in the Second World War*, Sceptre, London, 1988.

Fugger, Nora: *The Glory of the Habsburgs, The Memoirs of Princess Fugger*, George G. Harrap & Co Ltd, London, 1932.

Gage, Sir Berkeley: *A Marvellous Party, 1989* [copyright Ulrick Gage 2013].

Garver, John: *Chinese-Soviet Relations 1937–45: The Diplomacy of Chinese Nationalism*, Oxford University Press, Oxford, 1993.

Gerwarth, Robert: *The Vanquished, why the First World War Failed to End 1917–23*, Allen Lane, London, 2016.

Gibb, Harold: *Record of the 4th Royal Irish Dragoon Guards in the Great War, 1914–1918*, Saward, Baker & Co Ltd, Canterbury, 1925.

Gilbert, Sir Martin: *World in Torment - Winston S. Churchill 1916–1922*, Hillsdale College Press, Minnesota, 2008.

Gliddon, Gerald: *VCs of the First World War – Somme 1916*, The History Press, New York, 2011.

Gough, Hubert: *The Fifth Army*, Hodder & Stoughton, London, 1931.

Gough, Hubert: *Soldiering On*, A. Barker, London, 1954.

Guoqi, Xu: *Strangers on the Western Front*, Harvard University Press, 2011.

Haarr, Geirr H.: *The Battle for Norway April - June 1940*, Seaforth Publishing, Barnsley, 2010.

Hargest, James: *Farewell Campo 12*, Michael Joseph, London, 1945.

Hart-Davis, Duff: *Peter Fleming*, Jonathan Cape, London, 1974.

Hastings, Max: *The Oxford Book of Military Anecdotes*, Oxford University Press, Oxford, 1985.

Holt, Thaddeus: *The Deceivers: Allied Military Deception in the Second World War*, Weidenfeld & Nicolson, New York and London, 2004.

Howarth, Patrick: *Intelligence Chief Extraordinary, the Life of the 9th Duke of Portland*, The Bodley Head, London, 1986.

Howard of Penrith, Lord: *The Theatre of Life, Life seen from the Stalls*, Hodder and Stoughton, London, 1935.

Ironside, General the Lord (edited Colonel MacLeod and Denis Kelly): *The Ironside Diaries 1937–40*, Constable, London, 1962.

Ismay, *General the Lord: Memoirs*, Heinemann, London, 1960.

James, Lawrence: *Imperial Warrior - The Life and Times of Field Marshal Viscount Allenby*, Weidenfeld & Nicolson, London, 1993.

Jardine, Douglas: *The Mad Mullah of Somaliland*, Herbert Jenkins Ltd, London, 1923.

Jedrzejewicz, Wacław: *Pilsudski a Life for Poland*, Hippocrene Books, New York, 1982.

Jeffery, Keith: *MI6, the History of the Secret Intelligence Service 1909–49*, Bloomsbury, London, 2010.

Jones, John: *Balliol College, A History* (Second edition), Oxford University Press, Oxford, 1997.

Keegan, John: *The First World War*, Hutchinson, London, 1999.

Keegan, John (ed.): *Churchill's Generals*, Weidenfeld & Nicolson, London, 1991.

Keegan, John and Wheatcroft, Andrew: *Who's Who in Military History From 1453 to the Present Day*, Routledge, London, 2001.

Kersaudy, Francois: *Norway 1940*, Harper Collins, London, 1990.

King, Greg and Wilson, Penny: *Twilight of Empire*, St. Martin's Press, New York, 2017.

Kinvig, Clifford: *Churchill's Crusade – The British Invasion of Russia 1918–1920*, Hambledon Continuum, London and New York, 2006.

Kirby, Maj-Gen Woodburn: *The War against Japan*, HMSO, London, 1965.

Kiszley, John: *Anatomy of a Campaign, the British Fiasco in Norway 1940*, Cambridge University Press, Cambridge, 2018.

Kurtz-Phelan, Daniel: *The China Mission*, W.W. Norton & Co, New York, 2019.

Leeming, John, *Always To-morrow*, George Harrap, London, 1951.

Li, Laura Tyson: *Madame Chiang Kai-shek, China's Eternal First Lady*, Grove Press, New York, 2007.

Linderman, Aaron: *Rediscovering Irregular Warfare, Colin Gubbins and the origins of British Special Operations Executive*, University of Oklahoma Press, 2016.

Lindsay, Hsiao Li: *Bold Plum*, Lulu Press, Morrisville, North Carolina, 2006.

Lindsay, Michael: *The Unknown War – North China 1937–45*, Bergstrom & Boyle, London, 1975.

Liu, F. F.: *A Military History of Modern China: 1924–1949*, Princeton University Press, Princeton, 1956.

Lloyd George, David: *War Memoirs* Volume 2, Odhams Press Limited, London, 1938.

Mackenzie, Sir William: *The Secret History of SOE*, St Ermin's Press, London, 2000.

MacMillan, Margaret: *Paris 1919 – Six Months that Changed the World*, John Murray, London, 2001.

Malaparte, Curzio: *Technique du Coup d'état*, Bernard Grasset 'Les Ecrits', Paris, 1931.

Mann, Chris and Jorgensen, Christer: *Hitler's Artic War*, Pen & Sword, Barnsley, 2017.

McKercher, B.J.C.: *Esme Howard, A Diplomatic Biography*, Cambridge University Press, Cambridge, 1989.

Meade, C.: *Approach to the Hills*, John Murray, London, 1940.

Melnikau, Ihar: *Photographs of World War Two from the Archive of Ihar Melnikau*, Alfa Books, Minsk, 2019.

Messenger, Charles: *Broken Sword, the Tumultuous Life of General Frank Crozier*, Pen & Sword, Barnsley, 2013.

Mitter, Rana: *China's War with Japan 1937–45 – The Struggle for Survival*, Allen Lane, London, 2013.

Morgan, Kenneth: *Consensus and Disunity; The Lloyd George Coalition Government 1918–1922*, Clarendon Press, Oxford, 1986.

Mountbatten, Admiral the Lord Louis [ed. Philip Ziegler]: *Personal Diaries 1943–46*, Collins, London, 1988.

Murfett, Malcolm H.: *Naval Warfare 1919–45: An Operational History of the Volatile War at Sea*, Routledge, London, 2008.

Neame, Sir Philip: *Playing with Strife: The Autobiography of a Soldier*, George Harrap, London, 1947.

Nesbit, Roy Conyers: *The Battle of Burma*, Pen & Sword, Barnsley, 2009.

Newman, Robert P.: *Owen Lattimore and the 'Loss' of China*, University of California Press, Oakland, 1992.

Nicolson, Harold: *Curzon, the Last Phase 1919–1925, A Study in Post-War Diplomacy*, Constable & Co, London, 1934.

Noonan, William: *The Surprising Battalion, Australian Commandos in China*, NSW Bookstall Co, Sydney, 1945.

Orpen, William: *An Onlooker in France 1917–1919*, Williams and Norgate, London, 1921.

Petro, W.: *Triple Commission*, John Murray, London, 1968.

Piłsudska, Alexandra: *Memoirs of Madame Pilsudski*, Hurst & Blackett, London, 1940.

Piłsudska, Alexandra: *Piłsudski, A Biography By His Wife*, Dodd, Mead & Co, New York, 1941.

Plevy, Harry: *Norway 1940 Chronicle of a Chaotic Campaign*, Fonthill Media, Brinscombe, 2017.

Potocki, Alfred: *Master of Łańcut; The Memoirs of Count Alfred Potocki*, W.H. Allen & Co, London, 1959.

Powell, Marie-Jacqueline: *The Battleground of High Politics: A Comparative study of British and French Policies Towards Poland and the Baltic States, 1917–39*, Book Guild, Lewes, 2003.

Pratt, Sir John: *War and Politics in China*, Jonathan Cape, London, 1943.

Radziwill, Michael: *One of the Radziwills*, John Murray, London, 1971.

Ranfurly, Hermione: *Countess of: To War with Whitaker: The Wartime Diaries of the Countess of Ranfurly 1939–45*, Heinemann, London, 1994.

Ride, Edwin: *BAAG [British Army Aid Group]: Hong Kong Resistance 1942–45*, Oxford University Press, Hong Kong, 1981.

Ritter, Jonathan: *Stilwell and Mountbatten in Burma. Allies at War 1943–44*, University of North Texas Press, 2017.

Romanus, Charles F. and Sunderland, Riley: *US Army in World War II, China-Burma-India Theater, Stilwell's Command Problems*, Washington, US Government Printing Office, 1956.

Romanus, Charles F. and Sunderland, Riley: *US Army in World War II, Time Runs Short*, Washington, US Government Printing Office, 1956.

Roosevelt, Kermit (introduction): *War Report of the OSS*, Volume 1 and 2. Walker & Co, New York, 1976.

Rose-Innes, Cosmo: *With Paget's Horse to the Front*, John MacQueen, London, 1901.

Seaman, Mark: *Special Operations Executive: A New Instrument of War*, Taylor and Francis, London, 2005.

Shakespeare, Nicolas: *Six Minutes in May*, Vintage, London, 2018.

Slim, F. M. Viscount: *Defeat into Victory*, Cassell & Co, London, 1956.

Smith, Jean Edward: *Eisenhower in War and Peace*, Random House, New York, 2012.

Snyder, Timothy: *The Reconstruction of Nations, Poland, Ukraine, Lithuania, Belarus 1569–1999*, Yale University Press, Yale, 2003.

Snyder, Timothy: *The Red Prince – The Fall of a Dynasty and the Rise of Modern Europe*, Vintage, London, 2009.

Stephan, Enno: *Spies in Ireland* (translated from German by Arthur Davidson), MacDonald, London, 1963.

Sutherland, David: *He Who Dares, Recollections of Service in the SAS, SBS and MI5*, Leo Cooper, London, 1998.

Sword, Edward Roland: *The Diary and Despatches of a Military Attaché in Warsaw, 1938–1939*, edited by Elizabeth Turnbull, Andrzej Suchcitz, Polish Cultural Foundation, London, 2001.

Szejnert, Małgorzata: *Building Mountains – Stories from the Polesie Region*, Znak, Warsaw, 2015.

Tarnowski, Andrew: *The Last Mazurka*, St Martin's Press, New York, 2006.

Taylor, Jay: *The Generalissimo, Chiang Kai-shek and the Struggle for Modern China*, Belknap Press, Harvard University, Harvard, 2009.

Tommasini, Francesco: *Odrodzenie Polski*, F. Hoeswicka's Bookstore, Warsaw, 1928.

Tsang, Steve: *A Modern History of Hong Kong 1841–1997*, I.B. Tauris, London, 2003.

Tse-tsung, Chow: *The May Fourth Movement – Intellectual Revolution in Modern China*, Harvard University Press, Cambridge, MA, 1960.

Tuchman, Barbara: *Stilwell and the American Experience in China 1911–1945*, The MacMillan Company, New York, 1971.

Van der Ven, Hans: *War and Nationalism in China 1925–45*, Routledge, London, 2012.

Wakeman, Frederic: *Spymaster, Dai Li and the Chinese Secret Service*, University of California Press, 2003.

Wardrop, Major A. E.: *Modern Pig-Sticking*, Macmillan & Co, London, 1914.

Watt, Richard: *Bitter Glory – Poland and its Fate 1918–39*, Hippocrene Books, New York, 1998.

Wedemeyer, Albert: *Wedemeyer Reports!*, Henry Holt and Co, New York, 1958.

Weygand, Maxime: *Mémoires Vol 2 Mirages et Réalité*, Flammarion, Paris, 1957.

Wharton-Tigar, Edward: *Burning Bright*, Metal Bulletin Books, London, 1987.

White, Theodore and Jacoby, Annalee: *Thunder Out of China*, William Sloane, New York, 1946.

Wilkinson, Peter: *Foreign Fields*, I.B. Tauris, London, 1997.

Willmott, H.P.: *Empires in the Balance*, Naval Institute Press, Annapolis, 1982.

Willmott, H.P.: *Grave of a Dozen Schemes*, Airlift Publishing, London,1996.

Willmott, H.P.: *The War with Japan*, Rowman & Littlefield, Maryland, 2002.

Wingate, Sir Ronald: *Lord Ismay – A Biography*, Hutchinson, London, 1970.

Woodruff, Philip: *The Men who Ruled India – The Guardians*, Jonathan Cape, London, 1954.

Wright, Damien: *Churchill's Secret war with Lenin*, Helion, Warwick, 2017.

Wyrall, Everard: *The Gloucestershire Regiment in the War 1914–1918*, Penguin, London, 1931.

Wyrall, Everard: *The History of 19th Division*, Edward Arnold, London, 1932.

Yu, Maochun: *OSS in China: Prelude to Cold War*, Yale University Press, New Haven, 1966.

Yu, Maochun: *The Dragon's War – Allied Operations and the Fate of China 1937–47*, Naval Institute Press, Annapolis, 2006.

Zaloga, Steven: *Warsaw 1920 – The War for the Eastern Borderlands*, Osprey, Oxford and New York, 2020.

Zamoyski, Adam: *Warsaw 1920, Lenin's Failed Conquest of Europe*, Harper Press, London, 2008.

Theses and papers

Académie Royale des Sciences d'Outre-Mer, Biographie Belge d'Outre-Mer, T.VII-B, 1977, Bruxelles, Belgium, col. 48–61.

Adams, Mathew Lloyd: Herbert Hoover and the Organization of American Relief Aid to Poland in 1919–23, http://journals.openedition.org/ejas/7627 (accessed 18 October 2020).

Bajer, Peter Paul: Short History of the Radziwiłł Family, Rocznik Muzeum, Achivum Polonii Australia Vol. 4, 2010.

Bàtonyi, Gabor: *Britain and Central Europe 1918–32*, University of Oxford, Oxford, 1994.

Boyd, Louise A.: The Marshes of Pinsk, *Geographical Review*, Vol. 26, No.3 (July 1936), pp. 376–95.

Chervov, Victor: Joseph Pilsudski – From Socialist to Autocrat, *Foreign Affairs*, Vol. 14, No. 1, October 1935, https://www.jstor.org/stable/20030709 (accessed 18 October 2020).

Cienciala, Anna and Komarnicki, Titus: From Versailles to Locarno, Keys to Polish Foreign Policy 1919–1925, University of Kansas, ISBN 0-7006-0247-X.

Dubois, Marie-Laurence and Hendrick, Annette: Inventaire des Archives de la Famille Carton de Wiart, Valorscience, June 2016.

Durka, Jaroslaw: A Sketch of the History of the Radziwiłł Family Berlin Line until 1939, Museum in Nieborów at Arcadia Branch of the National Museum in Warsaw, Trzy Trąby Foundation, 2018, pp. 28–41.

Grimsdale, Maj-Gen G. E.: The War against Japan in China, *RUSI Journal*, Vol. 95, No. 578, 1950, pp. 260–7.

Harrison, E. D. R.: An Absolute 'Non-ducker – Carton de Wiart in the Great War', *Journal of the Society of Historical Research*, Vol. 91, No. 366, Summer 2013, pp. 98–119.

Harvey, Trevor Gordon: *An Army of Brigadiers, British Brigade Commanders at the Battle of Arras 1917*, University of Birmingham, August 2015.

Hodgkinson, Peter Eric: *British Infantry Battalions Commanders in the First World War*, University of Birmingham, August 2013.

Jackson, Geoffrey: What was the Point? Raiding in the Summer of 1917, *Canadian Military History*, Vol. 19, No. 4, Article 4. (Autumn 2010).

Kondrativk, Leonid: *The Ukrainian Galician Army in the Ukrainian Polish War 1918–1919*, Kansas State University, 1979.

Kopisto, Lauri: The British Intervention in Southern Russia 1918–1929, *Historical Studies for the University of Helsinki*, ISBN 978-952-10-6923-9 (pdf).

Manfred, Alexander: Marshal Foch's Trip to Warsaw and Prague in the Spring of 1923, *A Journal of History and Civilization in East Central Europe*, Vol. 14, No. 1 (1973), p. 507.

Onslow, Sue: Britain and the Belgrade Coup of 27 March 1941 Revisited, *Institute of Historical Research*, University of London, ISSN 1471-1443.

Rahimlou, Youssef: Aspects der l'expansion Belge en Egypte sous le regime d'occupation Britannique (1882–1914), *Civilisations*, 38, No. 1 (1988), pp. 101–78.

Rodriguez, Robyn: *Journey to the East – the German Military Mission in China 1927–38*, Ohio State University, 2011.

Stevens, Keith: A Token Operation: 204 Military Mission to China 1941–45, *Asian Affairs*, Vol. XXXVI, No. 1 (March 2005), pp. 66–74.

Theseira, Julian: When we spoke at Versailles – Lou Tseng-Tsiang and the Chinese delegation at the Paris Peace Conference, *Global Histories*, Vol. 1, No. 1 (December 2015), pp. 39–60.

Yousef, Tarik: Egypt's Growth Performance under Economic Liberalism, *Review of Income and Wealth*, Series 48, December 2002.

Yueying, Hu: Henry Wallace's Visit to China, an Ultimate Effort to Send the US Army Observer Group to Yan'an, *International Journal of Culture and History*, Vol. 3, No. 4 (December 2017), pp. 213–18.

Archive documents

Imperial War Museum (IWM)

Private papers Gen G Grimsdale Doc 8521a.

Liddell Hart Centre (LHCMA)

GB 99 KCLMA Jacobs-Larkcom.
OCONNOR 4/5/1 1941-1943 Escape Narrative of Lt-Gen Sir Richard O'Connor.
ISMAY 4/5.

Reading University Library (RUL)

Peter Fleming correspondence etc.
MS 1391.
A/24.
B/13.
B/14.
B/15.
B/16.
B/17.
B/44 Notebook.
G/7 Photographs.

Southampton University Library (HLUS)

Mountbatten papers MB1/C42 and C43.

The National Archives (TNA)

FO series

First World War

FO 800/112/67 Folios 254 - 256: Memorandum by Monsieur E Carton de Wiart concerning: Views on Belgium…
FO 800/215 Miscellaneous correspondence Volume 2 (1918).
FO 841/149/33 Probate: Leon Constant G Carton de Wiart.

Poland 1919-23

FO 371/5448 (Major General Sir H.C. Holman's Final Report of the British Military Mission, South Russia, April 1920).
FO 371/8143 Poland. Code 55 Files 2900 – 6134 (1920).
FO 608/57 British delegation, correspondence and papers relating to Poland (Political): Commission…
FO 608/58 Anglo-French Commission to Warsaw; its arrival at Cracow.
FO 608/59 Bolsheviks: Allied Assistance for Poland against Bolsheviks.
FO 608/265/17 Distribution of cyphers, containing: Cyphers for General De Wiart. Cypher for Warsaw and…
FO 608/267 Journey of General Allenby to Paris.
FO 608/268 Missions: Sir Harold Stuart's Mission to Coblenz.
FO 608/268/23 Poland, containing: Establishment of General de Wiart's Mission. Officer to be sent to…
FO 688/14/1 Cavan visit.

FO 688/14/4 Anglo-Polish relations.
FO 688/14 Ambassadors telegrams.

Italy

FO 954/13B/438 Italy: Lisbon telegram No 1755. General Carton de Wiart's departure.
FO 954/13B/436 Italy: Lisbon telegram No 1750. General Carton de Wiart's journey.
FO 954/13B/433 Italy: Lisbon telegram No 1741. General Carton de Wiart returning to England.
FO 954/13B/429 Italy: Foreign Office telegram to Lisbon. General Carton de Wiart should proceed to...
FO 954/13B/423 Italy: Foreign Office telegram to Lisbon No 1360. General Carton de Wiart should return...
FO 954/13B/417 Italy: Lisbon telegram No 1723. General Carton de Wiart to offer to return to Rome for...
FO 954/13B/415 Italy: Lisbon telegram No 1721. Arrival of Generals Carton de Wiart and Zanussi.

China

FO 954/7A/ 9 Far East: Foreign Office telegram to Chungking, No 2. AMUSE. Prime Minister to General...
FO 954/7A/63 Far East: General C. de Wiart and General Ismay. Talk with Madame Chiang Kai Shek.
FO 954/7A/45 Far East: Chungking telegram No 6 AMUSE. General C. de Wiart to Prime Minister Aircraft...
FO 954/7A/39 Far East: Foreign Office telegram to Chungking No 6 AMUSE. Prime Minister to General C...
FO 954/7A/261 Far East: From General Ismay. Copy of a letter from General C. de Wiart. The military...
FO 954/7A/254 Far East: Foreign Office telegram to Chungking No 16 AMUSE. Prime Minister to General C...
FO 954/7A/252 Far East: From General Ismay. Extracts from a letter from General C. de Wiart Gravity of...
FO 954/7A/2 Far East: Chungking telegram to Foreign Office No 3 AMUSE. General Carton de Wiart to...
FO 954/7A/192 Far East: Foreign Office telegram to Washington, No 9393. President to Prime Minister No...
FO 954/7A/113 Far East: Foreign Office telegram to Chungking No 13 AMUSE. Prime Minister to General C...
FO 954/7 Private Office papers of Sir Anthony Eden.
FO 954/6C/720 Far East: General C. de Wiart (Chungking) telegram to Foreign Office No 2 (for Prime...

FO 954/6C/719 Far East: General C. de Wiart (Chungking) telegram to Foreign Office No 1 (for Prime...

FO 954/32B/430 War (General): Chungking telegram No 3 AMUSE. General C. de Wiart to the Prime Minister...

FO 954/1B/542 BURMA: telegram from General C. de Wiart to Prime Minister. Chiang Kai Shek anxious for...

FO 954/13B/539 Italy: Foreign Office telegram to Washington, No 6509. Prime Minister to President, No...

FO 954/7A/47 Far East: Foreign Office telegram to Chungking, No 8 AMUSE. Prime Minister to General C...

FO 954/7A/113 Far East: Foreign Office telegram to Chungking No 13 AMUSE. Prime Minister to General C...

CAB series

Yugoslavia

CAB 121/674 Situation in Yugoslavia.

China

CAB 120/816 General Carton de Wiart.

CAB 127/27 Correspondence with General Sir Carton de Wiart, personal representative of the Prime...

CAB 127/28 Correspondence with General Sir Carton de Wiart, personal representative of the Prime...

CAB 127/29 Correspondence with General Sir Carton de Wiart, personal representative of the Prime...

CAB 65/6/39 Record Type: Conclusion Former Reference: WM (40) 94 Attendees: N...

CAB 65/49/4 Record Type: Conclusion Former Reference: WM (45) 4 Attendees: W...

CAB 65/51/4 Record Type: Conclusion Former Reference: Confidential Annex to WM (45) 4...

CAB 66/57/31 Record Type: Memorandum Former Reference: WP (44) 631 Title: South-East...

CAB 79/28/7 1. Situation in Greece. 2. Visit by Field Marshal Alexander to Moscow. 3...

CAB 79/39/10 1. Meeting with Sir Henry Tizard. 2. Military Command in Burma after full Resumption of...

CAB 79/39/13 1. Liaison with European Allies - Portugal. 2. Cessation of Censorship. 3. Supreme...

CAB 79/39/18 1. Examination of the Effects of the Bombing of Japan. 2. Combined Shipping Review. 3...

CAB 79/42/15 1. Situation in Java. 2. Java – Report by Daily Herald correspondent. 3. Progress of...

CAB 79/46/14 1. Directive to Commander -in-Chief , British Forces in Germany 2. SEAC - Internal…

CAB 79/46/15 1. Meeting with General Carton de Wiart. 2. Commander-in-Chief of the British…

CAB 79/80/5 1. Meeting with Directors of Intelligence. 2. Air Operations against South-East Europe…

CAB 79/83/20 1. Meeting with Directors of Intelligence. 2. Effects of Allied Attacks on the Enemy…

CAB 79/84/15 1. Meeting with Directors of Intelligence. 2. German Warning to Prisoners of War on…

CAB 79/84/22 1. Amphibious operations in South East Asia Command. JP (44)318(Final). 2. Entry of…

WO series

Somaliland

WO 32/5809 OVERSEAS: Africa: Dispatches relating to military and political situation.
WO 106/23 Synopsis of the Campaign against the Mullah.
WO 106/272 History of the King's African Rifles and the Somaliland Camel Corps, including the final…

4 Dragoon Guards

WO 76/1 4th Dragoon Guards.
WO 76/2/14 Name: Adrian C De Wiart. Regiment: 4th Dragoon Guards. Date of Service: 1901. Born: 1880.
WO 95/1112 2 Cavalry Brigade: 4 Dragoon Guards – war diary Feb/Mar 1916.

Lancs

WO 95/2080 56 Infantry Brigade: 7 Battalion Loyal North Lancashire Regiment.

8 Glocs

WO 95/2085 10 Battalion Royal Warwickshire Regiment.
WO 95/2085/1 8 Battalion Gloucestershire Regiment.
WO 98/8/262 Victoria Cross details of Carton de Wiart, Adrian Rank: Captain (temporary…

12 Inf Bde

WO 95/1502/4 12 Infantry Brigade: Headquarters (Jan-Mar 1917).
WO 95/1502/5 12 Infantry Brigade: Headquarters (Apr 1917).
WO 95/1503/1 12 Infantry Brigade: Headquarters (May-Jun 1917).
WO 95/1503/2 12 Infantry Brigade: Headquarters (Jul-Aug 1917).

WO 95/1503/3 12 Infantry Brigade: Headquarters (Sept 1917).
WO 95/1503/4 12 Infantry Brigade: Headquarters (Oct 1917).
WO 95/1503/5 12 Infantry Brigade: Headquarters (Nov-Dec 1917).

57 Inf Bde

WO95/2083 57 Infantry Brigade: Headquarters.

105 Inf Bde

WO 95/2486/2 105 Infantry Brigade: Headquarters.
WO 95/2486/3 105 Infantry Brigade: Headquarters.

113 Inf Bde

WO 95/2554/5 113 Infantry Brigade: Headquarters.

Poland 1919

WO 32/5422 ORDERS: General (Code 52(C)): Recommendations for awards for members of British Military.
WO 339/54561 Lieutenant Maurice Carton de WIART Welsh Guards.

Poland 1939

WO 202/117 Telegrams concerning supply of war materials.
WO 202/113 Order of Battle of the Polish Army.
WO 202/115 Reconnaissance reports.
WO 202/125 GOC's letters.
WO 202/121 Military Attaché Warsaw: telegrams in.
WO 202/114 Formation and policy.
WO 202/116 German tactics and Order of Battle.
WO 202/127 GSOI's telegrams and letters.
WO 202/120 Situation telegrams: in.
WO 202/124 Air Attaché letters.
WO 202/126 Polish identification and battle plan.
WO 202/122 Military Attaché Warsaw: telegrams out.
WO 202/123 Military Attaché letters.
WO 202/118 GHQ situation reports (Polish and English).
WO 178/68 British Military Missions: War Diaries, Second World War.
WO 216/47 The German attack on Poland: report from Major-General Carton de Wiart, British Military...

Norway

WO 106/2013 Namsos operations; report by Major General A. Carton de Wiart.

WO 106/1905 'Sickle' Force; reports by Maj. Gen. Carton de Wiart and other unit commanders.

POW

WO 32/10706 PRISONERS OF WAR: General (Code 91(A)): Vincigliata (Prison Camp No.12): Reports.
WO 208/3440 General De Wiart: publicity of escape stories.

China

WO 106/3484 Future activities of Service Reconnaissance Department, letters from General Blamey.
WO 106/3383 Chief of Imperial General Staff: letter from Lieutenant General Lumsden.
WO 106/3494 Assistance to China.
WO 106/3564 Personal letter from Lieutenant General Carton de Wiart to Chief Imperial General Staff.
WO 106/3579 Coordination and control of British military activities in China.
WO 106/3588 China: operations.
WO 106/3585A China: intelligence.
WO 106/3585B China: intelligence.
WO 106/3589 China: operations.
WO 106/4805 Special Operations Executive weekly situation reports.
WO 106/5027 No.203 Military Mission: Administration: General Lumsden and General Carton de Wiart.
WO 106/5015 No.204 Military Mission: Operational directive to General Carton de Wiart and the.
WO 106/5027 No.203 Military Mission: Administration: General Lumsden and General Carton de Wiart.
WO 178/ 53 War Diaries No.204 Military Mission (Forward Area).
WO 203/1012 No.204 Military Mission.
WO 203/206 No.204 Military Mission.
WO 203/3355 British Army Aid Group: liaison between South East Asia and Chinese Expeditionary Force.
WO 203/3357 British Army Aid Group: redeployment.
WO 203/3426 Special Air Service unit: employment in SEAC.
WO 203/3774 Special Air Service in S.E. Asia: Organization.
WO 203/4390 No.204 Military Mission.
WO 203/4391 No.204 Military Mission.
WO 203/4822 No.204 Military Mission.
WO 203/5381 Future policy of the 204 British Military Mission school and the British Army Aid Group.
WO 203/5629 Mountbatten visit to Chongqing March 1945.

WO 216/134 South East Asia Command: situation report from General Carton De Wiart.

WO 208/473 General Carton de Wiart: appointment as Head of British Services in China and relations.

HS Series

Poland 1939

HS 4/223 British military mission to Poland: despatch by Major General A Carton de Wiart.

Norway

HS 8/263 MI(R) War Diary 1939–40.

China

HS 1/4 SPIERS.

HS 1/5 SPIERS.

HS 1/9 FLIMWELL, AMHERTS, HAINTON.

HS 1/134 Operations: REMARKABLE, NONCHALANT, RESURRECTION, GAUNTLET, WALDORF, PELICANS.

HS 1/164 Commando group.

HS 1/167 BAAG.

HS 1/175 Operation CONWAY.

HS 7/257 India and Far East Jul-Dec 1942 (pages 1–123).

HS 7/258 India and Far East Jan-May 1943 (pages 125–281).

HS 7/259 India and Far East Jun-Dec 1943 (pages 283–514).

HS 7/260 India and Far East Jan-Mar 1944 (pages 515–634).

HS 7/261 India and Far East Apr-Jul 1944 (pages 635–786).

Index

Made in the USA
Coppell, TX
19 February 2024

29204177R00195